Mediator
in
Political Economy: Islamic and Modern
And
Corporate System: Islamic and Modern

Dr Ahmed Lissane el-Haq

The author is a member of the Islamic Conference and one of the ancient scholars of the Quarouine and Dar al-Hadith Al-Hassaniya , holds an Ph.D in Islamic economic and social – and works at the university as a professor of international political economy – in addition to his specialization as a researcher author in Islamic economics .

INTRODUCTION

The field of economics, a vital field, has come down with its weight in life, and has polarized global thought and its problems have eliminated the worries of countries and societies, due to the severity of its impact and its importance not only for study, but for life and its importance appear in the connection of human life and material destiny with its wheel, as it is not dispensed with by an individual, a family, a group or a state... A nation may live without literature or philosophy, but it does not live without resources that secure its life and ensure its continuity...Before we find its members thinking about entertainment and luxuries, we find them thinking about the necessities of life.

Economic activity is invading various classes, and is receiving increasing attention from countries and societies, as a result of the complexity and suffering of contemporary human life, and the family, social, political and international problems that economic conditions raise... It is not for the intellect to solve them, unless it throws weight into the system of acquisition and action.

Hence, it is clear that the study that we intend to complete within the framework of political economy deals with theoretical and applied economics, or the intellectual and practical aspect alike, and we will try to put it in a scientific framework that is not restricted by the restrictions of a particular doctrine, as imposed by the study of economics as a subject of scientific subjects.

Before he knew his way to contemporary doctrinal directions, it was an autonomous science. Science is neutral in nature, benefiting humanity as a whole, and the doctrine is biased by considerations that respond to the interest of a party or group... Describing it as political economy does not mean sectarianism, as much as it means that it is linked to the policy of an Eastern, Western or Islamic state, as it will come to the heart of the subject, as we will see that the caliph Omar bin Al-Khattab was the first to give the concept of state policy to the economy.

Behind the desired outcome, we will focus and spend time studying the basic principles, scientific approaches,and realistic theories.

Therefore, we started with what we see as the most important, and the most realistic, which is the basic economic issues raised at the level of theoretical knowledge on the one hand. Practical and applied effectiveness on the other hand...Followed by the human and natural economic problem posed at the level of public life: the lives of individuals, families, states and societies....

The study, with its methodology and design, and how it deals with current issues, will aim for the first time topresent the political economy in its general concept and put it within the framework of the general theory; to include both Islamic, capitalist and socialist economics. by theorizing and comparing

Basic principles and regulatory laws, as well as trying to analyze, highlight weaknesses, strengths, what is positive and what is negative, what is applicable, and what would go down in history...It is most targeted at the narrative of events and the rumination of texts.... Whether in economic systems or companies.

And that companies -especially those with shareholding or different nationalities - are considered in the present era the most powerful means of monopoly, influence, domination and influence.It is the largest field in which the meaning of political economy is manifested - it spent a weapon used by developed countries in addition to the weapon of the monetary system and modern technology in the face of the confinement of the economies of third world countries, including Arab and Islamic countries.However, in the aggregate —commercial, modern civil, Islamic, financial or personal, as will be mentioned in the second part - it is considered – locally and internationally – one of the most important pillars of commercial and industrial progress and the most powerful tool to achieve major economic projects.

All of these are positive considerations and strong factors that prompted the owners of capital in the world to contribute to its establishment. Therefore, the political economy in the concept we have put forward is not based – theoretically and practically - on study and application without companies.

Chapter One

This chapter deals with the basic issues that will help the reader understand the principles, laws and theories that may be presented to him. It enables him to follow the stages of research, and we start with the concept of the word economics and its link to politics, through the definition of science

Economics and learn about its branches and its relationship to other sciences.

The concept of THE WORD ECONOMY AND THE NATURE OF THE MAIN TRENDS UNDER IT

The word economics, a word used by the private and the public, so that its use, unlike many sciences, has deviated from the scientific framework and known its way to the popular circles.

This is because it is linked to a vital reality that imposes its existence and domination over the lives of individuals, families, states and societies... Its circulation and popularity was helped by the fact that everyone believed that economic progress was the basis or measure of overall progress. Its meanings and concepts, near and far, have not been defined, nor have they been scientifically or legally regulated, and they differ in ancient and modern times according to the trends of economic doctrines and the extent of their relationship with political and social doctrines and the objectives they are intended to achieve. As a model of this difference, we take a brief picture of the character that has characterized the major economic trends or systems represented in the capitalist, communist, and Islamic trend.

Capitalist system

The prevailing capitalist system in the West is an individual system that focuses on private ownership, capital, and factors of production in the hands of individuals and companies, as well as on production rather than distribution. It is a system imprinted with the character of personal interest as part of the public interest.

For its sake and to maintain the element of competition, the main driver in the development of production is the freedom of the individual to own property, the freedom of production and the freedom of consumption, the opening of free markets, and the file of speculation.

One of its negatives, along with the positives, is to exceed the limit in the individual's estimation and to take care of his personal interests at the expense of the group. He gave him the opportunity to "leave him alone "and released his hand almost infinitely freely, which enabled him to be able to use everything that his hand reached, and to enter it as private property.

As a result, wealth swelled among individuals, imbalanced and divided society into two classes: the class of rich owners of large companies and the class of vulnerable people in need, who were locked in their faces, and deprived of any compulsory law -except hard work and work that requires the rich to spend their money to alleviate their situation if they have never been workers or employees, unlike the Islamic economy, which decided to sponsor the employee, the pension and social security system worker, and legislated the rule of zakat in order to sponsor widows, orphans and the disabled.

In short, the capitalist system distinguishes that the individual is the master of himself, and that he is the sole owner of what he acquires, and what follows in it for others. He shall dispose of it as he pleases, and he has the right not to disburse the means of production under his control, except for what is in his personal interest. Its production does not control its price except the law of supply and demand, so it decreases if it is offered and rises if it is requested. If he prefers bank interests to trade, industry and agriculture... Despite the interest of the state and society, the results of thought printed in the nature of personal interest, instead of the public interest.

That was the word "economy" in the capitalist sense, as an international economic system. If we try to establish this doctrine in terms of living and the system of life, it seems that it is more effective and advanced than the Marxist doctrine, the more we compare the lives of individuals between the East and the West, so that the progress of the West is the result of productive power and the progress of the East as a result of austerity, and the strangulation of the system of life, as confirmed by the retreat of individuals from the communist system, and manifested in the migration from East Germany to West these days 2-10-1989, and if they were allowed to spend like their counterparts in the West, the East would be less advanced than the West. Therefore, the West is called the First World, the East the Second World, and developing or developing countries on the way to growth in the Third World. Like all doctrines, the capitalist doctrine has principles. Among its basic principles are:

- The Law of Personal Benefit
- Law on Free Competition
- The law of private property, and its adoption as the basis of competition in the field of production
- The Law of Supply and Demand, and the Freedom of Markets
- Bank interest system arising from the monetary system
- Wage law, which is the price of labor
- International Swap Law.[1]

COMMUNIST SYSTEM

The communist system, based on a collective materialist doctrine, is antithetical to the capitalist system as a basis and goal, a means and an end. Insofar as the capitalist system overestimates the individual and takes care of his personal interests, we also see the communist system overestimate the group and take care of its interests, which made the individual a factor of production that produces and consumes, as well as the machine produces and consumes. His

---

[1]- Quoted from the Approach of Islamic Economics in the Production and Consumption of Wealth 1/78 by the author

right may not be more than receiving necessities, as a reward for the work he does for the benefit of the group. Taking into account the principles of (those who do not work do not eat) and(each according to his ability, and each according to his work),[2] then there is no freedom of ownership, no freedom of production, no freedom of consumption, no freedom of expression, no freedom of opinion, no freedom of self-determination... On the subject, Gustave Laboune says:As for communism, it looks only at the food needs of the individual, and cares only for its judiciary. It goes without saying that this system requires that the government has a compelling authority to manage and distribute livelihoods, and that it uses workers as absoluteslaves[3]. " Thus, one of the basic principles on which the Marxist revolution, led by Lenin, was founded in 1917 was the confiscation of public freedoms, the prohibition of private property and the nationalization of all means of production on the face of the earth or in its interior to be replaced by collective ownership, on the day when the state alone supervises the production and distribution of wealth.

However, the principle of communism that fascinated the proponents of Marxist thought - once it was exported to the Third World - was nothing new. Plato, the disciple of Socrates and the elder of Aristotle in his republic, circulated it in money and women, and called for the abolition of the family system and individual property,[4] claiming that communism in money and women would eliminate the causes of conflict between human beings, the same idea that Mazdak said after him, apprenticed to his teacher Zardasht, where Plato's life was between 429 and 347 BC, and the life of Mazdak around 487AD, thenMarx said it and called for its application, and assumed that property in primitive times was common, and he saw that it would return to its origin in the twentieth century.

Like many of his opinions, he made no concrete document or material argument. Although he believes only in the sensible, and exaggerates his consideration, and denies the Creator on its basis, he even says: He cannot decide that the earth is under him until he knocks it with his foot, and that the table is in front of him until he hits it with his hand, and we do not know anything that he relied on to deny beyond matter, which the mind does not realize, but rather the sensible? And what went wrong in deciding that property was a common property of primitive man? However, he denied the existence of God because he did not see it, and he approved the communist regime with the beginning of life, even if he did not see it. And that's one of his contradictions.

Marx did not stop there, but went further in assuming at the expense of his theory of faith in the sensible, arranging regimes and covenants, and assuming

---

[2] Political economy of Leontiev p. 114
[3] The Spirit of Socialism by Gustave Bonn, p. 32
[4] History of Economic Ideas, pp. 15,11-1956, by Dr. Mohammed Aziz Al-Iraqi

communism in the primitive era, then enslavement, then feudalism, then capitalism, then socialism as a stage, then communism as a goal.

Although he did not live, and felt only the capitalist era, he decided on the basis of the contrary principle, which he quoted from the philosophy of the German philosopher Hegel, that each of those systems carries within itself the elements of its own annihilation. This is known as self-destruction, and it dies on its own, so that another system is based on its opposite. And so on, until the communist system spontaneously arises. And without interference...What happened at the end of 1989 from the popular uprisings against the Marxist regime, and the surrender of the parties and governments in the communist camp to the fait accompli, indicates that the communist regime is the one that carried within itself the elements of its annihilation, and suffered from self-destruction. Although Marx wanted to stop with it the historical development of systems, which he explains is natural.

Nothing of what he said happened, as the capitalist system in the West still carries elements of its strength and continuity, and the communist system in the East did not arise spontaneously, as he claims, but rather was a bloody revolution that did not witness the history of humanity like it[5] and what he theoretically called scientific socialism. Lenin practically called it compulsive socialism. What is imposed by force does not live without it.

The communist liberated from its influence, Milovan Djillas, explained in his book "The New Class" that "Communists in power exceed by their dictatorship the most tyrannical and terrorist dictatorships." In his book "The New Class", he[6] means that communism has eliminated the social class and created a new class for itself. It is the class of the party and the state, and so Marx's theories are still mostly ink on paper. So where is the principle of "each according to his work, and each according to his capacity" and who are the most active, the most powerful, and the most needy? Who is more comfortable, less employed, and more useful? The toilers or the ministers? And where is the principle of absolute equality, which Marx did not exclude anyone from considering? Is there a difference in the system of life between presidents, ministers, and ambassadors, as well as between the toilers between East and West? Where is his theory of the value and surplus of the commodity? He believes that it is formed by the amount of work spent in its production, and its surplus has increased. In fact, it consists of the factors of capital and labor, and the land from which it is produced or made is determined at the level of supply and demand. They are opinions that we recorded when the Soviet Union was alive, and we will analyze some of them within the history of economic ideas.

---

[5] Our economy for the rest of the chest 1/211
[6] - The new layer S-21 F1 - Beirut for Milovan Djilas

However, Marx's philosophy led to the creation of an international economic order. Founded in a revolutionary style, it aimed at expropriation and nationalization. Nationalization means making everything for the nation. In it, Muhammad Azza Darwazah said: "The socialist method makes the means of production, establishments, facilities and various works agricultural, industrial, commercial or services, which includes banks, transportation, hotels, swimming pools, clubs, treatment, medicine, engineering, schools and institutes. owned by the State, and under the direct administration of the Government, and all employees shall be employees. "[7]

That was the word economics in the Marxist sense, as a materialist doctrine. If this brief perception does not allow for the analysis of theories, both philosophical ones such as the class struggle, the materialist interpretation of history, and the dialectical materialism that frames its doctrine, and is interpreted as the history of societies, and the conflict between their classes ...Or economic, which is better to do as we did when diagnosing the capitalist system, and accelerate the abstraction of some of them, and postpone the analysis to their places, especially since the communist system is more ambiguous, and far from the understandings of the capitalist system. Its principles include:

- Adoption of the interest of the group in the person of the
- Expropriation of private property, and nationalization of all means of production in order to form state ownership
- Socialism of production and consumption and the reaction between them
- The principle of equality and equal opportunities for individuals
- Establishing a system of solidarity and preventing begging
- The value of the commodity, and what it consists of or determines
- Surplus Value and Overtime
- Theory of Economic Evolution
- International Swap.[8]

If we try to do justice to the two great systems by expressing what could be an advantage for one over the other, we will not discern an advantage for the capitalist system more than the preservation of the element of competition, which is of great importance in the field of production and labor. It is the element that the communist regime lost by expropriating and outlawing private property, in exchange for the privilege of this regime to lift the poor class and ensure the necessary amount of what life does, while leaving the privilege to the ruling class.

---

[7]- Islam and Socialism, p. 56, Muhammad Azza Darwaza
[8] On the Approach of Islamic Economics in the Production and Consumption of Wealth " by 1/78

The progress observed in science, industry, civilization and urbanism... It does not seem to return to the status of an Eastern or Western regime. It is primarily due to unity and work, although each doctrine sees no reasons for progress except what is related to its doctrine, as Muhammad Dawud said.[9] Therefore, Arabs and Muslims delayed, and others advanced, after they disputed and failed and their wind went away.

ISLAMIC ECONOMIC SYSTEM

The Islamic economic system in its principles -not in many of its societies - is a moderate middle system that is not an unjust individual, nor an extremist collective that has not been characterized by the character of capitalist extravagance, nor by communist association. Combine the element of competition with the advantage of lifting the weak. If societies adhere to his law -in moderation and balance - they will achieve social justice and equality. By virtue of which individuals and groups are equal in duties and rights, taking the interest of the individual as the interest of the group. So that no side rises to the detriment of one side, or that a right prevails over a right, or that an interest prevails over an interest.

It's a divine system. He organized the squares, codified the laws, and forbade halal and haram. Prohibiting what has been proven to be economically, socially, healthily or morally harmful...He guided our religion and created them to take care of rights, perform duties and work conscientiously...A system that enabled the individual to have the freedom to earn and work, the freedom to seek and own property, and the freedom to produce and consume, but at his disposal with discretion, and not to be naive, so that his work would no longer be detrimentalto the interest of the group. God Almighty said, "And **do not give the fools your money, which God has made valuable to you**"[10] by adding money to the group, instead of adding it to the individuals who own it according to the law, and they did not say nor give the fools their money.

Islam, in front of the freedom of the individual, despite the right of individual property, did not force him to squander what he had of the money of God, in which he succeeded his righteous servants, believing in the Almighty's saying: **"Spend what made you successors in it," nor did he have any opportunity under Sharia to suck wealth out of the hands of individuals without giving consideration or compensation, and eating people's money in vain.**[11] In the hadith, "Every Muslim against a Muslim is haraam: his blood, his wealth, and his honor."

---

[9]- Date of Tetouan 6/116- 1st Edition - 1970 by Muhammad Dawood
[10]- Surah Al-Nisa 5
[11]- Surat Al-Hadid 7

One of its advantages is that it imposes the necessary amount of what life does, a solidarity of society, the law of zakat, and others for its sake, and then otherwise allows the disparity of livelihood, which is one of the secrets of the wheel of life, and its rotation on every kind of honorable and humble work.

Some writers claim that Islamic economics is individualistic, knows individual property, and is ignorant of collectivism. Those who hold this view are not specialists in Islamic economics, nor in its legitimate sources. Rather, they issue judgments, based on the existing conditions.

In fact, the Islamic economy is neither a right-wing individual economy in the capitalist sense, nor a left-wing collective economy in the communist sense. Rather, it is a moderate middle economy in the Islamic sense. Combining the interest of the individual and the group, it allowed individual ownership in a circle of specific Sharia laws regulating individual and collective activity in the person of the state, in order to own public property, which benefits the group. In its general sense, a group means the nation with all its members, as it is permitted in the case of a tribal or local group. It was manifested in the lands of the joint tribal and Kish tribal groups in Morocco. The first of the foundations of collective property in Islam is the caliph Umar ibn al-Khattab. Where the open lands stood to be a common abscess between the former and the latter, [12] especially the lands of the blackness of Iraq.

However, the consideration of collective property, whether above or below ground, is more legitimate than the consideration of individual property... As for what is above the land, the state, in addition to foreign trade, and the factories and institutions it builds - it owns public utilities and natural resources, so it owns the seas, rivers, lakes, mountains, plateaus, deserts and forests, and everything that is not considered private property, as it is the owner of what has no owner and the heir[13] to who has no heir, and it is responsible for ensuring who has no guarantor, and as for the types of solid and liquid minerals under it, the state owns it in its entirety, even if it is found with private property.

In that, Abbas al-Ta'araji quotes Ibn Rushd as saying: "The matter is with the Imam. It was owned or not owned. "The[14] expression in the Imam in the first Sadr, takes the place of the state in this era, and Professor Abdullah Ali Hassan said: "The Imam has the disposition of metal, even if he is found with a certain king. "Sayyid Qutb[15] quoted Malikiyah in their most famous statements that minerals are not permissible funds"until those who found and seized them own them. It is for Muslims. "[16]

---

[12] - The abscess of Yahya bin Adam, p. 13.The Money Book of Abu 'Ubayd, p. 58.Futuh Masr wa al-Maghrib by Ibn Abd al-Hakam, p. 123. The Great Sunnahs of Al-Bayhaqi 9/139
[13] Book of Money by Daoudi Al-Asadi, p. 380
[14] - Adherence to the provisions of the feudalism of the judge, page 11
[15] - Legislative comparisons of Abdullah Ali Hassan 1/382
[16] - World Peace and Islam by Mr. Qutb, p. 115

After proving the private property of the individual or the company, and allowing the collective in the right of the state, or in the right of the tribal or local group, Islam has established a legitimate isthmus, separating the rights of the individual and the group, neither the state that represents the group, can steal the legitimate rights of individuals, under an authority supported by religion, nor the individual who is imbued with the spirit of Sharia, working under its laws, finds in himself free or spacious to operate with absolute freedom, and leads to his instinctive tendency, and his personal insatiableness to enrich and finance at the expense of the state and society.

This was the reality of Islamic economics, as there is no unjustcapitalism, no radical communism, no revolutionary socialism, and no private expropriation except for the public interest and with real compensation.... The researchers saw that the capitalist system radicalized to the far right, and the communist radicalized to the far left, and their voices rose in search of a just alternative that guarantees the rights of all, as the Islamic economy in its principles does not

In many of his communities, he is more fortunate than others to be nominated for this nomination as manifested in his principles.

If we have already inventoried some of the principles of the two systems: capitalist and communist in order to compare the three main systems, one of the principles of Islamic economics is:

- Adopting the interest of the individual and the group
- Take a moderate approach
- Equality in duties and rights, and equality of opportunity for all individuals. In it, Imam Ali bin Abi Talib said: "I have looked at the Book of Allah and I have not seen in it any bounty to the son of Ishmael on the son of Isaac."[17]
- The application of the Zakat rule, and the establishment of Takaful or social security, to benefit every disabled, damaged or unemployed person whose doctrines have been understood in life.
- Consideration of collective property in the person of the State, tribal or local group with the recognition of private property that has entered into the possession of individuals or companies by legitimate means.

- The development of money, and the investment of treasured money, according to the Prophet's saying: "No orphan's guardian has money, so let him trade in it, and do not leave it until charity eats him."[18]

---

[17]- The abscess of Abu Yusuf, p. 26 Ould Ismail is the Arabs and Ould Ishaq is the Ajam
[18]- Sahih Al-Tirmidhi 3/163, Money means money and charity means zakat

- The law of supply and demand, and the freedom of markets, according to the words of the Prophet (PBUH): "Let the people provide for God from each other."[19]
- Freedom of ownership, freedom of production, freedom of consumption, freedom of trade...Provided that it is within the limits of Sharia and the law, away from the taboos and prejudice to the rights of others.
- Encouraging international exchange between Muslims and foreigners alike. This is in regard to what may be traded, sold, and bought in Sharia.
- Whoever has a private agricultural land to cultivate it himself, or prevents its exploitation without origin for those who need it, or participates in it with others and does not disrupt it, according to the hadiths of the Messenger (PBUH) on the subject, he said in the novel of Al-Bukhari and Ibn Majah: "Whoever[20] has a land, let him plant it or give it to his modern brother." He said in the novel of Muslim: "Whoever has a land, let him plant it or let his modern brother plant it."
- "Whoever revives a dead land, it is for him,"[21] as the Prophet (PBUH) said.
- "Whoever builds up a land that is not for anyone, then he is more deserving," as the Prophet (peace and blessings of Allaah be upon him) said, and Omar spent the days of his succession.[22]
- Whoever was given land to exploit, and he gave it three years, it is for those who exploited it, as Omar spent the days of his succession, in other than private property, as well as from its stone to revive it and did not revive it in three years, it is for those who revived it and the quarantine is located in the lands of the dead, and it means placing stones as a source of what is intended to be built or revived
- Adopting work, as the basis for acquisition, and encouraging the element of competition in the field of production and work.
- Payment of wages in full, and without delay, and the Messenger ordered that the wage earner be given his wages. before his sweat dries out.
- No acquisition or benefit from the money of others, except through work, or giving consideration or compensation, or what pleases the soul in non-transactions...No injustice, no cheating, no usury, no gambling, no monopoly...[23] It was also decided at the level of the Qur'an, Hadith and Islamic jurisprudence.

---

[19]- Sunan Al-Nasa'i 7/256
[20]- Sahih Muslim: Abi version 4/216
[21]- Al-Bukhari: Al-Fateh version 5/415. The Great Sunnahs of Al-Baihaqi 6/143, Funds for Abu Obaid, p. 272
[22] Al-Bukhari: Al-Fateh version 417
[23]- These principles are also quoted from my book The Approach of Islamic Economics in the Production and Consumption of the Revolution 1/79

And what God has forbidden, He has forbidden for economic, social, health, religious or moral harm...As the reference progressed. And the heavenly religions could not prevent what is in the interest, or allow what is harmful.

It is clear from the above that the word economy, a word whose concepts are not defined, as manifested in the capitalist doctrine, which focuses on private property, the conditions of production and its factors, and the security of the freedom of the individual, taking care of his personal interest, thus preserving the element of competition... and the communist doctrine, which focuses on collective ownership to lift up the needy class...While we see the Islamic economy proving private ownership within legitimate legal limits, and collective in the person of the state or a tribal or local group... By production, it means taking care of distribution and how to consume, combining the element of competition that drives production and the recovery of the needy class, which is guaranteed by the right of zakat and others . Hence, it is clear that economic concepts are not determinable, except through each direction or doctrine separately.

THE ORIGINAL, LINGUISTIC AND IDIOMATIC CONCEPT OF THE WORD ECONOMY AND THE CHANGES THAT HAVE OCCURRED BETWEEN CAPITAL AND CAPITALISM... COMMONS, COMMUNISM, PARTICIPATION, SOCIALISM....

The original and linguistic reality of any word is natural, and the idiomatic is technical, and the ideologies that are emerging in the economic field are the ones that change the original and natural concepts, and subject them to a certain economic philosophy, as manifested in changing the original concept of the word economics about the meaning of moderation and moderation. Since the Islamic economy came into existence. Where it began in the seventh century AD, and the[24] contemporary - as a doctrine and science - began in the sixteenth century, and it was natural that the former would affect the later, we wonder about the extent of the impact of its principles on the contemporary economy in both parts, or the extent to which this economy was affected by its principles or what it could quote from its words and meanings.

The question does not target what the capitalist system has reached from injustice and communism from extremism, but rather aims to identify the nature of the principles before they are distorted, emptied of their original meanings, and tilted by extremism to the right and left, knowing that doctrine, capitalism, communism and socialism are contemporary words. It carries with it new meanings, and purposes that symbolize them. Either to economic doctrine, philosophical production, proposed principles, or a method inspired by the interest of an individual or a group. They are all concepts that flew from their original bases and flew into new atmospheres.

The Islamic economy has defined capital by the word and meaning referred to by the Qur'an in the case of repenters from dealing with usury, as it says: «**If you repent, you have your capital, you do not oppress or injustice» Do not oppress by taking usury or interest in the contemporary expression, and do not oppress by preventing the recovery of capital.**[25] The loan capital, whether little or much, is the lending capital, without its interest, and the trading capital, whether little or much, is its origin from which the profit is generated. If a person trades with ten dirhams and wins two, his capital is ten dirhams, and if he trades with one hundred million, and wins ten, his capital is one hundred million.

This was the Islamic economic perspective of capital. As for capitalism, with its T-word, its unfair economic reality, and its hegemonic exploitative system, as evidenced by the indebtedness of the third world, the principles of Islamic economics in justice and moderation to the contrary. If it means an economic doctrine based on the absolute freedom of individuals and companies, and depends on the multiplication of money and its exploitation by all legitimate and

---

[24] - The Islamic Economy of Sadiq Al-Abbari, p. 43, Book Seven
[25] - Surat Al-Baqarah 279

illegal means, the Islamic economy is not based on freedom that is not regulated by law, and does not rely on the many without the few. As long as the few are the root of the many.

The commonplace is defined by Islamic economics in the ownership of common property among members of a tribe, group or sect... Such as money common among heirs, common land between tribal groups, and the prevalence of resources or public utilities of the state. Bob Al-Bukhari to stop the commons, and he said: "A door if a group stands on common land, it is permissible" and Bob to sell it, and he said: "The door to selling land, houses and offers is undivided[26]."

As for communism, with its T-word, its extreme material and economic reality, and its enslaved system of the individual, Islam is at odds with it. If it means an economic doctrine based on the nationalization of all types of private property, and its transformation into state property, in order to spread it, the Islamic economy does not know this method and does not recognize it. Rather, it knows and decides that the individual has his ownership and rights, and that the state has its ownership and rights.

What is not disputed by two is that Islam and communism in the Marxist concept do not combine. The difference between them is atheism and faith, and the proof and prohibition of private property, and the difference between them is the principles and laws, especially what is related to the family system or the consequences of private property such as zakat, inheritance and ability to perform Hajj....

Participation in its Arabic derivation, and its Islamic meaning, was defined by the Islamic economy before it knew its way to the East and the West. In the principle of people's participation in basic needs, the Prophet (peace and blessings of Allah be upon him) says: "Muslims are partners in three: money, pasture and fire." Imam Shafi 'i, after enumerating the types of minerals, rivers and torrents,[27] said: "Muslims in all of this are partners." Abu Faraj al-Hanbali[28] said about the open lands: "And they are common among Muslims." He supported his words by saying that Imam Ahmed said that they are common among Muslims,[29] which is an extension of the words of Caliph Omar after its opening: "I associate with Allah those who come after you in this period." Muhammad Muntasir al-Kitani[30] quoted Imam Ahmed saying: "The land of the outside is common among Muslims." Abu Ubaid said: "Muslims are all partners in the same." Abu Ya 'la said: "All people are common in the apparent and

---

[26] - Al-Bukhari: Al-Fateh Version 5/312
[27] Sunan Abu Dawud 3/377 Sunan Ibn Majah 3/48 , Sunan Al-Kubra Al-Bayqi 6/151
[28] - The Mother's Book of Al-Shafi 'i 3/265
[29] On the Jurisprudence of Zakat for Al-Qaradawi 1/408
[30] - Extraction of the provisions of the abscess p. 74/108

esoteric minerals." They[31] want state ownership. Our scientists decided on the principle of participation and used its language.

In the event of the moderate balanced, who wanted him to enter Europe and develop into a radical materialist communist doctrine, Al-Hajjawi decides in the "Semitic Thought in the History of Islamic Jurisprudence" that the socialist thought of the companion Abu Dhar Al-Ghaffari is the origin of the socialist doctrine prevailing in Europe. He entered it through Andalusia.[32] The German philosopher "was" this fact, and said: "Islam is credited with placing its roots in Europe, which it crossed through the Pyrenees mountains, after the emergence of Islamic civilization in Andalusia."[33]

The Islamic economic trend approached its justice with intellectual currents, philosophical methods, and positivist doctrines, striking extremism and exaggeration, and departing from the subject of money. Where Islam put him, with the most arrow, and went with the freedom of man, his behavior, his faith, and the determination of his destiny, every doctrine, so he returned to us obliterated features mutilated features. He returned to us leading atheism after faith, and adopting domination after freedom, revolution after pacifism, and extremism after moderation, and his humanity evaporated. He had the right to refuse, even from those for whom he was placed. This is what has happened now (1991-90)

These were the changes in the original and linguistic concept of the word economy, and it is clear from the above, and whatwill come is that the Islamic economy in its principles printed with the character of moderation and moderation still retains its originality as a law and method, as it meant in the linguistic and original sense, and in its Islamic reality a commitment to the approach of moderation and moderation. It is said in language: Take care of things, say, work, sleep or walk... If he mediates between excessive and negligent

In the work system and the call for economic movement, Al-Bukhari narrates that the Prophet (peace and blessings of Allaah be upon him) said: "... Aim, approach, come, go, and something of perseverance, intent, and[34] purpose. Take the path of repayment and righteousness, and start from the workloads of the near destiny to your efforts and energies, and link in your movement between the becoming of days and their spirits early. Theintent is to reach. Economy The economy in the workloads as eight hours - reach the goal that you are throwing away, as Hafiz bin Hajar said in the principle of moderation and moderation, explaining the intent in the hadith[35].

---

[31]- Young Tariq and Al-Ghafiki, p. 133 . What is meant by "open land"?
[32]-Semitic Thought 1/140
[33]- Their participation and our Islam, p. 134
[34]- Al-Bukhari: Al-Fath copy 14/79
[35]- Fath Al-Bari 14/75

The Messenger refused to take the risk, and was guided to set the work program at the level of the energies and efforts of the workers, and the energies of the means used, citing the example of the traveler who carries his animal insufferable, so it perishes and is cut off on the road, so there is no animal left, and there is no distance... He said: "Do what you can afford, for the emanator, neither at noon, nor on the ground, is cut off."[36] He was asked, "Which works are better?" He said, "I will perpetuate it, even if I say," As Aisha was asked, "Which deeds are most beloved to the Prophet (PBUH)?" She said: Permanent....»[37] mundane or eschatological.

Sustainability, programming work, dividing it and mediating its amounts were among the reasons for the success of economic projects, as was risk-taking, improvisation and the accumulation of business. The analyst in Omar's book to his worker Abi Al-Ash 'ari said: «After: Do not delay today's work for tomorrow, if you do, business will catch up with you, and you do not know which you will take and you will lose»[38] from the reasons for its failure.

Consideration shall be given to the sobriety of the plan and the evaluation of the curriculum, and to the extent of the ability to develop production and improve its means, rather than the boasting of each individual of owning what he isunable to develop at the expense of the state and society, knowing that the limitation of each individual to owning what he can invest himself makes production steady, and the national income high. This is one of the theories of the caliph Omar bin Al-Khattab. He said to the Companions of the Prophet (PBUH): "Fix your property that Allah has provided for you, and for a little while in kindness it is better than many in violence[39]." This is one of the meanings of the word "economy" in the field of production and work, as put forward by Islamic economics. Production in the Islamic curriculum requires progression from stage to stage. An economist in this sense is a disciplined person who, if he walks at a balanced scientific pace, ensures success, and protects against the consequences of improvisation. You see all his works are disciplined and imprinted with the character of the sympathy that Islam brought...It is indiscipline to breach due diligence, or to rush without calculation or discretion. Al-Tirmidhi narrated that the Prophet (peace and blessings of Allaah be upon him) said: "Good azimuth, affection and economy are part of twenty-four parts of prophecy,"[40] as his statement will come.

This was the Islamic curriculum in the field of production and work and in the policy of spending, and in the face of the capitalist's character of extravagance and communism from association, we see it derives its strength

---

[36] - Plant: Discontinuous and back: Beast
[37] - Al-Bukhari: Al-Fath copy 14/74
[38] Life of the Companions 2/114. For Mohamed Youssef
[39] - Tabari History 5/27
[40] - Sahih Al-Tirmidhi 8/171

and effectiveness from the Qur 'an, Hadith, the biography of the Prophet (PBUH) and the behavior of his companions... It means good management and commitment to the approach of moderation and moderation. The frugal in this sense is the person who is known for good management, and the ability to create a balance between income and expenditure in order to overcome the conditions and factors of need. This is taken from the words of the Prophet, as narrated by Imam Aḥmad ibn Ḥanbal: "There is no high economy," that is, what I lack of the best behavior when spending. This was one of the meanings of the word economy. It has become clear from its features in the Islamic economy, unless it is clear in others, that it has the right to retain its original meanings.

In addition to what was decided by the hadith of the principle of mediation, in spending man's energy and organizing his work. In order to ensure the success of projects and the continuation and development of production, we find that the Qur 'an says in the method of consumption and recommending the policy of moderates in their economy: «**Those who, if they spend, do not overspend and do not marry, and between that** there is **strength**» and says: «Do **not make your hand tied to your neck and do not spread it all, so you sit blameworthy.**"[41]

The economist, according to these verses, is the person who is saturated with the spirit of the Qur 'an and applies its teachings, so that he does not overspend, nor does he make his hand chained to his neck, nor does he spread it all, whether when collecting wealth, or when spending it. His behavior is characterized by good economic management, and what is said in the individual is said in the family and the state.

The principles of Islamic economics, in front of the radicalization of the capitalist to the right and the communist to the left, were the first to carry the word "economy" in its original meaning.

Judge Abbas Al-Taraji, in his book "Enjoying the Provisions of Feudalism", reported that the caliph Omar bin Al-Khattab asked in the days of his succession a man: "How was your spending in your family? He said: It is good between two bad things, so extravagance is bad and the covetousness is bad and the consistency between them is good. Allah the Almighty says: And **those who, when they spend, do not spend extravagantly and do not marry, and there is strength in between.** "

Thus, the Islamic economy bears the banner of moderation and moderation, starting with the size of ownership and the method of work, how to produce, and ending with the method of distribution, and how to consume, in response to the plural word contained in the saying of the Prophet (pbuh): "The best things are the middle."

---

[41] - Surat Al-Isra 29.Shackled: Received

Hence, it is clear that the economic approach, deduced from the Qur'an and Hadith, and the mothers of Islamic sources, is not a capitalist, communist, or positivist system. Rather, it is by its identity, entity, constituents and exploitation. An Islamic regime with its warp and flesh. It was not imprinted with the character of Western extravagance or Eastern cohabitation, so it came as a good thing between two bad things, and an advantage between two zigzags: the slip of excessiveness and the slip of negligence, according to Allah, the Islamic countries to apply it and act accordingly.

These were the linguistic, etymological, and Islamic concepts of the word "economy" and its doctrinal influences, the polarizing ideologies of the origins and meanings of capital, the commons, and participation in the image retained by Islamic economics. It carried in its templates some of the first foundations of contemporary economics, and after verbal and moral distortion turned into what is known as capitalism, communism and socialism.

The first men of this nation did not twist on a meaning that was not mentioned in the law of their religion, or a word that was not corrected on the rules of their language. Today, everything has evolved, even concepts and languages. There may be no harm in pronouncing or using the word capitalism, communism and socialism, as the danger does not lie in the use of an Arabic word of hope, which still has an Islamic spirit. Rather, the danger is all the danger in promoting imported principles, saturation with the foreign spirit, and destructive dissenting opinions, which may not be enough to stop its sweeping current, to abandon a new word, or a term of contemporary scientific terminology, especially since the purposes of words, which are embraced by the Islamic economy, vary the purposes they carry in the foreigner's plan. There is no danger left in pronouncing what is meant by the statement, as universal words in circulation, as long as Islamic thought is a source of economic and social principles before they are finished with moderation, and as long as the meanings of Islam and its laws and linguistic uses are based on their origin, attesting to what is authentic and foreign. This was the linguistic and original concept of the word economics.

In terminology, it means the total wealth, in which society disposes, that is, the total productive projects and services related to the production, distribution, circulation and consumption of wealth, in accordance with studied scientific curricula and laws.

An economist in the terminological sense is a person who specializes in economic knowledge. That is, who knows the general theories and laws that govern economic efficiency, and it is true that he is described as an expert, a professor or a scientist specializing in economic affairs.

Among the Prophet's companions were two economists: Abu Zahir al-Ghafari in society, and Umar ibn al-Khattab in the name of the state. One of the theories of Abu Dharr al-Ghafari is that he called for the circulation and investment of cash, not hoarding it and[42] calling for spending the curiosity of money, an expansion on those who have not yet received enough,[43] which is the same as what Omar decided[44].

Omar offered his experience and specialization in the subject of money. He said: "Whoever wants to ask about the Quran, let Abu Ibn Ka 'b come, and whoever wants to ask about the obligatory laws, let Zaid Ibn Thabit come, and whoever wants to ask about jurisprudence, let Moaz Ibn Jabal come, and whoever wants to ask about money, let him come to me. God blessed and Almighty has made me a treasurer and a divider for him." This[45] was stated in his sermon in Al-Jabiyah.Economic efficiency is more practical than theoretical and knowledge is more theoretical than practical. Effectiveness means the sum of the activities carried out by the individual, the state and society for the production, distribution, exchange and consumption of wealth.

Thus, every person who has acquired knowledge through study, experience, and practice, and works in connection with the circle of production, exchange, or consumption, is a contributor to economic efficiency. Worked in agriculture, trade, industry, fishing or livestock raising...The work considered in economic activity, whether physical or intellectual, is the work aimed at producing material goods and goods, because doing physical and intellectual exercise is a significant work, but outside the economic field.

On the direct action of the project, the Islamic economy focuses on acquiring wealth and benefiting from the money of others. In it, the Prophet says from the narration of Imam al-Bukhari: "No one has ever eaten food better than to eat from the work of his hand. And that the prophet of God David ate from the work of his hand."[46]

---

[42]- Opening of the Bari 16/4 Flags of the Nobles 2/49
[43]- The life of Abu Dharr and the type of his socialism, p. 62. The major layers of Ibn Sa 'd 4/235 Hayat al-Sahaba 2/236 Haliya al-Awliya 1/163 .Al-Istiḥām fī Ma'rifat al-Ṣaḥā
[44]- Output of Abu Yusuf in Al-Kanz, p. 27History of the Islamic Nations of Al-Khadri, in Al-Fadl 2/36
[45]- Money for Abu Obaid, p. 123
[46] Al-Bukhari: Al-Fateh version 5/209.

THE LINK BETWEEN THE WORD ECONOMY AND POLITICS AND WHICH POLICY?

Some writers have linked the words economics and politics, because they have noticed the links between the two trends. The history of the link between the two words dates back to the early seventeenth century on the day the French writer Antoine Menkeritien issued in 1615 a book entitled Political Economy, based on the risk of some words. This link is not made in all circumstances and circumstances, especially since the word economy as a broader living reality is more circular, more emancipatory and free from being bound by the link to politics, unless it contains the economic policy of each country, or diplomacy for some countries that link them to economic cooperation, as evidenced by the policy of some developed countries, which refuse to sell some goods such as weapons to those who violate their policy.

Otherwise, the primitive man -for example, he was guided, and knew his way to the economy and its possible means in his hands, before he knew what we express in politics, and some economists even explained that many wild animals such as some birds, rats, bees and ants...It has been guided by instinct and inspiration to search for its living resources, and it may collect in the summer and save what it consumes in the winter, so it meets with man in the field of research and reality, and it is distinguished by the characteristic of crystallized thinking at the level of management, guidance and programming...In this regard, Dr.L. Leontiev says: Animals instinctively perform the most complex movements, but human action is a conscious activity. Work is a characteristic of man alone, "so[47] man specialized in conscious work, and others in inspiring movement.

If it is decided that the economy is the result of human thought - as understood by the expression of political economy - then man is the only frugal creature. Although the whole is moving, searching and rushing with inspiration of thought, instinct or inspiration towards securing his life, responding to his need. Note that the economy is associated with life insurance more than what is associated with thought and culture.

Although the responsibility is concentrated in the human being as a factor for himself and others. The Prophet (PBUH) said, as narrated by Al-Bukhari, Muslim and Al-Tirmidhi: "No believer plants a plant or sows a plant, so that a bird or a beast eats from it, unless he has a charity with it."[48]

If Marxism, which is part of political economy, describes man as a factor of production, he produces and consumes, as the machine produces and consumes, many animals, such as that taken for pearls and offspring...It is also produced and consumed, and if it is noted that some of them are produced with the help of man, and under his supervision, others are like bees that are found in caves and

---

[47]- The Political Economy of Leontiev, p. 11.
[48]- Al-Bukhari: Al-Fath version 5/400, Muslim: Father's version 4/231, Sahih Al-Tirmidhi 6/52.

forests that are produced naturally, and inspired by God, as indicated by the Almighty's **saying: «Your Lord inspired the bees to take from the mountains houses and trees and what they thrive and then collect from all the fruits, so walk the ways of your Lord so that a different drink comes out of their bellies, in which there is healing for people that in this is a sign for people who reflect».**[49]

Marx, in his book "Capital", expressed his astonishment at the precise system of bees, without expressing his opinion on their production, which is considered to be of use and exchange value without being related to abstract human work, which he focuses on but rather imposes in the production of values, despite the foregoing that the value of the commodity is formed by the factors of capital, labor, and land, from which it is produced or made, and not by the only factor is abstract human work, as he said.

Exchange value means that a commodity has a value equivalent to the value of another commodity it is exchanged for, and use means that it is not fit for exchange until it is fit for use. Used by the producer or others, and the work of natural bees, did not result in abstract human work, as his theory suggests. However, it carries use value when used, and exchangeability when replaced with another commodity. It plays an undeniable economic role, and zakat is obligatory for some imams such as Imam Ahmed and Abu Hanifa,[50] as it is obligatory for money, plowing, livestock and commercial performances...The topic will be detailed.

It became clear from this sense that economics in its broad concept, and at the level of life, nature and instinct, starts from the tangible reality, before it knows its way to organized thought, so it was natural to start with the stage of primitive reality, then the stage of stirring up thought at the level of reality, or stirring up reality to thought before it reaches the stage of organization and rationing, in order to become a science, linked to politics or other sciences. It will also come when dealing with the history of economic thought and even today, the individual is economical, the family is economical, and the state is economical. Everyone works and produces, and tries to balance income and expenditure... Thus, it is clear that the expression of political economy is clear only when it is related to the economic policy, internal or external, of some countries... If it obtains self-sufficiency, and can control its economy independently of the intervention, planning of international economic institutions, and directing it to the appropriate destination for its economic, social and political conditions... In order to secure its independence, develop its wealth, develop its economy, and create a balance between what it imports and exports on the one hand, and what it produces and consumes on the other.

---

[49]- Surat Al-Nahl 68.
[50] A Disclosure of the true meanings of Ibn Habira, p. 82, Al-Mizan Al-Kubra 2/6, The Raha of the Ummah in the Difference of the Imams of Damascus, p. 100.

Thus, it is clear that the phrase political economy, which some explain in Marxism, does not mean a special ideology, as much as it means that economic guidance is subordinate to the policy of an eastern, western or developing country, or the policy of an international association, such as the policy of the countries of the European Common Market.

Perhaps this is what Antoine Monchrestien means by political economy, so the economy in the West, for example, is linked to its policy, circumstances and the requirements of its doctrine, and the economy in the East is linked to its policy, circumstances and requirements of its doctrine...

On the other hand, the Islamic economy must stand out for existence, manifesting its identity, elements and independence, and is linked to the life of the Muslim, the conditions of his country, the requirements of his Sharia, and the policy of his state...

In the forefront of Islam, we note that Omar bin Al-Khattab has subordinated the economic system to the policy of the Islamic State, and this is considered the fiscal policy in the era of Omar. As part of his policy, he was looking at the public interest, starting from reality, and subjecting expenditures to income. It moves at its level, increasing each year or decreasing according to the revenues of the state, taking into account its financial conditions. This is only to be dispensed with, and depends on its resources to obtain self-sufficiency, which makes and does not require...

It [51] was this policy that led him to refrain from dividing and stopping the open lands and imposing an abscess on their neck, to raise the expenses of the state and society, and to have their production shared between the former and the latter, and he used to say, as asked by the division: «What is this, in my opinion, so what does it fill the gaps? And what is there for offspring and widows in this country, and in other lands of the Levant and Iraq? "[52]

Hence, it is clear that the policy related to the economy, before others, is economic policy; they called it economic policy, and the political management of the economy as they called it the political economy. All are expressions of the economic direction of the state.

Omar's decision to stop open land, and make its proceeds public property, to promote state expenditures in addition to the establishment of social solidarity, does not mean the expropriation of private property and its transformation into collective property, as the Marxist revolution did and a solution for some to promote it...Rather, it means drawing up a plan that ensures that its proceeds are put in the public interest for fear that it will always divide and become a state among the rich. Otherwise, the land was not divided and was not considered private property, in order to give it the concept of nationalization. Rather, it was

---

[51]- Kharaj Yahya bin Adam, p. 13
[52]- Al-Kharj in the Islamic State of Zia al-Din al-Rayyes, p. 103.

left in the hands of its original foreign master, who paid the state the abscess tax, in exchange for exploiting it. As Judge Abu Yusuf said: "All the lands that Omar stood, were of the kind that did not come into the possession of individuals, and[53] even if they came into their possession, they would not have been exposed to them, because expropriation is permissible only in circumstances related to the public interest, and with real compensation....

---

[53]- Kharj Abi Yusuf, p. 26.

Economics and its Branches

Definition of Economics

Defining economics accurately and specifically is not easy due to the overlapping of its concepts, its connection to human life, intellectual and social data, temporal and spatial conditions, and material conditions that sometimes agree and differ. It was natural for definitions to differ, depending on different trends, schools, and doctrines of economic and social life...

They defined it as "the science of wealth", "a science that studies the conditions of exchange", "a science that studies man's activity in order to satisfy his need", "a science that studies the facilitation of rare materials and the forms of conversion of these resources", "a science that studies the relationship of individuals to each other and to things in their quest for material well-being", "a science that studies production, exchange, distribution and consumption" and "the science of the laws governing wealth" ...etc.

Thus, the definitions differed, and each definition has a meaning that approaches or moves away from the other. Wealth science means that economics deals with the subject of financial wealth and does not go beyond it.

A science that studies the conditions of exchange, means pouring on how to exchange surplus production, types of goods, and various goods, after their production.

It is a science that studies the activity of man in order to satisfy his need. It means searching for the most effective practical methods by which man can meet his desires and satisfy his needs.

A science that studies the facilitation of scarce resources, and the forms of diversion of these resources, means trying to overcome the existing problem, between the scarcity of resources, the large number of needs or the lack of income and the multiplication of expenses, and the search for the most successful ways, and the most effective methods to transform relative scarcity to the level of needs, and the compatibility between the lack of income and the multiplication of expenses.

A science that studies the relationship of individuals to each other, and their relationship to things in their quest for material well-being, means that economics does not study human activity in isolation from things, or things in isolation from man, but rather studies the relationship between individuals, and then the relationship between them and things in order to seek to meet desires and satisfy various material needs. as dictated by the reality of economic activity. The relationship between individuals lies in work, especially in the field of production, consumption, exchange and distribution...and between them and objects located in the subject of nature and its raw materials.

It is a science that studies production, exchange, distribution and consumption. It means that economics studies the conditions of wealth at each of its stages, starting with production as the first stage in which materials turn into usable goods, then circulation, which is the stage in which goods are exchanged between producers and consumers, and then distribution. It is the division of income between the parties contributing to its production, and then consumption, which is the form in which needs are satisfied through the use of products.

The science of the laws that govern wealth means that economics does not mean wealth so much as the laws that govern it.

Economics

Economics is divided into several branches, the most important of which are:

I. THEORETICAL ECONOMICS

It means the study of economic approaches, projects, methods, programs, theories, laws and ideas, in terms of their concepts, and the type of links that link them, in order to determine or record what exists and is present for study, in order to select what is suitable for application. It is possible to summarize its most important approaches in the following areas:

a-Major economic sectors, including studies related to traditional and modern industry, internal and external trade, and food agriculture, which is intended to secure social life, and then commercial that is intended for profit or export.

b-General theories, including studies related to state public finances, national income, money and prices... It is the prerogative of the State through its institutions.

c-Economic planning, which is concerned with the process of programming, developing designs, and preparing and studying projects before entering into implementation. It is the right and competence of the State whenever it acquires a national character.

d-Economic policy, which is concerned with studying the principles, foundations, directions and choices that take into account the economic guidance of the state.... It varies from doctrine to doctrine and from state to state...It is objective and practical if

A country gained self-sufficiency, and was able to control its economy independently ofthe policy of the International Monetary Fund and the International Bank for Reconstruction and Development, as mentioned above, such as the policy of the countries of the European Common Market.

a-National accounting, which is concerned with studying how to "evaluate" production, control it, and estimate its results... The contemporary economy depends on it in terms of economic efficiency and the estimation of national income.

b-The history of economic thought, deals with economic principles, laws and theories from the point of view of their historical development, with the intention of benefiting later from the experience of the former. It is guided by its successes, avoids its failures, and learns about practical theories from intellectuals, as will be detailed.

II. APPLIED ECONOMICS

It means the application of laws, projects and programs studied by the theoretical economy, while working to use the most effective methods and the best means to develop and develop production...It deals with the economic reality as it is in a country or group of countries, based on applied economic geography, such as the distribution, production and consumption of resources in countries or regions...It embraces what is expressed in the descriptive economy, which is focused on the national economy in a limited period of time, as seen in the application of a pentagonal design. Certified by the highest circles in the country...We have presented theoretical economics on applied economics, because theory deals with topics from a theoretical point of view, before it deals with them from an applied point of view...

III. SOCIAL ECONOMY,

It means passing and adapting economic management, and taking it towards the impression of the nature of economic and social justice... This is done by means of equal opportunities and the establishment of the balance of justice when distributing wealth or benefiting from its resources, in order to improve the financial situation of individuals and solve their problems, especially with regard to addressing the situation of the working class, by imposing a system of determining working hours and minimum wages, protecting them from the exploitation of capitalists, and giving them the right to benefit from the social security system, in order to insure their lives against illness, old age and employment accidents...

Islam has established the primacy of establishing the rules of solidarity or social security, as evidenced by the words of the Prophet (PBUH) from the novel of Al-Bukhari and others: "Whoever leaves money, his heirs, and whoever leaves both of us" and in the novel "Whoever leaves money, his heirs,[54] and whoever leaves a debt or actual loss, and to me, and I give priority to the believers",[55] which is the origin of the legitimacy of general social solidarity.

---

[54]- Al-Bukhari: Al-Fath version 5/459, in which the Muslim was increased, agreed upon by Al-Bukhari and Muslim 3/179 Ibn Adam's Output, p. 79, Abi Yusuf's Output, p. 28.
[55]- Sunan Ibn Majah 2/41 , Al-Bukhari: Al-Fath 11/444 narrated by Mu'allaq.

Umar ibn al-Khattab established a system of general solidarity and a social security system to include foreigners and Muslims, as evidenced by the reconciliation contract concluded by the hero Khalid ibn al-Walid in his name with the people of al-Hirah, who are among the dhimmis, where he stated in his book: "We made for them any sheikh who was weakened from work, or who was afflicted with a scourge of pests, his tribute was thrown, and he was paid from the house of Muslim money, and his dependents who established the House of Migration and the House of Islam,[56] which is the origin of the legitimacy of social security in Islam.

Some may fancy that the social security system came as a result of human rights, which the West sees as the first to recognize, while it came as a result of the Muhammadan mission, and Islam transcended religious and sexual considerations and the framework that gave it in the Christian West to the level of social considerations and great humanities, which do not know the boundaries between a human being and a human being: a Muslim, a Jew or a Christian ...It was placed within the framework of social unity and the guarantee of the groups under the banner of the Islamic State.

However, the social security system or the existing pension system in the West, was not granted by Christianity or its countries, but was the work of the employee or worker, as a result of what is deducted from his wage during work, to grow and return to him when needed, so the result was that he guarantees himself in the event of disability by the return of his work in the event of ability, and when the employee and the worker end the effect of the social security system in the West, and does not go beyond what was stated by the Islamic economy, and applied by the Islamic State in its golden age, from the establishment of the system of general solidarity to shade all those whose doctrines are aware of life, regardless of religions and races, and without distinguishing between those who were previously an employee, worker or unemployed...as manifested in earlier texts.

According to it, the caliph Omar ibn al-Khattab spent on the sick, the blind, the damaged, the elderly, the widows and the orphans... Muslims, Jews or Christians. In this regard, Imam al-Sha 'rani, Abu Yusuf, Zia al-Din al-Rayyes and others report that Omar passed by a Jewish sheikh asking, so he gave it to him, and then ordered the treasurer of the House of Money to run on him from charity, and put on him a tribute and recounted that he addressed him by saying: "We ate your youth when we were young and we lost you in old age."[57]

And the youth that the state ate from the Jew in his youth, means what he was doing when he was strong and gained, and Muhammad Yusuf mentioned in the "Life of the Companions" that he had children, so Omar paid him ten

---

[56] Al-Kharj in the Islamic State, p. 163.
[57] - The darkness revealed to all the nation 1/237 Kharj in the Islamic State, p. 163, about which he placed a tribute: dropped it.

dirhams from the house of money, and said: "You cost him the tribute, so if you weaken, you let him taste it." Professor Abdel Moneim Al-Nimr[58] says in the same subject: "We also see Omar doing such a thing for patients who are disabled from work. He passed - on his way to the Levant -a leper Christian monk, so he ordered to give him a salary from the House of Money to ensure his need sustainably[59]. "

Rather, we have before us one of the rules of Islam, imposed by God in solidarity with the needy class, which is Zakat, the Almighty said: "**Alms are only for the poor and the needy and those who work on them and those who are composed of their hearts and in the necks and the debtors and in the way of God and the wayfarer, a duty from God, and God is All-knowing and All-wise.**"[60]

In many of its successive stages, humanity has not lost reformist preachers, or divine religions that have stripped themselves of themselves to call for spreading goodness and charity among people and asking the rich to help the needy, but its long history has not known a nation that deepened the concept of social solidarity, or a law that sat on one of its bases, or the religion of individuals one of its pillars, to serve this noble end, in the form decided by Islam. The Qur'an conflates it with prayer and says: "Establish prayer and give zakat." In this regard, the economist Dr. Mahmoud Abu Al-Saud says: "Islam imposes solidarity among Muslims...It is known that Islam has decided one of the principles of solidarity, unless it is mentioned in a law before it: celestial or status... This general symbiosis is reflected in physical terms. We review the banks of zakat, so we find the right of the poor, the needy, the worker of zakat, the offices, the author, the wayfarer and the debtor, all of these are an imperative duty for society to ensure them, and meet their needs. This imperative duty is part and parcel of the faith.

Abandoning it is tantamount to departing from religion, and reverting to what is below it, as zakat is one of the pillars of Islam. And if one corner collapses, the whole edifice collapses. Zakat here is a material solidarity bond. There is no Islamic society in which there is no solidarity. If this corner had been erected, I would have thrown every crow into socialism under the pretext of defending the poor, a stone that would silence him until the end of the age."[61]

If the social economy means that it is in the interest of all groups of society, and the issue of equality is the most important issue raised at its level, then the first to lay its foundations before the declaration of human rights, the principle

---

[58] The Life of the Companions 2/94.
[59] - Islam and imported principles, p. 109.
[60] - Surat Al-Tawbah 60.
[61] - Main lines in Islamic economics, p. 18.

of equality and centuries[62] before the emergence of material doctrines, is the Messenger (PBUH) and his successors.

On the subject, al-Bukhari and Muslim narrate about Abu Musa al-Ash 'ari that he said: «The Prophet (PBUH) said: « If the Ash 'aris were widowed in the invasion, or if their children's food was reduced in the city, they gathered what they had in one garment, and then divided it between them in one vase at the same time, they are from me and I am from them». Imam Ahmad, from Imam Ali bin Abi Talib,[63] recounted that he said:« The camel of charity passed over the Messenger of Allah (PBUH), so he fell down with his hand to a pile from a camel side, and said: «I am not worthy of this pile of a Muslim man» Abu Bakr[64] said when he was asked to prefer the people of antecedents, jihad and virtue in giving: "This is something whose reward is with God, and this is a pension, for example, it is better than egoism." Omar[65] said about the involvement of all people in the state's finances in time: "By God, who there is no god but He, there is no one but He has the right to this money, give it or prevent it, and no one is more entitled to it than anyone." Imam Ali[66] said to Orabiya, I noticed that he gave it to her like what he gave her lord from Ajam: "I looked at the book of God, and I did not find in it a favor to the son of Ishmael over the son of Ishmaq." The son of[67] Ishmael are the Arabs And Isaac was born. And the saying of Imam Ali is an extension of the saying of the Prophet (PBUH), all of you are from Adam and Adam is from dust, there is no merit of the Arab over Ajami except by piety and gooddeeds. "

IV. THE NATIONAL ECONOMY

It means clarifying the nature of the economy of each country in its homeland, highlighting its components, and what it can distinguish from the economy of another country, as a result of different capabilities, resources and life doctrines. It is therefore based on the economic situation of the state, and expresses its wealth and methods of production ...If the expression occurs in economic patriotism, instead of the national economy, it means achieving self-sufficiency and dispensing with national production. This is relative, not real, as not everything in the world exists within one state.

V. THE INTERNATIONAL ECONOMY

The international economy deals with the existing economic relations between countries, and the extent to which each country in addressing its

---

[62]- The brief in the constitutional law of Mustafa Baroudi, p. 206.
[63] Al-Bukhari : Al-Fateh version 6/55.
[64]- The compound of appendages and the source of interest 5/231.
[65]- Money for Abu Obaid, p. 24 Example: Equality and impact: preference.
[66]- Directed by Abu Yusuf, p. 26.
[67]- The life of the Companions 2/20 and the text is presented.

problems depends on dealing with another country, especially with regard to solving the problem of surplus and deficit.

This is because the state does not consume all that it produces in some sectors, so the surplus falls and in other sectors that do not produce or consume more than it produces, so the deficit falls, so it needs to export its surplus production on the one hand, and import what it meets the deficit on the other hand, such as Morocco exporting its surplus production of phosphate to Iraq, and importing from it what it meets the deficit in oil, and Iraq exports its surplus production of oil to Morocco and imports from it what it meets the deficit in phosphate. Every country has become a producer and consumer of another country: Morocco produces phosphate for Iraq and consumes oil for it, and Iraq produces oil for it and consumes phosphate...The more favorable the export and the import, the more the state controls its economy, the better its financial conditions, and it is the master of the situation, but the type of production and its value in such weapons gives the opportunity to developed countries, and its strength is likely to be on the third world countries.

Thus, it is clear that the economy of the state is negatively and positively affected by its foreign policy, and in the form that characterizes its relationship with others, and that the prosperity and prosperity of the world depends on spreading peace and creating an atmosphere of cooperation, confidence and good relations between countries, as the activity of the international economy activates the activity of the branch unless this or that country is bankrupt in its foreign policy.

The prosperity of the world is a reason for the prosperity of countries, and the prosperity of countries is a reason for the prosperity of families and individuals, and vice versa, as evidenced by what happened during the world wars. The economic recession occurred and materials were lost in the markets. He is not afraid that peace, security and stability are factors of progress, and wars, turmoil and strife are factors of demolition and underdevelopment.... The bestfor a state is peaceful, and the most successful policy is the one that opens up to the East and the West. What I lost on one side, I found on the other, opens up ways of cooperation, and the reasons for economic, cultural and scientific progress... Unlike the downsides of taking one side against another.

On these branches, all economic doctrines, including capitalism, communism, Marxism and positivist socialism, converge in all their different directions. In the Islamic economy, which is one of the legitimate aspects, we find what corresponds to all these branches, as manifested in its crystallization on the social economy. Omar bin Al-Khattab was asked within the framework of international trafficking, and within what is similar to the customs system about what is taken from foreign traders if they bring their goods to the Islamic countries, and he saw that what they take from Muslim traders if they come to their countries is taken from them, so it became[68] clear that Islam is a religion and a state, an economy and a system, a law, justice and a society... Allah has enabled Muslims to act accordingly.

---

[68]- Money for Abu Obaid, p. 18, the great Sunan of Al-Bayhaqi 9/136.

The economic field is a complex field with overlapping meanings and concepts to the extent that it is difficult to determine its areas of influence, and to identify all the links between it and other sciences. Many sciences help or create conditions or lead in the short or long term to the satisfaction of material needs. Medicine, for example, is not classified among the sciences related to economics, but given the incomes of clinics and laboratories, and what the imaging and analysis centers generate...What it requires from the construction of equipment and the establishment of laboratories to make medicine, has indirectly become one of the economic fields...The revenues of the free school in Europe are equal to the revenues of the laboratory, and the return of international athletes is better than the return of some commercial capital.

Therefore, it is difficult to determine the economic areas or fields, and it is also difficult for the practical, theoretical and applied aspects, on the basis of which the meaning of the economic is determined: is the scientist aware of the theories, or the observer of their application, or the practical contributor to the production of goods? It was also manifested in the difference between the teacher of economics and the practitioner of agricultural, commercial and industrial affairs and mineral engineering and extraction. There is no doubt that the engineer in the extraction of solid and liquid minerals is more economically useful than the preserver of theories without their application. If the other prepares the floor, and puts the tires.

However, economic knowledge or the process of wealth production was not limited to the theoretical aspect, the traditional method, or methodological studies, which may only benefit specialists. Rather, it is related within the framework of experience and at the level of contribution to economic effectiveness to the media, research, practical and technical methods and many aspects of public life, where people deal with business and economic opinions, where they do not know, so it was natural to ask about the economy: Is it science or not science?

Concepts have changed, and it is the rigid, backward mindset that does not change with life... The production of wealth has known new methods, and the old inherited theories, which are still being studied within the history of economic ideas, have lagged behind, and most of them are no longer valid to apply, as will be noted when studying the theory of naturalism "Phys and Hippocrates" that only the land produces, or the theory of mercantilism or "Mercantilism" that the source of wealth and the singing of the state lies in obtaining the largest possible number of precious metals of gold and silver, as will come in the Spanish Mercantilism, while the land today represents only one source of wealth. The singing of the state is the sum of the resources that make up its economy. Europe, from which the theory of physical and hierarchical doctrine was launched, does not rely on agriculture, as much as it does on industry, so that it is described today as industrialized countries. It was rational to focus research and studies on practical approaches, and on economic reality, as the approaches would organize processes, and the process, if started with a primitive approach became primitive, especially when moving to a new approach, as was manifested in the establishment of the Islamic Bank.

It may be better to go the usual way, and see - as others see it -that economics is a science, as long as it has principles, laws and foundations on which it is based. An economist is an expert, thinker, or scientist who specializes in economic affairs. They have linked it to a number of sciences such as sociology and its sciences, law and nature... This is because the qualities that it carries or is based on, could not but link it with the sciences that respond to those qualities, and we summarize them in the following

I. SOCIAL SCIENCES

Economics is one of the sciences without which society does not exist, and it is also not based, especially in its political character, except on social considerations. It was natural for it to be considered a social science. The life and sustenance of society depend on its surety. Its guarantee is based on economic effectiveness and the individual in order to secure his life, and the pursuit of material well-being within him, does notproduce alone and especially himself isolated from others. Rather, it is linked to society, and to its members, in many circles: the most important of which are the Department of Production and Consumption, the Department of Exchange of Goods, and the Department of Distribution of Labor and the division of its results...Then came the definition of economics as "a science that studies man's activity in order to satisfy his needs" and links it to social science, especially with regard to class structure, and is economically and socially related to the system of life, and also links it to some sciences known as social sciences:

a-History, especially the history of economic ideas. The suffix benefits from the experience, error, or rightness of his predecessor as mentioned above. It has become recognized that the length of the process and putting theories to the test of long practical experience is the criterion that can correct economic concepts and distinguish between what is practical and what would enter the midst of history.

b-Geography, especially economic and human geography, and what is known as demography, is related to the nature of life of individuals, their source of livelihood, counting their number, knowing who produces and who does not, who produces what is consumed, or more or less than it is consumed, and who lives on agriculture, trade, industry or livestock...This depends on the estimation of national income, and helps to develop economic planning by regions.

It seems that the progress or backwardness of the state is due primarily to the progress or backwardness of the individual, as the first building block of society. The economically, socially and culturally advanced individual is an advanced family, the advanced family is an advanced society, and the advanced society is an advanced state, and vice versa.

By total estimation, it can be said that the developed country is the one whose members consist mostly of the type that produces more than it consumes, then the type that produces what it consumes, or less than it consumes, and the least little is the one that does not produce... A developing country is one in which most of its members are of the type that produces what is consumed or less than what is consumed, then the type that produces more than what is consumed, and the rest does not produce... The underdeveloped is the one whose members are mostly composed of the type that does not produce or produces less than what is consumed, then the type that produces what is consumed, or more than what is consumed, so the progress of the state was dependent on the progress of individuals.

In this sense, the product does not mean what is known in the political economy as the work of the organizer within a factory or company...But I mean the worker in trade, industry, agriculture or livestock breeding...Or other free crafts and professions, along with those who represent ideals, within an integrated society, combining materialism and morale, and then what we mentioned of the class struggle, or the material interpretation of history, with which Marx interpreted the history of societies, and considered the individual within them a factor of production that produces and consumes, as the machine produces and consumes, is considered by the idealists to obliterate the reality of the individual and society.

a-Politics, whether it is economic policy or state policy, does not move or revolve except with the consideration of society. Events have shown that the economic situation is related to the political and social situation, which has improved and stabilized...It is troubled by its turmoil, as evidenced by the difference between the situation in Europe and Africa ...Some researchers even believe that political developments in the lives of peoples are due to economic reasons, and those who hold the theory of the materialist interpretation of history believed that the class struggle was for their sake. As is known to Marx and his doctrines. However, economy-driven or economy-driven politics does not mean party politics, or what is known as demagogic politics, but rather state politics.

Ibn Khaldun "Marx" preceded the establishment of the school of "materialist interpretation of history" as he preceded it to address the theory of the value of the commodity and its factors, as it will come. The difference between the two schools is that Ibn Khaldun believes that the economic element is one of the motives for which the conflict arises. It is one of the four reasons enumerated in his saying: "Either jealousy and competition, or aggression, or anger for God and his religion, or anger for the king and my endeavor to prepare it...".[69]

As for Marx, he limits the historical interpretation of man to the economic or material element alone, denying anything else. Thus, Ibn Khaldun's theory is more comprehensive as it is based on logical rules. It derives its existence from reality, while Marx relied on the exigencies of his materialism, so he assumed one rule for it, and the argument was not based on its own. Do we not know what answers the cause of the Crusades and the "ideological" conflict around Jerusalem? Is there an economic element in the holy site that deserves the destruction of nations?

a-Ethics, what is meant by ethics in the field of economics, is the behavior related to what is expressed in the social economy, which is the sincerity of individuals, their acceptance of the concept of economic and social justice, and the dictates of establishing the balance of justice whenever the distribution of wealth or the benefit of its resources, which is the readiness of the rich to volunteer and the participation of others, as manifested in the abdication of the rich supporters to exploit installments of their lands to the poor immigrants and their tolerance and acceptance of the concept of economic and social justice, the Prophet (PBUH) adopted the establishment of the first economic and practical association, which brought together their songs and the poor immigrants, which is known in the books of Hadith and biography as the Islamic brotherhood. He used to take Ansari's hand and the hand of[70] Muhajiri's hand, and say: «Takhya is two brothers». Ansari, if he had the virtue of land, granted its exploitation and gave its benefit to the origin of his immigrant brother,[71] and if he did not have a virtue in the books under his hand, or if the land is one of Ansari and the work of the Ansari and they are involved in production. The Prophet (PBUH) was the first of the Lord of production.

In it, Al-Bukhari and Al-Bayhaqi narrate that Anas bin Malik said: "When the immigrants came, and they had nothing in their hands, and the Ansar were the people of the land and real estate, so the Ansar divided them to give them from the fruits of their money every year and enough work and provisions,[72] so participation in production was on the basis of contributing to work, so the cohesion of society and its problems were solved. Thanks to the Ansar and the meanings of truth, justice and equality. Yahya ibn Adam narrated from Anas ibn Malik that the Prophet (PBUH) invited them to write something to them in

---

[69]- Introduction p. 379.
[70]- Nour Al-Yaqeen, p. 89.
[71] Al-Bukhari, Al-Fath Version 6/173, Sunan Maja 2/46, Musnad Al-Imam Ahmed, Part 5, Hadith 3135.
[72]- Sunan Al-Kibar Al-Bayhaqi 6/116.

Bahrain and they said: "No, until you write to our immigrant brothers in the same way[73]."

It is possible to decide that virtuous human ethics and the spirit of Islamic brotherhood made the economic system prevailing in the era of the Prophet (PBUH). There are no revolutionary or political principles or coercive laws, which require my supporters to give a part of his money to his immigrant brother, were it not for the truth manifested in the Almighty's saying: "**The believers are brothers, so reconcile between your brothers**", so she lived the principles of truth, justice and equality, without the need for a force to take care of her. Repeated experiences have shown that what is imposed by force does not live without it as mentioned above.

II. Legal Sciences

The economy has laws that limit - depending on the circumstances or expand the scope of its activity, foremost of which is the law of supply and demand, the law of prices, the law of rent, and the law of wages...Thus, it is related to legal sciences, and meets with them directly in such matters as property conditions, contracts and the organization of trafficking, as in the laws of Islamic jurisprudence...It may be associated with other laws in different scientific circles. Such as the law of botany, the law of physics and chemistry, the law of the development of society and other laws that must be known when addressing scientific, economic and social material issues.

Since the economy deals with economic life and the field of material production of society, every law has a relationship with society, or the study of matter and its use for material purposes that meet a need or respond to a desire, unless it has a direct or indirect relationship with political economy.

III. Natural Sciences

The economy has a relationship with nature and its materials, as the first stage from which the production process begins, and it meets it more in two basic places: the first is the geological science of the Earth and the second is the natural geography.

The first is concerned with studying the layers of the earth, and the minerals and solid and liquid substances they contain, and the second is concerned with studying the mountains, hills, plains, rivers, forests and soil types, and the amount of running, underground and descending water from the sky...This provides the indispensable field of economic activity in both places. It was about industrial, commercial or food production...

---

[73]- The book of abscess of Yahya bin Adam, p. 19.

If production in its current form has three aspects: a natural aspect, a technical aspect, and a social aspect, and within which the study of the relationship between man and man is imposed, then between nature and nature, that is, between one color and one of its colors, in an effort to identify the extent of the interactive effects in the production process, as understood from the definition of economics as "a science that studies the relationship of individuals to each other, and their relationship to things", then political economy in this point deals with it from a natural point of view, as well as socially and technically in other points.

The Economic Problem and Ways to Solve It

This chapter deals with the economic problem and its causes, its relationship to work, its methods and results on the one hand, and human needs, their type and difference, and their relationship to economic activity on the other hand. It also deals with the content of economic activity represented in the efforts made to secure material life and respond to its various needs... This is done through the system of acquisition and work. It involves three main processes: production, exchange and consumption.

ECONOMIC ACTIVITY AND HUMAN NEEDS

The economic problem, or what they call globally the economic problem, has human and natural causes: the most important of which are the scarcity of resources and the large number of needs, or the lack of income and the multiplication of expenses, or what Malthus called the imbalance between the population and the amount of resources sufficient to secure their lives... It is in this sense the problem of the individual, the family, and the state, and therefore the problem of the world. Global resources do not cover the needs of more than three to five billion people, especially as they have not been distributed regionally, internationally and continually according to the population, and that some of their incomes - as human causes - are spent in wars and advanced weapons, and in building space ships, factories of oppression and destruction, and in what harms such as drugs, instead of being spent on what pleases humanity and does not make it worse: tampering with the wealth of nations and deviating from the power of money, and the authority of science from the Sunnahs of the guided. The Qur'an has deplored such behavior. And that is in the saying of the Almighty : **"Do you adopt with all the proceeds of a sign that you tinker and take factories in order that you may be immortal, and when you oppress the oppression of tyrants, fear God and obey and fear Him who has provided you with what you know."**[74]

Had the world's resources covered all its needs, or been distributed fairly to its population, famine, unemployment and foreign debt would not have...Even industrialized countries do not relatively cover all their needs. This prompted it to cooperate and bloc and confront the millions of unemployed in its people. Unemployment is one of the forms of scarcity of materials and the abundance of needs. A statement clarified that the economic problem is a general and global problem, which is the deficit in the budgets of America and the Soviet Union before its dissolution. The developed countries were preoccupied with their problems, clustered around their interests, and their bloc resulted in the closure of the global economy and above it the international monetary system in their favor at the expense of the third world countries. Although working for the interest of humanity as a whole, especially securing food security, is the responsibility of man as a race, and his honesty towards God's vicegerency over him, God created the earth, and wanted it as a place of life, and a source of architecture, and chose it as a tool to build this architecture, and work to secure this life, not for some, but for everyone and what is on its back, starting with himself and his dependents, and then with what he owns of animals.

It is common for God's will that the movement of the universes be permanent, and man as a living being is special to the mind and the ability to organize the wheels of life. He could not stand with the movements of the

---

[74]-Surah Al-Shu'ara 132.

universes standing around him... Movement - whatever its type and source - could not have occurred, without motive, engine or reason, and every movement expresses its raison d'être, and bears the reason for which it arose. Although they differ in quality, they do not differ in responding to their physical and moral factors. The birds that the Prophet (PBUH) said about us and their affair: "If you trust God with a right that you entrust to your livelihood, as the bird's livelihood becomes dormant and goes to bed," did not retreat in their dens, and complain about the scarcity of resources, and the abundance of needs, but in a constant movement, so they search and move, and link in their movement between morning and evening expressing the meaning of trust in the success of the reasons, not in leaving them, so God blessed their endeavor, and they deserved to become hungry and go full. and other terrestrial and marine animals, looking and moving. The circumstances or need that prompted her to search for the resources of her power, and secure her life, are the same that forced man to work and search, and struggle with nature in order to take away his strength and clothing...

However, nature - with the will of God - does not curate man with all that satisfies his needs, and meets his desires for their abundance, and most of what it curates is not in its first form usable, so the process of work begins and a confrontation arises between him and nature on the one hand, and then between him and its materials on the other hand: confrontation in order to cut with nature what is commensurate with the level of needs and confrontation in order to turn it into goods or experiences...Among the many varied and unlimited human needs, the needs we study are material needs, the size of which contrasts with the size of economic resources.

They defined economics as "a science that studies the facilitation of scarce resources and their forms of conversion", which means trying to overcome the problem between the scarcity of resources and the large number of needs, and searching for the best and most effective ways to transform relatively scarce resources to the level of many needs. It seems that this definition, among the many definitions, is more related to the motivation to work, as the higher the level of needs at the level of resources, the more the movement imposes its existence, and the human being is forced to resist what suffers from the imbalance between the resource and the expenditure. It has been observed that those who have narrowed the field of life in their countries: either due to the lack of space, the stinginess of nature, or the lack of rainfall...They are the ones who find, work and succeed the most, as evidenced by the people of some European countries and the population of some Moroccan regions.

However, the needs are not determinable, neither in terms of quantity, nor in terms of quality, that there are material and moral needs, necessary and luxurious, social and international, civil and military, educational and health... If the response occurs to each other, the deficit occurs in others. Scientific discovery and demographic growth were only to extend its list, as whenever something is discovered or born, its need is created, especially since resources are scarce, some of which, such as minerals and oil, decrease and tend to disappear.

Thus, it is clear that the biggest problem faced by man, and the least of his efforts, in order to overcome his danger, is the scarcity of resources in front of the large number of needs, especially that the main resources adopted in nutrition, securing the lives of peoples are limited and the needs grow with demographic growth, and develop with the development of life, as manifested in the limited areas of agricultural land, in front of the growing population if it does not decrease with desertification and urbanization, in addition to the fact that its production may weaken or lag behind by rainfall, while the wheel of consumption is constantly escalating, and these are problems of the future, and taking measures does not contradict with the Almighty's saying: «There is no **animal in the earth except for God's sustenance**».[75] The Prophet, upon whom the verse was revealed, was saving the expense of a year for his people, as Al-Bukhari and Muslim narrated[76] to devote himself to the greater.

As for what is being proposed globally from trying to discover new resources and developing what is, in order to seek a solution, it may only be a relative solution, which comes to some countries and not to others, as it is objected to that the research does not guarantee the results and that the development of production, if possible, is determined at the level of balance between the quantities produced and consumed, so that the surplus does not fall at the expense of the product. If the surplus is less dangerous than the deficit, the solution may be to apply this same theory in addition to the good management of the Islamic economy and the approach of a national economic policy. Needs are subject to income, and income is not subject to needs, so one of the meanings of austerity is to dispense with what is missing, and to return from luxuries to necessities, and from satiety to half of it, as was the practice of Caliph Omar bin Al-Khattab in his global policy, where he made expenditures move at the level of income, increasing or decreasing according to the state's revenues. And if he is observed in case of deficiency, he says his famous saying: "If the generous person gets serious, he will get old." It means that he is not more than a Qasim for what God is good for. The year of Ramada "the year of famine in his reign" was determined to add to every person like him, and he says: "A man does not die of half his fullness" means that the rich does not die if he descends from fullness to half, saving the life of a poor person next to him, so that the food of one is sufficient for both.

His saying: "A man does not die from half his fullness" carries with him the theory of the division of needs, and he responds to the law adopted in the

---

[75]- Surat Al-Ankabut 60.
[76] Al-Bukhari, Al-Fateh Version 5/209.

economic analysis of needs, which is the law called "the tender power of needs", which was introduced by the German scientist "Joseon" in 1854 in the theory related to the limit of the benefit or pleasure that a person feels when dealing with a certain material, and accepting the need for it for division. He was quoted by Dr. Fathallah Al-Alou in his book "Political Economy".

According to this law, "Joseon" believes that the limit of utility or the intensity of the need or desire for something escalates in the early stages, and then decreases with the succession of use or intake of units of that thing until it reaches the point of satiety. Where it is necessary to take off, and if the continuation occurs and the limit is exceeded, the benefit turns into harm, and the desire into hatred. The result is that a certain amount of resources is sufficient to meet the needs. The problem is solved at the level of consumption if it is not solved at the level of production. The law is used in other ways.

For example, a hungry person needs to eat ten pieces of meat. His desire rises and rises from one to five and then decreases and decreases from six to ten. where satiety takes place... You see him eagerly receiving the first units and then after the fifth, which represents the last unit to the limit of benefit, he slackens little by little until he is satisfied and shakes his hand. In this case, it is more like a car whose movement escalates when getting up and decreases when standing, unless it is necessary to use the siege prematurely, and using the siege of necessity is like stopping the desire for necessity. The law, as it will come, has been adopted by the marginal school, which focuses in economic analysis on marginal utility, when dealing with, using, or using units in any economic field, based on the latter unit.

This is a form of the law of tender power for needs. Half the satiety that we tried to deduce in the light of Omar's saying: "A man does not die from half his satiety" is the point of separation between the use of the fifth and sixth units, where the border between the end of the escalation of desire and the beginning of its decline. It can be valued as much as necessary for what life does. There is no danger to the body in stopping it, but it needs protection. Some Arab doctors were asked about prevention, and he said: «Do not put your hand in food until you crave it and take your hand off it while you crave it» and what is said in food is said in others. Using only half of the need for something, or what is known as the necessary amount for what life does -as stated by Omar, Abu Dhar al-Ghafari, and other owners of the Messenger (PBUH) makes needs subject to resources, even if they are rare. This is what "half-life economy" means and responds to the austerity policy of governments.

Hence, it is clear that Omar's policy is a rational policy suitable for the individual, the family and the state, because the needs, whether the needs of the individual, the family or the state, are infinite and indeterminable, neither in terms of quality nor in terms of quantity and responding to all their requirements is not easy, as there are, as mentioned above, many different needs...If it is possible to respond to each other, the deficit will occur in others, especially as it varies according to time and place, and the level of economic and social life is different from one country to another and from one continent to another. Scientific progress and new inventions have only increased in size, as mentioned above. Whenever something is invented, the need for it is created, as evidenced by the need for radio, television, car and phone... which are not considered human needs before they are discovered.

The topic, then, has two aspects: one related to the scarcity of resources, working to bring their level closer to the level of needs, and one related to managing what is and exists, and working to adapt it to respond to needs. The measure is to preserve production and estimate it, and to know how to distribute it, believing the Almighty's saying: A tale about the prophet of God, Yusuf ibn Ya 'qub: "**He said, 'Put me over the treasuries of the land. I am a knowledgeable keeper.'" Two basic conditions: preservation of production and work by its means.**[77]

If some researchers believe that the economic problem has two basic elements: the scarcity of resources and the abundance of needs, its solution also has two basic elements: working to push scarcity towards abundance, and managing what is. Not only in the case of scarcity, but even in the case of abundance, considering that the scarcity of resources, and the resulting need is a problem, and their abundance and the resulting corruption are a problem.

Therefore, we find the Messenger (PBUH) seeking refuge from the evil of the sedition of the rich, and the evil of the sedition of poverty, and seeking happiness in the middle between the two seditions. Only good economic management of production and consumption can bring scarcity closer to needs, abundance from the middle, and the transformation of evil in both things into good.

This was the Islamic solution, which was to combine the work with the management of its results. As for the existing confrontation between economic activity and what they termed the economic problem, represented mainly by the aforementioned scarcity of resources and the multiplicity of needs, it seems that its fingerprints will not disappear on the pages of life, as long as the problem of scarcity with the large number of needs exists.

Each trend tried to address it from the angle of its doctrine, and the capitalist trend found its perception in the application of what is known as the idea of rational behavior, and saw that the individual can, if he moves freely, achieve his interest, and by achieving it, part of the public interest is achieved, as the public interest consists of the sum of individual interests, so the problem is solved. On the contrary, the communist trend believes that individual freedom, and the consequent freedom of production and consumption and the attempt of

---

[77]- Surat Yusuf 55.

capitalists to exploit the toilers, is the main reason for the crises that have afflicted the world, so the solution is to nationalize individual freedom, entrench the interest of the individual in the interest of the group, and transform individual property into collective property represented in the person of the state, so the individual's right to life remains limited to what he gives of food and clothing...in exchange for his work for the group.

The truth is that capitalist injustice is a problem, communist extremism is a problem, and the solution is to take the approach of moderation and moderation. It is the combination of the interest of the individual and the group, as stated by Islam, and it means the saying of the Prophet (PBUH) "the **best things are the middle**" and the middle: justice, or the situation that mediates between excess and negligence. Allah has described the Islamic Ummah as the middle Ummah and it should be so.

However, the level of problems in the countries of the third world, including the Arab and Islamic countries, is not easy to solve with the hoped-for assistance of the developed countries to the developing countries or the countries of the North to the countries of the South, or to accept the rescheduling of foreign debt, or to waive some of its benefits...Rather, they dissolve by relying on their resources and the arms of their children, and by developing a sober and sound economic policy, based on the national economy, and based on economic and practical strategies or balances, in accordance with what the Prophet (PBUH) said, "They paid, approached, went, and spirited, and some kind of perseverance and intentionality." The payment in everything is right and wrong. Any country that was not able to control its economy, and was unable to establish four equilibrium, had no choice but to stumble randomly. The four balances are as follows:

1. The balance between the labor force and its programs, and the work units are not intended to replace the monetary units, as it occurs in systems that do not adopt the monetary system. The balance is to be struck between them and the amounts of time, such as eight hours. The wage for work, whether with the state, a Muslim or a legitimate foreigner, in which Al-Bukhari said: "Al-Fateh version 16/271" is the door of the livelihood of the rulers and those working on it. The judge's slice was paid by the judiciary. Aisha said: The guardian - the worker - eats as much as his labor and the food of Abu Bakr and Omar» means from the state finances. A salary of between four thousand and five thousand dirhams per year. According to what Al-Baladzi mentioned in «Futuh Al-Balad, p. 436», however, the worker in the Islamic economy is different from the worker in the modern economy: the worker in the modern economy is a wage earner who is subject to the wage law on the one hand, and the law of supply and demand on the other.

In the Islamic economy, it has different situations according to the quality of its work: if its work is related to time, such as the day and the month, then it is a lease, and the Prophet (PBUH) was ordered to give his wage before his sweat dries, and if it is related to achievement, such as an agency to sell it. It is a type of leasing. The difference is that in the lease, it is worthy of the wage of what has been accomplished, even if it has not been accomplished, and in Al-Ja 'l, it is not worth anything except completely. If he is given money to work in it for a part of its profit, or land to work in it for a part of its production, then he is a partner. The difference between the employee and the partner is that the employee's right is fixed, even with the loss, and the partner has his luck in profit or production if it appears.

2. Balance between production and consumption, so that the surplus does not fall at the expense of the product, or the shortage at the expense of the consumer... And to take care of the interest of each of them from the complete care of the interest of the entire nation, as there is among its members only a producer and a consumer. It is the interest sponsored by Caliph Omar when he noticed that the companion Hatib bin Abi Balata reduced the price of raisins he sells, so he ordered him to raise the price or leave the market, so as not to harm producers...The rational policy in production is the one that is characterized by equilibrium, tenderness and gradualism from stage to stage, which is what is understood by the words of the Prophet (PBUH): "Good azimuth, tenderness and economy are one of twenty-four parts of prophecy" and improvisation is not a failure... It has caused legitimate, economic, political and military setbacks within the Arab world.

3. Balance between income and expenditure, an increase without a balance creates a deficit... And its absence or shortage with its presence harms the interests...Creating a balance between income and expenditure requires adopting Omar's policy of subjecting expenditure to income, so that it rises or falls as it rises or falls. Salaries, additional expenses and construction are unproductive... Subject to state revenues. It was Omar's policy not to give employees everything they asked for. Rather, it gives them what the state can ask for, and generalizes it at all levels. The Prophet (PBUH) told us that poverty comes from misbehavior, and dispensation comes from good economic management, which is what he understands from his saying: "There is no economy", that is, what I lack of the best behavior when spending.

4. The balance between export and import, if not more, as the more likely the export and the import, the better the conditions and the state controls its economy, but the type of production and its high value in such advanced weapons and modern equipment gives the opportunity to the industrialized countries today, especially since their production falls under demand, and the production of third world countries in such acids and minerals falls under supply.

It may fall under the need, and be sold at the price the buyer wants... Control of production requires that the quantities that are exported and the quantities that are consumed are estimated nationally... However, the control of economic policy is production and consumption, export and import. Itdepends on gaining self-sufficiency.

Therefore, it is difficult for a third world country to have a continental economic policy, as long as the International Monetary Fund and the International Bank for Reconstruction and Development are behind its policy. If Islamic countries had reached the level of approach, if they did not reach the level of repayment in the words of their Prophet: "Pay and approach", then the approach would be between the labor force and its programs, between production and consumption, between incomes and expenditures, and between export and import ....

Production, in its current conditions, is a process of coordination between certain proportions of factors of production, on which the conversion of materials extracted from nature into goods or bounties depends... The coordinator of these factors and the observer of their functioning within the institution is the organizer responsible for their phases and the uses associated with them. What a mind job. They can be summarized into three basic elements:

I. WORK

The work concerned in this field: The field of production is the sum of the activities and tasks carried out by man in order to extract or analyze natural materials and convert or reconvert them into goods or bounties that satisfy his needs and respond to his desires. It includes physical and technical work. For example, the process of mining and producing steel or steel depends not only on physical work, but also on knowing the chemical and technological developments that take place when materials are melted in the furnace. The advanced agricultural production process has also gone beyond the traditional stage of work, and depends on knowledge of agricultural engineering, which is capable of studying agricultural production processes from a technical point of view. It seems that every positive action aimed at obtaining a financial return would be placed within the framework of human activity in order to produce good things.

II. THEMES

Production topics are not determinable. And it will evolve - as the means and methods of work evolve with the development of production as manifested in the extraction of oil from stones, and butter from plants...It can be said that it is all that effort and work are exerted on, and includes in the first place what nature allows of raw materials, which are unusable in their first form, and their conversion into goods with use or exchange values, is what is expressed in the production process, and thus it is clear that the goods or goods pass before they reach the hands of the consumer in three stages: Cutting their materials from nature. Converting it ...exchanged or transferred to the market. We have deliberately expressed the conversion of materials deducted from nature into commodities, as there are many conversions that have not been included in the calculation of the production process, as seen in the conversion of flour into food, and fruits into juice... Unless there is a need to produce goods.

III. MEANS

The means of production are all the things that help the producer, through which he works for the success of his projects, and the development of his production, organization, control and control. Intellectual and material means include... From the intellectual adopted in the control of contemporary production, calculation, especially with regard to accounting in order to determine economic effectiveness, and from the material capital, and is divided in the contemporary concept, to the fixed or fixed capital, and circulating or mobile, as it is divided into human and material.

Fixed or fixed capital, means what is not transferred, or what is not missed at the will of profit, such as factories, machinery and production institutions... It is the property that gives production or income, its origin remains, and it depends more on human capital, which is essential in modern technology: it is strengthened by its strength, and weakened by its weakness. It is strong by its power in industrialized or developed countries, and weak by its weakness in third world countries. It is not only the inability of some of these countries to buy or acquire advanced devices, which are monopolized by the industrialized or developed countries. But it is also in the inability to form specialized frameworks at their level. You can use it efficiently. Hence technology was monopolizing and exporting, making money capital, and money capital not making it. You buy with it. This aroused the interests of the third world countries, and made them move towards it now.

Circulating or mobile capital means what is traded in such as wages, the purchase of raw materials and the performance of duties, in order to complete operations and services and the production of goods...It is the type that comes out of the ownership of its owner at the will of profit as it occurs in products and goods. It depends mainly on the use of monetary value or purchasing power of money. The monetary value or purchasing power derives its power from the power of resources, or the economic or productive power of any country, and includes in its entirety agriculture, trade, industry, mineral and animal wealth, fisheries, tourism, and various services...Which are considered as resources, and contribute to the development of production, and high national and national income. From its overall strength - or weakness - money derives its strength and weakness. This fact is what produced the strong money known in hard currencies, in the industrialized or developed countries, and weak in the third world countries, and as a result, the strong money dominated the financial markets and external agreements. The authority of the global monetary system fell into the hands of the developed monopoly, which closed in its favor at the expense of developing countries, or those on the path to growth, as evidenced by the "indebtedness" of the third world... This situation poses the problem of currency unification between two countries of different economic power. This may be the reason for the rejection of "Thatcher" days headed by unification among the European Community, in addition to the fact that unification may harm countries that choose to deal with each country separately...East Germany has benefited from its unification with the West, in exchange for ceding its currency, while fearing the dominance of the strong over the weak. Which can explain the position of Denmark, which refused to ratify the project of unity between the European Community... Weak purchasing power in Third World money has other reasons.

(a) Excess of money, without an economic or productive force supporting it. One of the positives of the old traditional golden guarantee is that it adjusts and determines values and works to unify the monetary system. After it was replaced by economic power or discretionary productivity, the papers began to flow at the level of cash liquidity to solve some problems, at the expense of monetary value, especially in some countries that do not have strong productive resources, knowing that the law of supply and demand deals with goods, workers and money. Strong money or hard currency was needed and weak money was on offer... The solution is to develop production and put money at its level.

B- In the presence of strong money, it excludes the weak from the financial markets, and affects their value, as each percentage increases in the value of the strong, decreases from the value of the weak, or decreases in it, and rises from the weak, so the weak decreases by the percentage of the rise of the strong, and rises by its decline, as is evident when conducting exchange operations.

C- The theory of inflation, and the impact of the value of materials on the value of money, as a result of the continuous activity in demographic growth, and the increasing demand for materials on an upward basis, as the greater the population, the greater the demand for materials, and the higher their value. The percentage that rises in the value of materials decreases or falls in the value of money, so what is known as deflation or economic melting falls in its values. If flour, for example, is sold in dirhams per kilo, then it turns into two dirhams, the value of flour rose by half, and the value of money fell by half, and if it turns into three dirhams, the value of flour rose by two-thirds, and the value of money fell by two-thirds...It is imposed on the level of population multiplication -that it was a dirham for what one person requested, and when two people requested it, it turned into two dirhams, and when three requested it, it turned into three dirhams. The process affects strong and weak money, but its impact on the weak is more, and the solution depends on the development of production to keep pace with demographic growth.

However, the monetary value, purchasing power or weakness of money does not stop when it is provided. However, in all circles related to the monetary system, the circulation of blood in the body negatively or positively affects balances, incomes, wages, profits, the values of things, the productivity of production, and the prices of exported and imported goods as manifested in dealing with the dollar, between its rise and decline.

This aspect is one of the common aspects between the Islamic and liberal economies because of the adoption of the monetary system, with the difference of laws between legitimacy and positivism. However, the Islamic economy has taken precedence to put cash in its real framework, and has given it importance that is rarely given to others, given its importance, and its role in the economic circle, especially in promoting goods and controlling their values. This requires preserving its value and image.

Within the framework of this importance, Muhammad ibn Ahmad al-Oqbani reports that the caliphs cut off the hand of those who defrauded in money[78]. Ali ibn Yusuf al-Fasi reported that Marwan ibn al-Hakam, one of the caliphs of the Umayyad dirham, cut off the hand of a man who cut off a dirham from a knight's dirham. According to al-Waqdi, the emir of Medina during the time of ibn Uthman was punished by cutting the dirham and hitting him with thirty whips. Al-Waqadi said: "This is with us whoever cut it, and planted the zeufs in it." Ibn Radwan[79] reported that the pilgrims fell in love with Mawla al-Hawari ibn Zarah by a thousand, and he was imprisoned to the succession of Umar ibn Abdul Aziz, as a result of finding a fake penny from among the pennies to sell it.[80]

Al-Qadi Ibn al-Arabi says in the «provisions of the Qur 'an» "The breaking of dinars and dirhams is a great sin, because they are the means of estimating the values of things, and the way to know the amount of money, and download them in the oppositions." It was narrated about Omar bin Abdul Aziz that he was given - the days of his emirate on the city - a man who cut off the dirhams, beat him and shaved his head, and ordered that he be circumambulated with him and it was said: "This is the reward of those who cut off the dirhams." He announced that he would cut off the hand of those who did like him after.

Ibn al-Arabi said: "As for his literature with the whip, there is no talk in it, but his throat was done by Omar, and as for cutting off his hand, Omar only took it from the chapter of theft. Because the loan (pieces) of the dirham is not broken, the breakage is the corruption of the description, and the loan is the diminution of fate. He took the money on the embezzlement side. " He said: " Our Maliki scholars said: The dinars and dirhams are the rings of Allah on which is the name of Allah. Had he cut - according to the people of interpretation - the hand of the one who broke the ring of God, he would have been worthy of it, as the one who broke the ring of the Sultan. On him his name is literature, and the seal of God is decreed by the needs. They are not equal in punishment, and I see the pieces in her loan, without breaking them, and I was doing so when I took office. "I[81] mean, the judiciary. This was a picture of the eligibility given to financial and monetary affairs in the Islamic economy.

---

[78]- The masterpiece of the principal, p. 120.
[79]- Doha, which is engaged in the controls of Dar Al-Sikka, p. 244.
[80]- Shining meteors in the beneficial politics of Ibn Radwan, p. 29.
[81]- Provisions of the Qur 'an by Ibn al-Arabi: Section III, p. 1051, Exiled Jewels Contracts in the Evidence of the Doctrine of Abu Hanifa, 2nd edition, 1309 AH, Paths of Peace, 3/27.

In order to preserve the value and voice of cash, and to preserve it from cutting, breaking, forgery and fraud. Besides adjusting the scales and scales, monitoring the prices and fighting the counterfeiters and cheaters...He embarked on the system of calculating and calculating, and it was important that the adult caliphs themselves took over his duties [82] and before them the Messenger (PBUH) took over himself, as evidenced by inserting his hand in the love of a merchant who hid his flaw and said: "Whoever cheats is not one of us."[83]

As for the function of money, it is not in owning and hoarding it, but in promoting and investing it. It is forbidden to freeze their values in gold and silver containers. The Prophet called for its investment, and said in what was narrated by Al-Tirmidhi and Al-Bayhi Haki: «Anyone who is an orphan has money, let him trade in it, and do not leave it until charity eats it»[84] and the wisdom that can be deduced from the texts is the use of money in what it was created from the movement, to be of common benefit, and its purchasing power is exploited in the circulation of production, and moving the wheels of economic and social life, as financial and economic affairs automatically move, by moving money, and frozen by freezing it, and there is no doubt that the production of goods and overcoming the problems of unemployment and the imbalance between income and expenditure, and not keeping pace with economic growth for demographic growth depends on the promotion and investment of money. It represents the working capital.

Production has its policy, and perhaps the best policy adopted by the state is the one that balances production and consumption, or between income and expenditure, in order to prevent the causes of deficit and its consequences -as stated by the Islamic economy, so it graduates from the stage of small industry necessary and food responsive to the needs of the people in securing their lives, then the medium dependent on medium incomes, then the large dependent on high incomes, as the last vehicle that drives it to develop its economy, as it occurred at the time of the European economic renaissance and was manifested in the Moroccan productivity policy. It focused on agricultural and livestock production, the food industry, and the necessary needs, such as the production of dresses, clothes, shoes, mattresses, covers, house equipment, and agricultural and construction materials...All of them are nationally-majority consumer production.

Morocco is among the developing countries that are candidates for self-sufficiency in national production, if it mobilizes all intellectual, practical and monetary energies... In order to achieve economic patriotism, placed on everyone's shoulders. Provided that this policy remains in the same line and the

---

[82] Administrative Arrangements 1/286-287.
[83] Sunan Abu Dawud 3/370 Sahih Al-Tirmidhi 6/54.
[84] - Sahih Al-Tirmidhi 3/136 Grand Sunan of Al-Bayhaqi 6/22.

balance between production and consumption, or between income and expenditure are two parallel policies.

The best thing I did was to focus more on the manufacturing industry, such as turning cotton into fabric and beetroot into scar. Agricultural production and industrial production meet at the table of national production, as seen in Moroccan economic policy. Where the factories are built next to the dams, and where the producer and worker in the agricultural field is Moroccan, and the producer and worker in the industrial field is Moroccan, and the exchange at the level of the market is Moroccan and the consumer is Moroccan. It is a good and successful policy, we have not known a failure like its approach in any country in the world. The international financial institutions interacted with them, at a time when they were wary of the tired policy in some third world countries, especially as they combined economic and social development, and opened up to the East and the West. Their effectiveness is reflected in the availability of necessary materials to the extent that some agricultural products sometimes overflow... Every country that wanted to devote itself to large projects had to focus on the necessary industry and food that would secure the life and stability of society.

As for focusing on the heavy, without its conditions and capabilities, and before it secures social life, and there is a ground for external consumption, it is not without risks, as it lacks material and technical capacity, national frameworks, modern equipment, and outlets for consumption...Especially since any huge project is not successful until it produces the amount of energy spent on it, if it produces half a loss in spending, and if it produces it and does not consume more than a loss in production, it seems that the consumption of heavy industry for a third world country is more difficult than its production, as it may find someone to help it to produce, and it does not find anyone to help it to consume.. It was in the interest of its economy to move at a balanced pace, graduating from one stage to another, or to have integrated economic ties between them that consume what it produces, as happened in Europe, and began in the Western world today. This was a picture of production and its physical means of mobile or circulating capital.

One of the physical means, such as mobile or circulating capital, may be what is consumed for production. values or consumables. Either it is consumed for consumption, such as what is eaten and worn and disappears from existence without leaving a trace in production, and it is called final consumption, or it is consumed for production, that is, in order to show it in new goods more than value, and it crystallizes in their values, and it is called intermediate consumption, through which production takes place. Machines, for example, consume energy to produce new goods, such as clothes.

Energy is of intermediate consumption, and clothing, if used from final consumption, the prevailing expression in the subject is that the machine "consumes and produces" and in fact it is "consumed and consumed to produce" in the sense that it is an increase in consumption that perishes in itself and its value decreases with its age, until it is destroyed, and needs to buy another in its place. If it is normal to count what is consumed in the calculation of the values it produces, it is also normal to count the depreciated percentages of its value from those values. So that it is not compensated without its production.

Suppose that its age is estimated at ten years, and its price is ten thousand dirhams, and what it produces in a year is one thousand commodity units, each commodity unit, takes from its strength and its value is a dirham that is included in the value of that unit. With this consideration, it will compensate itself, along with the expected profit in its use. Otherwise, she is like the mangy camel, what she gives of margarine is anointed with it, as it is said, so she works for herself at a time when it is believed that she works for others. What is said in the machine is said in many means of production that perish, and do not compensate itself with the expected profit from its use, such as a transport car if its life ends, and it does not provide its owner with what he buys in its place, so the answer is that he was eating from its value, and from his work if he was driving it with his hand...Hence the importance of accounting in production.

If we accept this theory, the machine, and the similar means and factors of production, are consumed and consumed to produce, and I say: to produce, because they are consumed only in order to produce, and not like the human being who consumes even if he does not produce. Passover is to say against him: Produces and consumes: if he is a producer or consumes. If it is unemployed.

Thus, artistic and physical work, and the subjects, factors, and means of production are considered. It is led by fixed and circulating capital, or intermediate consumption, which is the most important thing adopted by laboratories, companies and productive institutions.

The main modern companies are five: a joint stock company (anonymous or anonymous), a limited liability company, and a company limited by shares...Partnership Company, Limited Partnership Company...The main Islamic companies are five: Mudaraba and Lending Company,[85] which takes money, and trades it at a certain percentage of its profit, Al-Anan Company, in[86] which the participants work themselves, Al-Ojouh Company[87], whose capital - as its name - is that the participants acquire with their faces and their knowledge of honesty and honesty the confidence of traders and producers, so they buy goods at the deferred price, and a debt falls in their receivables until they sell and pay the

---

[85]- Mudaraba is the language of the people of Iraq, and Qarad is the language of the people of the Hijaz, and they are in one sense.
[86] Mufti of Ibn Qudamah 5/13
[87]- The book of jurisprudence on the four schools of thought 3/68.

price, and the negotiation[88] company in[89] which the negotiation takes place between the participants to include from their money other than Mai, and the business company[90] that does not depend on capital, as much as it depends on work, especially in the field of fishing, industry, minerals and the completion of construction projects...All of which are permissible to dispose of his property with a dispute between the imams in other than speculation and unleashing. The loss is always on money[91] and profit as agreed upon in all companies.[92]

These were the names of modern and Islamic companies, which the methodology here does not allow to analyze their laws and because of their importance, we will hold a separate chapter for them...The most modern works in industry, agriculture, trade, transport, minerals, services and trade in goods and securities. The most that Islamism works in is that it applies trade, industry, agriculture, fishing, transport, minerals, construction and the completion of urban projects. Each company according to its competences with the difference between Sharia and statutory laws, or between permissible and prohibited. If the laws of modernity conform to the Sharia laws, there is no difference, and it is also provided that the company may be established between Muslims and foreigners. In it, Al-Bukhari narrates under the chapter "Participation of Dhimmi and polytheists in sharecropping" about Ibn Umar, he said: "The Messenger of Allah gave Khaybar to the Jews to do it, and plant it. And they have half of what comes out of it. "[93] As is permissible between foreigners and Muslims, it is permissible between women and men and between women among them.[94]

It is known that Islam has lifted from women all kinds of quarantine and guardianship, and what she suffered in the prevailing laws, before its emergence, until this era, which was manifested in Roman law, which considered her as a boy. She is not entitled to act for life[95] and in French law, which considers that she is not qualified to contract, except with the permission and leave of her husband.[96]

As for Islam, it was granted full freedom and full disposition, so it had the right of manumission, mortgage, gift and charity, the right to sell and buy, the right to speculate and contribute to the establishment of companies, and the right to start and terminate contracts.[97] The scholars of jurisprudence decide that a rational woman has the right to read all contracts herself, and to entrust those

---

[88] - Beginning of Ibn Rushd 2/252 Jurisprudence Laws of Ibn Jizy, p. 209.
[89] - The beginning of the diligent.
[90] - Al-Mughni 5/3 Beginning of the Diligent 2/52 Jurisprudential Laws of Ibn Jizi 209.
[91] - The singer for Ibn Qudamah 5/62.
[92] Local for Ibn Jazm 8/126, singer 5/26.
[93] Al-Bukhari, Al-Fateh version 6/60.
[94] The Great Code of Maliki Jurisprudence 4/28.
[95] Muhammad al-Mithal al-Kamil, p. 267, by Muhammad Ahmad Jad al-Mawla Bey.
[96] - Same source and page.
[97] - Islamic Thought and Evolution, p. 24, Ahmed Fathi Othman.

who are common to her, and not to object to her. Rather, Malikiyah allowed her to be a guardian and a proxy. Al-Bayhaqi narrated that Maimouna, the wife of the Prophet (PBUH), had freed the child of God, without asking the Messenger (PBUH). This[98] was the right of a good and rational woman in Islam, but the foolish woman was entitled to quarantine, as was the right of the foolish man himself.

---

[98]- Grand Sunnah Al-Bayhaqi 6/59.

Production is traditionally divided into food production, commodity production or food production and commercial production. It is the food, sustenance, or pilgrimage production in which the head of the family produces what is consumed, and nothing is surplus to his need. He is a producer and a consumer of himself. This phenomenon is prevalent in ancient societies. On a day when the family was closed to itself, it did not care more than to produce what it needed in terms of love or vegetables to grow, clothes to weave, fats to squeeze, or animals to produce, and little more than its need. Its closure remained a loop around itself, sitting inside a narrow circle from which it could not get out until economic development began, and with it the desire to acquire wealth and raise the standard of life. This can only be done through joint efforts. The person felt the difficulty of the situation, felt the need to cooperate, and began to think about himself and those who followed him.

Perhaps the first obstacle that stood in his face was to realize that it is almost impossible for him to establish himself as the stature of society, and produce everything he needs from anything, so circumstances tended to divide work and move towards specialization, so each team specialized in a field of economic activity, so he found the farmer next to the factories and the trader. The process has shifted from the production of food, and what meets the needs to the production of goods, so the production of goods has multiplied, and it has exceeded the consumption of each product as much as the type it produces. At a time when it is in need of the production of others, the interest required that its surplus production be replaced by the surplus of the production of others, and automatically found itself in a circle in which it became a producer and consumer for itself and others.

Then the swap arose, and the swap is a process of conversion, by which goods are transferred from the producer or seller to the consumer or buyer, and their movement strengthens and increases as economic activity increases and stagnates, and usually takes place within the markets. It has laws known as trafficking laws

The market, whether locally, nationally or internationally, is concerned with a type of goods or with different types, which has no more status due to its old status than the meeting place of the exhibitors and the applicants for the goods. It is a place of covenant for the completion of operations and the conclusion of related agreements, and it is considered one of the public facilities of the state, which no one has a monopoly on, unless it acquires the character of a store or owned stores. Its existence is linked to surplus production, as there is no market without surplus production, which its owner dispenses with, and wishes to replace it with the surplus production of others.

The process is carried out directly by means of the barter known in ancient societies. It is the sale of one commodity by another, or by means of money, after a person has been guided to put it. The price shall be determined either by the state rate or by the law of supply and demand. The role of cash in the completion of operations, and the circulation of goods is like the role of oil in the engine, facilitates movement, not its elements, as he said: "Davidium" and preventing it from trading indirectly means stopping the movement of production, and the circulation of goods. The French philosopher «Proudhon 1809-1865» was asked about the reason for the lack of good things in the markets, and he said: «Cash is a guardian standing at the door of the markets. He gave an order to prevent anyone from entering»[99] He wants that cash from the force can stop the movement, if they stop moving him, as by losing him he loses the goods that ask for him...The economist Dr. Mahmoud Abu Al-Saud gave the role of criticism in the promotion of goods as an example. Hypotheses are not discussed, he said: "We impose a society consisting of a baker and a fisherman. The two were introduced to exchange at the end of the day a loaf baked by the baker with a pigeon caught by the fisherman, and then we assume that they were introduced to the use of a monetary unit, so the baker sells his loaf to the fisherman, and the cash unit is required from him, and then if the morning the fisherman sold it to the pigeon baker, and the monetary unit was required from him. and so on. . Then we assume that the baker decided to keep the monetary unit, so what is it? He will not buy from the fisherman his catch, and thus the fisherman will not benefit from his surplus production, and then tomorrow he will not be able to sell his excess loaf, as the fisherman has no other criticism, and so we find in this hypothetical society that the wheel of circulation must stand. "[100]

As for Islam, it set the exchange laws, encouraged production, called for the promotion of money, and denounced hoarding and monopoly, as the companion Abu Dharr al-Ghafari said in general: **"Those who hoard gold and silver and do not spend it for the sake of Allah, preach to them a painful punishment." One of the signs of production, investment and trading in money in the markets is what the Prophet (PBUH) said: "No orphan's guardian has money, let him take it and do not leave it until charity eats him."**[101] And the money that Zakat eats if it does not sleep and does not promote and invest and the Zakat comes out of it every year, is the money represented by the treasured money. As for the others, they develop and the duty of zakat comes out of them naturally.

It should be noted that the Islamic economy was the first economy, which set the laws of trafficking, opened the file of free markets and dropped the

---

[99]- On the main lines in Islamic economics, p. 25 by Dr. Mahmoud Abu Al-Saud.
[100]- Main lines in Islamic economics, p. 23 by Dr. Mahmoud Abu Al-Saud.
[101]- Surat Al-Tawbah 34.

intermediary between the producer and the consumer. The price is determined at the level of the law of supply and demand, according to the words of the Prophet (PBUH), as narrated by Muslim, Al-Tirmidhi, Abu Dawood and Al-Nasa 'i:«Hadir Labad is notsold. Let the people provide for God from each other. "He[102] does not sell Hadhir to Badad: He does not mediate or have a broker, as Al-Bukhari narrated," Al-Fath Version 5/275 " about Ibn Abbas. Al-Hadhir is the resident of Al-Hadra who knows its prices and Al-Badi is the Bedouin who imported his commodity and wants to sell it. Mediation means monopoly and opportunity. Prohibited mediation does not mean proxy for sale, but rather means monopoly at the expense of society, and the most dangerous mediation, mediation of communist countries. It shattered the Soviet Union and returned it to a market economy. Practical experiences have shown that freedom of production, freedom of exchange and freedom of consumption regulated by just Sharia laws are the best way to develop production and its factors.

It was the right of the Muslim to produce the commodity or buy it and sell it at a price that pleases him. He may choose the method of bargaining, Murabaha, auction or position.... We have detailed it with evidence in the "Islamic Economy Approach to the Production and Consumption of Wealth". It[103] may also sell at the accelerated or deferred price, or some of it may be accelerated. Some deferred in other than the sale of the ladder and[104] deferred is the one in which the commodity accelerates and delays the price,[105] unlike the sale of the ladder in which the price accelerates and delays the commodity,[106] which is a license excluded from the sale of what it does not own. Both are narrated about the Prophet (PBUH).

One of the conditions for selling the ladder is to mention its sex and type, and to know its destiny. By the criterion of Sharia, and to be in the dhimmah, and to be what is often found when the time comes, and to know the Muslim capital, and to be received in the contract council, and not to fall into the fruits of a tree, or to plant a specific orchard, so that there is no problem, if production lags behind. They allowed the difference in profit between the accelerated and deferred sale [107] if it did not reach the level of injustice, due to economic considerations such as the disruption of capital and the change in prices, so some

---

[102] Sunan al-Nasa 'i 7/256.
[103] - Al-Bukhari, Al-Fath Version 5/206, Muslim, Father's Version 4/295, Sunan Al-Nasa 'i, 7/303.
[104] - Muslim version of the father 4/296 Al-Bukhari version of Al-Fath 5/335 Sahih Al-Tirmidhi 6/48 Sunan Ibn Majah 2/22.
[105] - Ghaniya Al-Ma 'ar and the following on Al-Fashtali documents, p. 288.
[106] - Sharḥ al-Bī 'Alī Ṣaḥīḥ Muslim 4/296.
[107] - The jurisprudence of the Sunnah of the former master T-1-1977 - The approach of Islamic economics in the production of the revolution and the consumption of 1/418 of the author.

imagined that it was usury, and only the sale of the sample[108] or two sales in a sale[109].

One of the forms of selling the sample is to sell a commodity to another person at a deferred price, and then buy it from him immediately at a lower price, such as selling it for one hundred, and buying it for eighty and remaining twenty in the custody of the buyer, and the buyer does not want the commodity, but wants money ...It is a trick and a picture of usury ...One of the forms of two sales in a sale is that the knot combines the accelerator and the postponement, and it is not unique to one of them, or it falls on two goods, without specifying one of them, and it also falls on the one who terminates the sale, and then goes to consult, or consult about which of the two sales to work, or which of the two goods to take, and if one of them dies in that case, a problem occurs, as neither the type of sale nor the item is specified. The Prophet (PBUH) forbade them as he forbade all corrupt sales, which the research methodology here does not allow for analysis. I refer to the first part of my book, "The Approach of Islamic Economics in the Production and Consumption of Wealth, Especially the Chapters Related to Usurious Transactions and Corrupt and Correct Sales.

What is most striking today is the injustice in the prices of goods and their monopoly and the injustice in the price of the commodity, and the percentage of profit in them is estimated at more than one-third of the capital, and some, such as Ibn Rushd, saw that it is the price outside the usual prevailing in the market[110] and in French and Roman law is estimated at more than half and[111] famous at one-third. In it, Ibn Asim said in the masterpiece of the rulers:

| Whoever is ungrateful in what he has sold has the right to be ignorant of what he has done and when he is annulled by judgments | His condition is that it is not permissible for the public to be injured by a third, and what increased the impact, and it is not permissible for the knower to establish |

The monopoly of materials does not mean that the producer saves his production until the price and materials are available in the markets, nor does the trader who bears the difficulties in bringing goods, in the service of himself and society, and it was appropriate to be given the opportunity to choose and to act freely. So that people - as Zarkani said - do not refrain from bringing, unless people still have a need, and there is nothing that he has with others, so he is forced to sell at the price of time, in order to pay for the damage, as Zarkani

---

[108] Sunan Abu Dawud 3/373.
[109] - Sunan for women 7/295.
[110] - Sub-Mukhtaṣar of Ibn al-Ḥājib under No. 2374
[111] Legislative Approaches 1/189 by Abdullah Ali Hassan, 1st edition, 1946.

quoted from Qurtubi and Qadi Ayadh[112] and Al-Manjouri quoted Malik as saying: "If a person has food and people need it, the Imam ordered him to sell it and the[113] pronunciation of the Imam in the first chest is equal to the word state in this era.

Muḥammad ibn Ismāʻīl al-Sanānī explained the meaning of the monopoly of food. He said: «He bought it and imprisoned it to say and glue». He quoted Judge Abī Yūsuf about the generalization of the meaning of monopoly that he said: «All that harms people is his imprisonment, it is a monopoly. And whether it is gold or clothing. "Abdullah bin Ibrahim Al-Tamli[114] mentioned about Al-Mazouni that it is not permissible in the years of famine, except for the middle price, and that the seller must return the excess,[115] meaning the excess in profit over the middle price.

Thus, it becomes clear that the product or seller, who is normally waiting for the right opportunity to sell, is not considered a monopoly. Rather, the monopolist is the person who has treasures and curiosities of money that he does not want to trade in a normal way. Rather, it tries to monopolize materials because of them. Whenever something enters the market, I need it and wait for high prices, as is the case with some traders, and some companies today, especially when circumstances warn that an increase in the price will appear in the arena... The reward of the bringer and the monopolist was that the Prophet said in their regard, "The bringer is Marzouk, and the monopolist is cursed."[116]

Imam Malik narrated from Caliph Omar bin Al-Khattab that he said: "There is no monopoly in our market. Men baptize with their hands curiosity[117] to go to a livelihood from the livelihood of God, which descended in our yard, and they monopolize it for us until the price increases, but whichever bringer brought on the pillar of his liver in winter and summer, so that the guest of life will sell how God wills, and hold how Godwills. "It[118] came in the narration of Al-Bayhaqi that he entered the market, and he saw people monopolizing, and he said: " God Almighty comes to us with sustenance, even if our market descends, some people rise up and monopolize it thanks to their departure from the widow and the poor, if the jilb comes out, they sell as they want from control ...[119]

As a professor of Sharia, and in Islamic and political economics, I have said that I have not found anything in the modern economy that does not exist. First, there is an alternative to it in the Islamic economy, except that it is prevented by God from causing moral, health, economic or social harm. And that the social

---

[112]- Sharḥ al-Zurqānī ʻalá al-Mawṭā 3/299.
[113]- Answers to the jurisprudence of Ahmed bin Ali Al-Manjouri, p. 6 - AD - 4 - Juh No. 318.
[114]On the Paths of Peace 3/25.
[115]- Answers of the late jurists, p. 42.
[116]Sunan Ibn Majah 2/4 The Greater Sunan of Al-Bayqi 6/30.
[117]- Gathering gold.
[118]- Muwatta: Al-Zarqani Version 3/299.
[119]Grand Sunnah 6/30.

economy -if we exclude the actions of some violators - is practically Islamic. Rather, it needs the awareness of workers and an impartial scientific study, rather than a targeted personality. Disciplines in literature, history, philosophy, economics, and law are respected. In Islamic studies, he writes, discusses and opposes both Hub and Bear" without evidence or reference to a source. The Messenger of Allah believed, saying: "Ifthings are entrusted to other than their people, wait for the hour." The social economy, unlike the government, is mostly regulated by Sharia laws, without knowing a name for its employees... For example, in trade: a trader or speculator who participates with his money. In industry: wage maker or for sale... In agriculture: A farmer in his hand or a participant in his land. In livestock breeding: a breeder by himself or a participant with others. In construction: A building with a fee or a boycott. In transport: deceptive to a tanker or car, or a carrier with a guarantee. All are permissible in Shari 'ah.

This was the perception of the traditional method of swapping production in free markets and the role of cash within them. Today, the face of production has changed, and with it the face of exchange and the face and nature of transactions in the markets, as reflected in international agreements and financial markets.

Traditional markets depend on commodities, freedom of trade, and financial markets or "stock exchanges" rely on securities, such as stocks, bonds, and other newly developed and traded securities and financial instruments, in a way that exceeds the freedom of the market to sometimes disturb it, and they are divided into the primary market, or the issuance market in which various companies and institutions with financing deficits issue those securities and instruments, and into the secondary market or stock exchange.

A stock exchange is a place designated by the government to trade securities. It serves as a container for collecting information on the activity of companies, called the secondary market. Brokers and members involved in them trade the various securities included in the market list, before they move into the possession of the buyer, and they are used.

For the proliferation of transactions and types of securities, especially in recent years, we are limited to giving the model of stocks and bonds and selling options in their status and concepts in Western markets, and then in their Islamic perspective.

SHARE

Share in general, represents the share or part of the capital of the ownership of the joint stock company, with its profit and loss. It is in the capacity of a negotiable and transferable document, and it is often purchased at the nominal value, that is, the registered price printed on its face. There are types:

1-The ordinary share, which represents a share in the company's property and a common right in its assets, considering the nominal value, and gives its owner - in addition to his share in the profit - the right to participate in the election, and direct the company towards achieving its objectives.

2- Preferred share: It means preferred over the ordinary share, because of its owner's preference in the maturity of the profit, the guarantee of the nominal value, as included in the loan bond, and the right of precedence over the company's belongings when liquidating it. It may be closer to the common stock or bond: if you guarantee the nominal value, it is closer to the bond, and if you do not guarantee it is closer to the common stock.

3- **Enjoyment share:** The shareholder usually provides a share of money to the company, to obtain a share that continues to continue, and does not return to him, except when it expires, unless he sells it, but in the enjoyment share, the nominal value of the share is returned to the shareholder during the life of the company gradually or at once, with his entitlement to profit remaining. This process is called the depreciation of shares and is used by companies that are limited to a certain period, such as the completion of a project, or the exploitation of a mineral mine with a government concession specified in years. They go through the difficult stages, they check for success, and their expenses go down.

Option and Undertaking Sale and Purchase of Shares

This transaction occurs in commodities and securities, such as stocks, bonds and financial instruments traded on stock exchanges, and means the option to buy and sell them, during a specific date with a period of time, such as one month and two months, at a pre-agreed price, and the buyer of the option does not have an obligation to sell or buy. Rather, it is just a right that, according to what is required by his interest, he can exercise or leave within the specified period.

The company's goal is to sell by option, either in order to encourage senior managers and managers to dedicate themselves to serving it, or in order to obtain new investors, or to create difficulties for those who want to buy a high share of its traded shares in order to control them, so it gives the right of option to its shareholders to obtain shares in a new issue at a price, which may be lower than the prevailing price to be more committed to their old shares.

In addition to option sales, companies issue pledges to sell shares in a specific or absolute period, at a price that may be lower than the prevailing price, in order to obtain income, without affecting the size of their ownership by introducing new shareholders, as buying the share with the pledge is not related to the profit of its investment, but rather to what is expected from the profit in its high price. As shares in a successful company rise by themselves, regardless of the profit of its investment, the shareholder – for example, he may buy a share for a hundred, and sell it after years by a thousand.

From a legal point of view, a share in an Islamic company, or an institution between a Muslim and a foreigner, is a share in its capital provided by the participant or bought by those who have previously participated in it, provided that they bear their loss in exchange for the profit they receive, so they may own and profit. It is a bit that does not turn and does not trade, as trendy stocks do. Rather, it continues to continue, until it stops, breaks or loses and liquidates. Its owner has the right to sell it, as property is sold, after he offers it to his partners.

If they do not want to buy it, they authorize him to sell it to others, as stated in the hadiths of Muslim and Al-Nasa 'i.[120]

As for its purchase from the shareholding or its modern anonymity, it is permissible in the ordinary share, which does not guarantee its nominal value, if its activity is known and its transactions are directed and its laws comply with the Sharia laws, such as working in transportation, fishing, minerals, agriculture, industry or trading in licenses... Based on the permissibility of establishing a company between a Muslim and [121] a foreigner similar to what the Prophet (PBUH) did with the Jews of Khaybar. Where he gave them the land on the condition that it is produced, [122] but in trafficking, it is required that the management be in the hands of a Muslim or with his knowledge and record, so that the foreigner is not alone in the management, and deals with prohibited transactions. Scholars have authorized the purchase of the stock from the contribution, and did not prevent it - according to what Dr. Abdulaziz Al-Khayyat mentioned in his book "Companies in the Light of Islam, p. 60, except Taqi Al-Din Al-Nabhani and Dr. Issa Abdo. Whereas Sheikh Mahmoud Shaltut, Dr. Muhammad Yusuf Musa, Sheikh Ali Al-Khafif, Sheikh Muhammad Abu Zahra, Sheikh Abdul Wahab Khallaf, Sheikh Abdul Rahman Hassan, Sheikh Muhammad Al-Mahdi Al-Khalisi, and Dr. Gharib Al-Jamal authorized...

It seems to be right with the permissives. The stock gives a kind of independent ownership. as being sold, bought, transferred, and traded. It's like buying an apartment in a company-owned building. Therefore, it does not bear, or be measured on the share of the partner in the Islamic or joint venture company.

Buying the stock and selling it with the option, it seems, is not buying and selling. Rather, it is a promise or proposal from the company, and the buyer's choice in implementation, and differs from selling the option in Islamic jurisprudence, which relates to the opportunity of the option to conclude the contract and is divided into the option of the Council, pursuant to the words of the Prophet (PBUH) from the Bukhari and Tirmidhi novel: "The two sales by option unless they are separated, or separated" [123] and to the option of the condition, which the owner says, without the option of the Council...This is as if the seller says to the buyer: If you do not come up with the price on such a day, then there is no sale. Or the buyer says if I don't get the price on a day like this, don't buy. The judge's ruling is slicey and Bukhari narrated it pending[124] and it can be permissible,if the option is not for a consideration or price, and it is considered as a condition option in Islamic jurisprudence, the company used to

---

[120] - Sahih Muslim: Father's version 4/306 Sunan Al-Nasa 'i 7/301.
[121] - Completion of the advertiser for Ayyad Ali Sahih Muslim 2/6 under No. 2281C for Sheikh Al-Mazri.
[122] Al-Bukhari: Al-Fateh version 6/60.
[123] Al-Bukhari, Al-Fateh version 5/230, Sahih Al-Tirmidhi, and his pronunciation 5/254.
[124] Al-Bukhari, Al-Fateh version 6/183.

say: If you do not come up with the price of the share within thirty days, there is no sale.

BOND

A bond is a paper of financial value, purchased at its nominal value: It is issued by governments and some companies, and includes an undertaking by its issuer to pay a specified periodic interest on. below ninety days and above. It is a debt document whose holder is treated as a lender and to which the laws governing the relationship between the creditor and the debtor apply. He is not entitled to participate in what the shareholder participates in, such as administrative election, but some companies give him the right to vote, when they feel that investors' confidence in their management is weakening. Therefore, they accept to lend it sometimes if they accept to participate in voting.

Bonds now account for the bulk of securities traded in developed country markets. Its advantage is that it is guaranteed at its nominal value and its benefits by an obligation from its source. If the issuing company fails to pay the interest or the nominal value, the issuing authority shall sell its property in fulfillment of that obligation. Therefore, people tend to buy government bonds, because they are more secure and more profitable, if they are exempt from taxes.

However, the bond as a debt document, which is intended to obtain guaranteed continental benefits, may be subject to its benefits due to the factors of inflation and price volatility below us, so its value falls, and its benefits shrink, so the proposal was that the benefits move at the level of inflation and price volatility... Note that each percentage increase in the value of materials or increase in prices decreases in the value of the bond and its benefits. For example, if the interest rate is ten and the value of the materials increases, or the prices increase by ten, the return of the bond will be eliminated from the interest.

TRANSFERABLE AND RECALLABLE DEED OF ENGAGEMENT

The participation bond combines interest and profit potential, as it guarantees the specified interest rate, and it is distinguished from the loan bond by a promise from the issuing company to add another percentage if profit allows it to do so. It is described as a profit participation bond. If it is not achieved, its bearer is only entitled to benefits.

The convertible bond gives the bearer the right to convert it into an ordinary or preferred share or another type of securities issued by the company, if the issuance document so stipulates.

The callable bond, with a text from the issuance document, means that the company, especially in the indefinite, or long-term, requires summoning its holder whenever it wants to give itself the opportunity to repay the loan, but if it requires repayment at the nominal value, investors may not accept to buy it because it may call its holder at a time when its price is higher than its nominal value, so it does not benefit from selling it.

From the legal point of view, the bond, if it is called the participation bond in the Islamic concept, or investment certificates, and it is intended to contribute to a profitable productive project, and its owner bears his share of the loss, in exchange for his share of the profit, so its ruling - such as the share - is a ruling to contribute a share of the capital of the Mudaraba company. [125] And Islamic loans, as it means giving money to those who trade it in a common percentage of its profit: such as a quarter, a third or half.... According to what was agreed upon between the owner of the money and the worker. or between the moneylords and the company. The shareholder bears what his share represents in the loss, and takes his share by quota in the certain percentage of the capital of the profits...If it is on a loan fee with guaranteed continental interest, and its owner is given the judgment of the creditor, and the issuer is the judgment of the debtor, it may be the same as bank deposits in the first form, but not the second.

It was presented during 1989 for discussion in Egypt, under the title "Investment Certificates", which was prevented by the Sheikh of Al-Azhar, and authorized by the Grand Mufti Sheikh Al-Tantawi,[126] referring to the fatwa of Sheikh Shaltut, although Sheikh Shaltut repented of his fatwa before his death, as the late Abdul Rahim Abdul Bar told me...What determines the case is the cost-effectiveness in what way? Is it by profit and loss sharing, or by guaranteed continental benefits? This is the view that I adopted during the Islamic Financial Markets Symposium held in Rabat and during the Islamic Economic Thought Forum

Cezayir.

Then there are some problems that stand in the way of a Muslim, when he wants to buy shares and securities from modern companies. Examples include:

1- Different forms of transactions and concepts, between Europe and America, or between one company and another, as it may be permissible in one face and may not be permissible in another, which makes it difficult to sort the papers, and confuses non-specialists in Sharia and economics. This is the same as what Sheikh Muhammad Abduh signed, as a British company in Egypt presented him with a picture, which he saw as one of the forms of Islamic speculation, so he approved it, and rumored that it allowed life insurance.[127]

2-Based on the fact that a Muslim may not buy a share or a security from a modern company until he knows about its activity and transactions, does it work

---

[125]- Singer to Ibn Qudamah 5/24-31
[126]- Fatwas of Sheikh Shaltut, p. 353.
[127]Introduction to Economic Theory in the Islamic Curriculum of Dr. Ahmed Al-Najjar, p. 185.

in halal or haram? It is very difficult to know her situation and the secret of her profession, especially if she works in several countries.

3- The loss that may be suffered in the difference between the real and the simulated shares. The real share is funded, and the simulated share - its name -is exposed. His bearer only has the paper. Although it is legally prohibited to sell it, and the issuance of the bond in its form is also prohibited, the problem is that it is a confidential issue. It is practiced by some companies, when they are weak or feel the conditions of bankruptcy. If bankruptcy actually occurs, the victim of the loss that he began to buy is gone, and the unscrupulous does not lack a way to escape the grip of the law.

4 His debt to the company is linked to the fate of its capital, as the debts that it may have on the part of shareholders or others are not insured at the time of loss, because participation in anonymous, anonymous, or public name wrapping falls between funds... Its debts do not exceed its capital to the funds of the participants, except for Islamic companies, including Mudaraba and Qard, in which the partnership between persons has debts that fall into their receivables, and the debtor is not discharged except by performing what is related to it, so it exceeded its capital to the funds of the participants. This is a preservation of people's rights, as it is not possible to manipulate them, and to claim bankruptcy, as it occurs in modern companies, and this is one of the advantages of legitimate contracts.

SELLING CURRENCIES AND BILLS OF EXCHANGE AND DEALING BY CHECK

As for hard currencies, and gold bullion, trade occurs in them, as well as in various commodities: either through monetary exchange, between different currencies, or buying and selling gold bullion in ounces. Since what is bought and sold at the level of Islamic jurisprudence is commodities, we wonder: Is money a commodity, or a tool to express its values?

Economists differed on the nature of money: Is it "the apparent form that indicates the value of commodities, or is it the material by which society expresses the volumes of the values of commodities,"[128] as Marx said, or is it "like all other commodities an economic commodity,"[129] as Dr. Hussein Omar said?

In the Islamic economy, gold and silver are considered commodities when they are molten or embedded, offered for sale, so when they want to pay zakat, they evaluate commercial offers, and money when they are molten. In this case, they are considered a measure, "evaluation," or price of commodities, and an asset for the values of things, as Ibn Khaldun says, in addition to being an intermediary between commodities and the secret of their circulation. In its price, Abu Obaid al-Qasim bin Salam says: "The eye and paper are not suitable for anything, except that they are a price for it." Ibn Khaldun[130] says: "Allah Almighty created the two metals of gold and silver as a value for every financier. They are the ammunition and the cannula for the people of the world mostly."[131]

Gold and silver coins, bronze and copper coins can be considered commodities. As long as they are made, as goods are made.

Al-Muzni said about money: "Money is not the price of things," so[132] it is considered commodities. This view confirms that the companion Abather al-Ghafari, who generalizes the verdict in his Almighty saying: **"Those who hoard gold and silver and do not spend it in the way of Allah, inform them of a painful punishment." He buys it with gold and silver and saves it as he saves materials.**[133]

As for paper money, it is not a commodity, as it is not manufactured, as goods are manufactured, but rather it is a tool to express its values. Since the scholars of jurisprudence have determined that what is sold in the commodity is utility, that is, the use-value in economic terms, and that if it is devoid of permissible utility, or carries a harmful such as drugs, it is not considered a

---

[128]- Capital of Karl Marx 1/52.
[129] Money and Credit, pp. 4-5, 3rd edition, 1966, by Dr. Hussein Omar.
[130]- The Book of Money by Abu Obeid, p. 46, Al- 'Ain, Al-Baqar Baksr Al-Ra: Silver.
[131]- Introduction, p. 680.
[132]- Mukhtaṣar al-Muzzīnī 'alá al-Mawdūn
[133]- The major classes of Ibn Sa 'd 4/330 The Flags of the Nobles of Al-Dhahabi 2/53.

legitimate commodity, as paper money carries the values of commodities, and a surplus benefit, as the buyer can buy any commodity with a use-value, and a permissible benefit. It is considered a price when it is in lieu of the commodity, which is expressed by jurists in one of the two compensators, and it is a commodity when it is purchased in another currency, as is understood from the work of Abu Dharr in buying money in gold and silver. The process is as close as possible to bartering. It is selling a currency for a currency, and a commodity for a commodity. Bartering is a reward in sales.

With this in mind, it can be said that the sale and purchase of paper money is permissible if it is delivered from monopoly and smuggling, and it is the subject of profit and loss and applies the same provisions applied in goods. The research is not related to trafficking or the principle of development and investment, but to the difference between Sharia and status laws and between permissible and prohibited. This was the view on banknotes, and we conclude with the difference between a check and"campbells" and the way they are written and sold.

The financed check is a security. It takes the place of the banknote in dealing, performing rights and discharging receivables, without regard to history, whoever falsifies it or gives it an unfunded uncovered shall be punished, and whoever falsifies or falsifies the money shall be punished. Since the law of the state has sanctioned its work, as well as the work of the banknote, it is legally permissible to take its place in the form of dowry, pilgrimage expenses and the price of sales...

The"Kambiela" is a commercial paper, bearing the title of a deed of debt, traded in banks, sold and bought through endorsement, which is the signature on its back. It means that the website is obligated to pay its value if it returns to it, and it is released in the form stipulated by the law to include an order from a person called the drawer, to another person called the drawee, to pay a certain amount of money to a third person called the beneficiary. The beneficiary may want the money before the expiry of the bill of exchange, so he submits it to a bank in order to receive the amount, minus part of its value, such as its value is one hundred and receives ninety-five. The bank, in turn, may wish to obtain the amount and submit it to a second bank, and the second may submit it to a third bank, and so on, as long as the endorsement process continues, so it sells it. consistently undervalued.

Dr. Ali Suleiman Al-Obaidi says: "Campbells were purchased by deducting a certain percentage of their value. This is called a deduction. And when the bank needed money. Before the maturity date of the bills of exchange, he can deduct this bill of exchange from another bank. " He said about the endorsement process: " The beneficiary may not wait for the maturity date of the bills of exchange to be paid by the drawee, so he resorts to endorsing them and obtaining their amount from the endorser. Endorsement is the usual means of circulation of a bill of exchange, and every person who signed the bill of exchange bears responsibility or is obligated to guarantee its amount. "[134]

From the legal point of view, some believe that the sale of a bill of exchange is permissible and it [135] seems that there is a difference between the bank extracting it when the deadline comes with a mosquito, as an agent for the beneficiary and the agency with a reward, as stated by Ibn Jazzi - and selling it with a share of its value, so it falls in what is known in jurisprudence as "put and hurry": put part of the debt and hurry the rest, as if the principal of the debt is one hundred, and the debtor says to his creditor: put twenty and hurry eighty, that is, subtract twenty and hurry you eighty. It is usury, as Ibn Rushd said,[136] because there is someone who took money free of charge or compensation, and it is the opposite of lending more.

In the loan, the lender lends an increase against the term, and in "put and hurry" the borrower imposes a decrease against its deletion. This is as if the loan money is one hundred and the lender increases twenty and becomes one hundred and twenty. And the twenty plus or minus the borrower is twenty, and it recovers to eighty, and the twenty minus is usury, as in both cases he took money without consideration or consideration. The Islamic economy has developed a practical approach to the acquisition of money, based on the fact that there is no way to benefit from the money of others except by giving in return or compensation, or what pleases the soul in non-transactions. The consideration may be a work, such as fifty dirhams for a day's work or a day's work for fifty dirhams. It may be a material compensation, such as a hundred dirhams for a shirt and a shirt for a hundred dirhams and all the money taken outside this framework and did not fall within the framework of donations and humanitarian aid, it is to eat people's money wrongly.

Ibn Rushd says: «And the mayor of those who are not permitted to put and hasten that it is similar to the increase with the collective view on its prohibition. He drew his likeness to it that he had made time a measure of the price, instead of it in all two places. That is because there, when he increased in time, he increased in price, and here, when he was devalued, he devalued him in his interview with a price. "[137]

Ibn Qudamah says: "If he has a deferred debt, he said to his opponent: Put some of it away, and hurry up for the rest of it. Zaid ibn Thabit, Ibn 'Umar, al-Miqdad, Sa 'id ibn al-Musayyib, Salim al-Hasan, Hammad, al-Shafi 'i, Malik, al-Thawri, Hashim, Ibn' Aliyah, Ishaq, and Abu Hanifa hated him. Al-Miqdad said to two men who did this: "Both of you have authorized a war from Allah and

---

[134] - Commercial papers in Moroccan legislation, pp. 12/18.
[135] - On Islamic Thought and Evolution, p. 43 by Muhammad Fathi Othman.
[136] - The beginning of the diligent 2/142.
[137] - The beginning of the diligent 2/143.

His Messenger."[138] He wants to do this by saying: "**O you who have believed, fear Allah and give up what is left of usury, if you are believers, if you do not do so, then authorize a war from Allah and His Messenger.**"[139]

Thus, it is clear that the deduction that is subtracted from the amount of a bill of exchange debt, in order to collect it before the maturity date, is similar to the decrease that is subtracted from the amount of the debt in order to collect it before the maturity date, with the difference in the beneficiary between the two operations. It is the bank in the first and the debtor in the second. Sharia rulings are self-contained and are not subject to change of names. However, the prohibition is only related to the increase required by the lender at the time of the contract or the shortage required by the borrower at the time of performance. As for the increase that comes from the debtor upon performance, which is known as good judgment or the shortage that comes generously from the creditor, which is known as charity with some debt capital, it is permissible.

On the subject, Imam Malik narrates that he addressed a creditor who asked him: "If he gives you the like of the one you predicted, you accept him, and if he gives you the don of the one you predicted, you take him in rent, and if he gives you better than the one you predicted, he will be kind to himself. This is thanks to you, and to you is the reward of what you[140] have seen. "Al-Bukhari, Muslim, and Abu Dawood narrated from Jabir bin Abdullah Al-Ansari, who said: " I had a religion against the Messenger of Allah, so he saved me and he increased me. "[141] As Al-Bukhari, Muslim, Al-Tirmidhi, Al-Nisa 'i, Ibn Majah, and Al-Bayhaqi narrated from Abu Hurayrah that the Messenger of Allah borrowed from a man and[142] gave him a tooth over his age and said: "The best of you, or of you, is the best of you. "[143]

The prohibition was focused on the conditional increase, and it was confirmed by Ibn Umar's statement from Malik's account: «From the predecessor of the predecessor, it is not required only to spend it» Otherwise, Ibn Umar himself said: «If he gives you better than what I predicted good in himself, it is thanks to him for your thanks» as it is focused on the conditional shortage, as it is understood from the debtor's statement to the creditor: Put and hurry, otherwise, Al-Tirmidhi, Ibn Majah and Al-Bayhaqi narrated about Abu Hurairah that the Prophet (PBUH) said: «Whoever loves to be shadowed by Allah on a day when there is no shadow but His shadow, let him look insolvent or put on him»,[144] which is an explanation for His saying: «**If he is difficult,**

---

[138] - The singer for Ibn Qudamah 4/48.
[139] - Surat Al-Baqarah 278.
[140] - Footprint: Al-Zarqani version 3/336.
[141] - Sahih Muslim: Al-Nawawi version 11/30 Sunan Abu Dawood 3/337.
[142] Age : Camel.
[143] Al-Bukhari: Al-Fath 5/453 Muslim, Al-Nawawi 11/38 Sahih Al-Tirmidhi 6/56.Sunan al-Nasa 'i 7/291 Sunan Abu Dawood 3/357 Sunan Ibn Majah 2/42.
[144] - Sahih al-Tirmidhi 6/41 Sunan Ibn Majah 2/41 Sunan al-Kubra for al-Bayqi 6/28.

look at a facilitator, and if you believe, it is better for you if you know» then what the creditor puts on the debtor[145] was tanty as a ratification.

This was an analysis of the sale of a bill of exchange and its relationship to the process of putting and hastening in Islamic jurisprudence. It should be noted that those who can get rid of prohibited transactions at the same time are individuals. As for countries - which have been linked to global economic systems, and the consequent foreign debt and its benefits - they may be able to eliminate such taboos. As for getting rid of transactions related to the global monetary system, and the repayment of external debts that it requires, efforts and efforts are needed.

---

[145] - Surat Al-Baqarah 277.

Final, Intermediate, Immediate and Long-Lived Consumption

Final consumption is a utilitarian process, which enables the individual to satisfy his need and desire, and the values and benefits of the products are eliminated by annihilation, wiping out the impact of their use from existence: such as what is eaten and burned. Within the working capital - an analysis of the meaning and role of intermediate consumption in which landowners, or owners of companies, factories and institutions, mediate production. Both of them eliminate values, on the difference in the impact left by the second in production, without the first, which harms production, and affects its amount in capital, is the over-consumption of the final in its two parts: immediate and perennial, and the over-median, on the contrary, increases its amount in capital, and works to develop production and its factors, as will be explained.

It is possible to imagine that the values of products are generated by the process of production, and age during the process of exchange, to perish and die in the process of consumption. The forms of consumption and their benefits vary according to the needs, and the extent to which each benefit responds to its need appropriate to its nature. either immediately, or after different durations. The value of food products - for example, foods - ends as soon as the desire for them ends, and the value of clothes gradually ends with the end of their life, that is, with the duration of their use. The more immediate and continuous the benefit, as is the case with food, the more it burdens the human being and accounts for a large part of his effort, and the more durable it is, the less it is carried and the more opportunity it gives to others. It was also manifested in household needs.

Thus, consumption can be divided in consideration of each desire, and the nature of the benefit it meets into immediate and long-lived consumption, and we mean immediate and long-lived that is related to material desires and benefits. Otherwise, there are many moral, psychological and instinctive desires, which are met by things that have not been included in the consumption of material values.

Perhaps the first problem for the average consumer is the inability to use the economic account in order to create a balance between the resource and the expenditure of the above that resources are limited, and the needs are multiple and different. The distribution of the limited resource, over the unlimited expense, is a complex process, the solution of which requires estimating the percentage of each need, for the supplier, not for what satisfies it, as if we assume that the supplier is a thousand dirhams, we have to estimate the percentages allocated to nutrition, dress, rent or hygiene. Etc. In nutrition itself, we have to distribute the percentage allocated to it among the materials, according to their importance to the body, so as not to overdo secondary things at the expense of essential basic materials without which the body does not exist.

However, the use of economic calculation in order to unravel the complex of the consumption process does not mean the scarcity and abundance of resources, as much as it means how it is distributed to any situation, because the difference observed in the material life system does not lie in the principle of responding to needs at its basis. But it is in the quality and quality of the response, so we find that the rich responds to it if they want - with luxuries, and the average responds to it with necessities, and the poor who has no resource, has no system.

If the use of economic calculation, creating a balance between production and consumption, or between the resource and the sucking is necessary for the individual and the family, then for the state it is more necessary, and more urgent. The production and consumption of twins are linked to each other. The activity of the producer is linked to the activity of the consumer, and taking into account the balance would maintain the level of values and the stability of prices, and put the interest of the producer and the consumer in two parallel coffers, do not want one over the other, as the more the production cuff is weighted, and the consumption cuff is weighted, the stronger the supply, and the goods are depleted at the expense of the product, and on the contrary the demand increases, and the price rises at the expense of the consumer the more the consumption cuff is weighted.

Thus, it is clear that the law of supply and demand does not swing by itself, but rather swings the balance of production and consumption. It is negatively and positively related to the interest or harm of one of the two pillars of the economy represented in the product and the consumer.

One of the positives of the Islamic economy in the subject is to read in Imam Malik's footsteps that Omar ibn al-Khattab in the days of his succession ordered the companion Hatib ibn Abi Balata to raise the price of his raisins to the price set at the level of supply and demand, or to take it out of the market, when he saw that devaluing the price harms the product, and raising it harms the consumer. To take care of their interests is to take care of the interest of the entire nation, as there is among its members only a producer and a consumer, as provided.

What is said in national production is said in international production, and the countries most in control of their economies today, those that conduct economic calculation at the national level produce as much as they consume and export, in order to prevent the consequences of the chaos of production, and more than it controls the economy and politics, are those that have money that is produced only on demand.

Consumption is an overall term, including commercial consumption, if the production is to be sold and its profit is highlighted, and the final consumption in which the values are consumed in satisfying the needs and their percentage of the capital decreases. Intermediate consumption, through which production is carried out, values are developed, and their percentage in capital increases.

Thus, it becomes clear the difference between the positivity of intermediate consumption, which is adopted by the owner of a land, factory or company. In the development of its production, and between the negativity of the final consumption that burns values and kills them, the more the consumer deviates from good management and slips his behavior towards the knees of the extravagant ride, and the response to the life of extravagance and luxury. Overconsumption would drive development and overconsumption in the end would hamper it. It is also hampered by consumer loans, especially what is consumed in wars and overspending. where it is paid out of capital. As for productive loans placed on the path of development and included in the framework of intermediate consumption, they are paid from their production.

The wealth of the nation in any state, in any society, is of a single magnitude. It circulates between the state and society, the circulation of money between the producer and the consumer: the state is society and society is the state, two names for one name is the nation. It was best described as the wealth of the nation, a description chosen by the father of political economy, Adam Smith, for his book The Wealth of Nations.

Wealth as such is wealth, not generated by slogans, schematics, and ideologies. Rather, it is born of an intellectual and physical effort, and stems from the depths of society, and between its energies and limits its development, to collide with the lack of an economic policy, capable of tightening the linkage and creating a balance between the amounts of production and consumption, so that consumption does not fall at the expense of production and its factors. Consumption less than production gives way to economic development, and consumption like it creates stagnation, and consumption more than it leads to relapse, and the inability to control the course of things.

The productive creative wealth, behind the strength and weakness of the state, is the social wealth. In his book "The Enjoyment of the Provisions of Feudalism", Judge Al-Tartoushi said in the "Siraj of the Kings" that Caliph Uthman, when he isolated Amr ibn al-Aas from Egypt, and appointed in his place Ibn Abu Sarh, and Jaba from the levies unless Amr answered, said: "Do you know, Amr, that the vaccine has been administered?" Amr said: «That is because you have impressed her children» The amount of the vaccine means an increase in levies and the lean children means social wealth: the policy of Omar and my son was not demolished, as it takes into account the interest of the state and society, and the policy of Ibn Abu Sarh has been demolished and not built, as it takes into account the interest of the state at the expense of society.

Production and consumption are twin. Society produces and consumes continuously, and the state produces first, produces, consumes continuously, and spends in interests - whether through the management or processing budget. It was by drawing wages, or financing projects, most of which belonged to society, to grow a little, and then return, or return some of it to consumption.

The more you save, in the final consumption, and the individuals stay away from waste and waste of money, as society progresses, and its economy develops, as the more it consumes a decrease in its wealth, and goes with its profit and the practical space it occupies, the more unemployment increases as the shadow of production and work shrinks. It was in the interest of the State, which had the funds to release them, to make its way into the field of development.

The sultan in that Abu Abdullah Ibn al-Azraq says: "The money fluctuates between the sultan and the parish, if the sultan imprisoned him, the parish lost him, the Sunnah of God in his servants"[146] and the word sultan means the state in modern expression.

It was in the past. Today, most countries - plunged into a sea of foreign debt - may have nothing to hold back. Rather, it is held by some members of the community. What it can do is to economize on its expenses, in order to give the opportunity to the factors of economic development, especially since social wealth has an end to it and extravagance is an endless trait, it eats a lot, it eats a little, like fire devours a lot, it devours a little.

Before looking at a lot and a little, it seems that the lesson is serious about production and the economy when spending, as they become a lot less, and their bodies bounce a little more. People are between a productive worker who contributes to the construction of the edifice of the economy, and another wasteful wasteful, who demolishes what others have built. And money by nature, without its use and use is sterile. As Aristotle said, "Money does not give birth to money," but rather it is generated and grown by labor, and sterilized by hoarding and saving.

He has done better than raising her and vaccinating her, and he has harmed those who killed her and buried her values. The jurists described it as money growing by force, for its money from the power of development inherent in its nature. Therefore, zakat is obligatory in it, as it is in the already developed money, and as working capital, there is no production without its promotion and circulation. Intermediate and final consumption depends on the capital and its investment methods.

---

[146]- The wonders of the wire in the natures of King D100.

CHAPTER ONE

Economic Thought in Antiquity This chapter deals with the aspects of the search for the emergence of economic thought, and its development over the centuries, until the sixteenth century, the day it completed its maturity, organized its contract, and became a science in which studies are issued. Before that, we did not teach him an independent self-existence, but there are personal opinions, financial legislation, and agricultural organizations, contained in philosophical, social, and moral ideas...Or actions taken by tribal chiefs or written to those on their behalf in some matters. Therefore, we have passed through thought, instead of science, because thought is older than science as we have passed through the ages to include the era of the regularity of nations and before it.

THE EMERGENCE OF ECONOMIC THOUGHT AND THE EMERGENCE OF HUMAN LIFE

We express in economic thought, instead of reality or life, transcendence, and according to the practice of contemporary studies...Otherwise, the beginning of life on earth, and what the life of primitive man could be, for whom we did not know any source of knowledge, except instinct, instinct and inspiration. Or something of intellectual simplicity, which requires him to live as he agrees, and live a life that we can not define its features, and identify its components: is it intellectual or natural? Especially since researchers in ancient history have identified his first activity in hunting and hunting, picking what he can of legumes, and the fruits of prophetic trees, works that do not go far from the nature of the animal.

Feeling the difference between benefit and harm, between good and ugly or finding a solution to some problems, which some have tried to deduce from what I accept or avoid, is insufficient in justifying what has been attributed to it from economic thought and its upbringing, with the emergence of life, as long as the animal is also aware of the difference between benefit and harm and between good and ugly, and is guided to solve some of its problems.[147]

---

[147]- In the scenes, we saw the animal coming to its owner if it saw the fodder in his hand, and he fled if it saw a lamb sitting in front of him, and the cat sat in front of you quietly, to eat what you give him with the kindness of your mind, and if he kidnapped something, he fled with an unwitting mastermind, and about the monkey who Darwin sees as the supreme ancestor of man, according to him, much is said.

It is said that bees are carried on a beast or a carrier, so one of them flies right or left, and rises above the tops of the mountains, to caress the crowns of flowers, giving them an atmosphere of grazing and fun, and when they return, they do not return to their place of departure, but rather join the knee wherever they are, and just descend with their basket, and some have tried to discover the secret of God, and watch - inside the basket the process of converting the smells of flowers into filtered honey, which is a little conversion that takes them from the work of God to much in which there is healing, food and blessing.. He put their flies in a white bottle, which helps to monitor their work, and inspired them to start the bottle, before starting the production process, to hide their secret, which was true to his saying: «And your Lord revealed to the bees the verse» and the revelation here means inspiration.

The strangest thing I saw when I was young was that a housewife had a difficult dog, which no one else could approach, and she was the one who took care of eating and drinking it, and if it escaped from the mind, it went like seven, not twisting anything, until it attacked those who intercepted it, and did not stop its campaigns, until its voice was heard. One night he saw a ghost in the absence of the master of the house, and he attacked her with the ghost and did not listen to her words.

Although it is related to a relative who seeks a dependant to use in watering an orchard. This year, 1992, a jurist working in justice in my hometown, the jurist Shuaibi Abdullah, wrote to me telling me of such a case. Is that a person I know, Omar bin Bit, died, and he had a donkey riding him and spending on him, and when he was buried, it was noticed that the donkey entered the cemetery and stood on his grave.

With these examples and many others, it is clear that what explains the existence of economic thinking in primitive man is unclear, because the explanations put forward do not indicate economic thinking, but rather indicate discrimination and represent the common denominator between him and some inspiring animals, as manifested in the conditions of monkeys and bees...These are impressions that we have recorded, not for science, but for reflection and study

It is likely that the first nucleus of mental thinking arose in man during what is known as the Stone Age, the day he was guided to carving stones, and using them as a tool before the discovery of iron. Making the tool requires thinking about its work, according to the idea that making the thing falls under the pressure of needing it, knowing its task, and appreciating its results, and that its existence presents the idea of owning it in some way.

As for the crystallization of thought at the level of economic activity, it is likely to arise with the discovery of agriculture, as the first sector of the economy. Its discovery raises the idea of the discovery of iron, because agriculture depends on the plough and the plough as the first means of production depends on the use of iron. The use of iron would record the first production process, in which a natural material was transformed into a usable tool. Hence, it is true that economic thought begins, taking the principle of evolution, and is put next to it in the case of ownership of land and the means of its production. Was it individual or group?

The beginning of ownership between individual and collective

The opinions of researchers about the ownership of land were disturbed and are the only ones that can exist with the beginning of life - did they start individually or collectively? Some went on to say that it began as a collective property, popularizing the spread of light and air, and others saw that man, as a human being, is forced to altruize himself over others, and what he made, volunteered, or revived, he could only monopolize over others, so the ownership of the land, began individually. Notably, the individualists are the capitalists, and the collectivists are the communists. He also appeared when reading the detective, and Marx went to him.

Before we looked at the conditions of ownership, were they individual or collective? We had to identify the circumstances that create the idea of individuality or collectivity, to see the extent to which it was available to primitive man, who had to explain his circumstances in isolation from our circumstances and ideas, and what we used to shine the lights of contemporary doctrines, on what was before it came out of nowhere into existence.

Evidence indicates that the narrowness of the space, with the multiplication of those who need to exploit it, creates the conditions of congestion and fighting - as is the case with the well instead of the river - and this results in each individual taking over the amount they need, volunteering, or living, or it is agreed to leave it collectively, and exploited by common means.

This phenomenon is still present in the place known as al-Ma'dar in southern Morocco, where each tribe has a large or small area, which it obtained on the first day by volunteering, settling and defending. If it is narrowed from the need of one of them - after the population increases, they quarrel and quarrel, until it is divided, or it is agreed to leave it collectively, and if it expands and is above the need of individuals, everyone plows what he wants and how he wants, without being said individually or collectively, but they allow members of other tribes to plow the rest of those lands after exhausting their power, and what they have of seeds, provided that they do not keep plowing a specific place every year, for fear that they will covet seizing it.

Thus, it becomes clear that the conditions that create the idea of individual and collective property are not available to the primitive man who made God the globe his hand. The meaning of individuality is that each individual works on one hand, and the collective is not able to face the process of production, so the circumstances force him to cluster, and to seek the help of others, so primitive tribes arise, we do not know anything about their lives. Otherwise, the land has not been created in one form or another, and the assumption of individual or collective ownership on its back, necessitates the existence of an individual or collective system, and a supreme power or authority to nurture it, as manifested in the capitalist and communist system of this era. which no one can decide as life begins.

However, one of the proponents of collective ownership and its spread among primitive tribes is the writer «Wall Durant» in his book «The Story of Civilization». Karl Marx confirmed this claim, and included it among the developed systems.

It is known that Marx adopted the theory of the materialist interpretation of history, arranged systems, and assumed within the framework of economic development that property was common in the primitive era, then turned into the slave system, then feudalism, then capitalism, then socialism as a stage, then communism as a goal in the sense that it began communism with the beginning of life, and returns to its origin in the twentieth century.

He believes, on the basis of the principle of the opposite, which he quoted from the philosophy of the German philosopher Hegel or the law of self-destruction, that each of these systems carries within itself the elements of its own annihilation and destruction, without interference... Let another system be based on its opposite. And so on, until the communist regime that preaches it is established. On the contrary -it was achieved only by revolution and the use of force...Experience proved, after the dissolution of the Soviet Union, that the regime that carries within itself the elements of its annihilation, and breaks up on its own is the Marxist regime. The result is that communism has not been able to live with the beginning of life nor in the twentieth century, as he will show.

It is noticeable that Marx did not make any tangible document or material argument, although he does not believe, and does not say only the perceived knowledge. He exaggerates his consideration, and denies the existence of the

Creator on its basis, even saying: Hecannot decide that the earth is under him until he knocks it with his foot, and that the table is in front of him until he strikes it with his hand, as if all existence is limited to what he can see.

Although we do not know anything that has been adopted in the denial of what is beyond matter, although negation is like proof, it is accepted only on the basis of an argument, especially since the mind that used it as a tool for exile, is a limited creature, and the spirit world is the world of the uncreated, the infinite, and the limited creature that is the mind, does not control the world of the creature and the infinite, nor do we know anything that has been adopted, and what went wrong in deciding that ownership was in primitive man a common property. This was at a time when he did not see, and felt only the capitalist system that he lived through. He denied the existence of God, because he did not see it, and approved the communist system, with the beginning of life, even if he did not see it, which is one of his contradictions, as we referred to on another occasion.

Particularly in denying beyond matter, the mistake may lie in not putting things in place. It is natural to use mental power in the study of matter, and spiritual power in believing in what is behind it, as Ibn Khaldun decided, so they succeeded in the first, and overlooked the second, so they fell into error and confusion, believing in the Almighty's saying: "They know outwardly from the life of this world and they are heedless of the Hereafter" and the scientific progress they have reached, as manifested in the invasion of space, as evidenced by the appearance of the life of this world, and the denial of the existence of God is one of the signs of heedlessness about the Hereafter. The perfect man is the one who combines the material aspects based on mental strength with the moral aspects based on spiritual strength. There is no matter without spirit, and no spirit without matter.

THE ECONOMIC THOUGHT OF THE ANCIENT NATIONS OF GREECE

The regularity of nations, and the establishment of civilizations, dictates the existence of economic activity in one form or another, as there is no sovereign nation and civilization, without economic wealth based on it, as manifested in the Pharaonic, Babylonian, Greek and other civilizations. The absence of the economy as an organized, independent thought in those era does not mean that it does not exist as a reality, imposes its existence on life, and continues to continue or continues to continue, as there is no life without food, no civilization without money, working for it, and searching for its resources. The consequent production and consumption is the same as economic activity, whose fields - in quantity and quality - may differ according to time and place, and do not differ in the principle of responding to the necessary needs, without which life does not exist.... andits existence as a movement aimed at producing good things. It requires the existence of its subject matter and its possible means, as well as the existence of an economic thought or a just or unfair procedure that keeps pace with its development and keeps pace with its circumstances.

Wall Durant has been quoted in the story of civilization, and some researchers in ancient civilizations have quoted pictures and models that predict the existence of economic ideas, regulatory procedures, and government interventions that were embraced by ancient civilizations, and have a socialist, capitalist, or feudal character, due to the nature of the laws issued or applied in their regard.

GREECE

The intellectual energy of Greece focused on philosophical research, so they were famous for philosophy, before they were famous for economics, when they see that philosophical thought is an ideal thought, suited to the level of the excellent class, and they look at material thought through the prism of contempt and contempt, and they estimated that it is the task of slaves, and what they knew that philosophical production is a mathematical production of perfection, which may be dispensed with, and economic production is a necessary food production that is indispensable in any case, and that the philosopher does not produce what he believes in his life. It consumes what others have produced. Despite his scientific status, without slaves working in the fields, philosophers would not have been able to secure their lives. Even today, excessive philosophical and literary studies, instead of technical and technological ones, and taking care of the privileged class instead of the working class, may hinder the wheel of economic development or limit its effectiveness, as some of it occurred in third world countries. - And almost - by immersion in philosophical research, the absence of economic thought - oralmost - from the writings of Greece, and what was mentioned was not mentioned as an independent research. Rather, it is contained in philosophical, social, political or moral ideas, emanating from the general thought. Researchers believe that the first Greek to carry out an economic measure is "Licogoros", the uncle of King "Carlos", King of Sparta, who lived in the ninth century BC. He narrates that he abolished individual ownership, and divided the lands equally among the families, and one of the most famous Greek philosophers, Plato and Aristotle.

PLATO

The first thing that Plato - the disciple of Socrates and the elder of Aristotle in the field of economics - was famous for in his republic was to spread money and women, and he called for the abolition of the family system and individual property, claiming that communism in money and women would eliminate the causes of conflict between human beings. It is the same idea that Mazdak, the prophet of the Persians after him, said, apprenticed to his teacher Zardasht, where Plato's life was between 429AD and 347BC and the life of Mazdak around 487AD, then Marx said it, and called for its application, and assumed that the monarchy was in the primitive covenant, and hummed that it would return to its origin in the twentieth century as it was presented

The researchers explained that Mazdak's call created economic and moral chaos, and caused inhumane behavior, as his followers exploited the principle of spreading money and women, spreading light and air, so they rushed towards homes, plundering money and kidnapping wives, claiming that no one is more entitled than the other to what is in his hand.[148] Marx's call also ignited a Leninist revolution, in the course of which hundreds of thousands were killed, people's property was nationalized, and their freedoms were confiscated, including freedom of expression, freedom of opinion, freedom of ownership, freedom of production, and freedom of consumption...Baqir al-Sadr mentioned in his book "Our Economy" many times what we mentioned about the dead, as a result of the famine arising from the nationalization of private property

Islam, which proves its primacy to establish the rules of economic and social justice, as it legislated general solidarity, rejected hoarding, monopoly and exploitation of man by man, and decided the principle of right, justice and equality, and granting the right of equal opportunities to individuals, and the security of their freedoms, does not sanction chaos and disorder and opposes methods of violence, and the theft of legitimate acquired property, drawing the line between the rights of states and societies... Neither states, despite their power to impose surveillance and good guidance, can harm the rights of individuals, nor individuals, despite the laws authorizing ownership, can act in a manner detrimental to the economy of their countries, or the interests of their societies... "There is no harm and no harm" in his law. Freedoms are secured, but defined by laws that regulate them.

---

[148]- See the dawn of Islam, p. 109.

The Muslims economically and socially are equal as the teeth of the comb. There is no preference for an Arab over a non-Arab except by piety and good deeds. Likewise, Islam was in its principles, not in many of its societies. It is a divine force and an economic and social justice that moves on its own, neither capitalism nor communism nor competing materialist doctrines.

Plato's call did not apply. But it was ridiculed by many people, and even the comedian poet Aristophanes mocked him in one of his plays. Plato, as manifested in the utopia, felt that his system was more imaginary than realistic and that Athena was not ready to apply it, so he retracted some of his views in his book "Laws".

Some economists argue that his communism has nothing to do with socialism in its modern sense. He did not address the issue from the point of view of the popular class. Rather, he approached it from the angle of the privileged class, and gave it a social consideration, through which economic thought diminished. In his book The Republic, he divided society into three classes: rulers, army men, and the people or slaves. He considered the two classes of rulers and army men to be from the State Guard, and decided that the task of rulers is to rule the country, provided that they are philosophers, and the task of army men is to carry out defense affairs. As for the popular class of farmers, manufacturers and traders...They have the right to engage in physical labor.

He set up a social system that he called the utopia. It stipulated the need for the state to supervise the upbringing of children. In order to select talented people to teach them and prepare them as leaders of the country, and others go to physical work.

In order for the ruling classes and the military men to have the opportunity to devote themselves to serving the state, he called for the abolition of individual monarchy and the family system, fearing that they would be distracted from their main tasks. and they have the mansion of his communism. As for divorced people, they have the right to own and marry. Thus, it is clear that his communism is far from the socialist concept and its factors, as it is intended as a privilege and preference for one class over another. He was one of them. To describe her as an aristocratic communist...In doing so, he may be the first to lay the foundations for social class, and the difference between the Souqah and the nobility.

In general, Plato did not address economic thought except through philosophical, political or social views, as manifested in his opinion on how states exist. Where he discussed in his book "The Republic" the reasons for its inception, and the origin of its formation was attributed to the economic factor, noting that the individual has many needs that he cannot satisfy alone, so he is forced to join others, so human groups are formed. It is from these groups that the state is formed...This is the case because social entities are formed only on living resources...The mother of resources and their origin, as the "physiocrats" see it, is productive land and water.

ARISTOTLE AND HIS VIEWS ON ECONOMICS

It seems that Aristotle - a friend of Alexander the Great who lived between 384 and 302 BC - is more realistic, and more connected to economic thought than Plato. He tried to address some economic problems in isolation from philosophy, and opposed Plato in what he went to of communism, and instead proposed the system of private property and guaranteeing the freedom of individuals, and believes that the system of private property, and the principle of personal interest, leads individuals to compete and love of acquisition, increasing production, which is a capitalist principle, but criticized in his book "Politics", his teacher Plato, and attributed to chaos his statement of communism in money and women...He stressed that the idea would eliminate the competition arising from the love of ownership, which is the main motivation for the work. It is not long before his views are the first nucleus of capitalist doctrine.

One of his views is that there is a difference between the use value and the exchange value of the commodity, which is the theory adopted by Marx, and he analyzed it in his book "Capital" and became famous at his hands. Use value means that it is not suitable for exchange until it is suitable for use and exchange means that it carries a value equivalent to another value to be exchanged for it, which Mars called the equivalent between two commodities. Aristotle defined monopoly as the individualization of the seller to sell his commodity without the market price, and he believes that it is unfair. He also attacked usury and said that "money does not give birth to money," and so on. What will generate it is work, and whoever sheds his race, and burns his skin in investing it, will be more entitled to benefit from its results. Here he meets with the divine religions: Islam, Christianity and Judaism in the prohibition of usury.[149]

In the field of work, the methods of obtaining a pension are divided into three types: the first type is the one in which the pursuit of profit without remuneration or compensation from work or others is located, as is the case with interest-bearing lending...The second is the satisfaction of needs by natural means, such as fishing, raising livestock and the spoils of war...The third is through production. It is the attempt to extract good things from things that are not usable in their images.

---

[149]- The Knowledge Department of Al-Bustani 8/513 The Theory of Forbidden Usury in Islamic Law by Ibrahim Zaki Al-Din Badawi, 1st edition - 1383 AH - 1964AD - Cairo.

IN THE ROMANS AND IN THE MIDDLE AGES

As for the Roman Empire, it knew the procedures, laws and economic regulations carried out by the Emperor "Diocletian Janus", who tried to organize the state. After the turmoil that swept its states in the third century, it established public institutions in order to create jobs for the unemployed, put a number of commercial and agricultural sectors under the supervision of the state, set a system for industrial institutions, and obliged producers to abide by state prices, while making the right to import grain its prerogative. In order to ensure price stability, an observer was appointed in each state to supervise its activity. Some saw that its direction was socialist, despite the aristocracy of the state, but its measures did not indicate socialism, as much as the attempt to reform the economy. His work is closer to capitalism than to socialism.

Among his measures was the promulgation in 307 of the Law of Prices. He determined the prices and wages of workers, the prevention of monopoly, and the exploitation of traders and manufacturers. The result was that traders hid their goods, so prices rose, and goods decreased in the markets, and state revenues were affected as a result, so he found himself forced to impose exorbitant taxes, in order to be able to pay the wages of employees. Those who evade its performance are punished relentlessly and unequivocally, even resorting to torturing young children and wives, in order to extract from them recognition of the wealth of fathers and husbands, so a number of citizens were forced to flee, taking refuge in other countries.

Diocletian stepped down from the throne, retired from the political field and lived the rest of his life in his palace. About two hundred years later, a young emperor appeared on the stage of politics and rule, Justinian, who followed Diocletian's approach to the organization of the state. He extended his influence over the economic sector, encouraged government production, competed with individual production, and issued a decree setting prices and imposing a fair price. These regulations and laws were evidence of the existence of economic thought among the Romans, even if it did not reach the degree of knowledge studied and the literature was placed in it. At first, Rome knew agricultural activity, and after its victories in the third and second centuries BC, it knew extensive commercial activity.

Some researchers believe that Roman law, although it does not address the economy as an independent branch, has paved the way for some of its principles, such as freedom of contract and the establishment of individual ownership, towards the establishment of individual doctrine.

In the Middle Ages, the periodbetween the fall of the Roman Empire to the Germanic tribes in the fifth century, and the fall of Constantinople in the fifteenth century to the Turks. Exactly between 145 and 496 AD, the prevailing system in that period of the history of economic thought was the feudal system.

Its origins came as a result of the disintegration of the Roman Empire and its division into provinces in the form of statelets, which were occupied by tyrannical feudal lords, who needed wealth, monopolized resources, and took ownership of agricultural land, so they were known as masters and cultivators of slaves.

With this division, the bonds of Roman civilization split, and its current stopped, and the bonds of connection between the states dissolved, so that each submerged state or province within its borders remained folded into itself, in the form of separate circles, so it was normal for economic growth to stop with the cessation of its factors. This situation led to the emergence of a feudal individual economy, in which local agriculture replaced the commercial movement, which linked the east and west of the empire, and the economic reality shifted from a national economy run by the state, to an economy boycotted by the feudal lord and his aides, so the commercial and industrial stagnation, paralyzed the movement for centuries.

However, some emergency factors have removed some of the recession, and toppled some of the narrow limits...Starting in the late tenth century and the beginning of the eleventh century, the feudal economy began to emerge from the exclusive circle of the agricultural economy, to know its way to some trade exchanges. Among these factors are the Crusades, which restored the link between East and West and opened the file of commercial transportation between Europe and China. This is done through India, Iran, Iraq, Syria, Turkey, and the religious and social revolutions known as the farmers' or slaves' revolutions, which broke out in France in 1357AD - and in England in 1381 and then in Germany - 1525 - calling for the lifting of injustice, the liberation of necks, and the fair distribution of social wealth, have awakened the feeling, and inflamed the thought towards the demand for individual freedom, which is the first nucleus for the establishment of free doctrine.

If these are some of the factors of economic and social openness, then next to them is a factor of inertia and obstruction, which is the factor represented by the churchmen who contributed with their negative shrinking monasticism and their despised upsurge of material life in obstructing the wheel of economic development...Whenever the statesmen thought of establishing a project, or tried to establish an advanced economic system, they found themselves chained to the shackles of the church and its teachings. They did not breathe a sigh of relief and Europe did not rise up to its modern renaissance, until the so-called separation of religion from the state.

Some have been drawn with the idea of separating religion from the state, and its effectiveness in the modern European renaissance, so he put forward the idea for Muslims, and did not notice in the midst of admiration for what that renaissance reached that there is no church or monastic system in Islam, as reflected in the Prophet's saying: "Jihad is a monastic nation" and includes -

besides jihad with the sword - jihad of the soul on which every religious, economic, social or cultural movement depends...The chances of separating religion from the state have been practically realized in Islamic systems, where the clerics had their competence, and the statesmen their competence, and it has not been proven throughout history that the clerics hindered economic progress, or opposed something of interest, and God did not forbid it. What is said is that the religious economy is moral...It does not apply to the Islamic system, which is considered an international system, for which laws have been established, which are punishable for not applying them, contrary to what is required by the spontaneity of morals. Here, there must be a difference between what is divine and devotional, and in which responsibility falls on the shoulders of individuals, and what is mundane, meaning the system of material life, and in which responsibility lies on the shoulders of the nation in the person of those in charge of its affairs. And to him refers the saying of the Prophet (PBUH) in the issue of palm trees from the Bukhari narration: "You know the things of your world."

If it is noticed that Muslims are late and others advance, then peace does not bear the consequences of this delay...They worked hard on its economic and social system, and did not comply with the commands of God in union and work, at a time when the United and workers, regardless of their different systems and beliefs, progressed, and it became clear through this that linking the wheel of progress and delay to religion is wrong, and it was wrong for the illusion to rise to the point of linking Islamic systems that absorb all aspects of life, and between the inertia of churches and the monasticism of their men.

The previous monotheistic religions, headed by Judaism and Christianity, didnot have an equal character in caring for the interests of the two lives, and did not come with economic, social and political systems, societies proceed according to their laws, as is the case with Islam, but came with religious trends and moral teachings. For the most part, she called for righteousness and good manners, renouncing injustice, spreading justice, and taking the hand of the weak and charity to him...What is mentioned in life issues is from this framework. Perhaps it is the common denominator of all divine religions.

As for Judaism, the research records that the Old Testament books dealt with some transactions in a moral framework, such as the principle of fighting injustice. The most important of which is the prohibition of usury among Israelis and its authorization between them and others, unlike the generalization of its prohibition in Islam. It says in Deuteronomy: "To a foreigner you shall lend by usury, but to your brother you shall not lend by usury, that the Lord your God may bless all that is in your hand."

Despite the distortion and contradiction of the Jews to the commands of God, and the commands of their prophet, Judaism seems to be more connected to life than Christianity, as evidenced when reading the various Gospels. During the Middle Ages, some Christian writers tried to address some social problems, according to the opinion of the Church, and they did not reach anything significant in life, so it was considered a factor of inertia and obstruction.

Islam and the Beginning of Arab Economic Thought

The historical sequence of economic thought, prior to the sixteenth century, in which we held this chapter in order to study its phases, dictates the excitement of Islamic economic thought, within this sequence. Although not by its principles, which still insist on application - as was evident in the establishment of the International Federation of Islamic Banks linked to a stage of history except in terms of the time of its emergence.

If this brief presentation is not enough to give a picture of the Islamic economy, which we issued under the title "Islamic Economy Approach to the Production and Consumption of Wealth" in three volumes, it is no less than to hint at some of its principles, in order to draw the attention of those who have calculated that Islam is the religion of worship, far from the battle of economic and social life, and they saw that the first to inaugurate economic thought in Islam is Abdul Rahman bin Khaldoun in his introduction.

Whereas the source of Ibn Khaldun's thought is Islamic, and then personal. During the course, he dealt with the theory of population, its relationship to the civilizational and economic level, the theory of the value of goods and their formation factors, the theory of the division of labor, its impact on economic development, the theory of prices, the low price of necessary goods at the abundance of production, the survival of perfectionism retaining its price, the theory of state intervention in commercial affairs and its damage to the interests of individuals, and the theory of money as savings for the values of things...etc.

While the Islamic economic system is considered an international system that caused a coup d 'état in Arab life between before and after the mission. Through him, the Prophet addressed the economic situation and solved the problem of class between the rich supporters and the poor immigrants. Among his companions were prominent economic thinkers such as Omar Ibn Al-Khattab, Abu Dhar Al-Ghafari, and others. Through this, it became clear that the reality in the book entitled "Arab Economic Thought" is in fact an Islamic economic thought in its flesh and in its stamina, as was manifested in the source of Ibn Khaldun's own thought.

Although the Qur 'an is a book of legislation, guidance and guidance, it came in general faculties, and was sublime in dealing with particles and abstracting theories, it included a number of verses full of economic concepts. The interpreters showered it with a barrage of texts carrying economic thought. without naming it.

While the hadith and its annotations are considered the largest source of Islamic economic legislation or what is related to it in the law, as evidenced when reading the books and chapters dedicated within his books: We read, for example, in Sahih al-Bukhari: the book of zakat, the book of sales, the book of preemption, the book of peace "advances" for a known period, the book of sharecropping, the book of borrowing and performing religion, the stone and bankruptcy, the book of mortgage, the book of the company and the book of leasing. Etc.

The books of jurisprudence also dealt with the economic aspect within the jurisprudential studies, dealing with money, prices, accelerated, deferred, correct and corrupt sales, injustice, monopoly and loan, payment of debt and assignment in it, usury of the loan, usury of sale, provisions of speculation, loans, companies, farming, Musaqah, leasing, rent, land sector and revival of the dead...etc.

He wrote independent books outside jurisprudence and hadith, which may be considered the first nucleus of the Islamic economy, even if they do not bear his name. The most famous of these books are:

1- The Book of Money by Abū 'Ubayd al-Qāsim ibn
2- Kitāb al-'Amūl li Abī Ja'far Aḥmad ibn Nasr al-Dāwūdī
3- Al-Kharaj Book of Judge Abu Yusuf
4- Kitāb al-Kharāj liḥyá ibn 'Adam
5- Extraction of the provisions of the abscess of Abu al-Faraj al-Hanbali
6- Royal Rulings of Al-Mawardi

Thus, it is clear that the organized economic thought began with the Muhammadan mission, and upon returning to what preceded it, it seems that the economic movement known to the Quraysh, which is the domination of the Arab tribes, before the emergence of Islam, is the commercial movement, and the riba-based transactions that characterize it, for which seasons are held and markets are organized, and migration to remote countries takes place, especially to Yemen on the winter trip and the Levant on the summer trip. These are the two famous journeys that they make in security and reassurance, as they were the people of God's sanctuary and the sanctuary of his house, and thanks to him they gained prestige and respect, so that they were cutting off the Fiafi, without anyone harming them. And the people around them are between kidnapped and looted. Allah reminded them that understanding the two journeys and feeding them because of them from hunger, and he secured them during them from fear, so that they may realize that the virtue is his, and that he is the secure provider for their lives, so they turn after their Islam from attachment to the house to attachment to his Lord, where there is no deity except Him. The Almighty said: "To enjoin the **Quraysh** to envelop them for the **winter and summer journey, let them worship the Lord of this house, who fed them from hunger and secured them from fear.**"

Except for the commercial movement, the journey for it, and some agricultural work and livestock breeding, we did not teach the Arabs in their ignorance a distinct economic thought. Rather, we know for them a glimpse of morality related to courage, generosity, jealousy, loyalty, and the fathers of injustice. They were most famous for their generosity and love of spending, which in the sense of the public use of wealth goes back to its original origin.

It is possible to summarize the economic activity or resources of Arab wealth that Islam found to exist, so its invalidity was invalidated, and its favor was acknowledged in four magazines: dealing with usury, trade and agriculture, and raising livestock.

REVOKE THE USURIOUS SYSTEM AND ESTABLISH ISLAMIC COMMERCE IN ITS PLACE

Usury in language means increase and growth. It is said that the usury of sowing, if it grows and increases, as evidenced by the Almighty's saying: "**If we send water down to it, it will be shaken and patted**." In Sharia, it[150] means an increase in specific things, especially the increase that the lender increases on the borrower, in return for the term and[151] receives it without giving a reward or compensation from work or others. Therefore, it is considered wrong to eat people's money... Note that the loan in Islam, humanitarian assistance, prevents it from falling other than the face of God and is morally incompatible with exploiting the circumstances of need, and imposing an usurious increase under it.

This is because Islam has developed practical methods for acquiring money on the basis that there is no way to benefit from people's money except by giving a consideration, consideration or something that pleases the same giver, and the consideration may be a work as in the lease, such as a day's work for sixty dirhams, and sixty dirhams for a day's work, or it is compensatory, as evidenced by the process of netting between two goods, or between a commodity and its price, which is expressed by jurists in one of the two compensators.

This is in contrast to the work of the loan shark, who lends the needy - for example - one hundred and twenty until the end, so his hundred return is guaranteed, as if it remained under his hand and above it twenty of his brother's race... And money does not give birth to money, as Aristotle said and his parable of the gambler who beats one dirham and comes out with a car number equal to fifty thousand dirhams. The consideration or offer he gave is practically fifty-one thousand dirhams, except for one of the race of others, so it was completely fair and just that Islam forbade usury and gambling, and everything known to eat people's money wrongly.

In the context of research on how usury enters the land of the Arabian Peninsula, some researchers explained that Jews who are rarely present in a country, and survive dealing with usury, or there is a usury institution, and

---

[150]- Surat Fussilat: 39.
[151]- Singer to Ibn Qudamah 4/1 Introductions to Ibn Rushd 13/18

receive from the control of their capital or management, have settled in the north of Arabia, and practiced usury transactions despite its prohibition in the three religions: Judaism, Christianity and Islam, and its enemy walked among the wealthy Arabs, and they began to deal with it, despite the fact that the Arab element, was one of the most tolerant peoples of the world, and kept it away from the spirit of blackmail and monopoly.

They were lending with an increase that leads with the debt, and if the term comes, and the debtor is unable to pay what he owes, he says to his creditor: "See me your increase," or the creditor says: "Do you judge or raise?"[152] Do you perform or increase? The more the debtor fails, the more the creditor doubles the increase, until it becomes exponential. Allah has forbidden the believers to do so by saying: "**O you who have believed, do not eat usury exponentially**." Some fraudsters who resent Allah to please the wealthy have claimed that Muharram is the only multiplier. Sheikh Hussein Muhammad Makhlouf said in his interpretation, "The elite of the statement of the meanings of the Quran 1/125": "Allah has forbidden the origin of usury and its multiplication." Evidence shows that this dealing, which is prevalent in usury banks today, is what is meant by the usury of Jahiliya, which the Prophet (SAW) put in the farewell argument under his feet, as he[153] was standing at the time with his capital and his increase waiting for the coming of the term. Islam came and invalidated it, and ordered people to repent from dealing with it, and they were limited to recover their capital without increasing. The Prophet said: "The Riba of ignorance is a subject and the first Riba was placed by the Riba of Al-Abbas bin Abdul Muttalib, for it is a subject of all. In another narrative, all usury is subject, but you have your capital, you do not oppress or oppress. " Do not oppress by taking what is left of usury, and do not oppress by preventing the return of capital. This was a confirmation of the Almighty's saying: "O you who believe, fear Allah and give up what is left of usury, if you are believers. If you do not do so, authorize a war from Allah and His Messenger. If you repent, you will have your capital. You will not be wronged, nor will you be wronged."

Islam, when it appeared, abolished usury and gambling, and all transactions based on fraud, cunning, fraud, deception and human exploitation of his fellow man, did not leave a vacuum in life, a gap in production or a setback in consumption, but rather developed fair practical methods that dealt with all vital fields, and dropped the mediation between production and work, as evidenced in the lawsuit to convert money that is lent at usurious interest guaranteed at the expense of the weak into commercial capital, which the owners of funds bear the loss of, in exchange for obtaining profit. This is known as Mudaraba and Lending Company. Where the money is given to those who work in it with a share of its profit, and the worker bears the responsibility of the work, and the master of the money is responsible for the loss, and the profit between them is according to what they agreed upon, as will be stated.

---

[152]- Muwatta: Al-Zarqani copy 3/324.
[153]- See the book of jurisprudence on the four schools of thought 2/247.

One of the practical methods is the principle of earning money through direct action, as the best element on which to acquire in Islam. In this, Al-Bukhari narrates that the Prophet (PBUH) said: "No one has ever eaten food better than to eat from the work of his hand, and that the Prophet of God David used to eat from the work of his hand."[154]

The work of the hand includes trade, agriculture, industry, fishing, livestock breeding...Maordi saw his focus in trade, industry, and agriculture.[155]

REFORM IN THE PEASANT ECONOMY

The city's first Muslim community of immigrants and supporters was founded. Where the spirit of brotherhood generated by the work of the Messenger and the work of the emissaries of his companions prevailed before the migration, and the deep feeling was the strong interdependence and fruitful cooperation, and sincere brotherhood, between all his members. This spirit would not have been overflowing in those circumstances, and abound with such meanings, had it not been for the dawn of religion, making it a basic rule for the success of any reform attempt, guiding people and not forcing them, as manifested in the Prophet's curriculum:

In the first year of the Hijra, the Prophet (PBUH) separated the Ansar from the owners of property and among the poor immigrants who left their money in Mecca to flee their religion from sedition. He would take Ansari's hand and Muhajiri's hand, and say, "We are brothers."[156] So, the first seed of this process was launched from a moral religious reality, and when its merits in Islamic principles found fertile ground, it rested on its leg, and resulted in a material symbiosis, which turned the poor into rich people, and the procedure into participants. The process has two principles:

1- The principle of participation in production on the basis of work contribution. Under this process, the supporters were to put the money in the hands of the migrants, who had to take responsibility for the work, and the meeting was when the production was shared, as it actually happened.

2- The principle of volunteering for the benefit of what he preferred from the funds over the necessary amount known in the Hadith books as a grant of credit, according to which Al-Ansari would give his immigrant brother more than he needed, in order to exploit him, and benefit from his production without missing the original to its owner. The immigrants continued to exploit and benefit from these properties until the circle of possibilities in Islam expanded, and the Prophet seized the lands of the Jews of Bani Nadir, so he divided them into poor immigrants, and ordered them to return what they had of the Ansar's money.

Thus, the rich supporters would give up to their brothers, the poor immigrants, installments of their money, to work in it, to benefit from its mule,

---
[154] Al-Bukhari: Al-Fateh version 5/209.
[155] On the Paths of Peace 3/5.
[156] - Nour Al-Yaqeen, p. 89.

or to work in all of them, dividing production. Allah is true when He says in their altruism and love for immigrants, "**Those who have taken up home and faith before them love those who have emigrated to them and do not find in their chests a need of what they have received and affect themselves, even if they have special needs.**"[157]

As for raising livestock, which is one of the main resources of the island's population, it was encouraged by Islam - it also encouraged agriculture, trade and industry...He embarked on the principle of volunteering with benefits in addition to zakat, as he did with regard to the benefits of the land. In this, Abu Hurairah occurs in what happens to him about the Messenger (PBUH). He was asked: What is the righteousness of camels? He said: "You give the cream, you give the abundance, you pauperize the back, you knock the stallion and you water the milk,"[158] which is confirmed by what was stated in the hadith that the Prophet (PBUH) was asked what is the right of camels? He said: "Milking her on water, lending her bucket, lending her stallion and her plight, and carrying her in the way of Allah."[159]

ADVOCACY FOR ECONOMIC DEVELOPMENT AND ACTION

Islam wanted development, encouraged production, and called for the promotion of money, and denounced hoarding and monopoly, as the companion Abu Dharr al-Ghafari said in general: "Those who hoard gold and silver and do not spend it for the sake of Allah, inform them of the suffering of the day." One of the signs of the call for production and investment is the saying of the Prophet (pbuh): "No one who is an orphan has money, let him trade in it and do not leave it until charity eats it.[160]" That is, Zakah, and the money that Zakah eats, if he does not sleep, is the money represented in the hoarded money, as mentioned above.

For the sake of development, we find that Islam has opened the field of competition and security of freedom of ownership, freedom of production, freedom of consumption, freedom of trade, conclusion of agreements, and establishment of legitimate companies...It is the first economy that came with a market economy or market freedom and dropped the mediator between the producer and the consumer, as will be explained below.

Islam called for work and considered it the main starting point for earning money, in which the Prophet's saying progressed: "No one has ever eaten food better than to eat from the work of his hand. Etc.» He also ordered the payment of wages in full, and without delay. The Prophet (PBUH) ordered that the wage earner be given his wages before his sweat dries. Islam, the first celestial religion, came with a complete system of life, and was guided to work for the

---

[157]- Surat Al-Hashr : 9.
[158]- Sunan Abu Dawud 3/169 Grand Sunan 4/183 for Al-Bayhaqi.
[159] Grand Sunnah 4/183.
[160]- Sahih Al-Tirmidhi 3/136 Greater Sunnah 6/22 The Crown Collector of the Origins in the Hadiths of the Prophet 2/22-I 3/1971 by Sheikh Ali Mansour.

world and the Hereafter...In it, Abdullah bin Omar says: "Work for your world as if you were living forever and do the other as if you were dying tomorrow." Judge Abu Bakr bin Al-Arabi quoted him in the "Provisions of the Qur 'an" when he said the Almighty: "And **do not forget your share of the world."** Imam al-Ghazali, a Sufi, saw that the merchant's worship was to grow and strengthen his trade for the benefit of the nation. It is his leading theory in the subject that exceeds the treasure that harms production and work - the level of saved money, and put it at the level of frozen values in such as gold and silver pots, and his reason for the damage to the economic movement, as every monetary value frozen in the treasure, or gold and silver pots or antiques... By the amount of its value, it creates a vacuum in production and work. Marx's statement as a communist does not recognize capital, that capital without labor does not produce posits beside him that labor also does not produce without capital...The Islamic economy was the first economy to focus production on land, capital and labor factors...

Therefore, Imam al-Ghazali believes that the treasure, whether direct, represented in the saved money, or indirect, whose value is locked in the pot, is an injustice, an economic injustice and a social injustice. The role of criticism in the economic and practical movement has been likened to the role of the post, the judge and the ruler in the management of social interests. The[161] harm that arises socially from the imprisonment of the post and the ruler is equal to the harm that arises economically and practically from the detention of money and the freezing of its value.

---

[161] - See the approach of Islamic economics in the production of wealth and consumption 1/206 Author self-criticism, p. 214 for the late Allal Al-Fassi.

CAPITALIST TREND AT THE EMERGENCE OF MODERN DOCTRINES

This chapter briefly addresses classical doctrines, or traditional free schools: their beginning, thedate and place of their emergence.Its founders... Its basic principles...Evolution...Its positives and negatives.. With the analysis of what needs to be studied, compared or analyzed, in order to benefit from the subsequent right or wrong of its predecessor

Mercantilism

Economic doctrine is contrary to economics; because science as a common field aims to know economic facts, as it was before the emergence of doctrines...And the doctrine as a special trend -aimed at directing, intervening and influencing, and trying to change under the pretext of reform.... Science is neutral and the doctrine is biased because it is mostly personal thinking. It comes from economic, social, political, individual or sectarian considerations.

Like every beginning, the world economy arose with its two parts: capitalist and socialist, and then communist by the hands of those who are not specialists in economic affairs. The father of political economy, Adam Smith, was a professor of literature and logic, Ricardo was a banker and a broker in Bursa, François Kenai was a doctor, Louis XV, Karl Marx was a journalist, and Proudhon was a politician... before they professionalize research in economic affairs. Economic theories, regardless of their source, do not live, except at the level of scrutiny, and the test of practical experience. It is the practice that produces the papers, and differentiates between what is practical and practical, and what is studied within the history of economic ideas, in order to benefit the later from the previous experience negatively and positively.

This is what both the researcher and the practitioner of the Islamic economic system should know. Although it was the first international economy, and it was the only active economy in the Middle Ages when science froze for about a thousand years 1450-496AD, where it began in the seventh century AD, and built Islamic civilization on three continents and the modern - as a doctrine and science - did not begin until the sixteenth century...For colonial, internal, external and intellectual reasons, he was stalemated by the civil and social laws in Islamic legislation...And resurrecting it, it needs onthe part of researchers, leaders and investors to research, scrutiny, practice, experience, efficiency and strong determination...So we don't study it as history. Rather, we study it as a stagnant system that is beginning to regain its vitality.

As for the subject of introducing the doctrines or schools, which they termed modern, for the history before their emergence, it is possible to divide them into two main trends: the individual capitalist trend, and the collective socialist trend. In the capitalist trend, commercialism is located.

Mercantilism at its inception was known as the Mercantilist current, and Mercantilism means commercial sectarianism, embracing metal mercantilism, and commercial industrialism...A mercantile person means a researcher or business thinker. Thestream is divided into three main schools:

I. Spanish Mercantilism

Among her writers or thinkers, Ortiz, Olivares, Mariana, and the Spanish Pentecostals are betting that the only way to ensure the strengthening of Spain's influence is to work to bring as much gold as possible, and prevent its exit, after owning it.

The Spanish trend was known as mineral mercantilism, as they believe that the wealth that represents the strength and wealth of the state is measured by the amount of gold inside it, so they called for encouraging imports of gold, in exchange for exports of goods. Their aim in foreign trade was to import and hold gold.

The theory is primitive, superficial, deficient...It claimed that the wealth that represents the power of the state and its singing, is measured by the amount of gold that is inside it. While the wealth that represents the strength and wealth of any country is measured by the strength of its production at the level of the national economy, and called for the retention of money and the freezing of its values, without regard to the effectiveness of its use and the results of its investment for the benefit of the state and society.The owners did not notice that the money - if it is hoarded and its values frozen - is the same as the building stones in the negative.

This theory, along with the civil wars, may contribute to Spain's lagging behind the greatEuropean industrial renaissance, despite the huge potential available to it, after it occupied Latin America.In addition, it was finally infected by General Franco's seizure of power. and the modern European industrial renaissance in the wake of its youth. As a military dictator, he lost the economic, political and social experience.His long reign has given rise to factors of development in some sectors. If he succeeded in cultivating and building dams, he failed to keep pace with Western industrial development.

From the beginning, Mariana criticized the purely metallic trend and called for attention to public finances and the balance in the state finances. He called for financial reform through a decrease in the expenses of the Prince's Palace, the salaries of senior employees, and the imposition of a tax on luxuries used by the rich.

All of these are objective views that aim to develop a national economic policy that governs the link between income and expenditure and tries to solve problems at the level of expenditure if they are not resolved at the level of income. Thus, it is considered the first Spanish mercantile to get rid of the knot of gold saved, and brought it out of the darkness of hoarding into the light of development. Although his views are more focused on spending policy than production and investment policy. Although it is known economically that spending falls into the hands of investors.

Mercantilist ideas entered Italy in the early 17th century and took on a character similar to that of Spain. However, the attention of the Italians has focused more on the internal economic problems, especially with regard to the management of public finances, although some of them have gone along with the industrial mainstream at the time in France, so Antoniosera studied the means of industrialization and saw that industrialization is a tool for development. This being the case, what Italy has reached now in manufacturing confirms the validity of his theory.

SECOND- FRENCH MERCANTILISM

From her book "Jean Bodin " and "Antoine Monchrestien ", Bodin said the need for the state to intervene, and held it responsible for taking an initial initiative in order to establish a national industry, which would be the basis for a comprehensive renaissance, and enable the country to raise its exports, in exchange for bringing in gold coins. The aim of the commercial industry with abroad was to import gold and use it as a means of production.

The same idea was adopted by Antoine Monchrestien , who stressed it by saying: "Industry for the country is like blood for the heart."[162] He strongly criticized the policy of accumulating gold, and between its sterility and economic dangers, and focused on work, and saw that it is the secret of happiness, and that productivity is the only way to ensure the collection of wealth. He called on the nobles who own land and do not work to renounce old traditions, customs and social values, and to engage in the battle of work for the cultivation and reclamation of the land.

Menchritian's opinions are positive and practical, which have a great impact on economic thought, and it is sufficient that he was the first to write a book entitled Political Economy, so he imitated him from a thousand after him, as his statement presented. The first thinker in the French Mercantilist school whose efforts focused more on the field of work than on the opinions of a written blog is Minister Colbert, who worked as a statesman to implement the policy of industrialization, establish workshops, and protect French industry from crowding out others, especially English industrial production. In addition, he drew up a scheme to monitor the prices of products, according to the commercial and industrial laws codified in the economic legislation. He was rightly the first to focus the French economy on the industrial sector...Thus, the French Mercantilism is characterized by the trend towards industrialization.

III- ENGLISH MERCANTILISM

The English were not interested in pursuing industrialization, as the French did, nor importing gold, and preventing its exit from the country, as the Spanish did. Rather, their interest in that period turned towards foreign trade...Their first goal was to increase exports of goods and sell services to foreign countries, in order to obtain psychological minerals not to save them, but in order to buy raw

---

[162]Political Economy 88/1 by Dr. Fathallah Al-Alou

materials approved in British industry. Such as metals, cotton, wool, silk... Their slogan was "Let's sell more of what we buy"[163], which is a purely commercial slogan. Britain was later to be more industrialized.

One of the English Mercantilists is Tuman Moon, the first commercial writer since 1621 to conduct several studies on the balance of external performances. With the aim of establishing an economic, commercial and legal framework, in which payments are recorded with the outside in order to control the correspondence between what is exported and what is imported of goods, materials and services...

Among them is Gorias Schelde, who walked the same line as Tuman Moon and sees the need to pay more attention to foreign services, and to enable the country to have a strong maritime apparatus that enables the state to use its ships to transport its goods and rent its services in order to transport foreign goods. It is the plan under which he believes that working will generate revenues for the country from the gold coin. The purpose of foreign trade was to import and use gold.

The most famous English mercantilist of all was William Petty, who put forward many of the economic views adopted by the classics, physiocrats and socialists after him. He advocated economic freedom as advocated by classical free doctrine and believed - as did the physiocrats - that there are natural rules to which all economic data are subject, and he cared about the distribution of wealth, as did the socialists. He was the first to use statistics and mathematics in economic analysis.

Poti saw that wealth, when it is produced, depends on two basic factors: land and work. He said: "Work is the father and the driving base of wealth and real estate ownership is the mother." [164] If work is the father and land is the mother, then the child is production, but he has overlooked a third factor of production, which is capital, which as it revolves around raw materials, wages and additional expenses. Without it, the father and mother may not be vaccinated.

Based on the above, it seems that the Spanish Mercantilism is a metal printed with the character of gold collection and retention, the French Mercantilism is industrialized, printed with the character of industrialization, and the English Mercantilism is commercial printed with the character of foreign trade. The common denominator between the three schools is the commercial element, with different considerations, between these and those...This is not to say that other fields have been neglected. Rather, it means the first character placed on the activity of each direction or school.

In general terms, the views of the commercial doctrine in its three schools almost revolve around foreign trade and industry for its sake, and its monopoly by the state, and considering the profits from it as the main factor in strengthening the powers of each country that nature has deprived it of owning

---

[163] Political Economy 88/1 by Dr. Fathallah Al-Alou
[164] Political Economy 89/1 Fathallah Al-Al

gold and silver mines, with the difference between what each country does with it after owning it...The Italian writer Antonio Serra is one of the first to examine the foundations of the theory and its factors. In 1613, he published a book in which he examined the reasons why gold and silver are available in mine-free kingdoms.

Mercantilism arose with economic development, the movement of European countries towards colonialism, and the scramble for the bounties of vulnerable peoples.Spain moved towards the West, and the gold and silver mines in its colonies in Latin America [165] flowed to it without calculation, and thus reached the peak of greatness. Other countries realized that these two precious metals are the origin of all wealth, and began to issue legislation and laws warning people against exporting them, so that there is not less than what is available, and countries that did not possess these precious metals began to develop their resources and regulate their foreign trade, thus obtaining the difference between the values of exports and imports in gold currency. To support this system, high customs duties were imposed on imports. France has gone far in implementing this system, especially during the era of its Minister Colbert, who was said to have made France a country and a factory.

One of the disadvantages of this doctrine is that it suffocates society, restricts the freedom of individuals to trade, and establishes the state in the place of a single merchant, working to promote its goods and export them abroad... His death that the secret in the promotion of the state lies in the promotion of society itself. The state is society and society is the state: two names that touch one is the nation, and social wealth is more productive and effective than the public property of the state.

The theories of commercial writers did not agree on the economic views that they touched on, as evidenced by their disagreement on the theories of "value" and"usury".

On the theory of the value of the commodity, William Petty thought that it is based on production expenses. including land and humanitarian work, and Locke[166] saw that humanitarian work is the only source of value. Marx adopted it and criticized it, and Neoclass Barbon sawthat utility is the basis of value, and that useless things are worthless, and explained that the abundance of things makes them cheap, and their scarcity makes them expensive. John Law, for his part, gave an example of water and diamonds, which Adam Smith more after him than he hit him. He said: "We find water is very much used, but it is of little value, because the amount of water is much greater than the amount of demand for it, and diamonds are of little use, but they are of great value, because the demand for diamonds is much greater than the amount in it, so the result is that the values of commodities in his view are determined at the level of the law of

---

[165]Principles of Political Economy 115 / 1 - by Dr. Sayed Abdel Mawla
[166]History of Economic Ideas, p. 56 by Dr. Mohammed Aziz Al-Iraqi

supply and demand, and they rise with the rise of demand, and fall with its decline.

The commercial writers' disagreement about "usury" is no less different from their disagreement about the theory of "value". Thomas said by taking interest, he saw that the money loan enables small traders to rise, and helps to invest the money of widows and orphans. On the contrary, Josiah Glade saw that moneylenders are like males in the bee kingdom who live on work, and do not work. Aristotle once said, "Money does not give birth to money." However, the role it gave to the loan may not apply to this era, as it is difficult for the average investor today to face the problems of inflation and high prices, the performance of taxes and profits, and the consequences of the high cost of production. Including the high price of raw materials and wages, the price of machines with the performance of bank interests, and the success he wants succeeds.

Thomas's theory has lost its source of value at the level of experience and reality. After what is known as Third World indebtedness, and what has been proven by statistics that the bankruptcy of about 90% of traders was due to dealing with banks, it seems that the interest-bearing loan sits and does not rise, and that what rises is trade, industry, agriculture, and livestock breeding...The saying of the Prophet (PBUH) advanced: "Except for the guardian of an orphan whohas wealth, let him trade in it and do notleave it until charity eats him." It is the answer to the treasure that Islam and usury forbade.

Naturalism «Phys and Hippocrates»

Naturalism, or the natural free economic school, emerged in the second half of the seventeenth century by Dr. François Kenai, a physician of Louis XV, and spread, after [167] he published his book "Economic Tables" in 1750 and contributed to its publication along with its founder, "Mirabeau" and "Debon Dunmore" and helped to spread it that it appeared in conditions characterized by economic turmoil, which created the appropriate atmosphere for its spread. Despite its narrow scope in the field of production. He limited his subject to agricultural land alone. However, it dominated economic thought in France until after the revolution of 1789, and it may be one of the reasons for its acceptance, along with the lack of a balanced economic policy - that the land production it focuses on is the main resource of its time in Europe.

Physiocrats believe that there is a natural system that includes economic phenomena of all kinds and diversity, and that it is applied naturally on its own without the need for any intervention, provided that it secures the freedom of individuals, projects and types of property, and that the role of the state or government is limited to imposing respect for private property and individual freedom. They believe that by respecting property and freedom, and leaving man on his instinct and nature, he will work for his happiness and the happiness of others. From this principle began their famous phrase "Let people work and release the freedom of goods" and met with the principle of the free doctrine "Let it pass, let it work" and the principle in its origin is a physiocrat [168] said by "Vanson Corny" and adopted by the free doctrine.

The views of physiocrats, especially with regard to leaving man on his instinct and nature, to work for his happiness and the happiness of others, without the need for a system and authority sponsored by theoretical philosophical rather than realistic economic views, somewhat similar to the views of Plato in the "utopia", as their application to the image they see, depends on the existence of an ideal moral society, valid for all its members and groups. In it, esoteric scruples and the vigilance of conscience take the place of the state system and its authority. This is something that humanity has not reached. You may not reach it.

At the level of economic thought, François Kenai divided society into three layers:

The first class is the peasantry and farmers. This layer is the only one that is considered productive, since it is the one that produces what is called net product. It is the value of the quotient, which remains after subtracting the expenses, which are made for | agricultural production, such as the value of production is one hundred and its cost and the expenses of the product are fifty. It is represented by fifty.

---

[167] Lectures on Political Economy, p. 42 by Dr. Salaheddine Haroun
[168] Political Economy 93/ 1 Fathallah Alou

The same analysis is used in industrial production and limiting it to agricultural production is illogical. From the net product, Marx quoted the theory of surplus value. It is the profit or surplus in excess of value, which in his view is formed by the amount of work spent in its production, as will come.

Kenai saw the net product transmithted in the social form and revived it, just as blood does in the human body 169. In fact, the role it has given to the net product - despite its limitation to the production of a consumption material - is in fact the role of cash in the economic circle and the social body. It is the one who revives it, moves its wheels, and moves its debt, its mikes and purchasing power between the commercial, industrial and agricultural sectors...It flows between segments of society, as blood flows in the body...David Hume likened it to oil in an engine. Where the movement with its presence, and the impact of iron when lost. The oil rotates with movement wherever it is found.

The second layer, in Kanai's view, is made up of landowners. Although they were not classified within the productive class, he considered them the basis of the natural system, and felt that thanks to their continuous work and preservation of the foundations of civilization, they brought the land to what it was of quality and prosperity. In comparison with the concept that he gave to the first and second class, it seems that the first class, which consists of direct farmers to work, did not own the land. Rather, it owned the labor of its hand, and in fact it alone produces the net product, which is the basis of naturalism in production and labor. As long as the land is produced only by work... Thus, it is clear that the role it gave to the owners, who live on the work of others, as it was in the Middle Ages, where the feudal landowner owns land and uses slaves to exploit it, is in fact the role of those who work in the fields, as their efforts, their continuous work, and their preservation of the life of the land that lives by work and dies without it, have reached the quality and prosperity they have reached. Work is the secret of her life and she owns it without it, and they kill her and do not revive her. In Islamic law, land is owned, sold, bought and inherited... According to the work of man above it, and if it is abandoned and returns to the dead, the right of ownership over it will fall and it will return to the ownership of the state, and it will be for those who revive it.[170] The Prophet said, "Whoever revives a dead land, it is for him."

The third layer is called the sterile layer, and it consists of makers, traders, self-employed and users... He does not want sterility to be useless. Rather, it wants the values of its products to be equivalent to the values of its production and consumption expenses, without any net output. What he saw in this theory may have been for the seventeenth century, when agriculture entered the first row of European production and has now bounced back after trade, industry and services. to the third or fourth. However, saying that their products are

---

[169] Political Economy, p. 49, by Dr. Azmi Rajab, 6-1980- Dar Al-Ilm for Millions - Beirut
[170] See The Approach of Islamic Economics in the Production and Consumption of Wealth 305/2 and Beyond by the Author

equivalent to their production and consumption expenses is an opinion that lacks a firm argument as there is no trade, industry or craft without little or many returns to ensure their continuation.

Today, the net product, or surplus value that left production expenses in the land of cost, and rose to the sky of surplus values in a way that is not related to real value or exchange, nor to the law of supply and demand, is advanced industrial production, especially advanced weapons, or what we express with modern technology. The law that governs this species is political and ideological.

It was necessary to get rid of primitive opinions, bring the economy to the ground, and confront the complex reality now with practical approaches, as the approaches would organize the processes and process if they started with a primitive approach that became primitive...It is primitive for physiocrats to see that agricultural production is the work of God and industrial production is the work of man. [171] In fact, all the topics on which effort and work are practiced, whether in agricultural or industrial production, are the creation of God and production and its means in both fields of human work. The one who created the earth is the one who created the raw materials within it. What they saw was that the land is the mother of resources and their origin, and that each of them is insufficient to strike for the most important economic sectors, claiming that they are the work of man.

Physiocrats and their doctrine have been criticized, especially in limiting production to the net output of the land, and considering only the agricultural class as the producer...

In aggregate terms, naturalism is inherently at odds with other economic doctrines. Dupont, one of his leaders, defined it as the science of natural order. What comes to mind when hearing this expression is that it is the system that is different from the artificial social system. To push this illusion, we market what was conveyed by the specialist in the history of economic ideas, Dr. Muhammad Aziz, as he says about what is meant by naturalism: "It is the system chosen by God for human happiness, that is, the divine system. To find this system, we should refer to the esoteric system that God has placed in the heart of every human being to guide him to the straightpath. [172] It is an economic mysticism. They linked it to a material source, which is the earth, and they did not link it to a moral source, which is the heart.

The most effective way to implement this system in the eyes of its leaders is to leave everyone alone while securing freedom for them, to do what they see as good, and in the way they see as useful. They believed that the motive of personal interest is sufficient to guide man to what is best for him and for all, and that there is no conflict between his interest and the interest of all because the interest of all is only the sum of the interests of individuals, and they

---

[171] Political Economy p.51- Dr. Azmi Rajab
[172] History of Economic Ideas, p. 56 by Dr. Mohammed Aziz

believed that free competition would establish a good price between the two parties, and remove usurious profits in the field of the economy. These theories are as close to the theories of free doctrine as will come.

Based on the above, it can be said that one of the most prominent views of naturalists, which represents the backbone of their doctrine, is to limit "net product" or "net surplus" to agriculture alone. It follows from Kenai's analysis that production involves a certain amount of expenditure. This is the amount that should be subtracted from the productive wealth, so that the so-called net product increase remains. The amount of wheat harvested by the farmer at the end of the year usually exceeds the amount consumed for sowing and feeding.In their view, the trader does not create anything new, but his work is limited to the exchange of pre-existing goods, as well as the manufacturer. His work is nothing more than the modification of raw materials, and the mixing and addition taking place on them.

As for their views on the value of the commodity, economic historians have noticed that it is unclear, as they are in all the principles that they have called for, if we exclude the writer «Kundiak» who explained the idea, he said: «Value is not in the same thing as much as we have in our hearts of appreciation for that thing. This appreciation is commensurate with our need for it, so it increases and decreases, as our need increases and decreases, and the benefit is not the only element in the formation of "value", but the thing provided by it has an effective impact on "value" as well. The value of things increases in scarcity, and decreases in abundance. The value decreases when the thing is abundant until it reaches zero, like sea water on the shore of the ocean. "

Free Doctrine or Free Traditional School

Free or liberal doctrine is the doctrine that it is better to leave the individual alone, to work for his own interest, away from any external interference by the state or others, except in special circumstances. This is reflected in the principles of "one atom alone" and "one atom passes, one atom works"

In response to this theory, what has been proven by practical experience is that some individuals, most of whom are powerful, benefit from absolute freedom and many lose. It is the defect that Islam has addressed by preventing him from proving his foolishness from freedom of action, while defining it by laws that prevent the guide from infringing his right to the rights of others. If each doctrine has leaders and thinkers, one of the most prominent thinkers of the free doctrine is as follows:

Adam Smith

The father of political economy, Adam Smith, was born in 1723 and died in 1790. He was one of the group that believes in the existence of God with the denial of revelation and is rightly considered the first to lay the substantive foundations of political economy, and the greatest pillar of the traditional free school. He is also one of the most famous economists who played a key role in weakening economics in general, and freedom of trade in particular.

He was a professor of English literature and political economy at the University of Edinburgh, and a professor of logic at the University of Glasgow. His fame in economics came as a result of his book "The Wealth of Nations", which is the first source that caused a revolution in concepts and theories, as evidenced in his opinion that the wealth of nations does not increase as claimed by traders, by increasing gold and silver. It increases by increasing production.

His book The Wealth of Nations was divided into five sections: The first section was devoted to the subject of specialization, division of labor, exchange and money. The second topic was devoted to capital and methods of its formation, and the theories of rent and wages... The third and fourth were devoted to the study of the historical development of the wealth of nations. During which he criticized the views of the metal mercantilists and physiocrats, in defense of economic freedom, and devoted the fifth to the study of public finance topics...

Some economists believe that he was the first to say the theory of division of labor. In fact, Ibn Khaldun, who was born in Tunis in 1332 and died in Cairo in 1406, has already analyzed it for centuries, linking specialization and division of labor on the one hand and the difference in goods and quality of work on the other hand...Ibn Khaldun, even in the eyes of foreign researchers, especially in front of the scientific theorizing that he practiced in Al-Muqaddimah, is considered a science of the flags of administration, politics, judiciary, jurisprudence, literature, history, economy and society...

He was considered by some contemporary economists to be the first of the older economists. Especially since he dealt with various economic topics, three centuries before the great English economist William Petty. The contemporary French economist Louis Bodinwrote: "It is truly amazing to see the accuracy of Ibn Khaldun's scientific method based on the law of negativity, and the abundance of new ideas in his era, which he mentioned and analyzed four hundred years before" Adam Smith ", nicknamed the father of political economy. It explains the division of labor, professional specialization, money, value, population, and other economic theories… . Itis noexaggerationtoconsider him one of the greatest economists

The first two. "[173]

In addition to the division of labor, professional specialization, money, value and population. Ibn Khaldun dealt with important economic issues. Such as the value of the work, the factors of forming the value of the commodity, and the reason for the rise in prices or prices, and consider money as savings for the values of things and the return of money. He highlighted the importance of the division of labor, and its role in increasing production, and put forward before the physiocrats the concept of the natural system that runs the universe, and addressed, contrary to their theory, that only the land produces the subject of agricultural production, without paying more attention to it than industrial production.

If it is natural for the successor to benefit from the opinions of his predecessor, it is not easy - for lack of any argument - to decide that Smith was influenced or benefited from the opinions of Ibn Khaldun, especially since the match was not made in all opinions…We find out from the opinions named in particular that it integrates personal interest in the public or vice versa and sees that the producer -for example - only considers his interest. At the same time, it serves the public interest. He believes in economic freedom. In order to ensure it, he does not say that the state intervenes, except in such matters as the issuance of currency and navigation…In his view, the task of the government is limited to protecting the country from foreign attacks, securing justice among citizens, lifting injustice against them, and carrying out work and completing projects that individuals do not accept for some reason, such as being overstretched.

He sees in the production of use-values and exchange values that the value of a commodity is determined by work, that is, the effort exerted in its production. It is the theory that Marx adopted after him, and criticized him, as it criticized Adam named himself, for ignoring the workers of land and capital. However, Smith believes that humanitarian work is a measure of its order and is formed by the cost of production, such as the value of a commodity produced in an hour is equivalent to fifty dirhams, and another value produced in two hours is equivalent to one hundred dirhams… Marx sees its formation by abstract human

---

[173]Political Economy, pp. 7-9, 6-1970, by Dr. Azmi Rajab

action alone, in line with the nature of his doctrine, as a communist who recognizes neither private ownership of land nor capital.

Smith disagreed with the merchants that money is an excellent wealth, and considered it just an intermediary to facilitate the exchange of replacement values, and disagreed with the naturalists that agriculture alone produces the net surplus, and agreed with them that natural economic systems are divine, and that they are more righteous, and more just, and that divine care is what created in man the desire to improve his condition. It is from this desire that the natural social order emerges.

Contrary to Marxism, Smith sees the state as a bad manager. Because its employees are negligent and wasteful, they do not have a direct personal interest in management. They are paid from the public treasury. Based on this theory, the production of land will fall by half or a quarter, if it becomes all for the state and is placedat its disposal, which is a correct view of total nationalization. We find a place for it in what happened after the Leninist revolution in 1917, where land was turned into state ownership, so production fell by half, as a result of the peasants' strike, and the famine resulting from the strike killed six million people, so [174] the importance of private property and individual freedom in maintaining the element of competition became the main engine in the development of production.

ROBERT MALTHUS

Malthus (1766-1836) is considered the first pessimist, and the most prominent statistical writer in the traditional school. Famous for his research on the population, he noted the imbalance between their number and the quantities of resources needed to secure their lives, and sees in his pessimistic theorythat the required balance depends on the occurrence of disasters, wars and famines...Excessive destiny dies in them... His death to note, not only the imbalance between resources and population, but also the imbalance in the amounts of wealth in the hands of individuals, families, states and societies. Perhaps he did not hear the border of the padded ones next to the groans of the hungry.

The theory is a pessimistic theory, of the kind that discourages intentions, creates problems and does not solve them, if we exclude the aspect of statistics, and yet, it is still studying its negativity in the field of production and work. It is not long ago that objective and impractical approaches and more theoretical studies, rather than technical ones, contribute to the stagnation prevailing in third world countries.

As for the practical solution, or creating a balance that Malthus may be ignorant of its source, it lies in searching for new resources, developing production in what is and exploiting what God has deposited on land and sea in

---

[174] Our Economy 211/1 for Baqir Al-Sadr

the best way, and then distributing the wealth of the world to its population fairly and equitably, according to the words of the Prophet, peace be upon him, in Muslim's narration: "Whoever has more bounty, he should promise it to those who do not have more, etc." [175] and "Who" of the words in general includes individuals, families, states and societies... Especially food security, in which the Prophet said: "No one is safe who is full and his neighbor is hungry."

The leading theory – along with the financial policy of the caliph Omar - is the theory of the companion Abu Dhar al-Ghafari, calling for the application of the principle of equality, and the creation of economic and social balance. This is done by calling for spending treasures, and waiving the benefit of the curiosity of money, especially waiving the exploitation of the curiosity of agricultural land, without its origin, expanding on those who have not yet obtained enough, so the gap heals, and everyone gets what is the basis of his life.

The Qur'an has guided us that God created the earth, blessed it, and estimated its strength in the sense that He blessed its good, and estimated enough strength in it for its population, as explained by the interpreters when He Almighty said: "He **blessed it and estimated its** strength." International statistics [176] have indicated that the world's resources are sufficient for its population. Plus 10 percent if it is used efficiently, and its production is distributed fairly and equitably[177].

We do not know how Malthus saw the solution in the death of millions, and next to him are individuals who have enough millions? How did he miss the solutions of good, and see only the solutions of evil? How do you look at the calamities in order to die and not to work for life?

If he remains until today, he is witness to the solutions of his pessimistic theory of the types of disasters, wars and famines. And watch with her the ugliest form of imbalance...The wealth of the world is lost in boasting about the invasion of space, the invention of weapons of oppression and destruction, and its waste is burned in drugs. What remains is directed towards the suffocation of others as manifested in what is known as Third World indebtedness... It was natural for the imbalance between resources and populations to increase in underdeveloped countries, before developing countries, and in developing countries before developed countries, as the higher the income, the lower the imbalance. This is reflected in the course of life. Not only on the life of man, but his life, and the life of what God has mocked him of the animal, as long as all lifebelieves only in living resources.

However, the theory of balance between resources and population means necessities, before it means luxuries, and it targets food security, and creates a balance between the production of land and the amount of nutrition necessary

---

[175]Sahih Muslim: Al-Ibbi version 42/5 , and Al-Nawawi version 33/12 Sunan Abu Dawood 169/3 Sunan Al-Kubra 172/4-Lubaiqi

[176]In the Shadows of the Qur'an 118/24 by Sayyid Qutb al-Muṣāḥaf al-Muṣaf al-Safsir, pp. 630-i-1-1377 by Muhammad Farīd Wajdī

[177]Diligence Letter Magazine Issue 88 May 1190 AD

for the life of the population, before it targets the possession of antiques and precious things. Which may lead to the freezing of their high values to weaken production and create conditions of imbalance... This was a commentary on the pessimistic theory, which Meltos came up with from the theory of statistics, as a writer from the book of the traditional school. As for his views on the rejection of authority, let us postpone them until the socialist trend and the intervention of the state are discussed.

DAVID RICARDO

Ricardo 1772–1823 was a great businessman and financier, and a flag of the traditional school. He is classified within the group of pessimists, as a result of his influence on Malthus's theory of the imbalance between resources and population, and its adoption as a research tool. He was famous for his abstract style and interest in the distribution system after his predecessor Adam Smith was interested in production and its factors. He has several theories explained in his book "Principles of Political Economy and Taxation". Among his most important theories are the theory of rent, the theory of wages, and the theory of value or quantity of work...Marx took the theory of "value is labor" as well as its surplus of physiocrats in the net product of the earth.

The theory of rent means in the English concept at the time of its introduction one of two meanings: either the wage that the farmer provides to the owner of the land in exchange for exploiting it for a certain period, or the advantage that is unique to fertile land from another that is lessfertile, or more clearly it is the value surplus, or the cash abscess that the first achieves for the second. I'm doing something.

To clarify the theory, Ricardo believes that people began to cultivate fertile land, and when their number increased, they had to cultivate less fertile land. The difference between the first and second rents. As their number increased more, they were forced to cultivate less fertile land than the second, despite its high costs...The difference between the third and the second, as shown between the second and the first... He bets that the increasing rent with the population will lead to a very high level of prices, and thus to the misery of the working classes and economically vulnerable groups, and he ended up with a pessimistic view.

If we take a holistic view, it seems that the increase in areas, and the rise in production in parallel with the increase in the population, may lead to a balance between the population and the amount of resources sufficient to secure their lives, and prices are determined on average at the level of supply and demand. Rather, it is imbalance, not pessimism, if the increase in thepopulation, without the increase in agricultural land, then it is possible to talk about the rise in prices, as a result of high demand, and its impact on the purchasing power of the working class and economically vulnerable groups...Even today, the solution to the problem of food security arising from the scarcity of resources is to revive the soil and develop production in whatis already exploited.

The wage theory is also based on Malthus's population theory. It is summarized in the opinion of Ricardo that the multiplication of the population will lead to intense competition between workers, and thus to a decrease in their level of wages and standard of living, and that this level will soon stop at a certain limit. This is what he called the "minimum necessary for living", which is known as the minimum wage, as it takes into account the minimum necessary for living, and he believes that the fall of this limit from the amount of the minimum necessary for living will lead to malnutrition and the spread of diseases and deaths among workers, so he ended up with a pessimistic view.

It seems that what he called the intense competition between workers, and the low level of their wages and standard of living, is in fact their intense exposure to jobs, knowing that the law of supply and demand deals with workers, goods and monetary values. Themachine contributes to the intensification of their supply and the spread of unemployment among their ranks. The problem is due to the imbalance and imbalance between the number of workers and their positions of employment, or between the increase in labor power and the contraction or stagnation in the projects and services carried out by them. The problem is global, and the expansion of modern technology has contributed to its complexity. Hence, scientific progress - especially in war production, the disruption of human energies, and the waste of their bearers - is not all good.

Some economists were surprised that Malthus and Ricardo, who reached these dangerous results, continued to believe in the compatibility of individual and public interests, and decided on the principle of individual freedom, while saying that the state should not intervene in order to realize these dangers and solve the problems resulting from them.

It seems that the intervention of the state in order to impose order, solve problems, create jobs, and monitor the functioning of public and private institutions is necessary... Freedom is a double-edged sword that does absolute harm. They are exploited by the powerful, and benefit from specific laws that should not be bypassed. Achieving the public interest by achieving private interests may not be credible, and it has an economic value until all the interests of individuals are achieved, as long as the public interest begins with the individual, and awaits the end and the personality begins with some, and some are lost until the interest of all is achieved and the theory may not be fully realized.

In the theory of value or quantity of labor, Ricardo believes that labor is the basis of value, and that value comes as a result of the cost of goods and services. He wants the price to be represented by the costs represented in the values of labor and capital. In his view, capital is only previous work, that is, accumulated business values, and raw material. This raw material does not become a commodity ofuse and exchange value, until it is combined with humanitarian work, which gives it its required or useful final form, and wants humanitarian work as expressed by living work and the formation of capital from the values of accumulated work asexpressed by dead work. We have already mentioned that the professor of Marx in the theory of "value is labor" is Ricardo, and in order to avoid repetition, we postpone talking about the concept of value in general until the analysis of Marxist theories.

TRADITIONAL SCHOOL AT ITS PEAK

John Stuart Mill John Stuart Mill 1806-1873AD passed through the evaluation of the views of his predecessor, and added to the traditional economic heritage of the brainchild of opinions and principles of economic and social importance.In 1848, he published his book "Principles of Political Economy", which included a comprehensive presentation and a comprehensive evaluation of the most important traditional economic principles. The book, as economists have noted, is characterized by accuracy in the scientific method, and a clear presentation of the most important theories put forward by the older economists: the likes of "Adam Smith ", "Malthus " and Ricardo, and in the light of which new views were put forward.

On the subject of presenting opinions and theories, Mill accepted the existence of natural laws without returning them to divine Providence, as did the French physiocrats, and defended the principle of freedom, and considered it the first pillar, and defended the principle of free competition and the principle of non-intervention.However, it has put the state's intervention in its real framework, so it has decided to intervene in the issue of education, make it compulsory for parents, extend a helping hand to the weak, and protect children and young people by imposing control over public morals.To achieve social reform, it is proposed to define the inheritance system as a social system, and to confiscate the rent of land for the benefit of the group, by imposing the tax system, modifying the wage system, and encouraging production cooperatives.

The most important functions of the state in addition to the above in the view of the tendency to collect the necessary funds to cover public expenditures... Develop legislation and laws related to contracts. And securing the public bodies that ensure the implementation of laws, especially the judiciary, the police and the army...And to carry out projects and works that individuals refrain from or refrain from: either because they are not inclined to start them, or because they do not secure profit, or they are beyond their capacity as presented in the opinions of Adam Smith. All are viable economic and social views.

Jean-Baptiste Say Jean-Baptiste Say (1767-1832) represents the optimistic tendency within the traditional free doctrine of France. He previously worked in the field of banking, journalism, and an insurance company, and wrote books on political economy, or on ways in which wealth is created, distributed, and consumed. In 1830, he was appointed professor of political economy at the Collège de Firas. In the same year, he published his memoirs on political economy in six parts. At his hand, the teachings and principles of the father of political economy, Adam Smith, spread, and after their spread, the impact of French economists began to diminish.

Say defined economics as "the science of the laws that govern wealth" and [178] added that this science relies on observation and observation.He saw that trade was what distinguished human society from the animal world. Note that the

---

[178] Political Economy p.65 - Dr. Azmi Rajab

animalproduces and consumes...He explained that exchangeis not so much about the form of goods, as it is about their utility. He wrote in its subject to «Malthus»: «You claim that there areno non-material products, although there are originally, sir -only moral products, production is not a creation of matter. Rather, it is a creation of utility[179]. "His subjective theory of utility starved, to meet Malthus's objective theory of matter and to discern that the products are moral, but by means of material topics.

Say was influenced by industrial development and the atmosphere of freedom prevailing at his time in Britain and France. He divided the fields of economic activity into agriculture, industry and trade. Before him, Al-Mawardi preceded this division, and in Say's opinion, the divisionis only theoretical; he believes that the goal of the three sectors is to provide services. Agriculture, for example,is only a factory for agricultural products. It was natural to occupy the industry, which he believes is capable of accumulating capital, and automatic and technical development. The first place in his orientations, explaining that the owners of land and capital, who in the past were completing economic projects, have moved their task to the jurisdiction of the organizer, who has become playing the first role in production and investment processes. The new situation resulted in the separation between profit, rent and interest. The organizer collects the production elements and directs them to the correct destination. Sai is known for several theories, the most important of which are:

1-The Ports Law, or the discharge of products. According to him, products are replaced by products, money is only a means to achieve the exchange process, and production in itself, there is the possibility of disposal for goods produced in another branch. This means that once a commodity is produced, the possibility arises of obtaining a corresponding commodity of another type...He concluded from his analysis that there is no truth to the belief that the amount of money circulating in a given economic community, may at one time be insufficient to buy all the products within it. Therefore, he believes -in theory - that money, which is merely an instrument of exchange,cannot be the cause of the deficit.David Hume has previously likened its role in exchange to the role of oil in the engine, where there is no movement orexchange without the necessary amount.

It is true that money is a tool and medium of exchange, but we should not overlook the decision of the theory of cash circulation of the need to balance the amount of money and the size of projects or purposes by which they are accomplished, as will come in the theory of Gessel. Money as an instrument of exchange may not perform its task if it is weakened from resisting pressure and facing a force greater than its power. Economically, it is known that too much money, without an economic force supporting it, leads to a decline in its value, weakening its purchasing power, and affects the value of capital, and the

---

[179] The same source, p. 66

shortage of cash weakens the movement, and affects production and the exchange of surplus.

On the subject of production, we wonder: Is production in one branch the one that drives production in another branch, or is consumption, especially at the level of demand, the one that drives all branches at the level of the purchasing power of society? During the analysis of the theory of outlets, and the replacement of production with production, Sai was not exposed to the issue of barter or surplus problem...Rather, thereason for the non-discharge of some products is the deficit that occurs in the branches of production for others, where the deficit falls in the amount of sufficient quantity to seal the exchange process.We may note that the production of some branches. Such as large cars - for example, it may be disrupted by the lack of social purchasing power of a country, with the availability of production in other branches. Is it possible to produce vegetables, for example, to eliminate the deficit and there is an outlet for automobile production?

Say criticized the policy of increasing the monetary purchasing power of some consuming classes, such as workers and employees by raising wages and salaries or granting aid and compensation to some groups, and saw that this would lead to an increase in the amount of money circulating in society, without its equivalent in the amount of production circulating in the markets... While it is the purchasing power of workers and employees that strengthens their demand for products, and with the strength of demand and its increase, production increases, and diversifies into types that respond to various new requests. The increase in money only hurts when it is issued without a balance, guarantee, or economic or productive power based on its consideration. But if it comes from an economic power, its values respond to that power as an expression of it.

2-The principle of general economic harmony. According to him, every individual and every group has an interest in the prosperity and progress of others, and every field of economic activity has a direct or indirect interest in the viability of other fields. The interest of trade is in the prosperity of agriculture, the interest of industry in the prosperity of trade, the interest of cities in the prosperity of valleys, the interest of valleys in the prosperity of cities, and the interest of countries in the prosperity of other countries.

Likewise, the interest of the consumer in the success of the product, the interest of the producer in the success of the consumer, the interest of the baker in the success of the farmer, the interest of the farmer in the success of the merchant, and the interest of the butcher in the success of the livestock breeder...

Thus, it is clear that the individual, in order to secure his life and seek to reach material well-being, does not produce alone, and especially himself, isolated from others. Rather, it is related to society, and to its members in many circles. The most important of which are the Department of Production and Consumption, the Department of Exchange of Goods, the Department of Division of Labor, and the distribution of its results...It has been advanced from

Adam Smith's theory that the producer only considers his interest. At the same time, it serves the public interest.

With regard to production and consumption, whatis said in individuals, is said in countries and societies...The interest of the Bedouin society in the prosperity of civil production, the interest of civil society in the prosperity of bedouin production, and the interest of countries between export and import - in the prosperity of the international economy, and the spread of peace and good relations between countries, so that each country finds someone to cooperate with, especially in solving the problem of deficit and surplus...If cooperation does not reach the level of economic integration, within a regional association. And we are in the age of conglomerates, and inunforgiving circumstances the loners...

School of Freedom and Economic Analysis

The marginal school focuses its economic analysis on marginal utility, that is, on the limit of utility, when handling, using, or using units in any field of the economy, based on the last unit, at which utility is limited. The marginal wage is the wage of the last worker, the marginal price is the price of the last unit produced from a certain material, the marginal capital is the last invested amount of capital, and the marginal food is the last piece that responds to the desireand benefit of eating...

The use of the marginal analytical method during economic research is what the marginal school is characterized by, and has been provided by economists within other schools. It was adopted by Ricardo, who is from the traditional school, in proving his theory of rent. He considered marginal land the source of rent.

Beginning in 1871, three marginal schools emerged in Austria, Switzerland and England:

The Austrian Border School was founded in Vienna by Karl Manger (1840-1921), Bon Pavrik (1856-1914) and Von Wieser (1851-1926).

Karl Munger was interested in the theory of the concept of bounties and the source of value. In studies published in Vienna in 1871, he considered that defining the concept of bounties. It is related to the need for it, and that the thing that did not need to be eaten or used,is not considered a good thing. It is normal as long as the goal is the benefit, and the obtaining of the benefit depends on the need for its source.

In the theory of value, the "law of tender power for needs", which was introduced by the German scientist "Joseon" in 1854, is a marginal analysis that ends with the limit of the benefit of the thing, so the result is that the value of the material or commodity in his view is determined by the limit of the benefit it achieves. He does not look at the source of value or the factors of its formation, as he does not see that it is formed by the amount of work spent in its production, as Ricardo sees, followed by Marx, or by the factors of capital, land and work, as Ibn Khaldun sees at the level of the Islamic economy, or that it is determined in free markets by the law of supply and demand, as liberal doctrine sees. Rather, it looks at the extent of the benefit it brings.

Bon Pavrik has followed the same method, and used the same analysis, but he has become more famous for the theory of the investor regulator, and considering it the axis of economic growth. The presence of the organizer within a production institution is linked to the availability of factors or elements of production in order to be able to organize and coordinate them in certain proportions, and then to monitor their interaction, fusion and development during the stages they go through, during production processes.He distinguished between profit and interest, and saw that the wind is returning from regulation, and it means working at the level of economic activity, and interest is returning from capital, and it is fair to the saved cash capital. As for mobile capital, it falls within the framework of what is known as the work of the regulator, and gives profit. It is the focus of economic development.

The same analysis was used by Von Wieser, who gave a clear explanation of marginal productivity in the production of values. It was considered in its composition all the necessary factors: such as capital, land, labor... Focus on the last used unit of capital, labor, or other, representing the cost of production. The work is meant to be valued. Cost consists of intermediate-consuming core values. It mediates production, as evidenced by the value of physical and technical work, the value of bitumen and circulating capital, and the value of industrial land in industrial and agricultural production in agricultural production. The result is that the value is a container that collects the spent values in its production. It is logically clearer.

And on the core values, the institution rotates, to produce at the organizational level new values that are higher and higher than the core values. The difference between fundamental and new values is what Bon Baverick called profit, Marx called surplus value, and the physiocrats called the net product of the earth...The presence of the marginalists in the subject of value production, as in others, is focused on marginal analysis. It sets them apart from the traditional classics. He called them modern classics.

However, von Wieser's analysis was not limited to the factors necessary for marginal productivity, but went beyond them to develop a plan to find out the proportion of each factor that makes up the value produced. In fact, knowing the proportion of what each factor represents. Or what each of the raw materials represents, when producing a specific commodity or material as a type of medicine, for example, one of the most complex processes that is adopted in modern production. Second: The Swiss Border School was founded in Lausanne by the French writer Leon Vlras from1910 to 1834, followed by the Italian writer Villredobarretto from 1848 to 1923, who followed the same approach as Vlras, with an increase in the use of mathematical models.

Economists believe that the most important study issued by Leon Flouras is the "Elements of Political Economy". This was in 1896, in which he presented his theories. He is best known for theories of value, exchange, and general equilibrium. He considered that the exchange results from the overlap between the phenomenon of scarcity on the one hand, and the phenomenon of utility on the other. Meaning that scarcity and utility converge around determining the value of materials at the time of their exchange. Note that the request frequents rare objects, as well as useful ones. He defined marginal utility as the satisfaction of a particular desire, and focused the desire limit on the last unit that responds to the user's desire.

However, his theory of focusing on scarcity and utility in determining the source of value may be incomplete, as it overlooked the capital, land and labor factors adopted in the production of values along with the law of supply and demand. The value is rare, as in a sapphire picked on the beach, and determined by scarcity, or useful, as in a honey found in a cave, but most of what the world produces depends on the factors of production in terms of composition, and on the law of supply and demand in terms of specificity. Perhaps the flaw in his theory came from the differentiation between objective and subjective consideration of value. Factors of production are objective and self-interested. There is no conflict between them. As long as the goal of production is benefit.

The general economic balance in the eyes of Vlras is a general environment, or a large economic market that embraces all economic variables, production, consumption and exchange. He saw that prices are related to incomes, to the purchasing power of individuals, and that regulators, investors, buy factors from capitalists, workers and peasants. After production, it is sold at a profit, to the same people from whom its factors were purchased. The factors of capital, land and labor are not consumed, but their basic values are sold, and the consumption materials produced are bought at their price. The purchase of factors such as the purchase of capital at interest, wage labor and land by rent or purchase. And the sellers of its values to those who invest it, instead of direct investment, is like something that bears gold on its back and eats hay.

Third: The English Marginalist School was founded in Cambridge by Staley Givens in 1835-1882 from the writers who inaugurated the Marginalist School. He was known for criticizing Marxists in that value is formed by the amount of work spent in its production, without considering land and capital. Ara refuted them with clear practical examples. Alfred Marshall followed him in 1842-1924 from the professors of the University of Cambridge and from the two seats of economics.

Economists believe that the biggest thinker in the marginalist school is Alfred Marshall, who has been interested in the issue of prices, the theory of value, and the general theory of prices, with the difference of markets between crowded markets and confined markets...He said with rent, and did not link his source to the land. Divide it into the proceeds of production and the proceeds of consumption, which means the profit in production, and the savings in consumption.

In the theory of value, he tried to reconcile the traditional classical theory focused on the subject of cost, and the marginal theory focused on the subjective utility of value and saw that both contribute to the determination of price. He was the first to try to reconcile objective and subjective concepts.

But his theory of cost-benefit pricing also seems incomplete, as it overlooks the law of supply and demand, which has more power to control the pricing of values within free markets than cost and benefit. Goods produced at a cost and with a benefit may be demanded and offered. Its price goes up on demand, and it goes down under supply...

In total estimation, it can be said that the marginal schools' approach to focusing on marginal utility during economic analysis has had a great impact on the formation of economics, but its effect did not exceed the level of thought and theoretical studies to put forward at the level of effectiveness, and the completion of economic projects accordingly. Economics is more realthan theoretical.

KEYNESIAN THEORY IN THE METHOD OF ECONOMIC ANALYSIS AND GESSEL'STHEORY IN THE CIRCULATION OF CRITICISM

John Keynes (1883-1946), a pupil of Alfred Marshall, was the first to transform the method of economic analysis from traditional individual partial theories. to general macroeconomic theories, or from what is known as macroeconomics to macroeconomics... Before him, classical economists - and, in Keynes's view, classical economists were the ones who preceded him to put forward theories - proceeding from equilibrium and taking care of economic life through the actions of individuals, and seeing that it is they who control the economic equilibrium and the choices related to production and consumption.

While we see the Keynesian theory starts from the imbalance, and sees that the correct approach is to look at the holistic and total view of economic activity at the level of the state and society...After presenting his approach, economists in Europe and America focused - under the coverage of national accounting based on his approach - and expressed the national economy, national production, national consumption, national income and public finances of the state, and general theories of money and prices, and turned attention to the merchant, manufacturer and peasant to pay attention to the major economic sectors, which represent the backbone of the state's economy, represented in internal and external trade, traditional and modern industry, food and commercial agriculture.This helped the economic development.

In the theory of what is known as the "multiple contradictions", which is the number that measures the ratio between investment, which is considered an independent investment, and the increase in income determined by this investment, Keynes put forward it at the level of general theory, and gave it a strategic position in the process of determining the level of economic activity. Unlike others, focus on demand rather than supply. "Keynes cares about demand behavior, not supply behavior," says Samir Amin. Demand always creates its own supply, but supply does not always create its own demand.This is the axiom of the general theory. " [180]

---

[180] Global Accumulation p. 310- Dr. Samir Amin

Keynes based his theories in a 1936 book entitled "The General Theory of Money, Interest and Use", which was issued after the 1929 crisis that decayed the capitalist system and created problems that could not be solved. It resulted in a contraction in demand and widespread unemployment. within Britain and other capitalist countries. Keynes had to explain, through the general theory of money, interest and use, the causes and factors of the crisis, and put forward means of treatment in ways he saw as effective. He put forward new general theories that overturned concepts, and disparaged traditional classical theories.

Based on her criticism, the foundations of his approach were established, which is considered a basic rule. From them began the economic intellectual currents after the Second World War. The clearest evidence of the failure of traditional liberal theories, and the weakness of the foundations adoptedin their analysis, was that they were weakened in the face of resistance to the problems arising from the Great Crisis of 1929. Keynes focused in his book on the most important elements, especially the causes of unemployment, the role of money and state intervention.

In the causes of unemployment, Keynes began to criticize the classics in claiming that there is no unemployment of labor, because they believe under the cover of individual theory - that everyone who wants to work will find a job suitable for his intellectual and physical potential, given the competition in the material market, and the market of factors of production.according to their opinion. While the facts and events showed the opposite of what they see. Evidence that Britain and other capitalist countries knew the problem of unemployment from the beginning of this century until it exploded during the 1929 crisis, so Keynes proposed the solution at the level of economic activity as a whole, and the responsibility was placed on the individual, the state and society.

In money he criticized classical theory and its authors. They viewed it as a shallow theory, absent from its values, its role in promoting goods, and moving the wheels of economic and social life.They claimed that their role is neutral, and that it is only a veil that covers the truth, and they focused on exchanging goods for goods. Keynesian theory came to show the error of their perception, in addition to their error in unemployment. It places the center of money in the economy and the center of the heart in the body.

In the intervention of the state, the classical liberal opinion opposed state intervention except within a narrow framework, and considered that the state has an essential role in economic life. It manifests itself in ensuring full employment, raising demand, and says: "It shows us that the expansion of state functions is the only means to prevent the destruction of current economic institutions, and a condition for the successful exercise of individual pursuit."

As such, there is no economic, social, political, administrative or judicialsystem...Without a supreme authority to take care of it, the state is the one that sets the civil, commercial and criminal laws... It monitors the functioning of public and private institutions and ensures public order. It is able to solve the most difficult problems, social, and guarantee the rights of individuals towards the owners of factories and companies...Its intervention is rejected whenever it aims to harm legitimate acquired rights, such as the nationalization of private property or its expropriation without compensation and the public interest required by it.

From the foregoing, it is clear that Keynes, by criticizing the old classical or capitalist doctrine, does not oppose capitalism, or wish its demise. Rather, he wants to save her and put her wheels on the track of life... This may be missed by those who inquire about the nature of their approach.

After the analytical approach, wecan summarize the basic elements of Keynesian theory in three, which are as follows:

1-The marginal tendency to consume and the meaning of marginal progress in the marginal school, which means here that the total national income, including the income of individuals, is directed towards two uses: The first use is to direct most of the income towards the purchase of consumption materials. This is called final consumption. Where its values cease to exist, and the second use is to direct a lesser premium towards saving, and it is in order to buy capital materials, and it is called investment, or intermediate consumption, as it mediates production.

The existence of saving or investment depends on the application of the marginal propensity to consume theory. This is like an individual's income per month is one thousand dirhams, and his marginal tendency to consume is eight hundred, and to save or invest is two hundred. The achievement of the mandate in understanding the meaning of the marginal propensity to consume depends on understanding the average propensity to consume, which is the amount of the rate of consumption of the individual or the nation out of the total income of the individual or the nation, and the understanding of the size of capital depends on what Keynes called the marginal adequacy of capital. It depends on the achievement of comprehensive operation, and the level of demand for goods or investment materials.

2- Marginal effectiveness of capital. It is an essential element, an incentive, that pushes the regulator towards investing its capital. It has symptoms and seriousness, which may only appear during operations. He had to appreciate the results of the investment, before embarking on it. This made Keynes interested in the concept of incentive more than others, knowing that the organizer is anticipating the annual returns of investing his capital, or what Keynes called the expected return on capital. The price of the capital loan is included in the capital list to clarify what Keynes called the marginal effectiveness of capital. It is the measure that controls the ability of the regulator to face investment conditions, as the higher it is, the wider the investment horizons in front of it.

3 The interest rate is one of the elements adopted in Keynesian theory. The interest rate in the eyes of Keynes is a monetary phenomenon that is determined

first at the level of the amount of money in the market. Its size is due to the Central Bank, which, with its strongcontrol and legal privilege in issuing the currency, can affect the interest rate. However, his work is linked to economic strength and weakness. Second,what Keynes called individuals' attachment to cash liquidity, so they work to keep their property and money in the form of saved money, which Ibn Khaldun described as "savings for the values of things." Keynes saw that money is saved either for consumption, for investment, or for speculation in financial markets.

Although they all affect the amount of cash in the markets at the time of saving, what affects economic and social life in general and permanently, freezes monetary values, and deprives the state and society of benefiting from them is the treasure for the treasure. Islam prevented him, and called for his investment and treasure for the sake of treasure, itis not put, not within the framework of what is saved for consumption, nor for investment, nor for speculation in the markets and the truth of God, as he says: **"Those who hoard gold and silver, and do not spend it in the way of God, announce to them a painful punishment." The Messenger of God said: "Whatever gold or silver money is given to him is embers on his companion until he empties it for the sake of God."**[181]

The three elements: the marginal propensity to consume, the marginal effectiveness of capital and the interest rate, determine the amount of consumption, and the amount of investment. The propensity to consume depends on the marginal propensity to consume, the propensity to invest depends on the marginal effectiveness of capital, and the interest rate.

That was Keynes's theory of money, and its relation to consumption, saving, capital and interest ...The theory, although it put criticism at its center, did not highlight its role at the level of circulation, and the ability to attract economic movement from every side, as did the theory of «Gissel»

It is known that Gessel has called within the natural economic system for the circulation of cash, explaining that its purchasing power is not related to the amount of cash in circulation. Rather, as a means of transporting goods from dhimmah to dhimmah, and as an intermediary for their exchange, its amounts must be in line with the need of the markets, as well as the means of transport, such as railways, cars, carriers, aircraft and ships...The needs of its movables. If sufficient means of transport are to be provided for the packing of goods. In order to carry out a sound economic measure, we must reduce those means as little as possible, but the reduction should be compensated as much as possible by the circulation of means of transport, which imposes penalties on the state in the form of tax reimbursements on every transport car, ship or train that remains for a long time without carrying [182] and what is said in means of transport, similar to what is said in money. As long as the means of transporting goods

---

[181] Musnad Al-Imam Ahmed 165/5
[182] Dawa Al-Haq Magazine No. 7 - p. 6 - April 1959

from place to place, it is equal to transferring them from an asset to an asset. In both cases, the deficit would cause either disruption to the economy or disruption to society.

Professor "Irving Fisher" commented on the theory. He said: "The monetary circulation proposed by" Jessel " frees the country from the economic crisis in two or three weeks." This was evidenced in an experiment carried out by an economist, Michael, mayor of the municipality of "Forgel" in Austria, when the global economic crisis reached its peak and the "Gessel" system was adopted in the circulation of cash, so production and work moved by issuing local money suitable for spending, and not suitable for saving, so he saved his city from destitution and unemployment, but that local money did not live long because the central bank, which has the legal privilege to issue currency against it, was established. The same thing happened at the Bank [183] of France and al-Maqrizi explained that people hoard good money, not bad[184].

Dr. Mahmoud Abu Al-Saud, who was an economist at the Arab League, commented on the effectiveness of the theory of "Gissel" in the circulation of cash, and on the practical experience of Michael according to which: "Only a few months passed until the city flourished unequivocally, and trade and real estate expanded, and by expanding in it, the demand for workers increased, and their wages rose relatively, and with the rise in wages, their ability to buy increased, so the demand for goods increased, and some industries corresponding to the new demand were established, and the municipality expanded in the construction of public facilities, due to the availability of funds, and the municipality of" Forgel "became a proverbial rack. [185] Then he said:" This theory is completely consistent with what the teachings of the Quran require, and all the Quranic[186] teachings related to the subject should be enthusiastic to it. "It is the general saying of the Almighty:" **Those who possess gold and silver and do not spend them for the sake of God, so He will give them a painful punishment**. " It is known that the companion Abather Al-Ghafari has already put forward the theory of the circulation of criticism more quickly than his circulation in the theory of "Gesel" for centuries. Imam Ahmad narrated that he was asked about gold and silver coins, and he said: «[187] It has become no evening, and what is no longer has become». He is the first to carry the previous verse in general, and he forbade the hoarding of money, even after taking out its zakat, and he kept saying: «No one of you has a dinar or dirham, either to spend it for the sake of God or prepare it for a rival». The [188] comparison between the two theories after analyzing each of them separately -we discussed in the first

---

[183] Key Lines in Islamic Economics, p. 43 by Dr. Mahmoud Abu Al-Saud
[184] Political Economy 83/1 by Dr. Fathallah Al-Alou
[185] Key Lines in the Islamic Economy, p. 43
[186] Id. p.44
[187] Musnad Al-Imam Ahmed 176/5
[188] Al-Bārī 16/4 by al-Ḥāfiẓ Ibn Ḥajar Ibn Ḥajar Ibn al-Nubalīyah 49/2 by al-Ḥ

part of «The approach of the Islamic economy in the production and consumption of wealth».

Finally, we conclude from Gessel's theory - after Abu Dharr's theory - that criticism by the nature of its circulation and its charming purchasing power is the secret hidden from behind moving the wheels of economic and social life...The overall economic solution lies neither in the amount traded, as Keynesian theory holds, nor in the surplus hoarded, as metallic Mercantilism holds. Rather, it is in finding quantities that are in line with the needs of the markets.The problem of shortage, if it occurs, is solved with the speed of circulation, and the problem of lack of transportation is solved with the intensity of movement, and the multiplication of distances. At the level of circulation, and the ability of cash to make surprises, the more people manage to get it out of the darkness of hoarding and monopoly, and push it into the field of production and investment. For his benefit, not in his image. Hariri believes in his description, as he says:

I loved him to sleep, as if from the hearts I had tapped him, and the righteousness of my master created him. Had he not met me, I would have said that his ability was great.

THE MOST IMPORTANT LAWS OF CAPITALISM

That was the aggregate picture of what was expressed in liberal free doctrine or old classical capitalism, or the free traditional school.... Its aspects, principles and development, and the pros and cons that it embraces, or produces from classical intellectual theories or pioneering process...When intervention or study is called for, we have intended to do as much as possible, in order not to ruminate about historical events in the absence of what is meant by the study of the history of economic ideas. That is, to benefit from the work of the former. He is guided by his successes, avoids his failures and learns about the practical theories of thought, as mentioned above.

Because of the importance of the liberal free doctrine, which is considered the juice and butter of traditional doctrines, and the heir by adoption all the power, effectiveness and confrontation of life, we conclude the topic with a brief analysis of the most important laws that represent the common denominator between the various trends within it. It has already been stripped. They are as follows:

1- The **law of private property**, with securing the freedom of ownership for individuals and companies, and adopting it as the basis of competition in the field of production and work...Around it, all capitalist trends converge...It is the one that responds to the nature of souls, as socialist trends around collectivism meet, with the opposite of the nature of souls in their imposition, as manifested in the negative results and the revolution against them now.

2-The **law of personal benefit or private interest**, according to which every individual seeks by nature to bring benefit and to pay harm. In their view, he knows better than anyone else to serve his interests. This is the case, but often at the expense of the public interest, even if they theoretically see that the public interest consists of the sum of private interests, but in which country of the world is this principle achieved? Did it investigate the Europe from which it originated?

3 - **The law** of **free competition**, which is the most important element adopted in the movement and development of production. It was retained by the capitalist doctrine, as a result of the establishment of private property and individual freedom. He lost the communist as a result of her nationalization ...The codified view of the capitalist doctrine is that this law provides an opportunity in prices for the consumer, encourages competition between producers, and achieves justice by bringing values closer to the level of the cost of production. In it, Stuart Mill said, "Everything that determines competition is evil, and everything it can do is good."

4- The **Law** of **Supply and Demand** deals with materials that are not priced by the state, legally allowed to be traded, and is related to the freedom of the market... The freedom of the market means the freedom of the producer and the consumer in the sense that the product is free to produce it, and the consumer is free to consume it. Unlike the communist regime, which decided on the socialism of production and consumption and the reaction between them in the sense that the producers are themselves consumers as a result of the nationalization of individual freedoms. On the role of the law of supply and demand in determining values or the price of goods, Stuart Mill says: "The price is determined at the level at which the required quantities are equal to the quantities supplied." From this expression, it is clear that the law of supply and demand does not explain the same value andbenefit to the consumer, nor its subject matter and the conditions of its change at the level of the cost of production. Rather, it explains the change in its price and the conditions of that change. However, Mel explained only one case out of three...It is the case in which the required quantities are equal to the supply, and he did not explain the case of the high price when the demand for supply rises and falls when the supply for demand rises.

5-The wage law, which is the price of labor, is determined by the law of supply and demand. Demand means the amount of capital allocated to wages, and the number of workers seeking work. Cobden says: "The wage increases when an employer runs after one worker and decreases when three workers run after an employer, and unions that defend workers' rights have a consideration when an employer runs after one worker. If three workers run after an employer, as an expression of supply and unemployment, it loses its credibility, and the workers are paralyzed. Hence it seems that trade unions today, especially in Third World countries, are more formal than practical systems.

Thus, it is clear that the consideration of supply is the amount of capital allocated to wages. The demand is the number of workers looking for work, which is not commensurate with the problems of unemployment in the world. Note that the law of supply and demand deals with workers in the same way as it deals with commodities and monetary values. The appropriate consideration is that supply means the workers offered to work, and demand means the jobs required...If in the past the worker was required. Today it is on display. And if wages do not fall as much, then Kiva, as a result of inflation, plundering the value of money-valued materials, has fallen.

6-The law of rent: It has several concepts that predate each other, especially with regard to the rent of the land...This is where the law of supply and demand is born out of the law of free competition, which returns the prices of goods to almost the level of the cost of production. In this case, the price at the public level is determined by the price of a higher-cost, more expensive commodity.Despite their similarity in different production costs. If two identical goods are offered: the cost of producing one of them is ninety dirhams, and the cost of producing the other is eighty dirhams, the price for both of them will be set at one hundred dirhams. The owner of the cost of eighty dirhams gets ten dirhams before offering it ninety dirhams. This is one of the images of rent.

Access to production at the lowest cost is the strategy adopted by some factories and companies. Whenever you think about obtaining rents, or try to influence or exclude those who crowd out their production. It is favored by circumstances, if it obtains raw materials and services in its country, in exchange for those who import them, or reduces the amount of their most expensive, during the mixing and coordination process, or replaces them with others less powerful and effective, as evidenced in the manufacture of cars and the construction of buildings...The profit of the rent is at the expense of the consumer, andwe do not know whether the law can prevent it, as well as the methods of fraud, whenever it is discovered.

7- International Exchange Law: Economists of the free doctrine believe that the exchange between different countries is subject to the same laws to which the exchange between individuals is subject. and add to it by providing a measure of work to the swap state. If she had to produce that commodity herself. if you can. You may get a commodity that costs ten hours of work to produce, in exchange for a commodity that costs seven hours to produce. And vice versa. Thus, it is clear that both parties benefit from the agreement.However, the law governing international values...It is not the law of relative costs of production, but the law of supply and demand.

In fact, the laws that govern international agreements today are political, ideological, and economic considerations, especially between industrialized countries and third world countries, as evidenced by the policy of America and the Soviet Union when it was alive. The law of supply and demand governed agreements at the level of traditional materials and goods. Each party benefits in parallel with the other. Today, it has noplace in the sale of advanced weapons and the export of modern technology. The balance of performancewould not have tilted in favor of developed countries at the expense of developing, and rather underdeveloped, countries.

8- Bank interest system: The interest system is linked to the monetary system. The monetary system in its current state has not remained a global system that benefits all countries of the world on an equal basis. But through the International Monetary Fund and the International Bank for Reconstruction and Development - it became a special system monopolized by developed countries, and closed in their favor, as manifested in what is known as Third World indebtedness. Colonial countries came out as a matter of politics, and entered as a matter of economics. Economic colonialism is more complex than political colonialism, as it does not benefit with a fund or civil disobedience... The solution is for each country to rely on its resources and the arms of its people and get rid of the hegemony of developed countries. And it won't be, until you balance incomes and expenses.

These laws, if we exclude the interest system, and what isnot consistent with Sharia laws, represent the common denominator between the Islamic and liberal system, especially the establishment of private property, the monetary system, the freedom of the market, and the freedom of production and consumption...With the difference in regulatory laws, between legitimacy and positivism, as manifested in the concept of relatively absolute freedom in the liberal and specifically defined in the Islamic, it prevents the individual from exceeding his right to the rights of others.

SOCIALIST TENDENCY WITHIN MODERN DOCTRINES

This chapter briefly addresses socialist trends, associations, methods and opinions or their advocates. Createdby. Her circumstances ...her motives. Their owners...Her tendencies ...their development. moderation. Extremist ... Her social...Its internationalism...With the analysis of what needs to be studied, compared or analyzed.... Highlightingthenegatives and positives...

THE SOCIALIST TREND AND THE VIEWS OF TRADITIONALISTS AND INNOVATORS IN THE INTERVENTION OF

The state in favor of social groups The socialist trend was based on gaps, which opened up in the classical capitalist approach and caused criticism and appeals, which undermined its strength, and opened the file of the trend towards socialism. The most important of these criticisms are:

First, it focused on the interest of the individual, his freedom, choices and orientations, and overlooked in the sentence the role of the state, and its authority capable of monitoring the situation, protecting institutions, taking care of interests, and directing the economy in accordance with the interest of the individual and the group. Malthus and Ricardo said not to interfere, and Adam Smith called her a bad manager. Its employees are careless and wasteful. Some economists were even surprised by Malthus and Ricardo to prove the dangerous results they reached, while saying that the state should not intervene in order to realize the proven dangers and solve the problems resulting from them.

It was renewed «Keynes» to criticize the views of the traditional classics and oppose their opinion rejecting state intervention, and he saw that the state has a basic opinion in economic life and is more manifested in full use, and raising demand. He went on to say, "It appears to us that the expansion of state functions is the only means to prevent the destruction of current economic institutions, and a condition for the successful exercise of individual pursuit."

Second: It focused on microeconomics instead of macroeconomics, on the individual economy instead of the national economy, on individual income instead of the national economy, and on personal interest instead of collective economy. It was one of the weaknesses of the analysis of the classics, that they established branches in the place of assets. Despite the origins, it is she who moves and supplies the branches. The establishment of assets is linked to the authority and care of the state... They refused her intervention, and they underestimated her mission. Keynes transformed the approach of economic analysis from traditional individual partial theories to general macro theories, and criticized classical theories and described them as deficiencies...With his analysis and the response he received from economists in Europe and America, assets are regaining their status and the state is regaining its role.

The first economist who violently attacked the views of the classics, and focused on the national economy and the role of the state in protecting it, is "Frederick List". In 1841, he published a book entitled "A National Approach to Political Economy", in which he strongly urged free exchange between individuals and the reasons for protecting the state. The emerging national economy, which has not yet completed the elements of its power, needs to take care of it, and at this stage he likened the nation to a child in need of protection and care. He believed that free competition only benefits the strong and economically developed countries.

As such, every economic, social or political system...He needs a higher authority to take care of him. The existence of a supreme legislative and executive authority is the difference between the meaning of the state and anarchism, as will come in the anarchism of Proudhon, but the argument that free competition only benefits the strong and developed countries may not be believed except at the high level. Strong capital investigates weak, weak money, not ordinary producers, local artisans. Capital is converging in quantity and quality.Free competition between producers, not between speculators, monopolists and the creation of opportunities, is the gateway to the development of production and the rise of national income.

Third: It focused on the ways or methods of wealth production, and omitted how to distribute them even though production and consumption are twinned. The economy is not based on one, without the other. If production is for exchange, and distribution is for consumption, there is no exchange without production, and no consumption without distribution...Distribution is divided into an initial distribution, and it means the distribution of the results of wealth among the shareholders or the elements contributing to its production, or its entitlement as the state. Secondary, which means the distribution of the public finances of the state to its interests. The distribution system, whether primary or secondary, is carried out only by means of the laws of the state and ensuring their application. They refused to intervene. The conditions and means of distribution were absent...One of the reasons may be that individual production is due to the freedom of the individual according to their opinion, and distribution is collective, due to the state system and the state system is rejected. This gap is the largest door from which socialist principles flowed to the old capitalist doctrine. It soon turned into Marxist communism, and the views of the innovators inside it remained the secret of its continuation and progress untiltoday.

From these gaps, and the like, the views of innovative economists at the level of the national economy began to think about national and collective interests, instead of maintaining the freedom of individuals and taking care of their own interests, and they believe that the release in individual freedom has led to the ugly exploitation of workers by factory owners. This resulted in surplus production, with the weak purchasing power of social groups. There were crises after crises... They demanded the intervention of the state in order to rectify the situation. It is the same Marxist theory that the release in individual freedom, and the exploitation of workers by factory owners are the reason for the creation of crises, so it demanded state ownership.

The theory is lucky to be considered. Freedom without borders, as the classical individualist system sees it, is detrimental to social groups. where it is the subject of exploitation by the economically powerful. and nationalization - as the communist regime did harming the same groups. Where it is the subject of exploitation by the state. It is the imbalance that the Islamic economy has addressed by defining it by laws that regulate the activity of the individual and do not leave him the opportunity to exceed his right to harm others. The result was that individual freedom is absolute in the capitalist system, limited in the Islamic system and nationalized in the communist system, and the Messenger says: "The best things are the middle ones."

The first to call for the intervention of the state, and put forward the theory of distribution, and focused on the exploitation of vulnerable social groups, is the famous economist «Sesamondi» 1773-1842 In his book «New Principles of Political Economy», he criticized the classics for their interest in the production of wealth more than their interest in ways to distribute it and led to free competition, which he sees as pushing businessmen to reduce production costs by various means...These include the employment of women and children in inappropriate conditions, including the increase in the number of working hours, and the reduction of wages to the lowest level...He refused to recognize the harmony between private and public interest...

And here it seems - it's not all about free competition as much as it is about the lack of a law protecting workers from exploitation by employers, especially women and children. Knowing that the determination of working hours, the determination of the minimum wage and the establishment of labor laws are the prerogative of the State. He called for its intervention while placing the responsibility on the shoulders of free competition. His opinion on the lack of harmony between the private and public interest is the one that responds to reality, as it has been proven that the interests of individuals have been completely ruled, so that the public can judge through them, especially since the public is indivisible, as well as the private. The judiciary of the public means the judiciary of the interest of the last member of society. and work for it from the task of the state. Although it does not have the staff of Moses to eliminate it, as evidenced by the unemployment that exists in industrialized countries today.

For this reason, Sesame demanded the intervention of the state in order to protect the weak and alleviate the economic crises, but his campaign against the traditionalists. It has not reached the level of advocacy to overturn the existing conditions, and change the basic systems of society. Rather, it seeks to secure as much justice as possible among people, especially for vulnerable social groups, so [189] that it is described as a social reformer, albeit its views, and similar views calling for a focus on the national economy and the distribution of wealth. States intervene in the interest of society, as a farm from which socialist principles grew. He identified the first role of the state in two fundamental problems. It is not up to the individual, no matter how powerful, to solve them. One is social. It relates to the protection of the vulnerable from harm of any kind and source and the other is economic. related to mitigating crises whenever they occur.

In fact, when the situation is disrupted, crises occur, disasters and famines occur or the country is attacked... There is no force to resort to except the power of the state. Whoever refuses to intervene rejects the interest of the entire nation.

---

[189] Political Economy p.75- Dr. Azmi Rajab

provided it is led by a good and loyal national government. It lives for the public interest and for the public interest only.

Based on the principle of state intervention and the national economy, comprehensive economic planning was launched. as a result of changing global conditions. Since the First World War, events and political fluctuations have followed...Foremost among them is the Bolshevik Revolution in Russia in 1917, the Great Economic Crisis in 1929, fascism in Italy, Nazism in Germany and the last World War, and its impact on public life. The scope of state intervention has expanded, and governments have penetrated into the heart of economicandsocial life, intervening in important issues such as setting and monitoring prices. I went from the principle of intervention, to the system of economic guidance. The state is everything in the reformist sense, not in the Marxist sense.

CALIPH UMAR IBN AL-KHATTAB WAS THE FIRST TO ESTABLISH COLLECTIVE OWNERSHIP.

The first to impose globally the intervention of the state, and in the most important economic issue and social interest, related to the formation of collective property for the benefit of the state and society, is the caliph Omar bin Al-Khattab, when he refrained from dividing the open lands in the Levant, Iraq and Egypt... He stopped it so that its abscess or its proceeds would be public property shared between the former and the latter.

He encouraged him to exercise the right to intervene, and to present the public interest over the private interest, if there is anyone among the prophets who supports his opinion. Imam Ali addressed him by saying: "Let him be a subject for Muslims,"[190] that is, a public property that benefits everyone. This is what is understood by the words of Al-Hafiz Ibn Hajar: "He saw that stopping the open ground, and striking an abscess on it, would continue to benefit Muslims."[191] Judge Abu Yusuf said: "He was a success from God in what he did. And in it was the best for all Muslims. And what he saw from collecting the abscess of that and dividing it among the Muslims was the general benefit of their community. "Abu Obeid said:" He wanted to be a stopping place for the Muslims, what they have procreated, to be inherited by a century from a century, and to be a force for them over their enemy. "[192][193]

It seems from similar positions that the heads of the armies exchange Omar with the same feeling and need, and that the spirit of public interest is predominant among the Companions of the Prophet (r). Thewriters of money and abscess: Abu Obaid, Al-Dawudi, Al-Balazari, Abu Yusuf, Yahya bin Adam and Al-Bayhaqi, as well as Subhi Al-Saleh and Dia Al-Din Al-Rayes from the contemporaries, stated that the leader in the Levant, Iraq and Egypt, endowed

---

[190] Grand Sunnah 9/34 of Al-Bayhaqi
[191] Fath Al-Bari 450/5 by Hafiz Ibn Hajar
[192] Kitāb al-Kharāj liḥyá ibn ʿAdam,
[193] The Money Book of Abu 'Ubayd, p. 58

the situation, and they did not divide the two lands until they wrote to Omar. His answer was, as evidenced in his book to Saad bin Abi Waqqas : After that, your book informed me that people have asked you to divide between them their spoils, and what God has given them, so look what they brought to you in the camp from Kara and money, so divide it between those who attended from among the Muslims, and leave the lands and rivers to their workers, so that this is in the gifts of Muslims. If we divide it among those who attended, nothing will happen to those who came after them. "The [194] same is true for Amr ibn al-Aas in Egypt. He was sent to Omar, and wrote to him "to let her go" [195] and the same thing for Abu Ubaidah bin Al-Jarrah in Al-Sham. He wrote to Omar and the answer was the same as before. Al-Kalai said: "When the father of the book slaves came from Omar, he worked on it, and his opinion was about that, and Omar's opinion was one[196]."

This was the position of the caliph and the army princes, who viewed it through the prism of the public interest and intervened in the name of the state in order to achieve it. As for the soldiers, led by Bilal ibn Rabah al-Habashi, they did not quickly digest the issue of waqf in favor of the Muslims who will come. They demanded division, as the Messenger of Allah (PBUH) divided Khaybar.

Khaybar forcibly conquered - as he conquered the blackness of Iraq, where the conflict took place -and the Messenger divided it into thirty-sixshares[197].

Omar's answer was: "If you divide it, there is nothing left for you after you. How can one who comes from the Muslims find the land divided and inherited from the fathers? What is this, in my opinion, that fills the gaps? And what is there for offspring in this country, and in other lands of the Levant and Iraq? " [198] He returns to himself, and says: "O Allah, my soul is good for leaving it."[199]When the soldiers pressured him in the department, and the matter reached Bilal until he said: "To divide it or to give it freshness by the sword." He [200] only said: "O Allah, suffice me Bilal and the companions of Bilal," [201] which is all that the caliph was able to dounder Islamic democracy - Bilal ibn Rabah al-Habashi..However, the turmoil of opinions and the protest of the conquerors with the work of the Prophet in Khyber caused him to fall at the crossroads. The companion Muaz bin Jabal was afraid to surrender to the opinion of the soldiers in the department, and the public interest was lost, so he stood in his face and said: God willing - to be what you hate. If you divide it, the great rent becomes in the hands of the people, and then they annihilate it, and that becomes to the one man or woman, and then after them comes a people who obstruct Islam and

---

[194] The Money Book of Abu 'Ubayd, p. 58
[195] The Great Sunnah 139/9 Fattouh of Egypt and Morocco, p. 123 by Ibn 'Abd al-Ḥakīm
[196] The Approach of Islamic Economy in the Production and Consumption of Wealth 237/2 by the author
[197] Maad 137/2 for Ibn al-Qayyim increased the extraction of the provisions of Al-Kharaj, p. 22 for Abu Al-Faraj Al-Hanbali
[198] Al-Kharaj in the Islamic State, p. 102 by Zia al-Din al-Rayyes
[199] Book of Money, p. 279 by Daoudi Al-Asadi (12) Fath Al-Bari 415/4
[200] Kitāb al-Kharāj li-Abū Yūsuf, p. 20. Extraction of the Provisions of Al-Khar
[201] Book of Money by Abu Obaid, p. 59 Extraction of the provisions of Al-Kharraj, p. 9

they find nothing. So look at something that can accommodate the first and the last of them. "[202] He came to Ma 'an's opinion, and he strengthened his determination to stop.

In order for the decision to be collective, he established a Shura Council consisting of ten supporters: five from Aws and five from Khazraj, after he consulted the immigrants and gave their opinion on the subject and [203] he got up, so he praised God and praised his Prophet, and then said: "I did not disturb you except to share with me my honesty, in what I carried of your affairs. For I am one as one of you, and today you acknowledge the truth. Those who have disagreed with me have disobeyed me and those who have agreed with me have agreed with me..." [204] Then he presented the aspects of the case, and explained his opinion on stopping the land, to be a public property for all Muslim fighters and offspring and for those who come after them.The methodology in this brief theorization does notallow for the analysis of the economic and social opinions he has expressed and the various verses he has inferred in which he said: «The verses have absorbed all people, so how do we divide it among them and let those who come after them? I don't thinkso. " All of them answered after God enlightened their insights with what He had delivered from the arbitrator of the verses: «The opinion is yours. Yes, whatI said and what I saw[205]. "I analyzed the subject in the second part of the" Islamic Economy Approach to the Production and Consumption of Wealth, pp. 236-258 " under the title " State Intervention and Omar's Decision to Stop Open Lands, so that their production is shared between the former and the latter."

And what prompted Omar and his governors to intervene in the name of the state, and to violate the Prophet's biography of dividing the open lands on the conquerors alone? Without the spirit of public interest and the recovery of the lost groups on the one hand, and the expansion of the Islamic State, and the rise of its expenses on the other hand. "This was a very dangerous decision," says Dr. Mohammed Ziauddin Al-Rayes. In it, the lands that the Muslims opened, as well as what they could open in the sea, became suspended, that is, the publicproperty of the Islamic nation, instead of being a shared property among those who circulate it, and the children inherit it from the fathers. " The decision was applied in the Levant, Iraq and Egypt and worked in the disputes between the Ottoman and Ali; because they agreed to it from the beginning. When some elements from the people of Najran tried to carry Ali in the days of his succession to change him, he said: "Omar was a rational man of opinion. I will not change anything Omar did. "[206]The monarchy continued to be collective, performing its task in the expenses of the state, and establishing social solidarity. And about its loss, and turning it into private property, al-Mawardi and al-Bayhaqi say: "When the year of the skulls was, in the year eighty-two in the

---

[202]Kitāb al-'Amūl li-Dāwī,
[203]Al-Kharaj in the Islamic State, p. 103
[204]Id., p. 104
[205]Id., p. 104
[206]Abscess of Yahya bin Adam, p. 9

sedition of Ibn al-Ash 'ath, the diwan was burned, and every people took what follows them." [207] This is the result of sedition, disputes, disputes and coups. Lives and property are damaged and nations and societies are lost.These are the calamities that tore apart the Arab world, separated its sons and destroyed its strength and components. Until the day 1992/8/22became dependent on the West, and under its supervision. And that is the reward of not doing what the Almighty said: "Do **not quarrel with one another, lest you fail and your wind depart, and be patient. Indeed, Allah is with those who are patient."**

Omar's fiscal policy. After completing the procedures for stopping the lands of the blackness of Iraq. It represents the backbone in open lands, and ended its problems by imposing an abscess on Amerah and immersed him[208], and he spent his income, and the income of others between the interests of the state, and the rift patches in society. He swore by his oath: «By Allah, who there is no god but He, there is no one but Him in this wealth, a share to give or prevent it, and no one is more entitled to it than anyone» He [209] circulated it until it included the dhimmis of the Jews [210] and Christians, and one of his opinions was to say: «He [211]is in their midst, which Allah has ransomed. He is neither the age nor Lal Omar. Divide it between them, and me as one of them. By God, if you stay, the shepherd will come to Mount Sanaa with his luck from this money. It is his place[212]."

He said: "I hope that I have lived among you a little or a lot to work among you in truth, God willing, and that no one of the Muslims remains, even if he is in his house, but he has received a share of God's money, and he does not work in it himself, and he has never been appointed to it." [213] He said: "If I live, the shepherd will come with a [214] donkey cypress, his share will not sweat his forehead[215]."

It is Omar's policy, at the level of opening up the Islamic State and positively opening up its economy. If the rigid classical economists did not realize the importance of state intervention for the benefit of society, and they were unable to give a solution to the problems before their eyes, then the orientations of Omar and his governors, and the supporters of his policy from the Prophet's companions, have gone beyond the existing problems to think about what the days may bring. - What do you mean, no? He said: "As for those in whose hands is my soul, if I did not leave the last people a statement, they would not have anything. I would not have opened a village for me, except to divide it, as the

---

[207]Royal Rulings of Al-Mawardi, p. 170 - Greater Sunnahs 134/9
[208]Grand Sunnah 136/9 - Amer is not exploited, and the immersive is not flooded with water
[209]Kharj Abi Yousef, p. 26
[210]See Islamic Economy Approach to Wealth Production and Consumption 145/3
[211]See Islamic Economy Approach to Wealth Production and Consumption 145/3
[212]Larger strata 299/ 3
[213]History of Al-Tabari 26/5
[214]Cypress: Mountain
[215]Al-Mughni by Ibn Qudamah 402/6

Prophet P. Khaybar divided it, but I leave it a treasury for Muslims to share." [216] In Al-Bukhari's novel

"If it were not for the last people, I would not have opened a village except by dividing it, as the Prophet (PBUH) divided (Khaybar) and [217] said in creating an economic and social balance:" If I had received my command, I would not have turned around, I would have taken the curiosity of the wealthy's money and returned it to the poor[218]. "

The credibility of his policy is that it does not go to tribute and temporary solutions, as much as it goes to the continental systems, which are organized by the state system, and continue to continue and do not change by changing people, as it changes by changing the governments of the times.This is what is understood by his saying: "If I live for the widows of the people of Iraq, I will let them not lack a prince after me." [219] In Bukhari's novel, "If God hands me over, I will let the widows of the people of Iraq do not need a man after me[220]."

Thus, in the name of the Islamic State, Omar, who was the first to give the concept of state policy the meaning of political economy, bore all the problems caused by disasters, famines, crises, price turmoil, and disruption of the situation.He prevented hoarding and monopoly, exploited influence, established bureaucracies and distribution systems, estimated gifts and expenses, established general social solidarity, and equalized - as Abu Bakr has equated - between men and women, Arabs, loyalists, adults, young people and covenants, when distributing wealth or benefiting from its resources. He said: "The people are honorable and lowly in the same God," and Abu Bakr[221] had already said - when Ma 'aden Bani Salim opened up during his reign and asked him to prefer the former Mujahideen over the later ones: "This is only something whose reward is with God. This is a pension, for example, it is better than selflessness. " [222]

In the name of the state, Omar bears the responsibility of the poor, and the rich are left to bear the responsibility of themselves, [223] and it is generous to his morals that the distribution is not tireless in his presence to anyone. Rather, he sets himself the right of every poor person in his hand [224] and more than that heforbade himself in the year of famine to eat meat and ghee like the poor Muslims [225] and to complete his justice that he himself takes over the justice of the weak from the strong, especially from his workers. In that, hesays:

---

[216]Extraction of the provisions of the abscess p. 11
[217]Al-Bukhari: Al-Fateh Version 33/7
[218]Fatiya Tariq and Al-Ghafiqi, p. 134 by Muhammad Muntasir Al-Katani
[219]Kharaj Ibn Adam, p. 56 Widows: A collection of widows: a masculine widow
[220]Al-Bukhari: Al-Fath 61/8
[221]Life of the Companions 84/ 2
[222]The Money Book of Abu 'Ubayd, p. 24
[223]Al-Bukhari: Al-Fath 516/6 Book of Money by Al-Dawudi, p. 287
[224]Fattouh al-Balad, p. 446
[225]The beginning and the end on the date 7/135 The Book of Money by Daoudi, p. 228

"Whichever one of my workers wronged someone, his grievance reached me, so I did not change it, for I wronged him."[226]

Before him, Abu Bakr said: "The weak among you is strong for me, until I take the right for him, and the strong is weak until I take the right for him[227]."

In the absence of the perception of Arabs and Muslims, and their fascination with what comes from the East and the West and at the level of whatwe have seen of the weakness of classical economists and their countries in the face of economic and social life...It can be said that the first country that practically applied the principle of human rights is the Islamic State, and the first economy that achieved economic and social balance is the Islamic economy, and the first renewed economist, applied the concept of joint benefit - not socialism is the caliph Omar Ibn Al-Khattab...

We have looked closely at the negatives and weaknesses, and the resulting economic and social problems, which are either due to the exaggeration of caring for the interest of the individual to the extent that he prepares everything, as manifested in the capitalist trend or the exaggeration of caring for the interest of the group to the extent that it prepares everything, as manifested in the communist trend. Either reject its intervention and underestimate its mission of caring for interests and imposing order, as the classics did, or call for its application to acquired economic and social rights, as the Marxists did.We found it to be a balanced and moderate positive in the Islamic economic system. If there is someone who works with it with conviction, sincerity and sincerity... SPONTANEOUS

ANARCHISM AND THE REJECTION OF STATE POWER

It seems that it is not about the individual and the state, as an instrument of change, but about the goodness or corruption of the individual, and the goodness or corruption of the state. It is a given that an economic, social, political or legal system...without a supreme authority to look after him, as provided. Its presence is practically the difference between order and chaos.Hence, Proudhon, who rejected any authority whatsoever, was an anarchist, and his doctrine was an anarchist, and what was claimed of socialism was an anarchist socialism. We don't even know how to classify it, and in what context we put it. He is a politician in France without a political ideology and a socialist without clear principles. One of his contradictions is that he rejects the authority of the state. He is a parliamentarian who endorses its laws. His views were a theory of the sort that was unworkable.

And that one of the most liberal and evasive doctrines of state pressure and guidance is the anarchist doctrine that Proudhon is his true father and only

---

[226] Larger strata 405/3
[227] Sufficiency in the History of the Caliphs, p. 25 for Ibn al-Kardbus, Life of the Companions 299/2 Major Classes 183/3 Beginning and Ending in History 301/6 for Abu al-Fida

leader. One of his most famous books is "Bakunin", "Jean Krave", and all anarchists exaggerate the glorification of the individual and the demand for his rights, as it consists of the self-society. It is necessary for life and they abhor authority; because every authority in their eyes - except the authority of science and reason - is nothing but the exploitation of man by man...They see the state as the greatest instrument of injustice and corruption. You corrupt the rulers first, and you corrupt the ruled second .What is' state? And who represents it? The answer is in Omar's saying: "The people are still upright, as their imams and their calendars have been upright." His [228] saying to his workers: "Fix yourselves, people will reform you." [229] He told his worker Abu Musa al-Ash 'ari: "If the worker goes astray, his flock will go astray." And the people are against the religion of their kings, as it is said. It is all wrong not to differentiate between those who are qualified for reform, those who are qualified for corruption, and "whoever makes people alike has no medicine for his foolishness."

The doctrine of anarchists consists of a mixture of contradictory opinions. He took from the traditional free doctrine his economic criticism of the state, and his glorification of individual cling and took from socialism its criticism of private property, and its theory of the exploitation of the worker and characterized by making wealth an essential element for the renewal of social life, and the rejection of power and guidance of the state, claiming that man's goodness by nature, substitutes for all authority and guidance. This is a claim that becomes a figment of the imagination when we stand on the news of world wars, and what man has committed against his fellow man...

---

[228] Larger strata 192/ 3
[229] History of Islamic Countries 19/1

FROM SOCIALISM TO STATE SOCIALISM

Socialism is a broad term, the concept of which, as in capitalism, differs according to different doctrines with different and evolving aspects in time and space. Despite the diversity of socialist concepts and their different trends and tendencies, they all converge around opposition to the individual principle enshrined in traditional free doctrines and schools, as well as on criticism of private property, individual freedom, or what is expressed in capitalism and its factors, with their owners disagreeing on the concept of common property, especially between communists and collectivists. The Communists see the abolition of ownership of all funds, because of the socialism of production and consumption, and the reaction between them, as a result of the nationalization of private property and individual freedom, including freedom of ownership, freedom of production, and freedom of consumption...And the collectivists see their purpose in relation to the factors of production, without consumption materials... Opinions revolved around their nationalization, identification, or differentiation of factors and materials . The most disputed was the ownership of agricultural land.Ownership, whether individual or collective, absolute or specific, is the bedrock of the global economy.

It may be better to move beyond what is called imaginative, philosophical, literary, and natural socialism.For its lack of importance, and even for theoretical idealism such as that set by Plato for the ideal state, it remained a dead letter on paper, and did not respond to it until Athens, for which it was set, for its lack of applicability. So let's go to what they called realistic idealism...

The ideal socialists include the English writer Thomas Moras,Saint-Simon, and his students. The likes of Augustin Thierry, Auguste Comte and Saint-Simon - the first to open the file of socialism did not demand the abolition of private property and factors of production. Rather, he called for improving production, and improving the condition of individuals and society. This means applying the principle of economic and social justice, which is the open door to socialism...The principle of economic and social justice was first applied by the caliph Omar bin Al-Khattab, as reflected in the topic that we have finishedanalyzing. analyzed.

One of the most important views of Saint-Simon is that the political government must give up the rule and hand over the reins to an economic government, because it is the one that can solve problems and better manage the affairs of society. This type [230] is known as elite socialism or autocratic socialism, because those who say it is an elite. It is the first picture of a command economy.

Saint-Simon said with an economic government, at a time when the world did not know the least share of problems and crises, which it knew today. So it is. The reign of the treasurer of the House of Money is over, and the concepts of investment are complex, and overlapping between ministries. Medicine, for

---

[230] Political Economy, p. 75 by Dr. Azmi Rajab

example, was the furthest field from economics. Today, considering the incomes of clinics, laboratories, pharmacies, analysis and imaging centers, and the requirements for building laboratories to manufacture equipment and medicine, and the consequent establishment of sales and distribution companies. It has become an economic field, and the income of a free school in Europe and America may equal the income of a limited partnership. and an international sports income, which may be better than the income of a merchant... Hence, all ministers are investors. The Islamic economy was the first economy that managed the development of the state and society. The caliph Abu Bakr says in the investment of the state's finances, "I will master the Muslims in their money." Aisha [231] said: "The Muslims won over him and what they won over others." Omar [232] says: "I am a merchant for Muslims." [233] He knew Muawiyah by reviving and planting lands and [234] sings: Is not the boy a boy who is not satisfied with him and does not have traces in the land, and it may be one of the reasons for the underdevelopment of the third world, besides other reasons written that governments are mostly composed of people, led by political circumstances, to receive ministerial portfolios in the name of political parties, without experience and economic awareness, so they begin the experiment at the expense of the state and society...Others are military jumpers, occupying the position of general command, without economic, social, and possibly political experience. The movement stops, and the causes of underdevelopment gather.. It should be noted that the concept of economic government does not mean certificates or information at the level of economic knowledge. It means understanding, awareness and experience gained in practice at the level of economic effectiveness.

The proposal of "Saint-Simon" is an economic government, which in the eyes of others means the principle of socialism, and the management of the affairs of society in a different way. His followers-particularly Augustin Thiery and Auguste Comte-have expanded on analyzing his principles, eventually leading them to realist socialism. They see that individual ownership. Unfair, because in their view, it gives the right to a certain income, without doing fruitful work that corresponds to it, and that the state is the best heir to the means of production and its factors. It should distribute the results to the best working individuals.

However, their saying that individual ownership gives the right to a certain income without giving the equivalent of work, may not be true, except for the money loan with usury, in which Aristotle said during his exposure to usury: Money does not generate money, orrent, especially the rent of white land, which they called usurious land. [235] In the Islamic speculative company in which the lord of money does not work, he bears the loss of the worker in exchange for his

---

[231] Al-Bukhari: Al-Fath copy 5/207
[232] Kitāb al-'Amūl li-Dāwī, p.
[233] History of Al-Tabari 56/ 4
[234] See Islamic Economy Approach to Wealth Production and Consumption 377/2
[235] Main lines in Islamic economics, p. 65 by Mahmoud Abu Al-Saud, Social Solidarity in Islam, p. 44. Mohammed Abu Zahra

profit. Otherwise, it is acquired by the sweat of its brow. and the Islamic economy, it is not so much about ownership as it is about Acquisition and Work Approach. It was decided to benefit from the money of non-Muslims, whether Jewish or Christian, except through work, giving in return or compensation, or what pleases the soul in non-transactions.Then there is no cheating, no deception, no usury, no gambling, no monopoly, and no exploitation of man by his fellow man.

Then there are many socialist currents, not of great importance:

Some of them are known as the socialism of the platform. Founded by professors: owners of platforms or university chairs, and the founders believe that it is the duty of the state to supervise and regulate the economy, and contribute to the dissemination of economic and social justice...

Among them is what is known as the socialism of gatherings, which was called for by Charles Fourier and Robert Onn. This type requires the organization of human and labor societies, a new organization that achieves justice and happiness for all, in the form of socialist cooperatives. Fourier said that people should be gathered into groups or battalions, each group consisting of hundreds of people. Half of them are men and half of them are women...

Some of them are what is known as real socialism. They are the ones whose owners believe that they do not build on imagination, or ideal ideas. Rather, it builds on facts, on tangible material facts, and lives the material development of historical events. Its most famous founders were Germans. They are Roberts, Lassalle, andKarl Marx, who are the most fervent advocates of its application, and came out of it with a materialistic doctrine that worried the world for seventy years.

As long as we are presenting socialist currents, it is inevitable to rearrange anarchist socialism or anarchist doctrine. Which, as mentioned above, is a trend with no order. It is led by the anarchist Pruden and is unique in calling for absolute freedom and the abolition of all government authority.He calls his companions extreme and chaotic slogans, such as: A person should not be subject to any authority. Their goal with the warp of the road to it was to organize society fairly . It is done economically. To obtain surplus incomes, resulting from private property, and to distribute the prices of production and lending free of interest, while not recognizing the private property from which the surplus is generated, and rejecting the authority of the state, without which there is no distribution or economic or social system.

In aggregate terms, practical, theoretical or moderate and extreme socialist doctrines seem to be the most important advocates of their variation. It is the application of the principle of equality and the achievement of economic and social justice, and against individual freedom, personal benefit, individual property, and state intervention or not, with what is observed from the tide between direction and direction.

It was not until a little while ago that the law of personal interest, or personal benefit:«its atom is on its own» and«its atom passes its atom works», which was enshrined by the capitalist doctrine until its credibility began to shake in front of socialist trends...Simon and his students, who have expanded in the analysis of his opinions, call for the abolition of private property and inheritance. Socialists in cooperative societies, such as "Aven", "Fourier" and "Louie Bilal", are trying to replace personal benefit with voluntary cooperation. Proudhon, the leader of anarchism, dreams of reconciling absolute freedom with the socialist trend. The advocates of intervention, led by "Karl Marx", form a revolutionary doctrine in the name of "state socialism".

As for the beginning, the history of socialism began almost with the principles of "Saint-Sion" and its students, especially in criticizing private property, and examining its effects on the distribution and production of wealth. It is the basic idea around which all socialistdoctrines hover over the differences between them.This is according to the opinion of historians of economic thought...The fact is that the Islamic economy and its men were the first to open the file of joint usufruct in the world. He is the first to involve - socially in the charge of zakat - the poor with the rich in the distribution of the return of money, without participating in the work. He is the first to involve all social groups in benefiting from the public finances of the state: whoever does not get it by working, gets the social solidarity fee, as reflected in Omar's saying: "By God, who there is no god but He is no one but He, and He has a share in this money to give or prevent, and no one is more entitled to it than anyone." Socialists' critique of private property is initially confined to three types:

First - the distribution aspect - which is the neglected aspect in the classical doctrine and here refers to the distribution of the means of production or their results to workers, in order to obtain a measure of income without work.Soon, a large Arab state tried in the life of one of its presidents to apply the principle of involving workers in the profits of factories and failed, because the principle is theoretical rather than realistic.

Second- in terms of historical development. They say that monarchy is a moving system, and in continuous evolution, and that it is moving with the succession of days towards the final destiny, which it has collectivized. This is due to the fact that inheritance is confined to the state alone. It is one of the theories adopted by Marx, and Lenin applied it to a bloody revolution.

Third - Production area. They believe that private ownership of the means of production is incompatible with the interest of production itself, as long as those means are transmithted by inheritance, and they believe that the solution is that collective ownership replaces individual ownership, and that the state instead of the individual becomes the heir alone, and they symbolize in work and gain a rule that is "for each according to his ability, and for each energy according to its work", which is another of the Marxist theories. It was from Marx that he adopted revolutionary socialist thought, turning it theoretically into radical communism, as will be manifested through the analysis of his theories.

As for Proudhon's role in the socialist trend, he began as a whole socialists by criticizing private property, and distinguished them by exaggerating its description as theft itself. His attack is primarily on income, which is called interest "usury" because it gives the owner the opportunity to obtain income without work. He estimated that the interest paid on the cash loan is the root of all grievances.

Perhaps the first positive theory. It agrees with what was decided in the divine religions: Islam, Judaism and Christianity, and it responds to God's discourse for repenters from dealing with usury: "If you repent, you have your capital, you shall not be wronged, nor shall you be wronged." Youshall [236] not be wronged by taking usury or interest in modern expression, nor shall you be wronged by preventing the return of capital.

However, Pruden believes, as do some economists such as Marx, that the productive factor is human work alone. Land and capital, on the other hand, cannot produce anything without labor. And that the Lord of the land and the owner of capital get something for nothing is theft.

We may find a justification for his theory in lending cash capital with interest and in renting the white land, which they previously called usurious land, and linking Dr. Mahmoud Abu Al-Saud, Muhammad Abu Zahra and Abdul Hamid Al-Khatib between its income or revenue, and usury in earning by waiting... [237] But is it also possible for work to be produced without land and capital? Is the commodity produced and manufactured on Earth or in space? Is the production of land, cultivated by the owner himself, and the profit of capital, which his owner invests in trade and industry, considered a particular theft? Exaggerating and taking risks with phrases, indicates the immaturity of economic thinking at the stage we study its opinions... Although Proudhon was a politician and philosopher. Contributed to some labor movements, socialist organizations...

As we have seen, the eighteenth century did not manage, and the nineteenth was accepted until many socialist writers began to call for the intervention of the state and its guidance in the social economic system. Therefore, as we have already mentioned, they wrote a new doctrine that they called "State Socialism" and "Karl Marx", the brightest writer who was enthusiastic about the new doctrine, and his doctrine, which included the progression from socialism to communism, was the latest form known by the directed economy.

Based on the above, you wonder: Who was the first to open the file of joint benefit and applied the principle of economic and social justice, and intervened in the name of the state in favor of social groups? What does the Prophet's saying mean in the principle of the participation of all people in the original needs adopted in the island in the case of the mission: Muslims are partners in three: water, pasture and fire? " And what does it mean for Caliph Omar to say: "God has joined those who come after you in this regard?" He said: «If I

---

[236] transliteration
[237]

received from my command what I did, I would have taken the curiosity of the wealthy's money and returned it to the poor» and said - after the state had its collective ownership of the land -: «We have the necks of the earth», [238] which is the mother of resources and their origin, and their income or output is concerned in saying: «By God, who there is no god but He, no one but has a share in this money to give or prevent, and no one has the right to it from anyone» They are economic and social principles, applied by the Islamic State fourteen centuries ago..Is there a country in the world that applies it today?

---

[238] See Islamic Economics Approach to Wealth Production and Consumption 277/2

Marx and His Theories of Economics and Philosophy

A glimpse into Marx's life and what people think of him

Karl Marx was born in Germany in 1817 and died in 1883, descended from Jewish parents, both of whom belonged to the Rabbinical sect - his father was a religious jurist. He is a lawyer, and his mother is a descendant of Polish Jews, who traveled to Hungary in the eighteenth century, because of the large number of Jews in this country who have farms and money.

After the birth of "Karl Marx" about six years ago, his family turned father and mother from its Jewish religion to the Christian religion, in preparation for living opportunities, and to facilitate the means of the future, in front of their son, who did not exceed six years of age. It is the age at which the features of the religion of parents and grandparents are erased, and all opinions and beliefs are exempted, if this son is not destined to convert to the new religion: the religion of the state in which he lives. This has already happened. Professor Mahmoud Akkad said in his book "Communism and Humanity": "Karl Marx cannot hide the hatred of the Jews . On the slightest occasion, he pours a tongue of rage on them, in order to pay for the percentage of the Jew who sees him as adisgrace. "

His father oversaw his upbringing and education. After high school in the city of Treve, he joined the University of Bonn in 1835 to continue his studies in law. In 1837, he moved to the University of Berlin, where he continued his studies in philosophy until he received his doctorate in 1841. His father's death coincided with the completion of his postgraduate studies.

He chose to research philosophy, and showed a strong interest in the ideas of the German philosopher Hegel, from whom he quoted the foundations of his theories in materialist philosophy and the principle of the opposite...He entered the University of Bonn as a professor of philosophy, where he met with Iraqis and difficulties because of his extremist revolutionary views...In 1843, he was forced to emigrate to Paris, where he met Joseph Proudhon and his lifelong companion, Frederick Engels. He worked in the press as an editor in some newspapers, seeking to live, and at that time he was very mobile, between Germany, France, the Netherlands and England, which he would not leave, except to return to it again. where he spent about thirty years.

In 1847, he published The Misery of Philosophy in response to Proudhon's Philosophy of Misery, and in 1848, with the help of his comrade Engels, he edited the Manifesto of the Communist Party, which contained the views of the communist association called the League of Justice, which later became the proletarian Communist League.

His thinking was philosophical. Until 1845 he knew nothing of economics. He followed the advice of his colleague Engels in acquainting himself with economic thought, so he read Ricardo's works and took a lot from them, as will come in the theory of "value is work" so that some see that his theory is Ricardo's theory. After that, his work appeared at the level of economic thought. In 1858, he published his book "Criticism of Political Economy". In 1860, the theory of surplus value appeared. In 1876, the first part of his book "Capital" was printed, and after his death, his companion "Engels" printed the second in 1885 and the third in 1894, which is his Gospel, which is guaranteed by the essence of his doctrine, and the juiciness of his idea. Reading it, it seems a kind of contradiction between the first printed part of his life, and between the second and third printed after his death. The existing companiesD Marx began to abandon the daily work, and devote himself to spreading his socialist call and working to write down his views, and continued to do so until the emergence of his star, and became one of the star of social philosophy in the world. This qualified him to liberate the Communist Manifesto and establish the first state... People's opinions, even his disciples, are contradictory about his character. While we see some praise him and call him the prophet sent in the economy. If it is not economic in origin, we see others shaming it with the sting of phrases, accusing it of weakness, hatred, envy and chaos...

Professor Mahmoud Al-Akkad, in his book "Communism and Humanity", quoted the disciple of Karl Marx, "Otorohel", in his book Karl Marx, his life and work. He is a fanatic in the Marxist doctrine, he said: "He was a model of his suffering from the impairment of his spiritual activity, and he was always volatile, distressed and vindictive, still prone to poor digestion and bloating, and the frenzy of bile, and he was obsessed like all the obsessed in feeling his physical troubles, and as he relied on food, which is not regular, on the use of spices, bazaars, pickles, salted fish eggs, and so on.He also used the likes of that in his work and his relationship with others. It is no secret that bad eating is a bad factor and a bad colleague at the same time. Either he refrains from eating or overeats in it, or either he is lazy from work, or heexhausts himself in it in an unbearable way, or he is caught from cohabiting with others, or he takes a friend for himself from so-and-so and so-and-so and Badran and Zidane... Those in the vortex are extremists. Neither their equipment, nor their heads, nor their spirits can withstand the surprise of difference. Likewise, "Karl Marx, in his youth, was unable to persevere in studying his candidacy for a job that would help him to meet the demands of living, and in his old age he became unable to persevere in an effort of mental effort.He had no industry, no office and no regular occupation, no means of subsistence .He has nothing but chance, improvisation, and turmoil. Instead of regular lectures during his studies, he prepared for regular work, filling his stomach with philosophical and literary spices. He has always had a lack of patience for self-sport, a weak sense of order and a lack of ability to balance the resource and the expense. Months elapsed and he was notenergized to write one line, and then he threw all his strength on a serious work such as the works of the apostate and the Titans, so he skimmed nights and days, inspired by reading a whole library, stacking around him a pile of scraps, filled with commentary and writing pamphlets on pamphlets, leaving behind piles of manuscript writing. They start it and neglect it, and it does not end with a result or a crop.

That was the picture of Marx's life as the biggest driver of this troubled world. The text says that he is physically, psychologically and spiritually ill.If it loses capacity, and is unable to balance its resource and expenditure, it is to offer an economic doctrine that equates economic and social interests. It balances materialism and morale, income and expenses, and the interest of the individual and the group... I can't help it, no matter what, and despite the contradiction of opinions among those fascinated by Marxist thought when it was exported to the countries of theThird World, they added to the personality of its maker a loose suit of genius and innovation.Among those who resented his extremism, and were encouraged by his misbehavior, they postponed him in the ugliest form of helplessness and creek..Karl Marx actually left an intellectual legacy that developed into an economic and social doctrine that spread thanks to partisan fanaticism, political frictions, sectarian tendencies, and bloody revolutions.It has been reluctantly ingested since 1932, when famine claimed millions of lives. Practical experience has shown that it is unfit. They flogged in front of competing world blocs and doctrines...He remained steadfast until he was hit by the self-destructionpredicted by Marx for the capitalist doctrine, and «Gorba Chouf» in 1990 practically ended Lenin's inauguration in 1917 theoretically, as he was overcome by reality and unveiled the vacuum and contraction of the inflated economy, and practical experience for 73 years proved the failure of slogans and theories of impracticability and unrealism. The matter, as the Arab proverb said, regarding the drowning man, who did not tighten his kinship: "Your hands are octa and your mouth is inflated."

Thus, it is clear that the chances of success of Marx's economic philosophy are more revolutionary political than economic, and more biased than scientific.It must always be recognized, whether in science,economics, governance or war, that a man is his supporters and companions. It was narrated from Imam Malik that he said in Al-Layt ibn Saad Al-Masri: "Al-Layth hindered him from Malik, but his companions lost him."

THEORY OF VALUE, ITS SURPLUS, OVERTIME AND ITS TAKE-OFF

Returning to the overall view of the most famous capitalist and socialist doctrines, it is easy for the uninformed in economic affairs to diagnose the shortcomings of the most important theories adopted by Marx, and note their circulation among Muslim and foreign economists, before they became famous at his hands. Until now, we have not known a theory that he came up with, without being told by anyone who preceded him or his contemporary. be philosophical or economic. He may sometimes empty them of their true concepts among their owners, in order to suit the revolutionary trend and materialism that dominated his philosophy, as evidenced when analyzing the theory of matter that he cut from one of the two wings of Hegel's theory in the absolute idea.

Value

Marx began his book "Capital" by talking about commodities and money, and assumed that the value of any commodity was shoes, cloth, or wheat. It is expressed by one factor, which is the amount of abstract humanitarian work exerted in its production. Commodities, as use or exchange values, are only certain amounts of human labor crystallized in their values . Increases with decreases with decreases. Utilitarianism means that it is not fit for exchange until it is fit for use, and mutualism means that it carries the value of another commodity with which it is exchanged.

Surplus value

To understand the theory of surplus value. It is necessary to refer to Marx's concept of the value of a commodity. That is, work is not a factor of value, or a measure of its disparity, as Adam Smith sees it. It is its substance and its only factor. So, a worker who works eight hours a day to produce a commodity whose real, use or exchange value is the power of eight hours, the capitalist puts it in his pocket. And the wages he performs may be worth the power of four hours...It turns out that the values consumed are less than the values produced by half. It is the difference that he called surplus value, and saw that it is he who accumulates, and amplifies wealth in the hands of individuals, and proposed the solution in the ownership of the state.

The theory has a good chance of being considered, but what arises from state ownership of laziness and low production, as happened in the Soviet Union, is also a problem that must be solved...Perhaps the theory, which creates balance and eliminates the opportunity for wealth inflation among individuals, is theory of the companion Abu Dharr al-Ghafari, who called for spending treasures and curiosity of money to expand on those who have not yet received enough. The theory of spending treasure and the merit of money deduced from the Qur'an and Hadith is more comprehensive and broader than the theory of surplus value confined to the commodity. In the Islamic economy, it is known as the profit arising from industrial, commercial or agricultural work. It is not the benefit of borrowing money without work...Work is the basis of acquisition in Islam.

&Overtime

When we flip the theory of surplus value to another face, and we confirm that the worker only pays the power of eight hours to receive the value of four, the excess four, but works free for the capitalist account, which creates surplus value, and is called overtime in addition to the four that received their wage orvalue. These were Marx's explanations of the theory of value, its surplus, and overtime, and what about its origin andtakeaway? The theory was taken up by Aristotle from ancient times, and he gave it a psychological concept. It is the intensity of the need for the thing, or the intensity of the desire for it. His value is not in the things themselves, but comes from desire and need, and the commercial writer Thomas Aquinas [239] saw that the value of the commodity is equal to all the costs necessary to produce it. Including humanitarian work, which William Iotti [240] saw as based on all production expenses. Including land, capital and humanitarian work. It is the same as the theory of Ibn Khaldun. "Turku" built it from naturalism on utility, and on the degree of appreciation, which the different man makes him the things he desires. Value has a personal value. which is psychological. It differs from one person to another, and Kundiak, along with psychological appreciation, highlighted another element, which is scarcity and abundance.

The first to try to focus the concept of value on abstract humanitarian work alone «Locke» and followed by «Adam Smith» at the beginning, but the father of political economy «Adam Smith» hardly interrupted by trying to limit the formation of value to abstract humanitarian work until difficulties fell on him from every side:

1- Measuring the hardship and skill of work. The effort expended in an hour of hard work is greater than that expended in two hours of easy work, and the craft that teaches in a year, is different from the craft that teaches in a month.

2- It is impossible to produce abstract humanitarian work for a commodity without the help of land and capital.

3. The law of supply and demand governs commutative values. The value of a good increases if it is asked for more than it is offered, and decreases if it is offered more than it is ordered, regardless of its source.

4- The impact of lack of use and its abundance in values. He gave the example of water and diamonds. It is an idea close to the scarcity and abundance that Kundiak observed. "

The last person who proved relatively that the necessary work is the basis for the formation of value «Ricardo» followed the attempt made by «Adam Smith» at the beginning and disagreed with him in that the value in some things, such as rare statues, is determined by scarcity alone, as it is not possible for the work, even if it is great, to increase its quantity or change its value...

Bastia was pleased with the expression "Ricardo" with the necessary work, and considered it the clearest measure of values, but he was not fully convinced of it, because he did not explain why the pearl found on the seashore was of value, equivalent to the value extracted by hard work from the seabed?

For his part, Bastia tried to express an expression that reconciles multiple opinions such as need, benefit, scarcity, the cost of production, humanitarian work and the difficulty of achievement, and it did not succeed...His expression of "service is the basis of value" is more ambiguous thanRicardo's expression of

---

[239] History of Economic Ideas, p. 20 by Dr. Mohammed Aziz
[240] Id., p. 48

the work necessary to produce it, both of which do not go beyond the subject of cost, work and difficulty of achievement. The subject of need, scarcity, utility, appreciation, psychological and the law of supply and demand remain outside the two expressions.

In the pretext of this abundant sea of conflicting statements, and the different opinionsabout the factor of value and its source, «Marx» adopted the theory of «Ricardo» value is work»and imitated it and chose it as a teacher. He has advanced that he knew nothing about economics, before he read his books, but did not improve imitation, and did not succeed in imitating. He took what he hesitated to prove, and confirmed it with certainty. In that, the specialist in the history of economic thought, Dr. Muhammad Aziz, says: « ..We have seen before that Ricardo said this idea, but he was hesitant, but Marx confirmed it [241].

However, the concept that Ricardo intended and gave to work, as well as the incomprehensible capital that Marx modified in Ricardo, means the stock capital, and by the necessary work, every work that helps to produce the commodity, such as making tools and machines, building institutions, and direct humanitarian work...By capital, Marx means the same tools, machines and buildings, and he called it fixed capital or bitumen.As for the wages of workers and consumables. He called it variable or circulating capital - as an analysis of the capitalist system and restricts work to abstract human work and [242] is the only factor that has been assumed to produce value.This assumption was deliberately made. Despite its violation of reason and reality, because it is consistent with its doctrine of focusing on the human aspect.

As for the theory of surplus value, or surplus value, it was formulated from the theory of "physiocratic doctrine" in net product or net surplus. It is the difference in the agricultural wealth produced, over the wealth consumed in the cost of its production. Quote them and circulate them in the excess difference that usually occurs between each new commodity and its production expenses.

The theory of surplus value and overtime is one of the effects of the theory of "value is labor", which is proven to be proven, and abandoned or negated by its absence. In this regard, Dr. Mohamed Aziz says in his book "History of Economic Ideas": "Value is labor" has been abandoned today, even by most Marxists.Marx himself. Despite his emphasis on the theory of "value is labor", he was forced to sometimes implicitly and explicitly admit that value depends on supply and demand. Since Marx deduced the theory of overtime and surplus value from the theory of "value is labor", it is clear that the collapse of this theory calls for the collapse of the lasttwo theories. If it is decided that the work does not create value, or that value can be created outside the work. There is nothing that proves that work necessarily generates surplus value. "The professor's saying"abandoned today" means the day the topic was written. I, in turn, completed this research twenty-five years ago.

---

[241] History of Economic Ideas p. 227

[242] Id., p. 176

Thus, what Marx adopted from the juices of economic thought in his time was scattered in the hands of research, as a result of decomposition, and changing it towards a doctrinal orientation...As usual in many of the topics he analyzed in his book "Capital", he criticized "Ricardo" for not searching for the origin of surplus value without analyzing his opinion on its composition. "Ricardo never bothered to look into the origin of surplus value," he said. It discusses surplus value, as if it were something inherent in the capitalist mode of production, which is the natural form of social production[243]."

Apparently, comparing his expression with the work done and the expression "Ricardo" with the work necessary to produce value is enough to highlight the percentage of surplus value in the two expressions. What he criticized on Ricardo is that he discusses surplus value, as if it were something inherent in the capitalist method of production. He is the same one who simplified it while analyzing the theory of overtime. He explained that a worker who works eight hours is paid four. The other four operate free of charge on the capital account and create surplus value. The surplus in this regard is inherent in the capitalist method of production, as Ricardo implicitly agrees with him in one part of "capital" and criticizes it inanother part. This is one of his contradictionsbetween the parts ofcapital, what he built implicitly or explicitly in the part of his demolition implicitly or explicitly in another part. The difference was noted between what was printed in his life, and what was printed by his companion "Engels" after his death. And Landry, did the English act during the editing first? If the custom requires not to act, the difference usually occurs in the work of two people in an author who did not cooperate in all its stages, such as the death of one writer and the completion of another.However, Autoruhl explained what Marx suffers from obsession and psychological and spiritual disorder. May cause this difference.

In exploiting the theory of spending treasure and the virtue of money, some mesmerized by the Marxist obsession, when it was exported to the Arab world, tried to install the thought of the companion Abu Dharr Qantara to override it. They claimed he was a communist who forbade private property. In this, Mikseem Rodonson says: "The extremist trend in the medieval Islamic era was supported in the person of one of the Prophet's companions, Abu Zar al-Ghafari. The socialistand communist left found in him a teacher who had already, or at least had taken his story as proof that ideas with a socialist orientation were not alien to Islamic traditions. Some authors have even gone so far as to infer from his example that communism is the answer to basic Islamism[244]."

This is understood from the words of the author Hussein Heikal: «He was one of the companions of the Prophet (PBUH) in socialism. They make the earth and what it contains like water and air, it is not permissible to own anything of it. "[245]It is a slander against Islam, and a slander against the Companions of the

---

[243]Capital 9/2
[244]Islam and Capitalism p.63
[245]Hayat Mohammed Al-Hussein HeikalP-542-I-8-1963- Cairo

Messenger, and that no one in this world can prove in texts, and in a scientific way that among the Companions of Muhammad is one who says this opinion[246].

And after: Any relationship between the constant of Abu Dharr's opinions related to the call to spend treasures and the curiosity of money, and the application of the principle of equality. And the establishment of a system of social solidarity in light of economic and social justice and other views aimed at reforming society in its era, and between these partial theories in the hands of modern economists?

Where is the constant reality of the theory of "value is labor" and that the commodity in which the worker takes ten hours to produce, is equal to the labor force of ten hours, which takes five hours to produce, is equal to the labor force of five hours? Without regard to the factors of land and capital, nor to the law of supply and demand... He had felt that work was an uncontrolled sex. Strength and weakness, so he invented the labor force, and he lost sight of the fact that strength is also an uncontrolled race. A good produced by one worker in two days may be produced by another in one day.

If Marx estimated that the theory of "value is labor", it could find a place in the production of manufactured salt. He had lost sight of the natural salt picked in the desert. There is nowork in it. It is the finest and highest value made. We have already mentioned that in his book "Capital" he expressed his astonishment at the wondrous engineering of bees and the sobriety of their weaving, without giving his opinion on honey, which is found in caves, which is the highest value, without having anything to do with the theory of "value is labor".

The work may be the same, and the values vary. The fisherman who throws his net into the sea, does only one job, and gets things that are notappropriate among them in value. and the writer who writes two books. The work in each of them took a full year, the Ministry of his country may decide to use one of them in its schools, and ask, so its value rises and it is carried out, and the other remains neglected on the shelves of the two papers.... It is axiomatic that the difference in the values produced starts mainly from the difference in the values of the raw materials, which represent the aspect of capital in the formation of value. Work is work and time is time. The values differ between what is made of copper, silver or gold...As well as what is made of cotton, wool or silk...

Marx overlooked many fundamental theories of value: he overlooked the elements of land and capital, and saw that they would not produce anything without labor and forgot that labor would also produce nothing without them, and overlooked utility. It is the one that causes the patient to pay a high price in a drug that he does not take for free, and overlooks the need. She is the one who carries the thirsty in the desert over the preference for water over diamonds and the hungry over the preference for bread over gold, and overlooks the scarcity. It raises the price of rare things to the level of imagination, and overlooks the

---

[246] This theory is one of the theories that we have analyzed in our chapter on Islam and contemporary theories between p. 338and 403 of the second part of the Islamic economics curriculum.

difficulty and risk that are not measured in working hours, as is the case with the pearl extracted from the seabed. Hence, it was natural to ignore the law of supply and demand that governs the determination of substitution values.

In Islamic economics, it is almost self-evident that the value of a commodity, measured in money, is the mediator between substitutive values, and is determined by the corresponding consideration. Compensation is a total expression. embraces all the different theories. Including utility, need, difficulty, scarcity, the work done or necessary, and the cost of production, because the consideration is related to the law of supply and demand, which affects the change of values after their production, before it relates to their sources, or the factors of their formation. It rises with values when it rises self, invincibility, need, psyche, cost, or consideration ...and decreases as it decreases.

In any case, it is high when it is needed, under any pressure and low when it is displayed under any reason. Putting the consideration as a basis for substitutive values does not leave the commodity rigid and confined to one scope, but rather gives it strength and flexibility, to be a substitute for one time, and a substitute for another time. Hence, the jurists' expression "one of the two compensators" came at a disagreement in money, whether they are commodities or a measure of their values, as mentioned above.

The blacksmithh who makes a sword, and sells it to a peasant in an agreed amount of wheat may be said in his sword instead, or compensated for it. Considering what characterized his commodity at the level of the law of supply and demand. The conclusion of the agreement at the level of the two components approximates the cost of producing that amount of wheat to the cost of producing the sword if it is not equivalent between them. But if the sword had been resold on the battlefield, its price would have been twice as high as the cost of its production. If it is resold in the market after the end of the war, it returns to its previous price. Whereas wheat, unless there were supply or demand conditions, remained at its previous value.

And so was the consideration, solving all the problems. It is clear that the compensation of the sword in battle is not compensated in the market, and the compensation of the medicine in the patient is not compensated for when it is true, and the compensation in the scarcity is not compensated for in abundance, but instead of the pearl captured on the seashore. Equals instead of extracted is hard work, and the value is the value. And the consideration is the one that equates between the value of natural and made honey and the consideration is the consideration...It may be more comprehensive than the expression "Marx" in the equivalent of two exchange goods.

As for the theory of "value is work", it has failed to explain many fundamental factors in value. If we ask "Marx" about the value of the commodity in sugar, he would answer "value is labor", but what is his answer about the value of honey?

The natural one that is found in caves, as mentioned above? Isn't it more expensive and more valuable? He reminded us that he did not hide his surprise and admiration for the engineering of bees in his hives as a link between him and the engineering of the spider ...It is better for him to evade, so that he positions himself as an engineer, instead of an economist, who sets a standard for values. As long as the theory of "value is labor" is unable to explain the factor of | value and its source in natural honey. The believer hardly thinks about the source of the value of honey, until he throws in his splendor the Almighty saying: «Your Lord inspired the bees to take homes from the mountains and from the trees and from what they thrive, then eat from all the fruits and walk the paths of your Lord so that a drink of different colors will come out of their stomachs in which there is healing for people. Indeed, in this is the verse of the people thinking» and the problem of reconciling the two commodities, is dissolved from its basis by the theory of the mosquito, which automatically takes care of setting standards for both sugar and honey, without going back to reviewing the factors of values and the cost of producing them.

Thus, the weakness of what Marx adopted of principles and theories manifests itself, so that we may not find a theory for him now other than the principle of communism in which Plato, Mazdak and Redsht said - steadfast, and lived on the level of life and reality. In this, Dr. Mohamed Aziz says: "Marxist economic theories have been subjected to violent criticism that has destabilized them all, and even the most important of these theories has cracked, and collapsed from its foundation. Marx himself contributed part of the demolition process. His final volumes, which were printed after his death, moved souls with their serious contradictions, which are irreconcilable, and with what came in the first volume. With this face, Marxism suffered what it had predicted for the capitalist system, namely, the law of self-destruction [247] and true self-destruction, which did not take place at the time the author recorded this fact. Rather, it was the destruction and dissolution of the Soviet Union in 1990.

The famous French writer Gustave Labone says: "When the incidents belied the principles of Marx, who remained for a long time the greatest pontiff of socialism. His most loyal followers looked at leaving her.. For example, the statistics of different countries deny his theory, which has been fundamental to socialists for forty years, that capital will be confined to a few people. When the statistics proved that capital was divided among many people, instead of being limited, the leaders of socialism in Germany, England, and Belgium began to abandon communism, saying that it [248] was an illusory doctrine worthy of harming the Latin nations.

SCIENTIFIC SOCIALISM AND THE ELIMINATION OF SURPLUS VALUE

---

[247] History of Economic Ideas 235
[248] The Spirit of Socialism, p. 5, by Gustav Lepon

In contrast to the revolution and the use of force, in Russia Marx sees the system of private property, which prevails in the old societies, proceeding in a natural and spontaneous development towards a definitive new system. where collective ownership prevails. On the day when the state alone controls all means of production, whether on the face of the earth or in its interior. Thus, the surplus value that the capitalist benefits from at the expense of the worker disappears. In his view, it creates economic and social problems.

It is known that the theory of "Marx" based on the principle of the "opposite", which he quoted from the philosophy of "Hegel", says that every system is based on the opposite of its predecessor, and he claimed that the development of property to return began with the communist system, then slavery, then feudalism, then capitalism, then socialism, as a stage, then communism as a goal. The economic development of the world ends with him, and he claims that each system carries within itself the elements of its own mortality, or what is known as self-destruction, and it dies on its own...In practice, which regime carried within itself the elements of its annihilation or the strength of its continuation today? The capitalist or the communist? And to which end did the economic development in the world end? And which of them suffers from self-destruction?

This naturalistic method, which Marxist doctrine sees as explaining the developments that property has undergone, since primitive was commonplace-as claimed until it returns, as was common in the final system, which it decided. It is what Marx calls the principle of "scientific socialism". This principle was formulated and quoted from the natural laws of naturalism (physiocracy). The meaning of scientific socialism wants natural science - that it did not intend a new project, but was limited to explaining the conditions and circumstances in which property developed, within human societies, with reference to the point towards which it rushes. Marxist doctrine in this theoretical method is closer to natural political economy and its idea of natural laws than to revolutionary socialist doctrine.

The addition of the principle of the antithesis, which further helps to understand scientific socialism, shows the extent to which theorists disbelieve in the history they explain, and in the principles they lay down. They believe in it when it is a theory that concerns others, and they disbelieve in it when it is realistic that concerns them. Marxists believe, on the contrary, that every existing system carries within itself the elements of its own annihilation. And then inevitably another system is based on its opposite...But no one thought that belief in this principle necessitated the establishment of another new system in contrast to the communist system, as it had already happened. On anything Marxist doctrine was adopted in stopping the historical current, which he explains as natural.

Dr. Mohamed Aziz said in the "History of Economic Ideas": "Marxists blame the classical economists seriously: they have not shown the relative and temporal character of the social system, which they have been studying. These economists had calculated that ownership and renting people from the final systems, and they imagined that the world had frozen forever in its present state, that is, the capitalist state. And what they are common to see is a historical stage that goes on, as others have gone on. "

Do the Marxists themselves have the relative and temporal character of their system? Did they see it as a historical stage? Going on like the others? Did they not also imagine that the world was frozen forever? And can any system freeze forever, in front of the ability of the Creator who initiates and restores?

Once again, we return to the Marxist Arabs who were shielded by the thought of the companion Abu Dharr, in order to protect them from the attacks of the believers. On the day they promoted him as a communist... Let us ask them in terms of credibility: Where is Abu Dhar, who sets an example in standing on the principle of these principles that are troubled between vision and reality? Has it been proven that he has set a principle and denied it? orcriticized something andcommitted it? Or called for a doctrine, and he was not one of the first to apply it? Or explain a theory and reality was otherwise? Or developed a curriculum and practical experience did not prove its credibility? This is contrary to Marx's method of scientific socialism, which he describes as peace and natural science, so it is a military coup, and a bloody revolution that has killed millions of people, as happened in the revolution of 1917- Prussia. What Marx theoretically called scientific socialism, Lenin practically called compulsive socialism.

With the advent of the communist revolution, which Professor Mahmoud Al-Akkad described in his book "Communism and Humanity" that the history of humanity has never been known, all natural peaceful slogans, including scientific socialism, which are said to transform private property in a peaceful, scientific and natural manner into collective property, and eliminatesurplus value, have disappeared through the natural development from private to collective property. None of that happened. So-called scientific socialism did not transform private property into collectivism. The surplus value was not eliminated, except by dispossessing people's property and nationalizing it by force.The expropriation and nationalization of property by force without compensation, and without being imposed by a public interest as part of the road is theborderline between the Islamic and communist economies.

THEORY OF EVOLUTION BETWEEN ECONOMICS AND PHILOSOPHY

The principle of economic development was one of the theories on which Marx's philosophy of economics was based. It is an originally philosophical theory and analysis...He explained to her the natural development that usually accompanies economic affairs, and foretells their progress. What is new is that it has been put in a special form, as evidenced by the assumption that monarchy has evolved from the communist system, then enslavement, then feudalism, then capitalism, then socialism as a stage, then communism as a goal.

Like all theories adapted from the philosophy of his predecessor or contemporary, he proceeded to the theory previously stated by the Arab philosophers, and was famous by the American philosopher Darwin in evolution and evolution, and formulated from it the principle of economic development.

It is known that Darwin carried out experimental studies in the origins, during which he observed the continuous evolution mainly from dust to plants, to animals to humans. He also observed the apparent disparity, even between members of the same sex, rising and falling. This inspired him with his idea, according to which he believes that the human race may pass through stages of its life. in an original stage where there was a monkey, before he rose to this beautiful image that he enjoys ... The will of God made Darwin famous, and his theory collided with an ideological political current. He inspired America at one time to devote all its efforts to spreading his philosophy and to harness his propaganda to its cultural centers in the world, in defiance of Marxism, which borrowed the theory, and applied it in economic development. Although the idea of man's descent from the monkey is critical of science, reason and religion...Because it was not based on steady scientific bases supported by reason. The mind did not digest the established differences between the idea of the descent of man from the monkey, without taking into account thesearch for the descent of each animal from another close to him, nor did it digest the natural ascension of some members of the same race, while we see others, who did not ascend or become extinct...And even the one who said it hesitated in its merits. In that, Dr. Muhammad Sa 'id Ramadan al-Buti said: "Darwin died before he was cut off[249]."

The truth is that Professor Abdul Moneim Al-Nimr quoted from the book "The Progress of Human Evolution" and its companion among American scientists who say the idea of evolution and advancement: "The development of man without deriving moral strength, and his progress in the path charted for the advancement from animalism to humanity is impossible, just as it is impossible to collect a book of Shakespeare's plays by throwing letters, however agreed, without thinking. There is no doubt that evolution creates man, not from pure coincidences, but it is a development in which from the beginning to the end was the capable hand of God[250]. "

The idea of evolution was originally adapted from the general idea in which Muslim Arab philosophers dealt with the study of origins, before Darwin adopted it and formulated the idea of the descent of man from the monkey. Before Marx adopted it and formulated the idea of economic development. In this, Professor Draper, a university professor in New York, says: "The Arabs roamed the institutes of philosophy and science at a speed similar to the speed

---

[249]The Greatest Cosmic Certainties P-11-I 2- 1390 AH Beirut
[250]Islam and Imported Principles, p. 46

with which they roamed the Kingdom of the Romans. Sometimes we are surprised when we encounter scientific opinions in their books. We thought it originated in this century.Such is the evolutionary doctrine of organic beings. He was studying in their schools...The current Europe is not higher in taste, tenderness and circumstance in any of its things than what was in the Andalusian Arab capitals at the time we are talking about."This [251] was the case of our ancestors, and this is our case... Jamal al-Din al-Afghani was asked about the house of al-Ma 'ari, in which the wilderness was surrounded by a new animal from Jumada. Does he mean the rise of the animal from the inanimate objects in the way that Darwin went or does he mean something else? He replied - with some disposition -: "My father's intention is clear. He means evolution and upgrading, taking the doctrine of Arab scholars before him. It was mentioned in the letter of Abu Bakr ibn Bishrun to Abu al-Samih casually in the chemistry research that dust is impossible for a plant and plants are impossible for an animal, and that the highest birth is a human being. It is the last of the three transformations "[252] and the message was conveyed by Ibn Khaldun in " the science of chemistry" and the transformations were not communicated to man.

Thus, it becomes clear that "Darwin" was in fact only an adherent of a doctrine analyzed by Arab scholars before him, and they finished studying it centuries ago. Let's listen to Ibn Khaldun to tell us about the results he reached in his time, and he says: "...Then look at the world of formation, how it began with minerals, then plants, then animals, in a magnificent form of gradation: the last horizon of minerals from above is connected to the first horizon of plants from below. Like weeds, the mala sowing him, the last horizon of the plant from above like palms and vines connected to the first horizon of the animal from below: like snails and shells. There is only the power of touch[253]. "

Abdul Karim Al-Khatib commented in his book "The Issue of Divinity between Philosophy and Religion" on this text, and he said: "And you see here Ibn Khaldun has rushed behind this sequence to the furthest limits, and has made man an advanced link in the chain of origins, which began from the world of inanimate objects, and then gradually progressed to the world of plants, animals and humans. Man thus attributes his lineage to the world of apes, as Darwin decides, and even to what is lower than this. the world of apes evolved from a world below. And this world originates from another world without it. And so on until it becomes a world of algae and plants and then descends into the world of inanimate objects and corals...Thus, Ibn Khaldun forgot in the impulse this enthusiasm for the new scientific discovery: he forgot what is known about the creation of man, in what the Holy Quran came up with in the creation of Adam and his descendants[254]. "

---

[251] The Issue of Divinity between Philosophy and Religion 37/1 by Abdul Karim Al-Khatib
[252] Islam and Imported Principles, p. 46
[253] Al-Muqaddimah, p. 92 for ʿAbd al-Raḥmā
[254] The Issue of Divinity between Philosophy and Religion 183/1

In fact, it is the professor who rushed in his commentary, running after natural evolution, as Darwin said » and from his doctrine, imagining that Ibn Khaldun's research extends to the monkey and then to man. However, the text in our hands - which the professor conveyed and commented on - does not bear this burden. It stopped evolution on the doorstep of the animal world. It ended where it began with snails and seashells, as did other philosophers of Islam. If the snail had evolved into an ape, and then into a man, it would have declared it, but it was limited only to what scientific and practical experiments proved its permissibility, and did not return it to what was known about the creation of Adam and his descendants...He said:"And the animal is not impossible to something that is gentler than it is, except that it is reversed back to thickness, [255] which is the same as what Ibn Maskawiyadid. The [256] nicest thing to say is that a student asked his teacher: Is it true whathe says: "Darwin "that our great-grandfather was a monkey? He replied: For Darwin to decide that his great-grandfather was a monkey. As for you and I, we found the Most High, the Prophet of God, Adam, the Lord of Mankind.

In comparison, it is clear that Ibn Khaldun's research is more accurate and comprehensive, and it is based on Darwin's theory that it portrays the movement of existence, which is better able to move up and down.

In this, he says: "Each of them is ready to be impossible to the next up or down," and the decline as the plant world to the world of minerals is easier to perceive the minds than the rise. If we know that Darwin's doctrine allows the monkey to be impossible as a human being, Ibn Khaldun's doctrine permits even the opposite. It is that it is impossible for a man to be a monkey, which is known to the public as a monster, as they circulate that the monkey was a human being and God made him a monster for his misdeeds.

The theory of emergence and elevation in the heart meanings was circulating among Sufi and Islamic scholars, and they were placing it within the framework of scientific facts that are debunked in good and pure hearts. They tie its fate to time so thatthey are not distracted by it from the Sharia and its home. If evolution and progress in the meanings of God's honoring His servants, we wonder: Is the doctrine of organic evolution, away from the Sunnah of the monotheists, and from the doctrine of the first breath and its sanctity? Darwin himself answers this question, explaining the concept he gave to this breath, saying: "I see that the living people who lived on this earth all from one primary image in which the Creator breathed the breath of life."[257]The answer did not appeal to the materialists from thenatural scientists, because it denies the emergence of life by chance and naturally, as they wanted, and they revolted against him, and considered his statement a contradiction of the doctrine from its foundation.

---

[255] Introduction p. 985
[256] On the Story of Faith by Nadim Al-Jisr, p. 64, 3rd edition, Beirut

[257] Islam and Imported Principles, p. 49

Thus, the theory of evolution was circulating among the philosophers of Islam, before it became famous at the hands of Darwin and before Marx adopted it and formulated from it the theory of economic development. We may notneed to establish evidence that Islam has called since its emergence for economic development.Where the Prophet ordered the development of orphans' money, as charity does noteat them, and blessed the work of a companion who gave him a dinar to buy him a sheep, so he bought two sheep, so he sold one of them with a dinar and came to him with a sheep and a dinar. He said: «May God bless your right hand deal» to [258] encourage development, which made economic affairs develop from the era of the Prophet to the era of Abu Bakr, and from the era of Abu Bakr to the era of Omar, and from the era of Omar to the era of Othman. Economic development reached its peak and a nation was sold [259] with its weight with reservation in this seditious behavior. Omar is known to have encouraged production and cash exchange work. He said - and the money piled up in front of him -:«And God does not keep it a roof under the sky until he divides it among the people» and [260] wrote to his worker Abu Musa al-Ash'ari: «But after: The strength in the work is notto delay the work of today for tomorrow...»[261].

He addressed the Companions of the Prophet (PBUH) by saying: "Fix your property that Allah has provided for you. For a few, there is better than many in violence. "Development took place [262] and economic and social conditions developed. But not in a hypothetical imaginary way, starting with the beginning of creation, as Marx claimed, but in a logical and realistic way that starts with social life, as soon as you start in a country or Egypt... Ibn Khaldin refers to this by saying: "Know that the real estate and the many losses of the people ofcities and cities are not at once, nor in one era,as none of themhas the wealth with which to own property whose values go beyond the limit, even if their conditions in luxury are not reached. Rather, it shall be their property and their identification with it gradually[263]. "

Although the Qur'an deals with public faculties that struggle with time and kill it, far from dealing with partial theories, which hardly settle in the field of science until they are copied with another, Sayyid Qutb says in the "Shadows of the Qur'an" when interpreting the Almighty's saying: **Those who spend their money for the sake of Allah are like a grain that grows seven ears in each ear, a hundred grains. God multiplies for whom He wills, and God is all-pervasive and all-knowing**[264]. ""The mental meaning of expression ends in a calculation that doubles one pill to seven hundred times... As for the living scene, which the expression displays, it is wider than this, more beautiful, more

---

[258]Sahih Al-Tirmidhi 5/263 Grand Sunan 12/6 Sunan Abu Dawud 348/3 Beginning of the Diligent 171/2
[259]Absorption for Ibn ʿAbd al-Barr: Section III p. 1041
[260]Kharj Abi Yousef, p. 27
[261]History of Al-Tabari 27/5
[262]Life of the Companions 114/ 2
[263]Introduction p. 653
[264]transliteration

emotional, and more influential in consciences. It's a growing life scene…" It is fair to say that the first foundations of contemporary economics are Islam.

THE THEORY OF ARTANDTHE VIEWS OF SCIENTISTS, PHILOSOPHERS AND NATURALISTS ON THE SUBJECT

One of the theories on which Marxist doctrine was based is materialism and theconsequent materialist interpretation of history. Marx put this theory as a basis forhis philosophy and a rule of his doctrine. It is a theory that inherently contradicts every philosophical theory that says the absolute idea, orallows in one of its stages to think beyond matter, in search of its creator and organizer, and then where did Marx once again take this theory?

Professor Mahmoud Akkad said: "Marxist materialism is based on the doctrine of Hegel, the German philosopher of idealism or modern idea. The doctrine of Hegel is notconsidered to exist, except for the intellectual aspect. It explains the development of contradictions, and Hegel said: True existence is the existence of the absolute idea and that the idea is eternal and eternal capable of everything. Professor Abdul Karim Al-Khatib in turn [265] quoted Hegel as saying explicitly : "God is eternal and eternal and he is an absolute spirit of the constraints of time and space: a spirit that did not start in the time series at a certain moment, and will not end in the time series at a certain moment. It is eternal: that is God in the perception of the philosopher, but in his conscience and feelings[266].

The theory of the "absolute idea" has a broad framework, and distant horizons. It leaves the door wide open, to embrace all free opinions, all theories resulting from thinking about matter, or beyond, and is prepared with its liberating character,to explain all stages of human history, and the development of contradictions with ease and realism. It is about the material or its sponsor.

Marx, as Professor Akkad says, proceeded to the doctrine of Hegel in all its dimensions, horizons and phases, and imposed on him a purely materialistic concept, after he emptied his framework of all its contents.He moved it from a doctrinethat sees nothing in existence except the idea, to a materialistic doctrine. He sees only matter in it, and he called his impostor doctrine, cut from one of the wings of the absolute idea, "dual materialism" and called its laws that control human history "the material interpretation of history."

The theory of materialism, by its nature, requires the closure of all open outlets, and the resolution of every idea that aspires to viewbeyond matter, in search of its creator, and the cutting off of all dark necks to know the truth of this existence, through the postponement of free thought. The theory of "materialist interpretation of history" means the limitation of all causes, circumstances, conditions, conflicts, wars and developments… that has occurred

---

[265] Communism and Humanism, p. 93 by Mahmoud Al-Akkad
[266] The Issue of Divinity between Philosophy and Religion 145/ 1

to humanity until today, on the material element, and the disregard for every aspect has to do with the ideals, the eternal lofty meanings, the religious doctrines, the supreme publicity, his news, his messengers and his messages, or every person who used his idea in search of the truth, and the attempt to know himself and the truth of his Creator and the truth of this universe, which is one of his atoms.

In the Communist Manifesto, issued in 1847, Marx and his comrade Engels wrote: For the proletariat, laws, moral rules and religions are only bourgeois illusions. Behind her are bourgeois interests. "Engels said in 1877: "We reject all attempts, because we believe that morality is the result of socialconditions. The morality we believe in is every action that leads to the triumph of our principles. No matter how unethical this act may be[267]. " Lenin said in 1910: "The true communist fighter must be practiced with all kinds of deception, deceit and misinformation. The struggle for communism blesses every means of achieving communism, and he said in 1918: "If the communist fighter is not able to change his morals and behavior according to the circumstances. No matter how much it costs to lie, mislead and deceive. He would not be a true revolutionary fighter, and he said in 1920, that the true revolutionary communist fighter is the one who makes every sacrifice. imposed on him to achieve the communist goal. Even if it requires sacrificing morality, dignity and conscience. The true ideal is the realization and consolidation of communist society[268]. "

And where is the immorality of the Prophet's saying: "I was sent to fulfill the noble morals?" Anas said: "Peace be upon him was the best of people created[269]."

Stalin said in 1929 about personal and partisan dictatorship instead of whathe claims from theoretical democracy: "Literature, arts and sciences must be weapons in the hands of the party. Through the party's control of etiquette, we can raise people's feelings, and through the control of the arts, we can control their behavior. Public opinion must be just a reflection of our principles, opinions and behavior. " And the truth of God Almighty, as he says to his Prophet:" **Remember, you are a reminder that you are not destined for them**. "[270]And about individual freedom, which is the oxygen of life, Stalin says in 1937 :" Let me make it clear to you frankly that our communist system does notbelieve in individual freedom. Individual freedom means the elimination of the group, it means deviating from obedience to the law, and it means deviating from Marxism. This type of freedom, that is, individual freedom, is whatthreatens our system, and it is not pleasant to say the Caliph Omar bin Al-Khattab, as he says, "When you enslave people and their mothers were born free," and so on, there are no heavenly religions, noideals, no morals, nofreedoms... But there is dictatorship and control...All the conflicts and wars

---

[267]Their Socialism and Our Islam, p. 36
[268]Id., pp. 37-38
[269]Nour Al-Yaqeen, p. 284
[270]Surat al-Ghashiyyah 22

that have occurred in the history of humanity have been for the sake of matter and for the sake of matter alone. In response to this claim, we may notneed more than one case. They are the Crusades around the Holy House, so the theory of "material interpretation of history" evaporates, as thereis no material element in the holy spot, worthy of the decay of nations on it. but rather a clash between two religious beliefs... The truth is that denying the history of the divine religions andthe brotherhood and harmony they spread or called for from acts of righteousness and charity... Denial of the reality of the scenes. The philosopher Bergson said: "We may find in the past or the present human societies. You don't know science, art or philosophy, but there is no Baladin society. "

Professor Allal Al-Fassi explained in his book "Self-Criticism" that Ibn Khaldun preceded "Marx" to the establishment of the economic school in history. The difference between the two theories is that Ibn Khaldun considers the economic element one of the four motives that I have already enumerated, including religion, and«Marx» limits the historical interpretation of man to economics alone [271].

As for the positivist concept of Marx's theory of "materialism", it is that there is nothing in existence except matter, that is, the tangible that touches, sees and hears. The real existence in his philosophy is to strike with his hand on the table, and when it is there, or he knocks with his foot on the ground and he hears its voice. The exaggeration in believing in the sensible is what led him to say that he could not decide that the table was in front of him until he struck with his hand and that the ground under him until he banged his foot.. We do notknow what happened to proving that ownership was common at the beginning of life, nor dowe know what happens to Marxists whose father died while he wasstill in his mother's womb. Does his lineage prove imperceptible or remains unknown?

Marxism, because of economic and ideological factors, limited its faith to materialism in order to succeed its doctrine, and as such ignored everything about its maker and organizer. Lenin says, "Marxism is matter. Hence it is hostile to religion. "[272] He said,"It is not true that it is God who regulates the universes. Rather, it is true that religion is a superstitious idea[273]. "

If Lenin were asked to prove his claim that God is not the regulator of the universes, and the source of their organization and management. When he was able more than the only answer, which was often repeated on the tongues of the natural, that it was found by chance, and that these crimes may have been a single mass in time, and then the eons rolled, and they separated from each other. This view, if it is correct, requires that you walk in space adrift. It is an opinion that the mind rejects. His belief is equal to messing with the thought instead of the man. Nature is organized. and any entrepreneur who performs

---

[271] Self-criticism p. 182.
[272] Islam and Imported Principles, p. 18
[273] Their Socialism and Our Islam, p. 51

their task regularly. The mind is difficult to digest its existence by chance and without a regulator. Iron, which is found by chance, may be said to be natural, but when it is transformed by an action outside itself into organized clocks, taking into account the organization of the universe itself, it is impossible for a healthy mind to recognize its existence by chance, or to organize itself.. The rock on which the stubbornness of the naturalists breaks, they sometimes shout some truth, or stand in amazement. It is their collision with the system of nature, and its inability to regulate itself.

The sheikh of mathematicians and astronomers, "Laplace," said - after explaining the system of the solar system: "The mind-boggling system seen in the movements of the bodies, which make up the solar system, can not lead to coincidence, but coincidence is an inappropriate word in the language of science. Serendipity is non-existent, and impossible in this world in which we see everything subject to the laws of the budget, the laws of calculation determined by unseen will, and extreme wisdom. And what we call coincidence, is the sum of the unseen forces, whose impact we do not know anything about, even we do not know about their existence.

While she cares about us. Accordingly, it is not possible to bring this system, which we see in the solar system, to chance. It must be recognized that there is a general organized root cause for this system[274]."

Plato said: "Where did this complete system originate in its branches, which are fraught with greatness and majesty? It can't be a coincidence. If we can say that it arose on its own, we can say that Polyklet happened on its own. If we look at the elements that the objects contain. They are so many that the mind cannot confine them, it was impossible to hold the existence of all this to coincidence. Therefore, there must be a higher mind, which is the only creator; for nature is an effect that manifests the union indicative of the oneness of the creator, who implements his judgment, as the influence of thought at once, without any fault. He is present and absent. However, it is impossible to perceive it with the senses. It is like the sun that touches all eyes. But it does not allow anyone to look at it[275]."

The American scientist Cary Morrison said in his book "Man is not alone": "My purpose in writing this book is to draw the attention of thinkers to the facts that have become possible to prove, which aim to support the belief in that organization, and indicate its purpose... The Creator is signified by infinite arrangements. Without it, life would be impossible. And that the existence of man on earth and the luxurious manifestations of his intelligence. Rather, it is part of a program carried out by the cosmologist, then he gave an example of the impossibility of chance in organizing the universe and said: "Take ten pennies, each separately, and put serial numbers on them from one to ten. Put it in your

---

[274] Islam and Imported Principles, p. 43
[275] Islam and Imported Principles p. 42

pocket and shake it tight, then try to pull it out of your pocket in order from one to ten[276]."

Field Marshal Ahmed Ezzat Pasha Al-Turki said: "It is worth mentioning that the wider the scope of science, the more the minutes and secrets of nature are revealed. The philosophy of materialism has lost its place. These men of science, who have served humanity with their scientific revelations, have the greatest services: the likes of Nutty, Pastor, and other famous sages all believe and believe in a supernatural power that is transcendent and transcendent than that of humans[277]."

The American philosopher Royce said: "The larger universe is like the smaller man, body and soul. As for the flesh, it is the world of nature, but the spirit in which it resurrects movement, and walks with it here and there, it is God[278]."

Thus, we deliberately used the same weapon, and philosophers reject philosophers and naturalists from naturalists. The surprise caused by the palace of «Marx» his belief in inanimate matter only in the hearts of believers, from the class of philosophers, sages, scientists and others, its weight is reduced, if we know - on the contrary - the emergence of another doctrine, denying the existence of matter itself.. It may notbe strange to deny the testimony of the senses. As long as the denial of the creator of the senses is more strange than it is.. Their doctrine is based on the fact that true existence is eternal immutable existence. As for the accidental existence that appears and disappears or is and perishes, it is existence and does not exist.

Mr. Abdul Karim Al-Khatib asked: «Is it an illusion for anyone to deny the material world?He replied: The truth is that he found among thinkers who deny the material world or turn this world into a faint image. All there is is is a mirage and a deception. His image of sense and body is the illusion that evaporates from people's minds, and is created from their imagination. And do notthink that this theory to the material world is the theory of the mystic, which would belittle material life and belittle every great and glorious thing in it. No, it is one of the doctrines of the materialists, who have long looked at the world of assets and turned their attention to it. They ended up despairing of winning an established truth in it. When they saw everything they got, it did notprove the case, and it never settled on a situation. "[279] He added: "The Sophist philosophers from Greece were leading this philosophy, which invalidates every truth that comes through the senses. " At the end of his presentation, he quoted the philosopher Protagoras as saying: " There is no existence independent of what is in our minds. What appears to a person to be the truth, is the truth to him. If two people differ in seeing something, what each of them sees is right for him. "

---

[276]Id., p. 45
[277]Islam and Imported Principles, p. 41
[278]Idem 42
[279]The Case for Divinity between Philosophy and Religion 1-90-91

Ibn Khaldun said: "As for the proofs they claim against their plaintiffs in the assets, and present them to the criterion of logic and its law, they are deficient and inadequate. As for what was one of those proofs of physical existence, they call it natural science. Its shortcoming is that the match between those mental results that are extracted by borders and measurements - asin their claim -and what is outside is uncertain." [280]

According to "Descartes", the issues suggested by the testimony of the senses are doubtful, [281] and after that came "Berkeley", so his disinclination to question the testimony of the senses was removed. I deny all the fields in which our senses work, such as visionaries, hearing aids, tangents, and others. He asked him to say: "Matter does notexist on the outside. Rather, we imagine that they exist. There is only the soul and the mind, and he explains: Where is what we eat, what wedrink, and whatwe wear? Where is what our handsmake and what our tongues speak? " [282] All in the estimation of the philosopher are illusions, deceptions, and illusions of dreams.

That was one of the blunders of all rational materialists and naturalists. This is a manifestation of their confusion and disorientation. What these people believed, they disbelieved in, and what another exile team proved.. Marx and his companions denied what wasbeyond the material and proved its existence by the testimony of the senses, and others denied the material itself, and invalidated everything that wasproven by the testimony of the senses, so they have not yet fallen on the existing. And that if intellectual and mental power were used in studying the manifestations of the universe, discovering the secrets of matter, its dimensions, spiritual strength, and innate qualifications in discovering the metaphysical truth, there would be none.

The problem is due to its origin -it seems - that they exceeded by reason its natural field, and the limits of its knowledge in studying the manifestations of matter, and trying to discover its secrets and deprived themselves of the human balance represented - in addition to mental strength - in the spiritual and emotional qualifications and the nature of attachment to higher ideals inherent in every human soul. It derives its guidance from the unseen. It is permissible for them to use mental force - instead of spiritual - in discovering the unseen truth, and to rule logic in issues of faith, and the realization of the unseen. This resulted in confusion in thinking, confusion above the apparent, and instability within the subconscious, as a result of falling into the arms of the disturbed material world, instead of the stable spiritual one. Because they were standing in the face of the mirror of truth and in front of the dangers of the soul, obscured by the density of matter, the darkness of the soul, and the wildness of the mind, and the flame of the subconscious fell, and the emotional feeling was obliterated, and the innate talents were extinguished.

---

[280] Introduction p. 515
[281] The Issue of Divinity between Philosophy and Religion 1/98
[282] The Issue of Divinity between Philosophy and Religion 99/1

They are then qualified to perceive the truth, and to uncover the evidence. It has been absent from their minds in the vilification of these contradictory material views that believing in a hidden existence is easier and closer to the mind than denying the viewer of material assets, and considering their existence tobe non-existent.

The philosopher "Georgias" was deciding the Greek Sophist doctrine of denying material assets, and ended up saying: "Then nothing exists" and [283] thus deciding that it does not exist in itself personally.

This is the inevitable result, to which comes the stripping of all spiritual qualifications and preparations, running after the abstract mind, obeying its hypotheses and turning in the rings of its orbit. To confirm his inability even to perceive the reality of the viewer from the physical objects that impose their existence on healthy minds, and rather to perceive the metaphysical facts in the invisible world. Shankra, one of the philosophers of India, has denied the reason to reveal any truth, whether in matter or in its sponsor. After that, the philosopher Kant affirmed that man knows from things their phenomena. As for the things themselves, they are impossible to perceive, and [284] if the luck of man is the inability to perceive the reality of the material world he comes into contact with. It may not be his position in front of the spiritual world. He is notaware of it, except what God has shown some of his servants.

The philosopher Herbert Spencer says: "Behind the natural world is an aspect impossible for man to know."[285] The philosopher Nietzsche denied all the data of the mind, because between the mind and the truth is a barrier that the mindcan never see beyond. The American philosopher Bergson [286] says: "The mind is the natural extension of our senses. Therefore, his first subject is inanimate matter, and he [287] decided that one of the most special characteristics of the mind is its natural inability to understand life. The mind perceives things from the outside in an automatic way. Instinct perceives from within in an inorganic way.

Thus, it is clear that the mental strength adopted by Marx in believing in matter and denying it, Maura Ha, has collapsed its rules, and has become for famous philosophers just a tool to try to explore and explore.... In addition, his daring to deny was not based on any scientific or logical basis, which stands in front of what has settled in the soul and has been proven by conscience, and many philosophers themselves have recognized its existence. Even if they explain the inability of the mind to realize its essence, and the impossibility of the viewer through it, because the mind in this field does nottestify knowingly, and does nottell about an eye. Rather, it bears witness to what lies in illusion, and is captured by imagination. And watching without how is only in the spirit that came down from his world.

---

[283] The Issue of Divinity between Philosophy and Religion 1/98
[284] والصفحة المصدر نفس
[285] The Case of Illusionism between Philosophy and Religion 1/96
[286] Idem 1/97
[287] Idem 1/96

Abu Bakr al-Siddiq was asked: "What did you know about your Lord? He replied: "I know my Lord, my Lord, and if it were not for my Lord, I would not know my Lord." He wants – and God knows best - that knowing the unseentruth does not make sense. but with moral extensions that descend from the world of lights to the world of objects. And the knowledge according to which it proceeds from mercy and its teacher is absenteeism, which is the Sunday of steadfastness thatmoves everything and does not move, believing the Almighty's words in the story of Moses and his girl and the righteous slave: "**They found a servant of our servants to whom we gave mercy from our side and we taught him from our side with knowledge..**" [288] Dalib Al-Yamani asked Imam Alia: Have you seen your Lord, O Commander of the Faithful? He answered, "Shall I worship him whom I do not see?" Dalib said: How do you see it? He said: "The eyes do not see: by watching the eyes, but the minds remind him of the truths of faith." Minds that are aware of the truths of faith are not dark physical minds. Rather, they are rational,enlightened moral hearts. You read the verses of the component on the pages of the universes. The Almighty says: "**Have they not traveled the earth so that they have hearts with which to reason or ears with which to hear? For they do not blind the eyes, but the hearts that are in the breasts.**"[289]

In the material mind, Professor Abdul Karim Al-Khatib says: "Humanity has conducted the mind in this field: the field of the unseen world in ancient and modern times. He did not achieve a goal, nor did he achieve a desired goal, but it became an established fact that the mind will not realize the essence of existence, whether apparent or subconscious, and that if it perceives something from the world of matter. He would only perceive certain phenomena, which loom on its surface. As for its depths and depths. The mind does not reach any of them, as it appears in successive attempts day after day in the field of scientific discoveries. As for the supernatural world, the mind is behind it in absolute helplessness[290]. "

Other than one of the philosophers, he believes that all that the mind can achieve in discovering the world beyond matter is the perception of science in it, and the belief in its existence. As for knowing and watching it, it is impossible to perceive.

In Islam, perception - at the level of charity after Islam and faith - may be the position of knowledgeable people whose feeling and conscience did not stop at the necessary commands and prohibitions. Rather, God opened their insights before their minds, purified their hearts, purified their secrets, and removed from their insides the concealment of inattention and the density of matter, so they were guided by the light oftruth to know what others were trying to realize with the power of reason, and they saw with their insights what it was impossible for rational materialists to see with their own eyes. In this, Pascal says:

---

[288] Surat Al-Kahf 65
[289] Surat Al-Hajj 46
[290] The Issue of Divinity between Philosophy and Religion 1/99

"The heart has a desire for the mind to understand it[291]."

What is more, when we return to the repeated experience, we see that the material mind is the first major obstacle in the way of spiritual departure, and the most powerful leader of the soul to fight innate nature, and obliterate the features of finding the world of the unseen, and turn off the lamps of the hearts... As he disbelieved in the prophecies of the prophets, and what comes from the owners of messages and guidance, only the recalcitrant who use their minds in the issues of the unseen instead of believing in their hearts, but did not deny the enjoyment of the divine flood enjoyed by the unsuspecting believers, and the victim of confusion, anxiety and disruption - as we noted in the life of Marx - only those whose souls were disturbed. Depending on the misery of their confused minds... It returned to them with a scourge that hides them from the truth, after it was the greatest divine grace that man relies on in the management of life, and uses it to clarify the truth and determine the evidence. Imam al-Ghazali says: "I know that the Almighty honors and generosity of this human being. He said :" **We honored the children of Adam and carried them on land and sea and provided them with good things and preferred them over many of those who created us. "It was one of the greatest honors and generosity of the mind that he inflicted on the world of angels because of him.**[292] When knowledge qualifies him as innocent and creative by looking at his creatures[293]. "

In Islam, we notice the distinction between the mental fields in the management of life and the building of civilizations.... In deriving judgments from texts, studying all legal, economic, social and other sciences, and between the spiritual outset, which depends on innate spontaneity more than on mental hypotheses. In the field of research, we see the Islamic world using mental power and intellectual energy to devise as many judgments as possible in one text, and we watch it work hard to erect mental evidence, establish logical proofs in the field of monotheism, and knock the argument with the argument in order to prove the existence of God, and correct the doctrine with his oneness, but when he tries to know who he believes, he leaves the mind in its natural field, and returns to his heart, to address the issue from within, so that he improves his spiritual conditions and works to settle accounts with the tyranny of the soul and the might of the air.. Even if his heart is cleansed and his bed is described, and his interior is strengthened beside God, God opens to him the door of his mercy, and floods him with his torrents, and he sees with the light of insight what is impossible to see with the light of sight.. Let the materialists know that the attempt to discover the material truth begins from the minds, and the journey towards discovering the metaphysical truth begins spiritually at the end of the minds' perceptions...

---

[291] Id. 1/110
[292] Surat Al-Israa 7
[293] Risālat al-Imām al-Ghazālī (The Letters of Imām al-Ghazālī), pp. 42-I

In fact, mental power is only a tool for managing life, and a means for spreading cultures and building civilizations. On it relied humanitybetween East and West, its infidels and believers, inits inventions and scientific progress. In the past, the philosophers of India erred when they realized the danger of mental power and its circumvention without subconscious passion. They tried to extinguish it with the types of infernal mathematics to look through it on things that prove our neighborhood and sometimes disappear. The Sufis are also tired of those who try to walk the path of strenuous struggle by themselves, forcing them to exaggerate asceticism, austerity, the roughness of food, clothing and housing, and the need for seclusion and isolation... Instead of turning to God inwardly, and to the lawful of the world outwardly.

The truth is that in true spiritual education and devotion to God and good observation and devotion to Him in worship, and work to purify the heart, and strengthen the interior through remembrance and recitation of the Qur 'an.. Whatcan be a guarantor of the serenity of the bed and the enlightenment of insight without affecting the grace of the mind, and without straining the soul and depriving it of the blessings of God that He created for His servants. In effect, "All things are clear, and hearts are clear, mentioning Allah." He who sees the truth is the hearts enlightened by the light of Allah.

So, what sees the truth are hearts enlightened by the light of faith, not minds mixed with matter. The American philosopher Amersen says : "Man is able to see God in the depths of his heart... If he listens to his conscience with a listening and conscious ear, he hears the voice of God in the intrusion of himself[294]. "

The outcome of the previous discussion is that the field of mind is the awareness of knowledge of the existence of God and the task of the heart is to believe in Him and then know Him. It goes without saying that the place of faith and knowledge is higher than the place of perception: because faith is a divine light that throws in the heart of the believer, and guides him to the path of goodness and guidance. Consciousness is a conviction about a logical proof, or a normal psychological feeling, such as a hungry person feeling hungry. It is more convincing than proof, because a person may lie to others andnot to himself. And the feeling is material when the material and moral when the believer. They are in the field of life, whether they are separated in faith in it orbehind it... Therefore, the old people, because of their pure instinct and the integrity of the emotional feeling, were more faithful and more stable than some materialist philosophers. If the naughty people knew what isin the faith ofspiritual pleasure and what God has bestowed on those old people of tranquility, tranquility and inner stability without which there is nohappiness, they would rush to supplication to God, saying : O God, faith is like the faith of the old people, as attributed to the caliph Omar, believing in His Almighty saying: "It **is He who sent down tranquility in the hearts of the believers**" and His [295] Almighty

---

[294] The Case of Uluhiyyah between Philosophy and Religion 1/111
[295] Al-Fath 4

saying: "**Those who believe and whose hearts are reassured by the remembrance of God, except by the remembrance of God, hearts are reassured**[296]."

All the doors are locked in the face of Marx and his companions. Neither faith in the heart nor the attempt to perceive the mind, as other philosophers have done.. That is because his philosophy is focused on believing in matter alone, and that matter in his philosophy is what highlighted the mind through friction, and the time of its existence. It is not outside of itself. but rather one of its images. The field of mind in its philosophy is the substance that created it, and controlled it. He does notseparate from her except to return ... The same applies to studying them and harnessing them for the benefit of man. It is the field around which the atheist and the believer meet, as a field common to all humanity. Thus, the life of everyone on earth depends... Logic is notopposed to helping matter to form mental power, but not then evidence of its control over it; on the contrary, we see other philosophers, including "Kicker", who decide that matter is only the result of thought, and an effect of its creation, because the mind imagines and plans the thing before its existence, and then works hard to establish its entity, as manifested in the construction of the pyramids and seen in scientific inventions and revelations today. The meaning of this theory is that it is the mind that controls matter, not matter that controls it.

This theory is supported by what was reported by international radio stations, and published by the newspaper "El Alam" on March 18, 1968, with a number of -6510 under the title "The mind controls matter". The news stated that a woman in Moscow named "Melia Mikhailova" can stop the hands of the clock, or make them spin quickly just to look at them with a sharp focus, and she can also move food and eating utensils on the table... Scholars have studied this phenomenon and they all agree that Mrs. Melia Mikhailova has a supernatural power, which is "the control of the mind over matter," and it is wonderful coincidence that this miracle appeared in Moscow, the cradle of Marxist doctrine, when he was alive..... Allah the Almighty has spoken the truth, saying: "**There are signs in the earth for those who have faith and in yourselves. Will you not then see?**" [297]

And in everything he has a verse that indicates that he is the One

The rigid material cracked down on Marxist philosophy, and all of it descended on the minds of those who professed its doctrine, and imposed it for ideological factors. From it everything branches out, and to it everything returns. It is no longer possible to be free from its laws or to feel a truth separate from it, as they feel it and its laws they feel, and by its revelation they realize. In order to fulfill it, they denied faith in what was behind it. And even in the depths of themselves,they only feel the material side. You see some of

---

[296] Surat Ar-Ra'd 28
[297] Surat Al-Dhariyat 21

them saying: "My existence is what I have achieved, but God does not know it." The existence that has been achieved is the common physical existence between the talkinganimal and the prodigal animal. As for the real human existence, if he realized it, he would attach himself to the eternal lofty meanings and become a believer in God, you see them deny the existence of God; because they do not perceive it, as they perceive material assets, and he distracted from their minds that the place of faith begins when minds are unable to perceive.

The Danish philosopher Kirk Gord says: "If you could understand God, as you realize the aether, for example, you would not believe in him. And you must believe in it, not because you are aware of it, but because you are not aware of it. "[298] This view is close to Ibn Khaldun's saying: "Monotheism is theinability to perceive the causes. "Ibn Khaldun saw close to what was narrated about Abu Bakr al-Siddiq," The inability to perceive, "and the inability to perceive watching the beloved is the awareness and belief of his existence... Ibn Khaldun further clarified the idea. He said: "Do not trust what the thought claims to you that it is able to surround beings and their causes and stand at the detail of all existence, and I will regret your opinion on that. I know that the one who is at the beginning of his opinion is confined to his perceptions and does notcount them. The same goes for the opposite. right behind him.They missed your awareness and your perceptions in the inventory.. This is not a trigger in the mind and its perceptions. Rather, reason is a true balance, but do notcovet to weigh the matters of monotheism and the Hereafter, the truth of prophecy, the truths of divine attributes, and everythingbeyond its development, for that is covetousness in impossibilities. "

Therefore, those who deny what the mind does notrealize, and drop it from the account of existence are extravagant against themselves, are unjust to the mind; for the mind is a finite creature. And the finite creature is impossible in his right to surround the world of the uncreated and the infinite...

Through the previous presentations, we clarify a lot of the natures and purposes of Marxist communism, and verify the discrepancy between its principles and the goals of the Islamic religion, which received the harshest blow from the Leninist revolution in 1917, where about two thousand mosques were closed, and about eighty thousand people lostbetween the suitor, imam, muezzin and reciter of their source of livelihood. The Islamic religion is a divine religion that came to save man from the worship of matter and its authority and to remove its chains and shackles from the control of those who control its name. To open before him distant horizons of freedom. He worked to transform his thought, doctrine, feeling and conscience from submission to those who tried to enslave him, and control his fate in exchange for a piece of bread to the belief in the living sustenance, which, if guided to his belief in everything, he dispensed with other things, and was freed from the pressure of matter and its

---

[298] The Issue of Divinity between Philosophy and Religion 102/ 1

factors and the arrogance of the tyrants in its name, and called himself to where the soul has a starting point, and the faith has authority.. This is not compatible with the ideology of the doctrine of absolute control, as it is difficult to subjugate the young person in the embrace of religion, and its freedom, and a guarantee of livelihood, and freedom from thinking about destiny, to thedictates of the men of the doctrine, to ensure the livelihood of livelihood. Thus, one of the principles for which the revolution of 1917 took place was the fight against religions.

It was mentioned in the Youth Magazine No. 18 October 1947 "Wecannot stand a neutral position on religion".[299] It was mentioned in the magazine "Pravda", which died with the death of the Communist Party - April 26, 1949. We believe in three things : "Karl Marx", "Lenin" and "Stalin". We do notbelieve in three things: "God, religion and private property" In such people, the Almighty believes the saying: "**O people, strike a parable, so listen to it. Those who pray without God will not create flies, even if they meet him, and if the flies take something away from them, they will not save him from him, the weakness of the student, and what is required, God does not appreciate the truth. God is strong and dear.**"[300]

Where are Marx, Lenin and Stalin from the famine that afflicted the peoples of the Soviet Union after its dissolution? Marx, Lenin, and Stalin had gone, achieving nothing. Neither in the material, nor in what is its sponsor.. And God is one of the steadfast... Private property returned to Russia.. Religion is advancing, and believers in God are increasing... In this regard, the philosopher William James said: "It is likely that people will reach the end of time despite what science may bring about from the opposite." The philosopher Ernest Renan said: "It is possible that everything we love will fade away, and everything we prepare from the sanctuary of life and its bliss." But it is impossible for religion to be erased[301]. "

The attempt of the communist leaders - at the beginning of the revolution and after it - was focused on erasing the religious instinct from souls and uprooting its roots, to take its place in sectarianism and communism. Efforts were initially directed at building a bridge between the goals of the party in control, between the uprising of religion and its teachings in freedom, and not recognizing the need for human beings. It is a natural clash between matter and spirit or between freedom and enslavement. In the Islamic Baath, we see the Messenger of God working to free the individual from submission to any material force, and flying him in distant horizons of freedom: freedom of belief, freedom of ownership, freedom of action, freedom of expression, freedom of self-determination, freedom of the market, freedom of production, and freedom of consumption. Let Islam lift the stone from individuals, and subconsciously eliminate each other's control. All of them commented on the Almighty Ali, to whom only they feel

---

[299] Muslim Peoples in the Soviet Union p.104 Their Socialism and Our Islam p.51
[300] Surat Al-Hajj 72
[301] The Issue of Divinity between Philosophy and Religion 1/4

equal, and do not need others, bearing in mind his Almighty saying: «**Everyone who is on it is the face of your Lord with majesty and honor**» and the Prophet's saying from Al-Tirmidhi's novel: «**If the Ummah gathered to benefit you with something, they did not benefit you except with something that God has written for you, and if they gathered to harm you with something, they did not harm you except with something that God has written for you.**»[302] The pens have been lifted and the pages have dried.

The life of man, the strength of his personality, his rights, and the honor honored by God by saying: «And we have honored the children of Adam» is not achieved by eating, drinking, clothing and housing... which Islam imposed on the owner of the beast. And if it is damaged, [303] as Ibn Qudamah said, and Musa al-Hijjawi said in her regard: "If my father is or is incapacitated, the righteous ruler will act and accept him" [304] in her favor. Rather, positive individual freedoms and moral and voluntary elements are achieved... It is the nationalized and taboo aspect of Marxist doctrine. In this regard, Stalin said: "Let me make it clear to you frankly that the communist regime does notbelieve in individual freedom. Individual freedom means the elimination of the group, it means deviating from obedience to the law, and it means deviating from Marxism. This kind of freedom, that is, individual freedom, is the most dangerous threat to a regime. " He said in absolute control, and the hellish dictatorship: " Literature, arts and sciences must be weapons in the hands of the party. Through the party's control of literature, we can raise people's feelings, and through the control of the arts, we can control their tastes. By controlling science, we can control their behavior... Public opinion should be a mere reflection of our principles, opinions and behavior. "

In the confiscation of religious doctrine, Lenin says in his total works on socialism: "Religion is the opium of peoples and religion is a kind of spiritual wine in which the servants of capital drown their human form... The fight against religion shouldnot be limited to abstract doctrinal proselytism. This struggle must be linked to the movement of classes and its goal must be to uproot the social roots of religion. "[305] The year - 1927 - after the success of the revolution : "Now, we openly declare that we are atheists. We see in religions a threat to human civilization. Religions are opium[306]. "

Lenin explained fighting religion as the opium of the people. Capitalists drown in it their human form, and that it is a danger to human civilization. In Islamic reality, the argument is the opposite. The slaves of capital from the greats of Mecca are the ones who fought the Islamic call when it appeared, and chased the Prophet and his companions everywhere for its sake. History testifies that the Arabs on their island were drugged with the opium of ignorance and

---

[302] Surat Ar-Rahman 27
[303] Singer 7/135 by Ibn Qudamah
[304] Ibn Qudamah al-Iqnā' fī Fiqh al-Imām Aḥmad 155/2 by Musa al-Hijāwī
   [305] Muslim Peoples in the Soviet Union 104
     [306] Their Socialism and Our Islam, p. 50

superstition. They crouched before physical images that had worshippers for centuries, until Islam came and awakened their enthusiasm, and breathed into them the spirit of work, and the spirit of life. Theystayed but a little. So, for the first time in history, they crossed the borders of their arid island and rushed towards the countries of the world. They establish countries and civilizations... History repeats itself. The Arabs return to the same fate, if the Islamic religion has no influence and no authority.

And about the word capital slaves. In the sense of matter, we wonder: Is there a difference between matter in one form and matter in another? And about worship in the sense of submission, we wonder: Who is right? Are the believers who submit to the one who created man and created matter for him, or the Marxists who submit to the creature for matter, as manifested in their saying "We believe in three things: Karl Marx, Lenin and Stalin andwe do not believe in three things: God, religion and private property"...

They are, with or without feeling, submissive worshippers, but worshippers of people and drugged, but with love of matter and drunkenness but with love of control, fighting an instinct, mixed with their souls, and rooted in their feeling, so I deviated from them by worshipping God the right to submit to matter and to matter alone. People do not know that the instinct of worship is divine luck in every human soul. Whether it is used in what was created for him, or thrown by the tyranny of the soul, and turned it from its natural course into the worship of material things **that are also considered the work of God and the truth of Almighty God. "Everyone in the heavens and the earth except the Most Merciful comes as a slave. He counted them and promised them except**[307].

And that if we analyze any human soul, we will find among its original compounds the nature of worship. In the sense of undergoing something... It's an inherent emotional instinct... God created her in every human soul, to act in submission to him, and to achieve slavery for him. There is nothing material about His creation, as is understood from the words of the Prophet PBUH : "Woe to Abd al-Dinar,woe to Abd al-Dirham," but if we take a closer look, and look in general at the Almighty's saying: "I **did not create the jinn and mankind except** to worship," that is, to submit to one of the opinions, we would see in the innate qualifications, which are born with every human soul, whether Muslim, Jewish, Christian or Magian, a very clear expression of the noble purpose for which man was created, and we would be convinced thatworship in the sense of submission is a field common to all people. By the grace of true faith, some of them were pleased with God's guidance on the way of the apostles and their followers to worship the true God, and others were misled. The opportunity for guidance was lost, and they erred in the ways of guidance. Their insistent instinct of devotion led them to satisfy their insatiable desire to submit to static or moving material things. Itis not appropriate for the honorable status of man or his spiritual, intellectual and moral status... It is submission to matter,

---

[307]Maryam 94

instead of submission to its Creator, and an emotional worship that does notdifferentiate in nature between the one who is the god of inanimate objects, and prostrating to idols, idols, the sun, fire and cows. Norbetween Abdul Dinar and Dirham... Notbetween what God said in his regard, "**Have you seen who has taken his God as his whim?**" Norbetween who has submitted to matter and the God of the group, as Marx did, "as Abdul Karim al-Khatib said: " He deifies the group after he denies God[308]. "

Lenin once wrote to the great Russian writer Mikseem Gorky, "You have no God because you have not yet created him. The gods do notseek it, but they do. "This statement [309] reminds us of the words of the caliph Umar ibn al-Khattab:"One of us is in ignorance to make his god of food so that if hunger harms him, hewill eat it. "The gods in ignorance make food, and Lenin's time is made of iron. Everything is material, and everyone needs it and it is necessary.. The sophisticated gods, made in the Soviet Union, were sold after its dissolution, and their price turned into food. Food is more useful for the hungry than nuclear arsenal....

---

[308] The Issue of Divinity between Philosophy and Religion 1/83
[309] Islam and Imported Principles, p. 18

LEGITIMACY OF ISLAMIC CONTRACT COMPANIES

Contract companies, or contracts, are companies that rely on a legitimate contract that falls between two onwards. They are five: Mudaraba and Loans Company, Anan Company, Faces Company, Negotiation Company, and Business Company. All of them are permissible to act [310] with disagreement between imams in other than speculation and unleashing.

By focusing on the contract, the money companies come out. The funds here do notmean the funds in which the disposal takes place under the contract, as is the case with the capital of Mudaraba and Anan. Rather, it means the common property of a group or sect, such as participation in the money of the estate or the booty before its division. It is known to some as the compulsory company, as it forces each individual to hold on and not to act until he knows his share. The Prophet (peace and blessings of Allaah be upon him) forbade the sale of spoils until they [311] were divided. Abu al-Walid Hisham bin Abdullah bin Hisham inferred from them by saying: "So send **one of you with this paper to Medina.**" He said: "**This is the company of money.**"[312][313]

The money company, unlike the contract companies, imposed itself on the partners without choosing from them. Their installations within it are regulated by Sharia laws. There is no room for action. This is before the department. If it is formed by agreement afterwards, it is transformed into contract partnerships, which guarantees rights and eliminates the causes of conflict between brothers in God and the mercy of God.

Ibn Qudamah and Ibn Dhuwayan have inferred the legitimacy of the company by breaking the shin and the silence of the RA or the opening of the first and the breaking of the second [314] by saying the Almighty: «**And there is a lot of confusion to seek each other, except for those who believe and do righteous deeds and few of them**»[315]. It is fixed in the Qur 'an, the Sunnah, and the consensus, as they stated about the doctrine of Imam Ahmad. Ibn Qudamah explained the confusion with partners, and said after reviewing the evidence: Muslims unanimously agreed on the[316] company's passport. "It is a unanimous award. Ibn al-Mundhir mentioned him and narrated her permission from Omar, Uthman, Ali, Ibn Mas 'ud, and Hakim Ibn Hizam in famous stories, there is no contradiction to them, so it is unanimous[317]."

---

[310] Manār al-Sabīl fī Sharḥ al-Dalīl 'alá Madhhab al-Imām ibn Ḥanbal 398/1
[311] Sahih Al-Tirmidhi 58/7 Sunan Al-Nasa 'i 301/2
[312] Surat Al-Kahf 19
[313] Beneficial to the Ruler in what is presented to them of the **rules and rulings, p. 102**
[314] **Pathways to Peace 62/ 3**
[315] Surah 23
[316] Singer 1/ 5
[317] Manār al-Sabīl fī sharḥ al-Dalīl 'alá Madhhab al-Imām Aḥmad ibn Ḥanbal 400/1

In the eyes of Ibn Qudamah, and Musa al-Hijjawi, it means meeting in the merit of disposition and in the "Book of Fiqh on the four schools" that it confuses one of the owners with the other. The expression goes to the company of Anan, where money and work are on both sides.

As for the Sunnah, Abu Dawud, al-Bayhaqi and al-Hakim narrated and corrected it about Abu Hurairah that the Prophet (peace and blessings of Allah be upon him) said: Allah says: "I am the third of the partners unless they betray one another. If he betrayed him, I went out betweenthem[318]. "

As for the two truths about Abu al-Manhal, he said: "I and my partner bought a hand in hand and a mischief, so Al-Baraa bin Azeb came to us, and we asked him, and he said: I did this with my partner Zaid bin Arqam, and the Prophet asked us about it, and he said: "Whatwas hand in hand, take it, and itwas not in mischief, so leave it. "

Musallam, Al-Nasa 'i, and Al-Tirmidhi narrated from Jabir bin Abdullah Al-Ansari that the Messenger of Allah (peace and blessings of Allah be upon him) said: "Whoever has a partner in a quartet or a palm tree, it is not permissible for him to sell until his partner's permission, so if he is satisfied, he takes it[319], and if he hates it, he leaves." Al-Bukhari, commenting on Abdul Rahman bin Al-Aswad, said: "I used to share with Abdul Rahman Ibn Yazid in sowing[320]."

Imam Ahmad, Abu Dawood, Ibn Majah and Al-Bayhaqi narrate that he was the partner of the Prophet (peace and blessings of Allah be upon him) in Ignorance. On the day of the conquest, he addressed him by saying, "Welcome my brother and partner." In the novel of Ibn Majah and others, he said, "Welcome my brother and partner... I was my partner in Ignorance and I was the best partner, Iwas neither amanager nor a practitioner. "[321]However, Muhammad bin Ismail Al-Sanani said: " He was the partner of the Prophet, peace be upon him, in the beginning of Islam in trade. When it was the day of the conquest, he said: "Welcome to my brother and my partner, who was neithera manager nor a mariner." [322] Commenting on the text, he said: "The hadith is evidence that the company was fixed before Islam, and then the Sharia decided on whatit was."

The company was established by the Book, the Sunnah, and the consensus, and known to the Prophet and his companions. If the jurists divide them into joint stock companies in the origin of their ownership and into contract companies subject to the requirements of the contract, what is intended to be clarified and defined in this research is contract companies, and we start with the speculation and loan company for its importance.

---

[318]**Sunan Abu Dawud 348/3 Grand Sunan 78/6 Ways of Peace 62/3**
[319]Muslim: Father's copy 4/306 Sahih Al-Tirmidhi 51/6 Sunan Al-Nasa 'i 301/7
[320]Al-Bukhari: Fath Al-Bari copy - 408/5-I - 1378AH - 1959AD
[321]Sunan Ibn Majah 23/2 Grand Sunan 78/6 Zad al-Maad 41/1
[322]Pathways to Peace 62/ 3

Ruling on Mudaraba and Lenders Company, its Pillars and Conditions

RULING

Mudaraba is the language of the people of Iraq, and Al-Qarad is the language of the people of the H They are in one sense. It is said that his hitter is a speculator, and he loaned him a loan and a loaner, if he pays him money to be traded in it with a common part of his profit.

The meaning of speculation is taken from striking at the ground, and walking in its shoulders, in order to seek the grace of God by trading on its back. This is what the Almighty means: "**He knew that some of you would be sick and others would strike in the ground, seeking from the grace of God.**" He said: "**If you strike in the ground, you do not have a wing to exclude from prayer.**" It was said that it was taken from beating in money in the sense of disposition, with the intention of trading in it. Muhammad al-Amir al-Sanani said: "**It is called speculation taken from beating in the ground, because the profit was often earned by traveling, or from beating in money.**"[323][324] which is to act[325]. "

The meaning of the loan is taken from the loaner in the sense of the boycott, from the mouse loan of the garment, if he cuts it, as the lord of money cuts off a piece of his money to the worker to work in it with a share of his profit as explained by Ibn Qadamah, [326] which – as the meaning of speculation - is permissible in Sharia. In it, Ibn Rushd says: "There is no dispute among Muslims about the permissibility of loans and that what was in the pre-Islamic era was approved by Islam[327]."

The Hanbalis defined speculation as a contract on the company in profit with money from one side, and work from the other, and the Hanbalis defined it as the owner of the money to pay a certain amount to those who trade in a known part of his profit and the Malikis [328] defined it as a power of attorney issued by the Lord of money to others, provided that he trades in his money[329].

The contractis not without either between two or more money lords, and between the worker or employees... The contract of the Mudaraba company, as it was signed between joint funds, before it falls on the funds and the work, or it falls between the owner of the money and the worker, so it is called by some a pure Mudaraba contract. The worker is an agent of the lord of money, and does not turn into a partner, until the profit they share appears, because these people consider that the company falls between the funds.

---

[323] Al-Muzzammil 20
[324] Surat Al-Nisaa 100
[325] Pathways to Peace 75/ 3
[326] Singer 22/5
[327] The Beginning of the Diligent 233/2
[328] Persuasion in the jurisprudence of Imam Ahmad 259/2
[329] The Book of Jurisprudence on the Four Madhhabs 38/3

But what appears from the definition of Hanifa is "a contract on a company in profit, it is a start-up company contract. This is what is understood by Sahnoun's statement about Ibn al-Qasim, that the company may not be without money from one of the partners, [330] his concept is that it is a company that is rewarded with money from one of them and work from the other, especially since there is a company of money, and a business company and the combination of them is a company between money and work, and the rule is that what is permissible separately is permissible collectively, so what they called pure speculation is a company. This is what Ibn Qudamah decides, as he said: «All that is permissible in the company is permissible in speculation, and what is permissible in speculation is permissible in the company, and what is forbidden in one is prohibited in the other, because speculation is a company» and [331] Qadi Ibn Asim means in the masterpiece of the rulers as he says:

A company in which money or work is permitted, not for the sake of the Prophet who worked in Khadija's money with the bulk of the makhzoumi: «I was my partner and I was the best partner» Evidence that money from one person and work from the other – or with his business partner - is a company, evidenced by the fact that it occurred between two people: the Messenger and Khadija. From its money to the Levant, some scholars extracted the legitimacy of the speculative and loan company.

In its origin, Ibn Majah narrated only under the "Chapter of Mudaraba Company" that the Prophet (peace and blessings of Allah be upon him) said: There are three blessings in it: selling for a time, speculating, and mixing righteousness with barley for the house, not for sale. "[332]But in his title, Saleh bin Suhaib, his talk about Al-Aqili is not preserved, and when Al-Bukhari is unknown, they saw that it is one of the legislation established unanimously.

In that, Muhammad al-Amir al-Sanani quotes Ibn Hazm as saying: "All the gates of jurisprudence have an origin from the Book and the Sunnah. We did not find him originally in the Sunnah, but he is unanimous, and he cuts that he was in the era of the Prophet, and he knew about it and approved it."

Ibn Hazm says that he did not find an origin for the loans in the year at a time when he proved that he was in the era of the Prophet and approved it, and that the Messenger made a speculation in the money of Khadija. Knowing that the reports of the Prophet PBUH and his work are of the Sunnah. As for the Qur'an, it seems that trading in the money of the helpless and others is included in the Almighty's saying: «Others strike in the ground seeking from the grace of God» and from it he took the word speculation. Speculation is lending, and lending is speculation. as manifested in the uses of scholars.

---

[330] The Great Code of Maliki Jurisprudence 22/ 4
[331] Singer 46/ 5
[332] Sunan Ibn Majah 23/2 Paths of Peace 75/3

Ibn al-Qayyim said: "The Prophet (peace and blessings of Allah be upon him) has approved speculation on what it was before Islam, so he beat his companions in his life and after his death, and the Ummah unanimously agreed on it." Ibn Qudamah[333] said about Ibn Mas 'ud and Hakim bin Hizam: "They are opponents and there is no contradiction between them in the companions, so he made a consensus[334]."

Ibn Hazm himself used both words, and analyzed the idea with economic and jurisprudential importance, but in a way that does not agree with his opinion of its origin, he said: "The loan was in ignorance, and the Quraysh were the people of trade. They do not have apension from others. Including the old sheikh, whocan not bear to travel, the woman, the young, the orphan, the jobless and the sick... They give money speculation to those who trade it for a certain part of the profit, so the Messenger of Allah (peace and blessings of Allah be upon him) acknowledged this in Islam, and the Muslims did a certain work with it. Undisputed. Had there been a disagreement in it, he would not have paid attention to it, because he transferred all from all dimensions to the time of the Messenger of Allah, peace and blessings of Allah be upon him, and informed him of this. He went out in Khadija's money[335]."

Hence, the importance of the speculation and loan company, and its role in moving the wheels of economic life, and promoting the development of social wealth, which did not give its owners the physical or intellectual ability or economic experience to invest directly, especially since trade is travel and presence. Many groups of the kind mentioned by Ibn Hazm are in need of someone to grow their wealth. The Prophet (peace and blessings of Allaah be upon him) says, "Anyone who is an orphan has wealth, so let him trade in it, and do notleave it, until charity eats him."[336]

Ibn Qudamah says in the subject: "People need speculation, dirhams and dinars do notdevelop, except by stirring and trade, and not everyone who owns them improves trade, nor everyone who improves trade has capital, so I need it on both sides, so God Almighty legislated it to pay for both needs." [337]

The non-implementation of the Islamic economic system in indirect investment has left a vacuum, which sees that usurious banks fill it, and it is considered one of the justifications for its existence and is blocked by the system of Mudaraba and Loans Company, and Islamic banks based on its approach, as it is the one that gives money to promote it with a share of its profit. Promoted in trade, industry, agriculture or livestock breeding... All are permissible, and they

---

[333] Notification of Signatories 16/ 4
[334] Singer 23/ 5
[335] Local 8/247
[336] Sahih Al-Tirmidhi 136/3 Grand Sunan 22/6 Crown of the Collector of the Origins in the Hadiths of the Prophet 22/2-I-3 - 1971/by Ali Mansour, Progress
[337] Singer 23/ 5

are included in the system of Mudaraba and Lending Company. As long as its capital is commercial and its system is the system of the commercial company.

ITS PILLARS

The pillars of the Mudaraba company: The contract in the affirmative or its equivalent, the acceptance or its equivalent, the two contracts, the capital [338] and the work, and how to divide the profit. [339]It is held in the terms of Mudaraba and Qarad or what is in their meaning. It is [340] required for the owner of the money to be permissible to dispose of his property, and like him the worker, because he is his agent, and a disposer with his permission, and whoever prevents the disposal of his property with a stone or otherwise, it is prohibited to dispose of the property of others.

TERMS

1- The capital shall be of the two currencies, or what takes their place in dealing and authorizing itshall be more expensive with money [341] as permitted by the offers denominated in both sides[342] if it is of two or more or with money on one side [343] and shall be null and void without being denominated for ignorance of the capital.

2-The capital must be present with the owner at the time of the contract. It is not valid with mortgaged or extorted money, nor with the debt owed by the worker, nor with the deposit under his hand until he repays it or receives the debt,[344] except that Imam Shafi 'i and Imam Ahmed have allowed speculation in the deposit with the permission of its owner. In it, Ibn Qudamah said - commenting on the words of al-Kharqi: If he has a deposit in his hand, he may say: strike with it - "The deposit belongs to the Lord of Money, so it is permissible for him to strike with it against it, as if it were present," and the 345 permission and acceptance of trafficking is tantamount to its return.

---

[338]Pathways to Peace 75/ 3
[339]The Book of Jurisprudence on the Four Madhhabs 38/3, The Beginning of the Diligent 250/2
[340]Singer 22/5
[341]The beginning of the diligent 235/ 2
[342]Faculties in Matters under Work in the Maliki Doctrine, p. 120 by Ibn Ghazi
[343]Al-Mufīdī for the rulers in it is presented to them from the verses and rulings, p. 102 - Hishām ibn 'Abd Allāh ibn Hishām
[344]Singer 68/ 5
[345]Kitāb al-Fiqh ʻalá al-Madhāhib al-Arba'

3- That the property is known in a certain amount and value. Do not wake up in the unknown, such as saying : Beat what is in this bag [346]while he is ignorant of it.

4- To pay the money to the worker in the event of the contract, and the delay ruins it. If some attend and some are absent, delay the work until it meets, and if the initiation occurs before its meeting, divide the profit over the present, without the absentee[347].

5-The capital shall not be guaranteed by the worker, unless it is excessive, infringing or contrary to a permissible condition. The lord of money stipulated it and accepted it. In one of these cases it is guaranteed, and in the other it is notguaranteed .[348]

6- The worker's share in the profit shall be known in proportion, such as half,one-third or one-quarter... Common in every trade money. If it is not known and common, the contract shall be voided, as it does notfall on an unknown person, or whatcauses the worker to be deprived, as if the profit occurred in some, without some.

7- That noone of the owner of the money and the worker shall be entitled to anything in excess of his appointed share in the profit. If the worker stipulates a wage in excess of the agreed percentage, except for what will come at his expense, or the owner of the money stipulates something that he has jurisdiction over, or makes the share of one of them a dirham known in amount, or with his share a dirham known as half and ten dinars, the contract is corrupted [349] for violating the laws of the company, and the profit cannot exceed what the owner of the money stipulates, so he has jurisdiction over it, or what the worker stipulates, so he has jurisdiction over it or not at all, so the worker requests it from the capital.

8- That the worker is competent to start the work, without the Lord of Money, and the Hanbalis allow to work, if it is not a condition of the Lord of Money, but other than the Lord of Money, it is permissible to enter into the work, and take his share in the profit.[350]

9- That the owner of the money does notstrike the worker for a term, because of the damage he may cause, as he may see the profit in leaving the sale of the commoditybeyond the term, so he is forced to sell [351]unlike Abu Hanifa.[352]

---

[346]Manār al-Sabīl fī sharḥ al-Dalīl 'alá Madhhab al-Imām Aḥmad 401
[347]The Jurist's Book on the Four Madhhabs 82/3
[348]Persuasion in the jurisprudence of Imam Ahmad 259/2 Beginning of the Diligent 234/2
[349]Singer 48/ 5
[350]Muwatta Imam Malik 347/3
[351]Singer 63/ 5
[352]The Beginning of the Diligent 236/2

10- That the master of money does not restrict the worker in his work, such as saying to him: Do nottrade except in the summer, and the Hanafi allowed to be restricted to one of the seasons such as the season of dates.[353]

If he loses one of these conditions, the contract is corrupt, and the Lord of Capital has his capital with theapparent profit, because he has grown his money and the [354]worker has a wage like him or a loan like him in a dispute between the imams. The difference is that the lease is worth it. Even of capital and lending,he deserves it only in profit 355 as it will come.

---

[353]Kitāb al-Fiqh 'alá al-Madhāhib al-'Arba'
[354]Manār al-Sabīl fī sharḥ al-Dalīl 'alá Madhhab al-Imām Aḥmad 401
[355]Beginning of the Diligent 240/2

THE FOUNDATIONS OF ITS FORMATION: WHAT IS THE LORD OF MONEY AND THE WORKER, AND WHAT IS NOT ONE OF THEM OVER THE OTHER

FOUNDATIONS OF ITS FORMATION

It is valid to establish a company between a Muslim and a foreigner, between men and women, and between women among them [356] if - between a Muslim and a foreigner - the requirements of the Sharia provisions are observed, and it does not fall on the taboo, and the act is in the hands of a Muslim or in his presence, so that the foreigner is not alone and deals with usury or other prohibited transactions.[357]

The Prophet participated with the Jews in the lands of Khyber, which is considered by the land speculation company, such as speculation with money, as it is in money, in order to participate in profit and land in order to participate in production. In it, Ibn al-Qayyim, speaking of the communion between the Prophet and the Jews in Khaybar, said: "Out of participation. It is the counterpart of speculation as well. Mudaraba profits, and it is free. He made a distinction between two symmetries[358]."

In the participation of the Prophet PBUH to the Jews, Al-Bukhari narrates under "the door of the participation of Dhimmi and the polytheists in the sharecropping" about Ibn Umar, he said: "The Messenger of Allah, may God's peace and blessings be upon him, gave the Jews the Khaybar to do it and plant it, and they have the condition of whatcomes out of it.[359]

Thus, it becomes clear that dealing with foreigners is permissible in Sharia. In addition to participating in the planting, Al-Bukhari, Muslim, Al-Nasa 'i, and Al-Bayhaqi narrated from Aisha: "The Messenger of Allah, may Allah's peace and blessings be upon him, bought food from a Jew for a term and mortgaged it with an iron shield."[360]

Al-Tirmidhi mentioned in the "Muhammadan Qualities" that the name of the Jew is Abu al-Shahm al-Ansari from Aws. His account about the amount of food[361] stated that he is twenty and Ibn Majah that he is thirty[362] and with the [363] participation of the Prophet to the Jews in the lands of Khaybar, Ibn Hazm inferred that it is permissible for a Muslim to participate in dhimmi [364] and what is permissible between a Muslim and a foreigner.

---

[356] The Great Blog in Maliki Jurisprudence 27/4
[357] Local 8/125
[358] Returned increased 143/2
[359] Al-Bukhari Al-Fateh Version 60/ 6
[360] Al-Bukhari: Al-Fath 206/5 Muslim, Al-Ibbi 295/4 Sunan Al-Nasa 'i 7/303, Al-Sunan Al-Kubra 19/6
[361] Al-Shama 'il al-Muhammadiyyah, pp. 174-173
[362] Sahih Al-Tirmidhi 5/219
[363] Sunan Ibn Majah 2/44
[364] Local 8/125

especially between the Prophet and the Jews and polytheists. They are the ones about whom God addressed him by saying: "Let the most hostile people find you the ones who believed in the Jews and those who associated with them." [365] It is worthy of being allowed between him and the Christians. They are the ones who addressed him about them by saying: "Let the closest of them find affection for those who have believed, who said that we are Christians, that some of them are priests and monks and that theyare not arrogant.[366]" Rather, it is permissible between a Muslim and a Muslim, between a Muslim and a Muslim, and between a Muslim and a Muslim.

It is at a time when Roman law considers that a woman, like a boy, is notentitled to act, and French [367]law states that she is not qualified to contract, except with the permission of her husband,[368] we see that Islamic law has lifted all kinds of quarantine from her, and authorized her to act in full. She had the right to manumission, mortgage, gift and charity, the right to buy and sell, the right to speculate, as Khadija did with the Prophet, peace be upon him, the right to contribute to the establishment of companies, with men or with women among them, and the [369] right to conclude and terminate contracts. Scholars of Islamic jurisprudence decide that a rational woman has the right to recite all contracts herself, and to delegate whoever she wishes. Indeed, Malikiyah allowed her to be a will and a proxy. [370]In general, she has the right to act without her husband's permission. Al-Bayhaqi narrated from the crepe of Mawla Ibn Abbas that Maimouna, the daughter of Al-Harith, freed a newborn for her, without asking the Messenger of Allah, peace be upon him, [371] but what we know in speculation is that a woman gives money to a man to work in it with a share of his profit, as Khadija did with the Messenger, peace be upon him, and we did not know a man who gave it to a woman. And if we know that a woman trades her capital, as did the tribe of Umm Bani Anmar during the era of the Prophet, peace be upon him, Sunan Ibn Majah 12/2.

WHAT IS THE LORD OF THE WORLD AND WHAT IS NOT HIS

The master of money has rights over the worker, just as the worker has rights over the master of money. Among the rights of the capitalist over the worker:

1-To designate the place of trafficking, such as Mecca and Medina, and to be prevented from a certain country, such as Haifa and Talbab in order to preserve his money.

---

[365]Surat Al-Ma'idah 82
[366]The same aya and number
[367]Mohammed Al-Mathal Al-Kamil, p. 267
[368]Mohammed Al-Mathal Al-Kamil, p. 267
[369]Al-Mudawwana al-Kubra fi al-Fiqh al-Maliki 28
[370]Islamic Thought and Evolution p. 24
[371]Grand Sunnah 159/6

2 - To determine the type of trade that he wants, such as clothes and grains, or does not want, such as vegetables and eggs, to pay the reasons for the loss.

3- To appoint the persons with whom he wishes or does not wish to deal, and on the persons the companies are measured. Consideration is based on experience in good and bad treatment.

4- To prevent the sale at an uncollected price, since it is possible for the capital to be converted into debts, some of which are difficult to repay.

5- To prohibit travel with his money at all or at sea, in order to avoid danger or high expenses.

6 - To restrict work, with a season of seasons, as the season of grain, as provided at the tap to take advantage of the opportunity to expect profit.

7-To prevent taking his money to a frightening country, such as a country of war, or taking it on an unsafe road. This was due to terrorism, road blocking or prohibition of passage, in order to prevent the causes of damage.

On the subject of these rights, which come in the form of conditions, Musa Al-Hijawi says about the doctrine of Imam Ahmed: "It is correct to stipulate that he does not trade in a type of goods or a specific country, orsells only in cash, or does not travel with money, or does notsell orbuy only with someone372."

If the worker violates one of the conditions that the owner of the property has the right to stipulate, he shall be considered an infringer and a guarantor of the property. He has the right to impose a condition, which is not in his favor, or he is unable to fulfill it, and the contractfalls only on mutual consent.

It has been erred by those who believe that deposits are guaranteed in the usurious bank, and risk capital in the speculative and loan company, crystallized in the Islamic bank and illusion that their owners put them at risk. In fact, bank deposits are guaranteed by their interest on the supposed account, and the visions of the Islamic commercial capital are guaranteed conditionally, and with successful and safe precautionary methods. The legislator of the Islamic economy, did not overlook this aspect, in order to see it as an advantage of theusurious bank.

Al-Bayhaqi and Aldar narrated cotton, while Al-Hafiz Ibn Hajar adopted it in "Bulgh al-Maram in the hadiths of judgments" and said: His men are confident, about the companion Hakim bin Hizam that he stipulates that a man, if he gives him speculative money: "Do notput my money in a wet liver, do notcarry it in a sea, and do notland it in a liquefied belly. If you do anything, I have guaranteed my money." They[373] were conditions that correspond to the conditions of his time, and each age has conditions and conditions that require it.

---

[372]Persuasion in the jurisprudence of Imam Ahmad 257/2

[373]Sobel al-Salam 51/3 Manar al-Sabeel in explaining the evidence of the doctrine of Imam Ahmed 402/1

In a similar way, Al-Bayhaqi narrates from Ibn Abbas, that his father Al-Abbas, the uncle of the Prophet, peace be upon him, if he paid speculative money, he stipulated that his companion should not take a sea with it, nor take down a valley with it, norbuy a wet liver with it. If he does, he is a guarantor, and he raised his condition to the Prophet, so he approved it[374]. "

Animal mortality, sea hazards, and flood losses are the foreseeable risks in the event of legislation. The owners of capital must take care and stipulate everything that pays the risk for their money, in order to ensure its existence, in front of the guarantee of bank deposits... Islamic legislation has laid the foundations for its preservation.

8- If the speculative money is stolen or extorted, the owner of the money shall have the right to claim and litigate for the worker, if he is absent, and if he leaves the claim and litigation. At a time when he stopped, he was his guarantor. Because he lost it by neglecting it. If its owner attends, he is entitled to defend his property, and the worker is not obliged to request it, nor to guarantee[375] it, as it is notguaranteed unless he exceeds, excessive, or violates one of the permissible conditions included in the agreement between them.

These were some of the rights or conditions prescribed by the various doctrines of the Lord of Money for the worker, and he is notentitled to:

1 It may not stipulate that dealingis only with a specific person, or limited to a specific commodity. Malik and Al-Shafi 'i prevented him, because of the narrowing of the field of work and was authorized by Imam Ahmed and Abu Hanifa, based on the requirements of the permissibility of the condition and the right to refuse and accept. The subject is a subject of dispute between the imams, as conveyed [376] by Ibn Rushd and confirmed by Ibn Qudamah, and [377] even today we notice thosewho trade only in love, clothes, or a special type of tools.

2- He may not stipulate trading in something that exists at one time, and loses another, because of what may affect the course of profit. It is similar to the requirement to deal with a specific person or to be limited to a specific commodity. Malik and Al-Shafi 'i prevented him, and Abu Hanifa authorized him for his commitment to the principle of the permissibility of the condition, and the right not to accept it.

On the opinion of Malik and Al-Shafi 'i, Ibn Qudamah says: They said: If the condition is to buy only from a specific man, a specific commodity, or something that does not exist, such as rubies and gloomy horses, it is not correct, because it prevents the intent of speculation. It is the flipping and the demand for profit. "[378]However, Ibn Qudamah approved it according to Abu Hanifa, and

---

[374]Grand Sunnah 111/6
[375]Singer 50/ 5
[376]The Beginning of the Diligent 236/2
[377]Singer 62/ 5
[378]Singer 62/ 5

he saw that it does notprevent profit, but rather reduces it. The worker may notaccept a condition that is not in his favor.

3- He may not condition the purchase on debt, as it may notbe theequivalent of the capital and the worker is drawn into his problems.

4- He may not stipulate working with the worker. Malik, Al-Shafi 'i, Al-Awza 'i, Abu Thawr and the opinion-makers prevented him, and Imam Ahmad authorized him, if it was not a condition [379] and the dispute related to the Lord of Capital taking his work - in addition to the percentage allocated in the profit to the capital - his share in the percentage allocated to work. As for volunteering and helping, I did not see who prevented him.

5-He may not stipulate anything in excess of his share in the profit, as provided in the speculation conditions, and if he signs, the contract shall be void.

6- He may not require the worker to guarantee the money, or bear the loss or some of it, and if he signs, the contract is corrupt with Malik, Al-Shafi 'i, Abu Hanifa [380] and Imam Ahmad, and a narration about Malik that the contract is valid and the condition is void. In this, the son of his foot says: "When the speculator's condition is to guarantee money, or between them the inferiority, the condition is void and the contract is valid. Do we not know there is a disagreement? It was stipulated by Ahmed, which is the saying of Abu Hanifa and Malik, and it was narrated about Ahmed that the contract is corrupted by him."[381]

The result is that the contract is corrupted while the condition remains, and it is valid with its nullity. What Ibn Qudamahmentioned about Imam Ahmed from his corruption in the first place is notin line with his statement: «We do not know otherwise, and it is known that the Lord of money deserves to profit by bearing the loss, and that the worker does notguarantee, unless he exceeds orexcessive, or violates one of the permissible conditions accepted by him, and the requirement to guarantee money or bear the loss is one of the prohibited conditions, and therefore there is no guarantee and does notbear the loss.

7- He may not require the worker to pay Zakat of the Mudaraba capital, as Zakat of the capital and what he deputizes for in profit is due to **its owner**. [382]In it, Ibn Rushd said in the introductions: The scholars agreed - as far as I know- that the capital of the loans, and the share of the Lord of Capital in the profit, is recommended to the owner of the Lord of Capital, and in the "Grand Code" of Maliki jurisprudence, "It is notpermissible for the Lord of Capital to require the worker to give zakat of the money of the loans, and it is permissible for him to

---

[379] Ibid., p. 25/5
[380] Beginning of the Diligent 236/2 Book of Jurisprudence on the Four Madhhabs 55/3
[381] Singer 62/ 5
[382] Introductions 255/ 1

require the zakat of the profit, and the worker may also require the Lord of Capital to pay his zakat, that is, the profit[383]."

In fact, we – in profit - are ignorant of the inference in the permissibility of requiring the Lord of Capital or the worker to pay his zakat to his partner, as long as zakat is a personal worship that must be paid by the Muslim in his possession. The scholars of the Maliki doctrine differed:

Is it on the owner of the money or in the money of speculation, or in the money of speculation with his profit, or is it considered an expense, and the account does not fall on it?[384] It is the novel of Ibn Abd al-Hakam. His narrative is clearer. Because it comes out of the capital, if it is not profit, it belongs to the Lord of Capital, and if it comes out of the capital and its profit and the profit between them.

WHAT IS FOR THE WORKER, AND WHAT IS NOT FOR HIM

The worker has rights against the owner of the money, which are:

1-To act in full manner. Provided that he behaves well, unless he is bound by one of the permissible conditions and accepts it.

2- To sell at the deferred and accelerated price, according to whathe deems profitable, in accordance with the doctrine of Abu Hanifa and at Al-Shafi 'i, he shall notsell at the deferred price, except with the permission of the Lord of Capital because of the danger therein.

3 - To return a good, if he finds a defect in it, and if the Lord of Capital accepts it, he may also buy the defective, if he sees it as a profit, because the profit is the lesson.

4- To buy, at the usual level, a live animal on which he carries, and he may not buy a ship except with the permission of the owner of the money.

5 - To delegate others in the sale and purchase.

6 - To travel with money by land and sea, according to the doctrine of Malik, Abu Hanifa and Imam Ahmed and contrary to the Shafi 'i doctrine, if the permission is absolute, and not restricted by condition, then it is disbursed to what the customs of trade dragged. The customs of trade are travel and presence by land and sea, especially since the word speculation is taken from striking at the ground, as Ibn Qudamah sees it[385].

7-To leave the speculative money with whoever he wants. He is entitled to his entire disposition.

8-Not todeal with the lord of money, such as selling him any of the company's goods. We do not know whether the sale is by profit or by capital. Malik hated

---

[383] Grand Blog 237/ 1
[384] Provisions of Zakat for Al-Fihri p. 103
[385] Singer 36/ 5

it, and Abu Hanifa permitted it at all, and Al-Shafi 'i restricted it, provided that it is a subordinationthat people do not like. "[386]If he bought something and did not pay its price, it fell from his capital, if it was not a deferred sale.

9-To accept the transfer at price, if the debtor refers it to whoever pays for it.

10- To spend more of the company's capitalat his expense. With regard to travel, spending for rent and clothing is necessary for travel, and this is calculated from the profit and if the profit does not occur, return from the loss; because his travel was for the trafficking of money, so it was his expense, as Ibn Qudamah quoted Malik, Ouzai, Hassan, Al-Nukha 'i, Ishaq, Abu Thur, and those of opinion[387].

If he carries with him another trade, for himself or for others, he spends from the two money together, and whatis said in travel regarding his alimony, it is saidin Hatra. Working in speculation does notleave him the opportunity to acquire from another side. He had the right to spend likehim with kindness, but with permission or on condition. Ibn Qadamah said: Or usually. Thus, the custom has been practiced in Morocco to this day. They disagreed if it was not a permit or a condition: Does he have alimony first? And is it in travel without urbanization? He showed what Al-Shafi 'i, Ibrahim Al-Nakha 'i, and Al-Hassan went to, that he has alimony.[388]

11 - To sell and buy without the currency of the country, if he sees the profit in it as a result, as he may sell an offer, on the contrary, unless the owner of the money says to him: Work in your opinion and settle the dispute, and he has the right to act.

12 - To rent from Mudaraba money a land that he cultivates, and profit between them as evoked by Ibn Qadamah from the words of Imam Ahmed, [389] as the lesson is the principle of investment, in order to obtain profit.

13- To buy for himself speculative money. He was approved by Imam Ahmed, Malik, Al-Thawri, Al-Ouzai, Ishaq and Abu Hanifa, and Abu Thur saw that the sale is invalidbecause he is a partner and Ibn Qadamah saw that it is true, because the money is not for him, but rather as an agent who buys with his client, and [390] perhaps it is about the price: efor capital or profit? It seems that the profit is for the share of the Lord of Money in the profit of each commodity.

This is one of the rights of the worker against the owner of the money, and he is not entitled to:

1- He may not buy more than the capital, except with the permission of the owner of the capital.

2- He may not lend from the mudaraba money except with his permission.

---

[386]The Beginning of the Diligent 239/2
[387]Singer 5/37
[388]Bidāyat al-Mujtahid 238/2 al-Mughni 64/3 Manār al-Sabīl fī Sharḥ al-Dalīl 402/1
[389]Singer 39/ 5
[390]Idem 53/ 5

3 - It is not permissible for him to travel with speculative money, a travel that people avoid, or carry it in a way that does notsecure its danger, and if the Lord of Capital gives him absolute permission in trade [391] as mentioned above, the Lord of Money may stipulate that. If he violates within the money.

4- It is not for him, if he works in the money of the master of money, to work in the money of another person. If he acts without his permission, and there is harm, to affect the profit, the dispute between the passport and not. It was said: Whathe won in the two money is between them. However, if it is authorized, or if there is no harm, it is permissible without dispute[392].

5 - It is not permissible for him to sell at the deferred price, without the permission of the Lord of Capital, contrary to the doctrine of Abu Hanifa and according to the Shafi 'i doctrine, and it was narrated by Imam Ahmed that he[393] guarantees money if it is not a condition and violates it... If it is a condition, it is a guarantor. The issue, as quoted by Ibn Rushd, is due to their disagreement about the need to act: Does it include selling on credit first? Likewise, to borrow money that is not traded with the money of the loans and profit between them. Malik prevented it, and Al-Shafi 'i and Abu Hanifa allowed it, and the [394] problem arises when the loss occurs: Is the money owed to the Lord of money or the worker, or to them both?

6 - It is not permissible for him to sell for less than the price of the parable, nor to buy more than it. If he does, the sale is valid with Imam Ahmad, and the shortage is guaranteed, and with Al-Shafi 'i that the sale is invalid, because it is a sale in which he was not authorized[395].

7- He may not speculate from the speculation money of another person, except with the permission of the owner of the capital. If he was allowed, the profit would be between them. When he said to him: Do with your opinion, or with what you see, God tells Ibn Qadamah about Imam Ahmad that it is permissible to give him speculation, because he may see to give it to someone who is more sighted than him by means of his investment.[396]

8 - It is not permissible for him to mix the money of speculation with his money, if he acts and does not distinguish himself within it, because it is a trust in his hand, and the trust does not prejudice others. If it is lost by a divine order, it is not guaranteed, because the trustee is not included, unless he is an infringer. Ibn Rushd quoted al-Shafi 'i and al-Layth Ibn Sa 'ad that his work in mixing is considered an infringement, so he guarantees, and Malik that he is not infringing, so he does not guarantee, and Ibn Qudamah[397] saw that he may see

---

[391] Ibid., 37/5
[392] Idem 46/5
[393] Singer 35/ 5 -36
[394] The Beginning of the Diligent 239/2
[395] Singer 38/5
[396] Ibid., 45/5
[397] The Beginning of the Diligent 239/2

the mixing as more suitable for him and memorized, so he enters in the generality of saying: Work in your opinion. andjustification for the opinion of Malik.

9- He may not stipulate for himself the whole profit. This is what usually happens between brothers, when a brother gives his brother money that he does not trade with, and is freed from the responsibility of helping him, so it is required that all profit be for him. Malik authorized him, and saw that he was a benefactor and volunteered. He works in it without collateral, [398]as is the law of loans, and Al-Shafi 'i thought that he was deceived, because if the loss was the Lord of money and Abu Hanifa [399]saw that it was a loan, not a loan,[400] and to consider it a loan, not a loan, the Hanbalis went in agreement with Abu Hanifa, [401] which is the most obvious.

If the dispute occurs between the worker and the master of money, the saying is the worker's saying; because in Sharia, he is faithful, and because the master of money did not trust him, until he put his trust in him. Trust and trust with disbelief do not combine, especially since the trustees do not guarantee, that the treason is from one of the hypocritical verses: "If a lie occurs, if a promise is made, and if a khan is trusted," as stated in the Bukhari novel and[402] not from the verse of the sincere believer, but Ibn Dawayan says about the doctrine of Imam Ahmed that the worker believes with an oath, and Ibn Rushd[403] mentioned about Malik, the revolutionary, Abu Hanifa, and his companions that saying it is because he is honest, if he comes up with what looks like, as mentioned about Al-Shafi 'i that they are allies.[404]

---

[398]Grand Blog 48/ 4
[399]The Beginning of the Diligent 239/2
[400]Ibid., 236/2
[401]Singer 30/ 5
[402]Al-Bukhari: Al-Fath 32/6 Grand Sunan 288/6
[403]Manar Al-Sabil in Sharḥ al-Dalīl 'alá Madhhab al-Imām Aḥmad 404/1
[404]Beginning of the Diligent 241/ 2

CANCELLATION

The mudaraba contract is not required, before starting work, and one of the contractors: the worker or the owner of the capital can terminate it on his own. They differed in the ruling after the start, so Malik said: It is necessary and[405] when Imam Ahmad is not necessary, as he sees it as one of the permissible contracts, it [406]is not a duty to work.

However, the necessity or lack thereof is not related to the requirements of the contract, but rather to the right of annulment... It follows that neither of them has the right to rescind it, unless one of its reasons is available. One of its reasons is that one of its pillars is absent, or that one of the conditions of its validity is corrupted. Ibn Qudamah divided it into three sections: what is contrary to the contract requirement or due to ignorance of profit or is not in the interest of the contract and its requirement.

If the contract is broken, it must be rescinded, and the money returned to its owner, and the worker is given in exchange for his work: either Ijara al-Mithal or Qardat al-Mithal. The difference, as mentioned above, is that the lease is worth it, even from the capital, and the loan is not worth it, except in profit. In the Ijarah, al-Shafi'i, Abu Hanifah, and 'Abd al-'Aziz ibn Abi Salamah from the owners of Malik, and Abdul Wahhab was quoted as saying that it is a narration about Malik, and Ibn al-Majshun went on to tell him about Malik, that he returns to the loans of the proverb. It is also his saying, and the saying of Ashhab, which[407] means the loan of the proverb, that the account falls, and if the profit appears, the worker takes it by the amount of loans like him, and if the profit does not appear, the money leads to its owner.

If there is a debt in the money, the worker must pay it, whether a profit appears in the money or not. With it, al-Shafi'i said, and Abu Hanifiyah said: If a profit appears, he must sue him, otherwise he will not. Ibn Qudamah tailed the two opinions by saying, "He needed to return the money, as he took it. Therefore, he must suehim[408]."

This is because the debt is of his disposition, unlike the stolen and the extorted, which he is not obliged to request, except in the absence ofits owner, and if he dies and does not know the speculative money in particular, he becomes a debt owed by him, and if he is in debt, the Lord of money is like the debtors[409].

---

[405] The Beginning of the Diligent 2/237
[406] Singer 58/ 5
[407] Beginning of the Diligent 240/2
[408] Singer 59/ 5
[409] Idem 65/ 5

The annulment includes damage to the property, for which the contract is signed between the owner of the property and the worker, before or after the commencement of the work, as it is done. Before and after starting work with Imam Ahmad - at the initiative of one of them or his death, madness or interdiction[410].

If the Lord of wealth dies, the heir takes his place, taking money and profit and bearing the loss. The worker has noright to act, except with the permission of the heir, who has the right to approve it. Its approval is considered by the Shafi 'is and Hanbalis as a way to complete speculation, not from its inception, and it[411] seems that it is a beginning; because the worker is an agent and the agency is invalidated by the death of the principal. This requires the renewal of the contract, and the renewal of the contract raises the idea of new contractors.

Likewise, if the worker dies, the owner of the capital - if he wishes - may start speculating with his heir if he is rational, and the money is ripe, and if it is offers that are not permissible, unless they are made, and the capital on the day of the contract in monetary value is considered a[412] payment for ignorance of the capital, because of which the contract is corrupted. Perhaps the difference between the heirs is that the heir of the owner of the property has been transferred to him by inheritance, and he has the right to dispose, as well as his perished property, from which he inherited profit and loss, unlike the heir of the worker who is not entitled to dispose of the property of others except with his permission. If he has a right, he is to claim profit if he appears.

HER LOSS AND HER DEBTS

The loss is always on the owner of the capital, and if it is agreed with the worker that the profit and loss between them[413] is incurred – except byproviding the capital that is provided even in interest - his share in the profit is due, as the worker deserves by his work. Personal agreements do not affect Sharia rulings... The Sharia law has made it entirely on the capital, whether it is for one person, it bears it alone, or it is for two or more people, so it is divided - as profit is divided - by the percentage of participation in capital formation. This is what is meant by the saying of Al-Kharqi: "The inferiority is worth as much as money."

Even positive laws may not exempt one of the partners from bearing his share in the loss. Dr. Ahmed Mohamed Ibrahim, quoting the memorandum published with the Egyptian Civil Code, stated that one of the legislations that does not allow for this is the legislation of the following countries: Poland, Article 590 Tunisia, Article 1035 Spain, Article 1690 Portugal, Article 1249 Netherlands, Article 1672 Argentina, Article 1686 Austria, Article 1196 Brazil, Article 1372

---

[410]Idem: 68/ 5
[411]Idem 59/ 5
[412]Singer 60/ 5
[413]Singer 62/ 5

Quebec, Article 1831 and the [414] debts that often result from the loss of capital, are related to the debt of the Lord of Capital, and the worker has nothing to do with that, unless he violates one of the previous conditions or behaves in a manner that comes on the capital and increases it, as if he was deflating his trade in a country and carrying it to another country with more than its price, he had to fine the rest of the rental duty.[415]

We say that it is related to the Lord of money, because the Mudaraba company is a partnership company, located between people. Its debts are owed. The debtor is justified only by performing what is related to it and not as a modern joint stock company, which is located between the funds, and its debts are limited to its capital, as will come, and as profit and loss are divided by quotas on the amount of participation in the establishment of the capital, the debts are [416] divided.

In the event of the bankruptcy of the owner of the capital or the company, the debtors divide what they find by the amount of their percentages in the debt. In it, Al-Bukhari, Al-Tirmidhi, Abu Dawud, Ibn Majah, and Al-Bayhaqi narrate, in what Ibn Rushd adopted, that the Prophet (peace and blessings of Allaah be upon him) said, about the man who surrounded religion with his wealth during his reign: "Take what you found, and you have nothing but that." The[417] talk is about Abu Hurairah, Abu Saeed, Aisha, Juwayriyah, and Anas.

And the fines, no one of them may possess anything unless he finds his commodity a certain list, so he is more entitled to it than others. In it, Al-Bukhari, Al-Tirmidhi, Abu Dawood, Al-Nasa 'i, Ibn Majah, and Al-Bayhaqi recount, in what Ibn Hazm adopted, that the Prophet (peace and blessings of Allaah be upon him) said: "Whoever finds his own belongings with a man who has gone bankrupt, is more entitled to it than others."[418]

Ibn Hazm believes that the rights of God are superior to the rights of slaves[419], and Ibn Qudamah believes that the worker's share of the profit is superior to the right of the debtors, because it is a right that the lord of money does not have, [420] especially since bankruptcy may arise from other than the amount in which the worker worked.

SPLIT HER WINNINGS

---

[414] Journal of Islamic Banks No. 15, p. 82
[415] Muwatta: Al-Zarqani copy
[416] Nawazel Al-Abbasi, p. 180, manuscript
[417] Al-Bukhari Al-Fath Version 7/265 Sahih Al-Tirmidhi 3/55 Sunan Ibn Dawood 3/37 Sunan Ibn Majah 2/33 Sunan Al-Kibr 6/50 Beginning of Al-Mujtahid 2/186
[418] Al-Bukhari: Al-Fath copy 460/5 Sahih Al-Tirmidhi 266/5 Sunan Abu Dawood 392/3 Sunan Ibn Majah 33/2 Sunan Al-Kubra 44/6 Sunan Al-Nisa 'i 265/7 Al-Muhalla 75/8
[419] Local 74/ 8
[420] Singer 56/ 5

The division of profit is subject to agreement, whether in pure speculation in which the capital is from one person, or in a speculation company in which there are two or more persons, and any percentage agreed to be considered on the day of the contract, shall be necessary on the day of division. In that, Ibn Hazm narrates about Abu Haseen, who said: "Ali bin Abi Talib told me in Mudarib and in the two partners: Profit is what they are called." He said: "This is a companion who does not know his companions."[421]

Commenting on al-Kharqi's statement, Ibn Qudamah said: "Profit is what they meant" in all sections of the company, and there is no dispute about that in pure speculation. Ibn al-Mundhir said, "The people of knowledge unanimously agreed that the worker may stipulate one-third or one-half of the profit or what they collect on it[422]."

In the Great Blog, Sahnun said, Ibn al-Qasim asks about the profit of Mudaraba: "Did you see Mudaraba on the half, the fifth, and the sixth, or less than that, or more? He said, "It's okay with Malik."[423]

Malik confirmed this in the Muwatta, and his tail by saying: "Everything that is named from that is halal. It is the loans of Muslims»[424]and profit in any case, shall be the subject of the agreement between the Lord of money and the worker.

If profit appears, and one of them asks for division and the other refrains, the abstainer shall be forced, as Ibn Hazm saw, and the small, insane and absentee shall be entrusted with whoever isolates his right[425] and with Ibn Qudamah that the one who submits his statement is the abstainer, because - ashe said - if he is the Lord of money, it is because he does not believe in loss, it is forced from profit, and if he is the worker, it is because he does not believe that prima is obligated to take it at a time when he is unable to respond. If they agree to divide some or all, it is their right.[426]

If the dispute occurs about the agreed percentage, then the statement of the worker is clear and [427]if the work is delegated, without assigning the percentage, as it usually occurs between brothers and friends, it is returned to the loan of the proverb. And if the Lord of Capital says:

You have what the condition of so-and-so. They know that, it is permissible, and if they do notknow it, or one of them does not know it, then the contract is corrupt, because it is an agreement on an unknown.[428]

---

[421]Local 8/126
[422]Singer 26/5
[423]Grand Blog 48/ 4
[424]Muwatta: Al-Zarqani Version 3/349
[425]Local 8/128
[426]Singer 57/ 5
[427]Muwatta: Al-Zarqani Version 162/3
[428]Singer 30/ 5

Accounting for profit may not take place except in the minutes of the owner of the capital, and the capital and its profit shall be fully accumulated by the worker [429] and the accounting shall be on money, not on goods, because the price of goods - as Ibn Qadamah says -increases and decreases, and [430] if it happens that the worker took his share of the profit, before accounting, before the capital was collected, or in the absence of the owner of the capital, he was his guarantor.

Ibn Qudamah reasoned that profit is a protection for capital, as it does not believe that loss occurs, and is forced from it, and that the property of the worker in profit is unstable before division and that the master of capital is his partner, soit is not correct to divide for himself without him. It became clear from Hanbali jurisprudence that profit is worthy of accounting, not its appearance. Therefore, if it appears, the worker may not take anything from him except with the permission of the owner of the capital [431] because the capital holds the profit until it is received.

At Hanifa, the division of profit is not valid, before the owner of the money receives his money, and if it occurs, it remains suspended, until the capital is received, it is valid, otherwise it is invalid, and at Shafi 'i that the division is valid, but if the loss appears, after the division, the worker has to return what he took, as well as the property, they decide that the division if it occurs, and the loss appears, the profit is recovered to compensate forwhat was lost from the capital.[432]

This was the view on the system of the speculation and loan company. In some of its topics, we deliberately recorded the opinions of scientists in their pens, in order to prevent what occurred in some of the analysis mixed with personal opinions, and not deduced, on the subject ofjudgments.

It is noted that some specialists in the contemporary economy wonder, in light of the division of modern companies into solidarity and shareholding -: Are Islamic contracts companies, especially Mudaraba and loans joint venture or shareholding? Which seems to be in solidarity in terms of the contract and its provisions, as it falls between people, not money, but it seems to agree with the contribution in some laws, and disagree with it in others, so they agree

1-In the principle of contributing to capital formation, and not limiting the number of participants, even if the contribution starts from seven and speculation from two onwards, and if the contribution is open, the Islamic system tends to close, as it does notopen to the public, except to the extent that the participants accept it.

2- Not requiring the similarity of the participants' shares.

---

[429] Muwatta: Al-Zarqani Version 359/3
[430] Singer 55/ 5
[431] Idem 57/ 5
[432] See the book of jurisprudence on the four schools of thought 61/3-62

3- Dividing profits and losses by the percentage of financial shares.

4- Participation of foreigners, Muslims, women and boys' money in its establishment.

and they differ

1- The contribution is mainly based on the financial element, and the Islamic element is based on the human element, as is solidarity.

2- The contribution consists of money, and the Islamic consists of money and work, as evidenced by the difference between their definitions. He progressed in defining the Mudaraba company at the tap as a contract on the company to profit with money from one side and work from the other. Mustafa Kamal Taha defined participation in the shareholding as a declaration of the will to participate in the company's project, with a pledge to provide a share of the capital represented in a certain number of shares[433]

3 - In the contribution, the profits are divided into money, and in Islam, they are divided into money and work.

4 - The loss of the contribution and its debts relate to its capital, and do notexceed it to the other funds of the participants[434] and in the Islamic related to the receivables of the participants, as is the case with solidarity. Liability is justified only by performing what is related to it, as mentioned above. This preserves the rights of people, as it is not possible to manipulate them, or to claim bankruptcy... This is one of the advantages of Islamic contracts.

5-The contribution isnot affected by the death, insanity or interdiction of one of the participants, unlike the Islamic one, which is dissolved, if the heir of the deceased does not agree to its continuation. In the sense that the account is located and gives its share of the capital with its profit, and resumes work, if it consists of more than two.

6 - In the shareholding, one of the participants can sell his share orhis share, without the prior permission of his partners, and in Islamia he is notentitled to do so, except with their permission, if they do not want to buy it.

7-In the shareholding, the shares are appointed in the form of equal amounts, and the participants are known as shareholders, and in Islamic, the shares are considered for the participants.

8- The shareholding shall set its basic laws according to legal and interest requirements, and Islamic laws shall be regulated by Sharia laws subject to them.

---

[433] Broker in Moroccan and Comparative Commercial Law 285/2-I-2-1980
[434] Id. 262/2

As for the anonymous name, it seems to be a commercial term, otherwise, it is known to the participants and its legally agreed name is known. If it does not carry an address consisting of the names of the partners or one of them, as is the case with the partnership company, that is, the joint venture, it is, as a capital company, carrying a name derived from its purpose. Ignorance , which harms or corrupts the contract of the Islamic company, is ignorance of the amount of capital or the percentage of profit allocated to both the owner of the capital and the worker.

The issues of name, social headquarters, management, board of directors, valuation of shares, and capital appreciation are organizational issues. There is nothing in Islamic jurisprudencethat contradicts its requirements. In general, joint stock companies in their system and laws are Western companies that violate Sharia laws, and Muslims must rely on themselves and their economy and establish Islamic companies that meet with modernity at the table of production and investment. We hope that we will be successful in removing the confusion between the contribution and the Islamic, as required by the research.

FORMATION, PILLARS AND CONDITIONS OF ANAN COMPANY

COMPOSITION

In the previous chapter, we focused on the speculation and loan company, as it is the one whose affairs the Prophet (peace and blessings of Allah be upon him) started, as a worker in Khadija's money, and as a speculator in the lands of Khyber. Because it represents the backbone, and we can offer it as an alternative to the usurious system, because of its ability to invest the wealth of those who know the investment and its means. However, it is important to complete the investment system, indirect and direct, to add it to the content of companies outside its circle. They are unleashed, faces, bargaining and business.

Perhaps the closest company to the provisions of speculation and loans, as will be noted during the research, is Anan Company. The main difference between them is that speculation consists of money on one side and work on one side, such as money from Khalid and work from Saleh and profit on what they agreedupon, and unleashing consists of money and work on both sides together, such as money from Muhammad and Said and work from them, and profit on the proportions of money and business, as decided by some or according to the agreement, as permitted by others.

In its composition, Ibn Qudamah said of the jurisprudence of Imam Ahmad: "To share their wealth and profit between them." He[435] quoted Ibn al-Mundhir, as quoted by Ibn Dawayan, and it comes within the words of Ibn Rushd that it is a unanimous award, [436] but the dispute occurred in some of its conditions. Since the worker's work in speculation is based on agency and trust… Ibn Qudamah says in the work of the partner: "Al-Anan Company is based on agency and trust, because each of them pays money to its owner. Thus, his security and his permission for him to act and all of it. It is a condition of its validity that each of them authorizes his owner to dispose of it. If he is absolutely authorized to dispose of it in all trades, he shall dispose of it, even if he assigns to him a nationality, a species, or a country in which he disposes of it, to the exclusion of others, because he is acting with permission. He stood on it like a proxy[437].

They differed in calling it unleashed. Ibn Qudamah, quoting Fur, stated that the word is derived from the thing, if it is presented, because each partner does not have to contribute to its establishment. It seems that they were not known to Malik, and the people of the Hijaz by this name, even if they found their rulings and knew a name among the jurists of his doctrine. In the great blog about Sahnoun, Ibn al-Qasim asks: «Does Malik know, Anan Company? He said: "I

---

[435]Singer 13/5
[436]Manar Al-Sabil in Sharḥ al-Dalīl ʿalá Madhhab al-Imām Aḥmad 398/1
[437]Singer 13/5

have not heard from Malik, nor have I seen any of the people of the Hijaz who know it."[438]

In addition to what Ibn Qudamah quoted from the fur, it is also mentioned that it is called unleashed similar to the equilibrium of the money of the two partners, the equilibrium of the horse with the other, if they are equal in view[439] of what some scholars have stipulated that the shares of the partners in the capital are equal to their amounts of work, based on the equal shares when sharing the profit. In it, Ibn Ghazi said: "Every company in which each of the two partners has shown the same capital and work as its owner, it is correct and the profit between them."[440]

Ibn Rushd conveyed this opinion, without interrupting it, and said: «I think that some scholars do notallow the company, unless their money is equal, so they turn to work, they see that the work is mostly flat, and if the money between them is not equal, there was an injustice to one of them at work. Therefore, Ibn al-Mundhir said: Scholars unanimously agreed on the permissibility of the company in which each of the two partners produces money like the money of its owner of his kind. I mean dinars or dirhams, and then mix them until they become one money thatis not distinguished from selling and buying what theysaw, from the types of trade, but what was of virtue is between them in half, and what was of loss is so..." .[441]

Thus, Ibn Rushd thinks that some scholars require equal amounts of money. to which others have gone that it is not a condition. Rather, it was the subject of consensus on the health of each company in which it was found, and it is true with its absence. Muhammad al-Amir al-Sanani quoted Ibn Battal as saying: "They unanimously agreed that the right company is to come out each one as its owner did, until he said: This is called the Anan Company, and it is valid if one of them comes out less than the other of money, and the profit and loss are as much as the money of each of them, and it is [442] stated in the"Book of Fiqh on the four schools of jurisprudence that is permissible between a Muslim, an infidel, a boy and an adult, and it is notrequired for equal partners in capital. "[443]

ITS PILLARS

The pillars of Anan Company are the contracts, the money, the work, and the face of profit sharing... That is, knowing the amount of work from the amount of money, knowing the amount of profit from the amount of money and work... As for the conclusion of the contract between the contractors, it represents the common denominator between the companies. It has been submitted that the

---

[438]Grand Blog 37/ 4
[439]Singer 13/5
[440]Faculties in Matters under Work in the Maliki Doctrine, p. 119 by Ibn Ghazi, Manuscript
[441]The Beginning of the Diligent 251/2
[442]Pathways to Peace 64/ 3
[443]Kitāb al-Fiqh ʻalá al-Madhāhib al-Arbaʻah 68

pillars of the Mudaraba company are the contract of offer and acceptance, the two contracts, the capital and the work, and the direction of profit sharing. The two contracts are not required to be more than one who may dispose of his property. It's money, work, and profit. It is the one that is the subject of agreement and disagreement. By comparison, it seems that whatis true in a speculative company is true in an unleashed company, as advanced in the words of Ibn Qudamah, where he said: "All that ispermissible in a company is permissible in speculation, and what ispermissible in speculation is permissible in a company, and what is forbidden in one is prohibited in the other, because speculation is a company."

TERMS

1- The capital shall be of the two cash or their equivalent, as they are the values of the losses and the sales prices, and they[444] have agreed that they are permissible with the union of sex, that is, in dinars or dirhams of one kind. It is the doctrine of Imam Shafi 'i, who looked at the adjective that enables the application of what he required from the confusion between the two money, and facilitates the process of articulation when necessary, [445] but they disagreed about different offers, or dinars on the one hand and dirhams on the other hand, [446] perhaps because of the difference in values, as it is located between two different currencies, or between materials of different value... Imam Ahmad authorized him when the two coins differed, as evidenced by Ibn Qudamah's statement: «Itis not necessary for their validity to agree on the two coins in sex, but it is permissible for one of them to issue dirhams and the other dinars. stipulated by Ahmad. Al-Hassan and Ibn Sirin said, " He saw that they were one race; if they separated, each one returned with the sex he paid on the basis that the offers would cash the country, and share the profit. "And to us that this is a valid company," he said. Capital has prices, so the return of the sex of capital is as if the sex was one, "[447] which is the most obvious lesson in terms of value.

If the order to participate in cash is delivered, opinions are available about the permissibility of participation, starting with offers, on the basis of considering their values. Rather, they prevented it from falling into its eyes, because of the company's requirement to return at the bargaining table. Either to the capital or like it, and the capital in the notables is of unknown destiny, and homosexuality is impossible. Therefore, Imam Shafi 'i allowed him in the proverbs and prevented him in others [448] and Imam Ahmed that the same value is not achieved, as the offer may be more or less than its value, so things are relative, and the price is non-existent, asthey do not have it in the case of the contract, so the solution is for everyone to sell his commodity, and participate in its price.

---

[444] Manar Al-Sabeel 398/1
[445] Singer 16/5
[446] The Beginning of the Diligent 2/249
[447] Singer 16/5
[448] Same source 14/ 5

It was in the past, and in some imams. Today, the prices and values of goods are known to factories and companies, and some of them are priced by countries. The values of money, as noted by exchange offices, are known, especially to specialists in their affairs. Whatis raised from the formation of the company's capital or detailed in it on the basis of accounting for values, there is nothing in itthat contradicts what isdeduced from the opinions of jurists.

This is one of the meetings of the Mudaraba company with Anan Company, as it istrue that what is said in the two Mudaraba partners, we cooperated to form the capital and give it to those who work in it with a share of its profit, it is true that it is said in the two partners of Anan. We cooperated on its formation, in order for them to work in it, and to divide the profit... The loss, whether speculative or unbridled, does notfall on the business, but rather on the basis of the participation in the capital. Thus, it is clear that Ibn Qudamah's saying:«It is notpermissible for the company's capital to be the capital of speculation» is correct.

We may note that the first, second and third conditions, respectively, in the two companies are: that the capital is cash, that it is present in the case of the contract, and that it is known as a prescription. Returning to the case in which the speculativecapital consists of two or more in exchange for the unleashed capital, which is only composed of two or more, we find that what is boughti to be of the two cash, has been interceded in the two subjects that exceeded its composition with the offers. This means Ibn Ghazi, as he says: "Every company that signed the goods on the values is correct," and he said about the cash on the one hand, and the corrected offer on the other hand: "Every company that signed their house from one of the partners, and with a corrected offer from the other, is an award[449].

Ibn Asim says in the masterpiece of the rulers:

The offer is permissible if theygive such food to a party that does notrefrain	On one hand or two actors and an eye or a symptom in another

It was the health of the company that the capital should be in cash, or considered as values in others. Abu Zaid Abdul Rahman Al-Fassi authorized, as stated in the company's Nawazel, that each of them pay an thousand, and one of them increases a prepared shop, in exchange for the other being enough for the hardship of work. He considered that the lesson of equality in values [450] and the contemporary economy divides the capital into fixed, which is construction and

---

[449]Faculties in Matters under Work in the Maliki Doctrine, p. 120
[450]Nawazel Company for Abdulaziz Al-Zayati Manuscript

what is not transported and mobile, and it is represented in the money placed at the disposal of the participants. Values include them.

Thus, it is clear that the formation of capital through evaluated offers - which is many today - is permissible among the classes of scholars, in which Ibn Qudamah said, in a novel about Imam Ahmed: "The company and speculation are permissible by offers, and make their value on the day of the contract the capital." [451] And we do not know how it was agreed to consider the value of offers at the will of Zakat and differed in its consideration when the will of capital formation. Although the right of God is more important than the right of human beings.

2- The capital must be present at the time of the contract. First, unlike what will come in the company of the faces, the company will not fall on the receivables. Rather, it falls on the funds and requires the presence of the capital when it is established, which requires that it not be mortgaged or extorted, nor by debt owed by one of them, nor by the deposit, before it is returned to its owner, as provided in the Mudaraba company. This is what M understands from the saying of Ibn Qudamah: "There is no money absent or religion, because itcannot be disposed of immediately. It is the intention of the company"and the [452] second is that some of them stipulated for its validity that the Malan mix an indistinguishable mixture, as taken from the saying of Ibn Rushd, quoting Ibn al-Mundhir: " They mix them until they become one money that does not complete ", which is the Shafi 'i doctrine. This calls for the capital to be seen in full view.

However, they disagreed about the image of mixing. Is it intended to mix directly or to enable each partner to act? Malik and Abu Hanifa argued that the appointment of money and bringing it is sufficient in the health of the company, and Malik increased to be within their reach, and Al-Shafi 'i argued that the confusion is carried out by annexation and reaction, and Ibn Qudamah believed that the conclusionof the contract in order to act is sufficient in the health of the company and its convening. This may be the case, because they are held by contract, not by confusion. Therefore, al-Shafi 'i's opinion was not approved, and he turned towards the opinion of Malik and Abu Hanifa al-Nu 'man. He said: «I do not buy the mingling of the two owners; if we see them and bring them. Thus, Abu Hanifa and Malik said... For us, it is a contract intended for profit, in which it is not required to mix money like speculation, and because it is a contract to act, it was not a condition to mix like agency»[453] And so it is, the contract is the one that imposes the meaning of collection, and turns all the shares into one thing called the company's capital.

These are jurisprudential views, generated by economic, social and monetary conditions. It requires its knowledge as assets and sources whose provisions are required... And if economic, social, monetary and regulatory conditions

---

[451] Singer 21/5
[452] Same source 16/ 5
[453] Singer 16/5

change... The legitimacy that is taken from the first chest, and according to which it works, has not changed, and there is nothing in its flexibility that impedes or hinders the course of contemporary economic development. Money is always currency, andcurrency is cash, and the participants are the contributors and the values of things are equivalent to their values. It is sufficient forwhat is said about raising or mixing capital to establish a company; its contract is based on the requirements of Sharia, and a bank account is opened for it, in which capital is deposited, before starting its work.

3- Each of the owners or funds must be known by a certain amount of prescription. Do not convene anonymously. Whether issued from one or two sides. It is as if one of them, or each of them, says to the other: I share with you what is in this belly button. It is similar to him in speculation that the Lord of Money says to the worker: I am speculating with you, including this bag. Itis not valid in the two pictures, because the contract is ignorant of the capital. If it falls, it falls corrupt, for the loss of one of its conditions. In it, Ibn Qudamah says: "It is notpermissible for the capital of the company to be unknown orindiscriminate; because it must be referred to at the point of separation, and it is not possible to return with ignorance and indiscretion," and[454] this type of ignorance is the one who does not accept Sharia. As for the anonymous in contemporary expression. It is not so much about her name as it is about her system.

4-That each of the two partners or partners has a part in the profit, and is it according to the amount of his money, or according to the agreement? So that's what we're going to look for in dividing the profit.

---

[454]Singer 16/5

Cancellation

The company is dissolved because of the nullity of the contract, or at the initiative of one of the partners or partners or his death, insanity or interdiction; because, as Ibn Rushd said, "One of the permissible contracts, there are no necessary contracts for any of the partners to separate from the company whenever he wants. It is an uninherited contract. "Ibn Qudamah [455] says: " It is invalidated by the death, insanity and interdiction of one of the partners, and by the dissolution of one of them, because it is a permissible contract, so it is invalidated as a power of attorney [456]. "

On the provisions of death, Ibn Qudamah says: «If one of the partners dies, and there is no heir to Rashid, he may reside on the company, and the partner authorizes him to act, and he has the right to claim division, and if he is loyal to him, his guardian takes his place in that, but he only does what is in the interest of his guardian. If the deceased is a guardian. With the company's money or some of it to a certain person, the legatee is like the heir in what we mentioned, and if he bequeathed it to another person, such as the poor, the testator was not allowed to act, because he had to pay them to isolate their share; and he differentiates between them, and if the deceased has a debt related to his estate, the heir does not have to sign the company, until he settles his debt. If he spends it without the company's money, he has the right to complete it, and if he spends it on the company's money, the company shall be null and void for as long as it remains. "[457]

If the partner dismisses his partner, his permission to act stops, and the dismissed person has no right to dispose except of his share, as he follows one to dispose of the property of others except with his permission and agency. Withdrawal of permission from one of the partners means the suspension of his share in the capital. That is, if the money is ripe. If it is an offer, then what Ibn Qadamah recalled from the words of Imam Ahmad is that he is not cherished, and that he has the right to act until the money is spent, by analogy with the worker in speculation, if the owner of the money dismisses him. He explained that profit and loss are not shown except by selling goods, and spending money as it is deduced from the opinion of Imam Ahmed, but Ibn Qudamah has quoted Abu Talib - as is the doctrine of Imam Shafi 'i - that he is isolated on the grounds that the contract is permissible and not necessary, so it is similar to the agency [458].

---

[455] The Beginning of the Diligent 253/2
[456] Singer 21/5
[457] Singer 21/5
 "Same source"
[458] Singer 21/5

If he wants to bargain before the money runs out, and they agree to sell the offers or divide them, the matter is clear, and if one of them requests to sell, and the other to divide, the applicant for division is answered without the applicant for sale; because the sale is first when the will of profit appears, and division when the will of bargaining. If it is said that the worker in speculation is answered to the sale, the answer is as Ibn Qudamah said: «The right of the worker to profit, and the profit isshown only by selling, so the worker deserved it because he obtained his right to it .... In our matter, each of them is redeemed for his share of the goods, so he was not forced to sell[459]. "

Earned

It is submitted in the Mudaraba and Loans Company that the division of profit is subject only to agreement between the owners and employees of the funds, due to the difference in business, as a result of the different types of trades. In Al-Anan Company, which consists of money and work from each side, we find that the owners of money are themselves the owners of business, so it is agreed, not between the owners of money and business, as is the case with speculation, but between the participants with money and business. Is participation on the basis of equality in the amounts of money and business, dividing profit and loss equally, as presented in the opinions of some scholars, first buy equal contribution, dividing the profit according to the agreement: either equally or otherwise?

This point is one of the points where the speculation and unleashing companies differ. In speculation, the owner of the money bears the responsibility for the loss, and the worker is responsible for the work in return for the profit that each of themobtains from the profit, according to whatthey agree on. The owner of the money may not stipulate it or some of it on the worker, and if he stipulates it, the condition is void. In it, Al-Kharqi said: "If the lord of money and the speculator agree that the profit between them and the position on them, the profit between them and the position on the money will be"...

Each partner shall bear his share in the loss, to the extent of his contribution to the capital, in return for his share in the profit. Either by equal shares, according to the equal amount of the contribution or according to the agreement on equal or non-equal. In it, Ibn Rushd says: "They agreed that if the profit is subordinate to the capital: I mean, if they are equal in the origin of the company's capital, the profit between them is half, and they differed, is it permissible for their capital to differ and equal in profit? Malik and Al-Shafi 'i said: It is not possible, and the people of Iraq said: It is permissible... and mayor to prevent that from likening

---

[459]The Beginning of the Diligent 250/ 2

profit to loss. Just as if one of them stipulated part of the loss was not permissible, so if he stipulated part of the profit outside his money. "[460]

It seems from the opinions of Hanbali scholars that equality does not buyi, neither in the amounts of money nor in theamounts of business. Rather, the profits are divided according to the amounts of money and business, or they are the subject of an agreement, as evidenced by the statement of Ibrahim bin Dawyan: "That two or more people participate in money that they trade in, and the profit between them is according to what they agree on."[461]

The agreement could not have been made, except by mutual consent between the partners. The power of openness will ensure the expansion of the scope of the establishment of companies and the contribution of each individual to what is under his hand, and in a manner that satisfies him: if those who have the physical and intellectual ability, he contributed to Al-Anan Company, and if he is among the elderly, the elderly, orphans and intellectual minors, he turned his money towards the Mudaraba Company, now embodied in Islamic banks. She was guarded by the masters, and the saboteurs took her away.

It is clear from many opinions that the Hanbalis did not distinguish much between speculative and unleashed companies. It was about the formation of capital or the division of profit, as it is understood from their saying that speculation is a company in which what is true in the company they want to unleash. If it is advanced that equality regarding speculative capital is unconditional, Ibn Qudamah says about notrequiring it to be unconditional: «Ido not buy equal to the two money. Thus, al-Hasan, al-Sha 'bi, al-Nukha 'i, al-Shafi 'i, Ishaq, and those of opinion said, and some Shafi 'is said that this is required. "Musa al-Hijjawi [462]says about not requiring him to work, and the profits section according to money and business: " Two or more people share their money to work with their bodies, and profit between them or one of them works, provided that he has more profit than his money. A condition for him is the amount of his money that is not valid, and a condition for him that is less than it is also true, to take part of the profit of his owner's money without work. "[463]This is one of the advantages of justice in the Islamic economy.

In order not to require equal amounts of money and business, they also did not require equal shares when sharing the profit on the funds, and they allowed it to be the subject of an agreement, as is the case with speculation. In speculation, I do not buy more than to assign to each of the master of money and the worker an agreed part in the profit. This is what Ibrahim bin Dwayan decided for Anan, as he says: "To stipulate for each of them a part of the profit, whether a condition for each of them according to the amount of his money, or

---

[460]The Beginning of the Diligent 250/ 2
[461]Manar Al-Sabeel 398/1
[462]Singer 16/5
[463]Persuasion in the jurisprudence of Imam Ahmed 252/2

less or more," [464] which is the same as what Ibn Qadamah decided. The Hanbalis are more open in the corporate door.

This was for the right company, but the corrupt - as if it falls on the receivables - Ibn Qudamah says: «When the company fell corrupt, they share the profit according to the amount of capital»[465] In which Ibn Asim says:

And if I fall on the receivables   and divide the profit by a committed judgment

HER LOSS?

That was for profit. As for the loss - whether speculative or unleashed - it is permanent depending on the participation in the capital. In it, Ibn Qudamah said, commenting on the saying of Al-Kharqi: "The inferiority over the amount of money" means that everyone loses in the company as much as his money, there is no difference in this. According to him, Abu Hanifa, Al-Shafi 'i and others said, "In the sense that they are divided by the amounts of money, without regard to business, and related to the receivables of the participants, not their shares in the company, as is the case with the modern anonymity. This guarantees the right of debtors to stand up to fraudsters on the pretext of bankruptcy. This is one of the advantages of Islamic contracts.

As for debts, and in the event of the bankruptcy of the company, the debtors divide what they find on the amount of their proportions in the debt, as advanced in what was narrated by Al-Bukhari, Al-Tirmidhi, Abu Dawood, Ibn Majah, and Al-Bayhaqi that the Prophet (peace and blessings of Allaah be upon him) said to address the creditors in the case of the man who surrounded the debt with his money: "Take what I found and you have nothing but that." Unless one of them finds his commodity a certain list, he is more entitled to it than others, as advanced in what was narrated by Al-Bukhari, Al-Tirmidhi, Al-Nisa ', Abu Dawood, Ibn Majah, and Al-Bayhaqi, and Abu Ali Ibn Hazm adopted it that the Prophet (peace and blessings of Alla be upon him) said: "Whoever finds his own belongings with a man who has gone bankrupt, he is more entitled to it than others."

PARTNER'S RIGHT TO ACT

The partner has the right to act in his name in a manner that benefits them, so he has the right to sell bargaining, bidding, Murabaha, moderation and assumption... And how he saw the interest in what was done with the customs of trade, as he had the right to receive the price; if he sold and the sale if he bought and disputed the debt, and demanded its performance, and referred and referred,

---

[464] Manar Al-Sabil in Sharḥ al-Dalīl ʻalá Madhhab al-Imām Aḥmad 398/1
[465] Singer 17/5

and responds with injustice to his guardian and the guardian of his owner of the purchase of goods.

If the commodity is returned to him by an adult, he must accept it, and he may demean the arsh of injustice or devalue the price, or delay performance because of it, and he may also rent, rent, claim and pay the wage. What isrecognized in such damage as injustice, the survival of some or all of the price, the reward of the caller or the porter, or other matters considered as a consequence of trade, obliges its owner, and he is obligated to borrow what he borrowed in favor of the company, in exchange for his share of his profit, as decided by Ibn Qudamah for Hanbali jurisprudence[466].

On his right to spend, spend, lend and deposit, Ibn Rushd says: "Their alimony and their clothing of the company's money, if they converge on the children, and they do not deviate from alimony like them, and one of the partners may buy and lend and deposit if the need arises." [467]

They disagreed about such things as dismissal, mortgage, traveling with money and participating in it... This is within the scope of the usual permission in trade. But if he releases his hand to act freely: Ibn Qadamah says: «If he says to him: Work in your opinion, it is permissible for him to do all that is necessary in the trade of goods and speculation with money, and to participate in it and mix it with his money and travel with it and deposit and mortgage and mortgage and mortgage and dismissal, and so on; because he delegated the matter to him in the conduct required by the company, so he was allowed everything in the trade»[468]

Therefore, if he gives speculative money or participates in it, he profits for the company and loses it to it, and if he takes it as a worker for another person, his profit is for him, and his responsibility is for him, as he is only obligated by what the contract was signed for. Rather, it is stipulated that itdoes not insist on harming its owner, so that it does not affect the development of profits. It has been submitted about the work of the worker in speculation - and therefore the son of the seniority of the partner's work – that it is permissible for him to work in the property of another person, if it is with the permission of the owner of the money or if it is without his permission, and there is no harm to his trade. If he acted without his permission, and the harm was to add his share of the profit in the second capital to the first capital profit, because the goal of the company is to obtain profit. Every work that hinders it in whole or in part, is considered a harm that hinders the development of its capital. They said that the second capital gain is refunded in the first capital gain, and they share all, given what

---

[466]Singer 18/5 -19
[467]The Beginning of the Diligent 253/2
[468]Singer 20/5

the contract was concluded for, and what is said in the worker is said in the partner, whether equally, as represented by Ibn Qudamah.[469]

If the partner has the right to act on behalf of his partner, he also has the right to intercede if he sells his share in a joint property between them. The verdict of preemption is an agreed upon verdict. It contained consistent hadiths, as Ibn Rushd said, and it was mentioned that its pillars are four: the intercessor, the supporter, the supporter, the supporter, and the prescription for intercession[470].

Malik, Al-Shafi 'i and the people of the city said that there is no preemption except for the partner who did not share, and the people of Iraq said: Preemption is for three in a row: for the partner who did not share, and then for the partner who shares, if it remains on the road or the plate, a company that combines them, and then for the adjacent neighbor, it was agreed to prove it for the non-size m, and the difference about the dividers and the neighbor.

The mayor of the city, what Al-Bukhari, Muslim, Al-Tirmidhi and Abu Dawud narrated about Jabir bin Abdullah Al-Ansari that the Messenger of Allah, peace be upon him, "ruled by preemption in everything that he did not swear. If the borders fall and the roads are diverted, there is no preemption."[471]

They deduced from the text that preemption does not fall except in the joint before dividing it, and the mayor of the people of Iraq in proving preemption for the neighbor, which some began with the partner or the dividing partner, what Al-Bukhari told Abu Rafi that the Prophet (peace and blessings of Allaah be upon him) said: "The neighbor is more entitled to pour it out,"[472] so they inferred with him the proof of preemption for the adjacent neighbor... Al-Bukhari narrated in the Book of Preemption under "Which Neighborhood is Closer?" On the authority of Aisha, she said: "I said, 'O Messenger of Allah, I have two neighbors, so which one should I dedicate?' He said: The closest one to you is Baba»And the[473] text -apparently – is not the half of preemption.

As for its conditions, as decided by Ibn Jazy for Maliki jurisprudence, they are five:

1-To be located in the property, and disagree on what is not divisible like a bathroom. Dividing goes back to income.

2-That nothing shall be issued by the preemptor indicating that his right to preemption has been extinguished. As if the buyer bargains in the hardship he bought from his partner, or is silent for a year or more, with his knowledge and presence, and accepts his apology for the absence and lack of knowledge.

---

[469]Singer 21/5
[470]Beginning of the Diligent 2/253
[471]Al-Bukhari Al-Fateh Version 5/342
[472]Al-Bukhari: Al-Fath copy 343/5 and Al-Saqab in Alsin and Alsad, and Al-Fath Al-Qaf and its proximity and adjacent housing
[473]Ibid p 345

3- That the accompanying rift has become the subject of a netting such as the sale and the dowry, and with Abu Hanifa, it does notfall except in what was sold, and it does notfall in the inheritance by agreement.

4- To fall into the common that has not been divided. 5- The intercessor should be a partner and not a neighbor. If the company owns real estate.

AUTHORIZATION PARTNERSHIP

A bargaining company, a commercial company, whose contract is based on the authorization or negotiation between the partners, and the release of each partner, his partner's hand, to act in his name freely, not knowing the difference betweenwhat was in his property, or the property of his partner, whether in his presence or absence. Is there anything in all that they have, as is understood from the words of some scholars, or in what is suitable or useful for trade, as is understood from the words of others other than? Disagreement about its meaning, the research leads to disagreement about its permissibility or non-permissibility.

In the principle of its occurrence in all properties and the disagreement of the imams about its permissibility, Ibn Rushd says: "They differed in the bargaining company, so Malik and Abu Hanifa agreed wholesale on its permissibility, although they differed in some of its conditions, and Al-Shafi 'i said:It is not permissible. The meaning of the bargaining company is that each of the partners authorizes his owner to dispose of his money, with his absence and presence. This is true for them in all kinds of properties. Omda al-Shafi 'i said that the name of the company applies to the mixing of funds. Profits are branches. It is not permissible for the branches to be joint, except with the participation of their assets. However, if each of them stipulates a profit for its owner in the property of itself, this is from gharar, and it is not permissible. This is the capacity of the bargaining company, and as for Malik, he sees that each of them has sold part of his money with part of the money of his partner, and then each of them is his owner to consider the part that remained in his hand, and Al-Shafi 'i sees that the company is not a sale and agency, and Abu Hanifa here on his origin in that he does not take into account as in Anan company only cash, and as for what Malik and Abu Hanifa differ in from the conditions of this company, Abu Hanifa believes that it is a condition for bargaining equal capital, and Malik said: It is not a condition for that, similar to Anan company, and Abu Hanifa said: One of them has nothing but to enter into the company. Their mayor said that the name of the negotiation requires these two things: I mean the equality of the two money, and the generalization of their king. "[474]

Thus, according to Ibn Rushd, the bargaining company is located on all properties. Therefore, the dispute occurred in its regard, and the Shafi 'is absolutely prevented it, the Hanbalis in some of their forms and the Hanafi nuts with conditions, and the Malikis with the dispute in some of their conditions. The most eminent imams emphasize its invalidity, Imam Shafi 'i. He said: "If the bargaining company is not invalid, there is no invalidity that I know of in this world.[475]

---

[474] The Beginning of the Diligent 251/1
[475] Singer who needs to know the terms of the curriculum 212/2

We - and if we realize the reason for the dispute - will not realize the reason for the invalidity at the level of distortion observed from the words of Al-Shafi 'i, as long as the contract did not lose one of its conditions and as long as the mixing of funds, whether in the form of development, facilitating the monitoring process, or preserving its values was not prohibited in whole or in part between one Muslim and another, and the explanation that the name of the company stems from the mixing of funds, and that the profits are branches, and the branches may not be joint, except with the participation of its assets is unclearbecause the term of the company requires that the assets stipulated in the contract be necessarily joint, it is related to the principle of participation: either some or all of the money, andwe do not see that a company with a capital consisting of the shares of the participants is held without it.

When talking about the capital of the Mudaraba Company, it was submitted that they allowed Mudaraba with money, evaluated offers, and assets that remain its property, as well as the capital of the Anan Company. If the circle expands, and it is agreed to contribute to all of them, it is a contribution of some kinds, none of which has been prevented from participating. It is not permissible to separate, it is permissible collectively, except that what will come from the negotiation involving scarce gain will be void. We also did not digest Imam Malik's opinion that each of the two partners had sold part of his money with part of his partner's money, and then each of them had to look at the part that remained in his hand. It may be, as Imam Al-Shafei said, that the company is not a sale and agency. This is whatappears when considering the different requirements of the two contracts, and what ismeant by them separately, and it is known that the sale is for the transfer of ownership and the company for profit and development, and combining them with the agency in one node that we have not identified.

Perhaps the closest opinion to understanding is that of Imam Abu Hanifa, who authorized it with equality and generalization. These are logical matters, which are required by the subject, as by mixing the funds and their participation with the discrepancy in their amounts, those with more money are lost and by generalizing them, negotiation is distinguished from unleashing, because they do notdiffer in the requirements of the contract, the elements, the conditions or the profit and loss...It's about how capital is formed. This is because the unleashed capital is determined on the basis of the contribution in amounts agreed upon and no partner has theright to act except with the permission of his partner, and within the framework that they have specified other than the negotiation according to which the money of each partner becomes the money of his partner, he has the right to dispose of it as he wishes, and what he did obliges its owner, as understood from the words of Ibn Rushd.

Despite what Ibn Rushd quoted from Malik, what was mentioned in the Great Code of Sahnoun about Ibn al-Qasim, indicates that negotiation may be in all things or concern some kind of trade. In this, Ibn al-Qasim says: "What they have in common, if it is in all things, they have negotiated, and if it is in common to buy one kind of trade such as slaves and beasts, they have negotiated in that kind."[476]

The result is that negotiation in all things is for the sake of absolute negotiation and includes capital and the commercial field, and negotiation in some is in order to participate and act in that some, and as long as negotiation means exchanging permission to act, its limits end with agreement between the contractors. Thus, it is clear that there is a common denominator between negotiation and unleashing.

Even in this era, two merchants may resort to their money and their offers, shops, tools and trucks... They agree to place it in the capital of a company held between them. I met two merchants who were involved intrade, construction and everything they own... So that there is nothing in the custody or ownership of one of them that was not in the custody or ownership of the other.

even as if they were one in two. It is this spirit that Islamic texts have called for its nourishment. And the company that they contracted, and gave it mutual trust and indissolubility, we did not find from the original texts anything to invalidate it. He started it by trading, and from it it branched out into other properties. In the end, it is not permitted to subscribe to it at the beginning, if the capital is in cash and the values of what it is worth.

As for the Hanbalis, they allowed it, except in some rare pictures. It is the one that includes in its calculation what itmay own or perform of the rights outside the circle of participation in capital formation. Their opinion on this is clearer, as the contracts of financial companies do not fall on those who are not owned in the case of the contract, and their owners are not involved or responsible for each other, except within the framework of the contracts concluded between them. Therefore, they divided it into correct and corrupt. In that, Ibn Qudamah says:

«As for the bargaining company, there are two types: one is to participate in all types of company, such as combining the unleashed, the faces and the bodies, so this is true, because each type is valid with its own Passover with others, and the second is to enter between them in the company to participate in what happens to each of them from a inheritance, or finds it from a concentrate ora snapshot, and each of them is obligated to do what is necessary for the other, such as bribing a felony and ensuring the extortion and fine of the guarantee, this is corrupt. Thus, Al-Shafi 'i said, and Al-Thawri, Al-Awza 'i, and Abu Hanifa allowed him to do so, and he told this about Malik. " Those who allowed him did not seemto look at the contract in terms of capital formation. Rather, they looked at it in terms of what was agreed upon. If the agreement for the contract company does not find its place in the unknown or nonexistent, Ibrahim bin Dawyan and Musa Al-Hijawiconfirmed the opinion of Ibn Qudamah, with a

---

[476]Grand Blog 4/37

difference in expression. They said the text to Ibn Dawyan: "It is to delegate each to his owner a purchase and sale in the debtor, a negotiation, a power of attorney, a traveler with money and a mortgage. It is an award, because it does not go outside the strike of the company, which has applied. If they enter it with a rare gain, such as the presence of a cat, a concentrate, or the inheritance obtained, or if one of themis obligated to ensure the extortion or bribery of a felony, a naked guarantee, or the need for a dowry with a slow pace, then it is corrupt, because it is a contract that the Sharia did not reciprocate, and because of the large number of damages. "[477]

We did not know for the tap such a division, it was natural that their opinion contradicted the opinion of the Hanbalis, especially with regard to the introduction of rare earning. After Ibn Qudamah explained that the tap stipulates equality and generalization, and that they invoke what they said that the Prophet (peace and blessings of Allah be upon him) said: "If you negotiate, do well to negotiate." He stated that he does notknow it, he said that it is a contract thatis not valid and[478]carries the corrupt type, and as for the right, he allowed it and what he allowed, it is notnatural to return it to others. If it is proven to him that "if you negotiate, do well to negotiate" to bring him to the right that did not fall on the rare gain.

It is deduced from the analysis of Ibn Qudamah that the four imams agreed in the sentence on the permissibility of the type expressed in the correct company, and Imam Ahmed and Al-Shafi 'i stressed the type expressed in the corrupt, and about the corrupt, it is true that the statement of Ibrahim bin Dawyan about the doctrine of Imam Ahmed: «It is a contract that the Sharia did not respond to similarly» with the saying of Imam Al-Shafi 'i: If the bargaining company is not invalid, there is no invalidity that I know in this world» and it: carries his reasoning not to mix funds; because the rare gain does notexist in the case of the contract, it is mixed with other capital assets.

Otherwise, it is not permissible to separate,it would not have prevented a society, as Ibn Qudamah said, especially since the contemporary economic movement, requires the collection of jurisprudence sundries, to be able to confront the new regulations, so it is safe to say that the company that carries out the activity of several companies with the negotiation of their owners, as is the case for some contemporary companies, the negotiation company is considered: The work of the shareholders within it, the activity of the unleashing company, and if you give money to those who work in it with a share of its profit, the activity of the speculation company, and if it works in the example of fishing and construction, the activity of the business company, and if it gains the confidence of the owners of the factories, and takes the goods to sell them and

---

[477] Manār al-Sabīl fī Sharḥ al-Dalīl ʻalá Madhhab al-Imām Aḥmad ibn Ḥanbal 406/1 al-Iqnāʻ fī Fiqh al-Imām Aḥmad 273/3
[478] Singer 5/ 5

pay the price, the activity of the company of the faces, and if it does all these activities, the negotiation company in some of its forms. Doctrinal scholars have not prevented the work of them collectively, if the laws and conditions prescribed for their validity are taken into account.

As for expanding its circle and introducing types of property, which it does not usually contribute to when forming capital, the right company may branch out to it, after the success of its projects, so it owns land, livestock, real estate and fishing vessels... This is all of its capital. What the capital devolves to at the end,it is not right to prevent its introduction at the beginning: either in the form of money or its consideration in the valued things, as mentioned above. Since scarce gain, because it is notvalid in the case of the contract to be considered a capital, its exclusion or the corruption of the contract for its sake is clear, because participation in what may happen from an inheritance, or is required from the arch of a felony and the guarantee of extortion. And a fine for guaranteeing... It is not with money that the capitalist company can be held, whether speculation,unleashing or bargaining, as one of its conditions is that the money is known to be present, and it remains only to listen to the opinion of the Shafi 'is and Hanbalis who invalidated the company, that the contract be signed in consideration.

This was the view of the bargaining company, and it was stated in the book of jurisprudence on the four doctrines "about the difference between it and the unleashed saying: "The difference between bargaining and unleashed is that each of the two partners in the bargaining is eligible for bail, that they are free and rational adults who agree on the religion, and that their capital is alike, unlike the unleashed company, "they said[479], and the text did not fulfill each statement and the previous texts more than a statement.

---
[479] Kitāb al-Fiqh ʻalá al-Madhāhib al-Arbaʻah 68

GOODWILL PARTNERSHIP

In this era, many companies trade without capital. But with money that debts fall in its debt: it buys goods, sells them and pays their price, and it is known in Islamic jurisprudence as the Faces Company.

And the company of faces – as its name – is located between people, who know in their faces that they are of goodwill, honesty and loyalty... Their capital is to gain the confidence of traders and producers, so that they take the goods and sell them, and then pay for them, so that their participation in the responsibility of the debts that arise in their receivables, including the purchase of goods and the performance of their price, in addition to practically contributing to their activity, and selling - such as buying - may be at the deferred and accelerated price.

Among what is stated in the "Book of Jurisprudence on the Four Doctrines" about its system "is that two or more people who do not have money participate, but they have a reason to be trusted, provided that they buy a trade at a deferred price, and what they earn is between them, and the company of the faces is divided into negotiation and unleashing: negotiation that they are among the people of sponsorship, and that the buyer between them is two halves, each of them has its price, and that they are equal in profit and that they utter a negotiation. The power of attorney of each of them is verified against his owner in what he has and his guarantee in what he has. He wanted to miss some of these restrictions, such as one of them buying a quarter of the commodity and the other the rest. "[480]

It differed in its permissibility, and was authorized by Imam Ahmed and Abu Hanifa, and was revoked by Malik and Al-Shafi 'i. In it, Ibn Jazzi said about the Maliki doctrine: "As for the company of the faces, it is to participate without money orwork. It is the company on receivables. So that if they buy something, it is owed to them, and if they sell it, they share its profit. It is not permissible, unlike Abu Hanifa»[481]..

It will come in the words of Ibn Qudamah that Abu Hanifa requires for its validity that the partner assigns to his partner the type of commodity, the amount of money and the time of his performance... This is because they share the responsibility for performing in a timely manner, and that Malka and Al-Shafi 'i require the mention of the agency's tapes, which makes it clear that their opinion is suspended by the condition. Although the scholars of the Maliki doctrine are fired in nullity. In that, Ibn Rushd says: "The company of the faces of Malik and Al-Shafi 'i is invalid, and Abu Hanifa said it is an award. This company is the company on receivables without workmanship ormoney. The mayor of Malik and Al-Shafei said that the company is only concerned with money or work.

---

[480] Kitāb al-Fiqh ʿalá al-Madhāhib al-Arbaʿah 68
[481] Jurisprudential Laws of Ibn Jazī, p. 209

Both are non-existent in the matter, with all the gharar... Abu Hanifa relies that it is a business, so it is permissible for the company to convene on it[482]. "

Abi Hanifa's view seems to be clearer, that there is a business involved in buying and selling goods. This is the same asthe employees of the speculative and loan company. If there is a difference, then those working in speculation trade with capital, and divide the profit with its owners, in exchange for bearing its loss, and in the company of the faces, they buy goods for a period and are independent by profit, in exchange for guaranteeing their price. That's what Ibn Qadamah means, and he talks about the guarantee in the transportation company.

He said, "The company is contracted on the guarantee as a company [483] of faces," and Hanbali authorized itunconditionally. In its subject and the views of the imams around it, Ibrahim bin Dawyan, Musa Al-Hijawi and Ibn Qudamah say:

As for the company of faces, it is that two people share what they buy, and the trust of traders in them, without having capital. However, what they bought between them is two halves or thirds or quarters or so, and they sell that, so what God Almighty has divided is between them. It is an award, whether one of them appointed to his owner what he buys, his destiny, his time, or his class, or he did not appoint any of it, but said: What you bought is between us, and Ahmed said in Ibn Mansur's novel in two men who shared their capital onwhat each of them buys: It is an award, and thus said the revolutionary, Muhammad bin Hassan, and Ibn Al-Mundhir, and Abu Hanifa said: Do not shout until time, money, and class of clothes are mentioned, for example, and Malik and Al-Shafi 'i said: It is required to mention the agency tapes; because the agency tapes are considered to be from the appointment of gender and other agency tapes.And for us that they participated in the purchase, and each of them authorized the other in it, so Passover and whatcame to be between them, as ifhe mentioned the tapes of the agency. They say: "The agency does not ratify until the amount of the price and the type is mentioned. It is forbidden for a novel to us, and if we hand it over, it is considered in the individual agency, but the agency within the company is not considered in it. In the guide of Anan and Mudaraba Company, some of the conditions[484] were not seen by others, so the balance was tilted towards the passport.

That was the look at the meaning of the company of faces, and the controversy surrounding it. As for the division of profit within it, it is subject to agreement, as evidenced by the statement of Ibn Qudamah: «halves, thirds, quarters or so. He confirmed this in connection with the division of profit in companies. He said: «As for the company of faces, the words of the clerical in general require the permissibility of what they agree upon in terms of equality

---

[482] The Beginning of the Diligent 252/2
[483] Singer 5/6
[484] Singer 12/5 Manar Al-Sabil 404/1 Persuasion in the jurisprudence of Imam Ahmed 2/270

and differentiation. It is the measurement of the doctrine; because all other companies have profits according to what they agree on, so too is this;because they are held on work and others, so what they agreed on was passed, as an unleashed company. "[485]

The point has been made that equality in the division of profit responds to equality in the amount of work, and differentiation responds to its difference, and the agreement would take into account the conditions and quality of work.

Thus, as Muḥammad ibn ʻAbd al-Raḥmān al-Dimashqī titled his book "The Mercy of Imams in the Difference of Imams," we find the opinions of one Imām, or one agreed opinion thatis unable to confront our difficult and complex complex problems. It may be that the research is facilitated besides the compassion represented in the difference, and the multiplicity of opinions: what is lacking in an aspect that has expanded in one aspect - thatthere is no economy of Maliki, Shafi 'i, Hanafi, and Hanbali, to which a follower of one of these doctrines adheres, as is the case for worship, for example. Rather, it is an Islamic economy, at whose table the views of our imams converge, who, if they differ in understanding, taking and deducing from the texts, did not differ in relying on Islamic sources of legislation.

---

[485] Singer 27/5

ORIGIN IN THE BUSINESS COMPANY AND ITS ACTIVITY IN THE FIELD OF EARNING AND COMPLETION OF URBAN PROJECTS

The era in which we live, the era of economic and international conglomerates, and the era of establishing companies, with different trends, so the Islamic Ummah had to emerge, search for its own values, its basic components, and impose its existence on the global economic movement... Its economy, with its strength and flexibility, and its principles of inclusiveness and moderation, is the strongest base from which projects of large and medium sizes are launched, including the establishment of companies.

If contemporary companies know the fields of trade, industry, agriculture, air, land and sea transport, as well as the fields of fishing, the search for solid and liquid minerals, and the completion of construction works, such as buildings, the construction of dams and arches, the Islamic economy is earlier to lay the first foundations for these companies on a difference in the requirements of contracts, and what may occur from conflict or consensus.

If it is submitted that among the Islamic commercial companies, the speculative company in which money is given to those who invest it with a share of its profit, the Anan company in which the owners of the capital work themselves, the bargaining company, which is based on the exchange of authorization to act, and expands to include from the funds of the participants other than what they trade, and the company whose capital is to gain the confidence of the producers and take the goods and sell them, and then pay the price, the business company that concerns us in this chapter, does not depend on the capital or the confidence of the producers. Rather, it relies on work, and it earns through what it tries to do, make, or accomplish from projects.

The imams authorized: Malik, Ahmed and Abu Hanifa, the business company, and Al-Shafi 'i prevented it, when he believes that the company is concerned with money, explaining that the profit in the same business is unrealized, unsecured, and the work of its participants may differ, so it is held according to what is in Gharar, but the reason is unclear, because the profit - whether in the same money or the same business - is unrealized, and unsecured; if the subject of the attempt, livelihood and work in the same money may differ, depending on the forms of goods and types of trade practiced by each individual. This is evident in the conditions of workers in the speculative and loan company, as they participate in work, not in money, and the profit in it is unrealized and not guaranteed, and the work is not uniform in form; as the person may buy and sell the other, so things are based on mutual consent, and the requirement of the agreement.

As for al-Malikiyah, Ibn Jazzi mentioned that it is an award, unlike al-Shafi 'i,[486] and Ibn Rushd attributed its passport to al-Malikiyah and the Hanafi and prevented it to al-Shafi 'i, ignoring the opinion of the Hanbali in its passport. It

---
[486] Jurisprudential Laws of Ibn Jazī, p. 209

was stipulated by al-Kharqī in his acronym. He said: "The company of the bodies is an award." Ibn Rushd [487] says: "The wholesale company of the bodies is in the hands of Abu Hanifa and al-Malikiyah is an award, and al-Shafi 'i was prevented from it. The mayor of Al-Shafi 'i said that the company is concerned with money, not business...The mayor of al-Malikiyah shared the booty with the sheep. They deserved it at work, and it was narrated that Ibn Mas 'ud participated happily on the day of Badr, so Sa 'd hit two horsemen, and Ibn Mas 'ud did not hurt anything, so the Prophet (peace and blessings of Allaah be upon him) did not deny them, and also speculation was held on work, so it was permissible for the company to be held on it, "[488] meaning the business company.

The hadith of Ibn Mas 'ud[489] was brought out by the women under the chapter of "the company without money" [490] and Abu Dawood under the chapter of "the company without capital". Muhammad al-Amir al-Sanani stated that he [491] was cut off and protested against his contact in other ways, and the spoils company was proven to be frequent. On a labour contribution basis, the principle of vesting was. This is what is understood from the words of the Prophet (PBUH) from the narrations of Muslim, Al-Tirmidhi and Abu Obeid: "They have nothing in booty and loyalty except to strive with Muslims." And because the work[492] and its quality are considered a division of the man with an arrow, and the knight has two arrows. Islam does notfight for money. Rather, he fights for the supremacy of the word of God, and treats his enemies as he treats them, so they sheep as they sheep and steal as they steal.

The text was invoked by Imam Ahmad, as by others.Thus, Ibrahim bin Dawayan inferred the company of the bodies in his doctrine, and he said - after clarifying its field -: "This is permissible for the words of Ibn Mas 'ud:" I, Sa 'ad, and Ammar participated on the day of Badr, so I and Ammar did not come with anything, and Sa 'ad came withtwo prisoners. Abu Dawud narrated it and Al-Athram and Ahmad protested against it and said, "I associate the Prophet (peace and blessings of Allaah be upon him) among them, and this was in the Battle of Badr, and its spoils were for those who took them before God shared them."[493]

If the subject of Islamic companies is divided into two main parts: trading and labor, and the subject of trading in speculative companies, unleashing, bargaining and faces, the subject of the business company is divided into the company for profit, industry or transport.

---

[487] Singer 3/5
[488] The Beginning of the Diligent 252/2
[489] Sunan Abu Dawud 349/3
[490] Sunan An-Nasi 7/319
[491] Pathways to Peace 63/ 3
[492] Muslim: The copy of the father 46/5 Sahih Al-Tirmidhi 118/7 Money for Abu Abed, p. 412
[493] Manar Al Sabeel 405/5

First: The company for profit, and includes every activity carried out by companies for permissible profit. The permissible gain is either by trying or by completing construction projects with compensation or making it agreed upon.

A- The company of earning by trying, which means searching for the secrets of the land and the wealth of the seas, including the marine fishing company, the company of solid and liquid minerals, groundwater extraction, the company of finding building materials, raw materials, the logging company, the extraction of coal from stone and oud, the company of medicine and education, and the company of loot. Even in digging graves, burying the dead or spying on the enemy, and transmithting news, as manifested in the opinions of our imams and scholars. They demonstrate that they are open to life in their times, and we are frozen with life in ours, despite these principles that give us legitimacy in establishing modern companies with different directions. On the subject, Ibrahim bin Dawyan says about the jurisprudence of Imam Ahmed:

To participate in what they possess in their bodies of permissibility, such as nesting, logging, hunting, metal, snooping on the enemy, and stealing what they kill with, "[494]which is the same as what Musa Al-Hijawi and Ibn Qudamah[495] confirmed by saying:"If they participate in what they gain from permissibility, such asfirewood, hashish, fruits taken from mountains and minerals, and snooping on the House of War, this is permissible. It was stipulated by Ahmed in the novel of Abu Talib»and[496] the hadith of Ibn Mas 'ud was written for him.

In the Great Code of Maliki Jurisprudence, Sahnun asks Ibn al-Qasim: "Is it permissible for the two partners to participate, provided that they collect firewood, and what they collect is between them in two halves? He said: If they all work in one place, then it is permissible. I said: They also participated in fishing, bird hunting, and monster hunting? He said: Yes, it is permissible if they are all working.

I said: "Did you see that they were involved in digging graves, digging minerals, wells and eyes, building buildings, making mud, beating milk, cooking graves [497] and cutting stones from the mountains? He said, "All of this is permissible with Malik, because they all meet in this."

I said, "Is it permissible for the doctors' company to share two men to work in one place? They are treated and work, so what is the livelihood of God, so they are divided into two halves? He said: I asked Malka about two teachers, who participate in the education of the boys, but what God has given them is between them in two halves, and he said: If they are in one council, it is okay... As well as my doctors, if the medicinesthey share, if he has the capital, they will be the same. "Abu Dawood inferred [498]from what Al-Bukhari brought out about the

---

[494]Manar Al Sabeel 405/5
[495]Persuasion in the jurisprudence of Imam Ahmad
[496]Singer 3/5
[497]One of its meanings is camel ball
[498]Grand Code 26/4-27-28 in previous texts

prince who was bitten by the scorpion, and he was riding from the Prophet's companions, mosquitoes,[499] where they participated in what they took ... In the advertising company, Musa Al-Hijjawi says: "As for the mere appeal, offer and bringing the customer, there is nodispute about the permissibility of participating in it."[500]

Thus, it is clear that the Islamic economy has opened the door to the establishment of types of companies, and put the responsibility of underdevelopment on the necks of Muslims; as it did not leave any modern company permissible, without laying the cornerstone of its legitimacy.

B- Company earning through the completion of urban projects, such as the construction of roads and the construction of dams and the construction of archways, factories, hotels and buildings... And the work inside it is either by leasing, and it falls by the day, by the month, or by misanalysis, as in the Almighty's saying: «**I want to make you one of these two daughters to rent me eight arguments**» [501] or fall in meters or so, instead of time, or by making the project be interrupted at an agreed price, as indicated by the Almighty's saying:«**Shall we make an exit for you to make a dam between us and them**».[502]

And making is a kind of leasing, and the difference between them is that the worker in the leasing is entitled to the wage of what has been accomplished, even if what has been agreed upon has not been done, and in making he is not entitled to anything except by completing it. This is like being leased to build a wall for fifty dirhams a day or to build every square meter with ten, so it is worth the amount of days spent or built of meters... Or he may make a thousand dirhams for him to build it, and he does not deserve anything before its completion, and he notes that the lease and the rent may meet, such as he may rent for thirty dirhams a day and make him five hundred dirhams with it, after completion, so the lease is given its ruling and the rent is his ruling. Therefore, the lease is related to time, and what is forbidden to it from counting in meters and making it completely related, except that the project is divided into stages, so it is worth making each stage completed, as an independent one. This is the tradition of contemporary contracting. And the guarantee in the lease on the project owner, and in the rendering or what is known as the boycott in building on the obligor to accomplish it.

From what was stated in «Ghaniya al-Ma 'ar and the following on the documents of al-Fashtali» about al-Lakhmi, he said, "Work in construction on two sides: Ijarah and intersecting, a work on Ijarah was for him whenever he built with his own amount of rent. And he doesn't have to delay catching that.

---

[499] Sunan Abu Dawud 261/3
[500] Persuasion (Jurisprudence of Imam Ahmad 273/2
[501] Surat Al-Qasas 27
[502] Surat Al-Kahf 94

Until the work is done, and if what was done is destroyed before it was completed, he will be paid as much as he was, and the rest will be rescinded... If it was a boycott, and he said: His entire structure, you had the wage, otherwise nothing was for you, it was like a boycott on sewing, if he built some of it, he deserved nothing except its complete and if it collapsed, he must build it from the beginning. "[503]

The difference between Ijarah and al-Ja 'l was clear, and his statement in the Ijarah indicated: If what was built was destroyed before it was completed, he had the wage in his capacity, and the rest is revoked, "in addition to his statement in al-Ja 'l, and if he was destroyed, he must build it from the beginning," that the worker in the Ijarah bears the responsibility for the work, and does not guarantee the success of the project to its owner, and in al-Ja 'l bears his responsibility until its owner receives it. This is what is required of companies that build dams, arches and other construction projects.

As for the building materials, what used to be in the lease is on the owner of the building, and in Al-Ja 'l, it is the subject of the agreement, but Al-Wansharisi has quoted Sahnoun's "Grand Code" from Ibn Al-Qasim as saying: "It is not ok to lease him to build this house, and the plaster and the wage from him", so he used[504] the term "lease" andwe do not know whether he means lease or make because Al-Ja 'l is a type of lease. It has its meaning and its meaning, especially since the employee does notbear more responsibility than the work of his hand unless he is of workmanship working by meter, so it is negotiable about who the materials are.

Thus, it is clear that thepractice of contemporary business companies to conclude contracts on the basis of boycott and completion of projects by making, in return for being charged with the natural and industrial materials required for construction, physical and artistic works, and the reconstruction of what has been destroyed, before delivery, is considered to be at the heart of the Islamic economy. He was adopted by others and evolved on his own.

As for the rendering or the price, it is subject to the agreement, whether in its amount or the time of its performance, and it may occur in stages, some of it is provided and others are delayed. If the materials are included in the works, as taken from the words of Ibn al-Qasim. However, if it has a consideration, it is clear from the words of some jurists that it does notdelay performance, unless the building is its creator, then criticism is permissible.

and delay, but they did not explain the reason for the difference betweenwhat he would buy. Or he makes them and enters them at the price of the market. Rather, they said in support of Ibn al-Qasim in one of the two aspects of its passport: "Either the wage earner is a craftsman, working as a wage and plaster, and delaying cash becomes permissible, as it is permissible to take from the

---
[503]Ghaniya Al-Ma 'ar and the following on Al-Fashtali documents, p. 245 under No. 2479D
[504]Ghaniya al-Ma 'ar and the following on the documents of al-Fashtali, p. 245

butcher and the baker every day meat and bread, and the price is late, so that this interpretation is permissible, cash was provided or else." This [505] is what companies that build houses and sell them on deferred salehave been doing. Some make materials, some buy them.

And offering the price is known as selling peace in the language of the people of Iraq, and advances in the language of the people of the Hijaz, and providing goods is known as selling for a period, and working together by combining two prizes...The jurists did not differentiate between the ladder in materials, manufactures and construction, as they did for the deferred sale. On peace in construction, Fashtali presented a model document. He went on to point out some of them and said: "So-and-so and so-and-so paid dinars from the rail of such-and-such a ladder, in the construction of a house that described it as such in a so-and-so position. He delivers it to him at such a time. The builder has to do all the machines and do the work for them... And what was destroyed from this house before its completion and its handover to its Lord, the committed builder must return it. "[506]

This was the ruling, if matters are on the basis of contracts and concord and what istrue in individuals is true in companies. As for if trust is mutual, as sometimes happens between friends and relatives, the matter is said by Al-Wansharisi: "If he does not stipulate cash ordelay, he criticizes what hemet with the machine, and whenever he does something, he pays him as much as he can."[507]

---

[505] Id., p. 277
[506] Ghaniya al-Ma'ar and the following on the documents of al-Fashtali, p. 289

[507] نفس المصدر والصفحة

ITS ACTIVITY IN THE INDUSTRIAL FIELD

Second - Industrial Works Company. Islam was the first to encourage industry, and called for its mastery, as evidenced by the Prophet's saying: "May God have mercy on him who does something and perfect it." Bukhari narrated in honor of the work that the Prophet (peace and blessings of Allaah be upon him) said: "No one has ever eaten food better than to eat from the work of his hand, and the Prophet of Allaah David used to eat from the work of his hand." [508]

It is known that David was making war shields. In it, Allah the Almighty says: **"And We made iron for him that I should do sabbat and do what is predestined in the narrative and do righteous deeds. Indeed, I see what you do."** He says in another verse: **"And We taught him a work of workmanship for you to protect you from your strength. So are you grateful?"** Ibn Majah recounted that the Prophet (peace and blessings of Allah be upon him) said: **"The Prophet of Allah was Zakariya, a carpenter."** This is only so that the concerns of his companions and members of his nation may rise towards learning the crafts.[509][510][511]

The Arab and Islamic nation had to wake up from its heavy sleep, and shake off the dust of helplessness and laziness, or at the end of it, believe what Ibn Khaldun said and Ibn al-Azraq confirmed by saying: "The Arabs kept people away from the crafts, because they are more ancient in the Bedouins, and further away from urbanization, and what theycall for from the crafts and others." [512]If the cause of the old age of the Bedouins and the distance from urbanization is removed, there is no excuse for fighting the battle of industrialization and its factors.

and an industrial business company that would include the fields of liberal professions and large, medium and small industry... In its activity, it is divided into what ismade for a fee or produced for sale:

A What is made for sale - which is most of what is produced by factories - needs tools, machines and construction... It is accepted by technical and technical expertise in addition to physical work, and is known as commercial production in addition to Hajji production, as it is said in agriculture: food production and commercial production. The original contribution to the establishment of this company, whether in what it manufactures for a fee or for sale, is by work before it is equipped, asonly manufacturers participate in it, i.e. specialized employers or specialists in each type.

In focusing on work, Ibn Qudamah says: "The company of the bodies is that two or more people participate in what they acquire by their own hands, such as

---

[508] Al-Bukhari: Al-Fath copy 5/209
[509] Surah Saba '10-11
[510] Al-Anbiya 79
[511] Sunan Ibn Majah 4/2
[512] Bad 'i 'al-Salab fi Nabat al-Malik, p. 457

the makers participate to work in their industry." Ibn Jazzi says: "As for the company of the bodies, it is in the works and works," if they work with their hands, or contribute their experience. [513][514] As for giving money to those who invest it in industry, and the makers use wage earners, this is a company that speculates with money in industrial production, similar to speculating in agricultural production.

Therefore, the contribution that the contract takes into account, and the negotiation of other tools and machines, is mainly professional work, which is what Ibn Qudamah means by saying: "The company of the bodies is based on abstract work."[515]

If it is new in its subject, from the fact that it was based on physical work, it was called the company of the bodies, as it was called the business company. Today, it has become dependent on the physical and the artistic. In the sense that the maker was working with his body, and today he may work with his body and his mind, or with his mind only, and the work is a gender that includes them. The responsibility for what arises from its production, commitment and guarantee lies on the necks of the participants.

Under Sharia laws, producers are free to sell their production: either as a value, or at the price specified at the level of supply and demand, if it is not of the type subject to the prices of the state; because the laws of the state, while targeting the public interest, are sanctioned by the Sharia in its sent interests, the more it is permissible and desirable, as it is understood from the words of Ibn Mas 'ud: «Muslims see it well, it is with God good» and Muslims consider Sharia to be the workers of the Book of God and the Sunnah of His Messenger.

BWhat is made with wages, and raw materials, such as gold and silver for crafting, linen for sewing and oud for carpentry... Either you are the owner of the commodity and it is the predominant, so the agreement is on the wage of the work, and it is guaranteed by the manufacturer if he loses it or corrupts it. When Bayhaqi was taken away from Imam Ali bin Abi Talib, "he used to guarantee the pigment and the jeweler, and he says:" Itdoes not reach people except that "[516]or it is from the maker at a price, and the agreement is based on the model and weight in such a formulation, and the model and the meter in such a carpentry, and the model and shape in such a sewing... In this case, Ibn Rushd requires that the manufacturer and the manufacturer be appointed, so that the workmanship does not differ in terms of different materials and work. In what was reported by Al-Wansharisi, while commenting on the documents of Al-Fashtali, he stated that there are four aspects, the most correct of which is to appoint the manufacturer and the manufacturer.

---

[513]Singer 3/5
[514]Jurisprudential Laws of Ibn Jazī, p. 209
[515]Singer 27/5
[516]Grand Sunnah 22/ 6

It was in the past. Today - the laws and models governing the manufacturer and the manufacturer have been established, and the duration of the achievement - many factors of disagreement have been displaced and the agreements concluded between producers and consumers have become tight.

The craftsman must observe Allah in his work, especially in the industries that are subject to cheating, as indicated by the saying of the Prophet (PBUH) from the narration of Ibn Majah: "The people who are pigments and jewellers are liars." He[517] recalls his saying in what was brought out by Muslim, Abu Dawood and Tabarani: "Whoever cheats, he is not one of us." He[518] increased in the narration of Tabarani, "and deception and deception in the fire." He must also take into account the order: the first, the second, and the third... Unless the town custom is not arranged. According to Nawazel Muhammad bin Abdul Salam Al-Nasseri, "Is it permissible for the owner of the Raha, and the owners of the industries, to introduce those who have spread or must be relayed? He said: Abu al-Qasim bin Dhaju was asked about him, and he answered what Ibn Farhun said in Al- 'Atabiyyah, quotingIbnHabib

It is for the owner of the land, as well as the makers, to provide whoever they want, unless that means injustice and procrastination, but if that is the custom of the country, there is no harm. "The [519]conditions of submission are manifested in the distant, the traveler, the old man, and the needy, if things are normal.

For the health of the industrial business company, Malikiyah requires that the subject matter and place of industry agree, as mentioned by Ibn Rushd, in [520] which Ibn Jazzi said: "But two conditions are permissible: one of them is the agreement of industry as tailors and blacksmithhs, and it is notpermissible with the difference of industry, as a tailor and a carpenter, and the second is the agreement of the place where they work, if it is in two places it is not permissible, unlike Abu Hanifa in the two conditions. If one of them has the tools of work, without the other, if it is trivial, he canceled it, even if it has a greater danger than his share of it. "[521]

As mentioned above, the contribution is based on physical and intellectual work, tools, machines and buildings, whether in what is done or made for pay or for sale - it has become dangerous and dangerous. Therefore, if the participants' shares are equal in ownership, it is clear, and if they differ, negotiate. It was mentioned in the Grand Code about Sahnoun asking Ibn al-Qasim, on a subject related to its difference in the field of earning, knowing that its ruling on earning as a branch of the branches does not differ from its ruling on what is made for a fee or for sale, or accomplished in urban projects, as all of them are fields that branch out from the business company. He said: "You see, if we share three

---

[517]Sunan Ibn Majah 4/2
[518]Sunan Abu Dawud 370/3
[519]Nawazel Al-Nasseri, p. 2
[520]The Beginning of the Diligent 252/2
[521]Jurisprudential Laws of Ibn Jazī, p. 209

people: I have a house, my companions, and my other mule companions, but what we have done is equal between us, and we are ignorant that this is permissible. So we worked on this, and we made money. He said: Money is divided between them in thirds, if the rent of the house, the animal, and the carriage are moderate. I said: If it is different? He said: The money is divided among them by thirds. Their capital is the work of their hands, and they have parity in it, and those who have the virtue of renting their belongings return to their owners. »Rent [522] means the value of the belongings if the rent is determined for them.

Perhaps the issue of homogeneity of work within the factory and the unification of its headquarters and the problem of machines, tools, buildings and workers' wages... This is what is known to economists as fixed and mobile capital, which no longer exists thanks to contemporary regulations. Where the factory is purchased on the basis of its competence and headquarters, or it builds and equips, and knows its competence and the shares of the shareholders in its establishment, before starting the production and work process and the jurisprudentiallaws governing the business company, I do not see it rejecting whatis good and permissible.

It was stated in the "Book of Jurisprudence on the four sects" about its permissibility with the non-union of industry, and between those who do good and those whodo not, they say: "Two or more makers agree, as carpenters or blacksmithhs, or one of them is a carpenter and the other is a blacksmithh, provided that they participate without money, provided that they accept the works, and the gain is between them. The judgment of this company shall be that each of them shall be an agent for its owner in accepting the works. It is permissible, whether the agent improves the conduct of business first. "[523]

However, what is required by Al-Malikiyah of the homogeneity of the industry and the union of its place, was not required by the Hanbalis, nor was it required by the Hanafis. It is the most obvious, that the lesson is that there is a contract that combines a maker and amaker, not a contract that combines a type in one place. After Ibn Qudamah clarified the opinion of those who say the condition, he pointed out that the difference may occur, if not in the type, in the difference of skills. His words go back into the past. Today, the industry has been unified, and the capabilities and skills in the laboratory have been merged, which means that the study of the views of scholars is legitimacy. As for the industrial system and its development, it is entrusted to Muslim businessmen.

The Hanbalis approved the company's contract with the difference of industry and its location, and focused on joint responsibility and contribution, even on behalf, and established the equality of participants and their equality in action, guarantee and commitment, in place of the administration that works in the

---

[522] Grand Blog 25/ 4
[523] Kitāb al-Fiqh ʿalá al-Madhāhib al-Arbaʿah 68

name of all; unless it is related to what is not the right of one of the partners, or arises from infringement or negligence. In this, Ibn Qudamah decides what Musa Al-Hijawi affirmed by saying:

The company of the bodies is: to share what they accept in their bodies in their receivables from work, it is a correct company. Even with the difference of trades, and what one of them accepts from the work, it becomes in their guarantee, demanding it, and obliging them to do it, and obliging those who are not aware of it to establish his place. If one of them says: I accept and you work, the company is correct, and each of them has a claim to the rent, and the tenant may pay it to each of them, and the payer is absolved of it. If it is damaged in the hands of one of them without negligence, it is their guarantee and what is damaged by the infringement or negligence of one of them or under his hand in a way that requires security, it is on him alone. If one of them acknowledges what is in his hand, he accepts it and his partner and does not accept his acknowledgment of what is in the hand of his partner, and it is obligatory on him." [524]

In any case, the guarantee between the company and one of its members is hesitant due to negligence or lack thereof, and it does not affect the owner of the commodity in preserving his right. His goods, whether lost or corrupt, are guaranteed to those who receive them. It has been proposed that Imam Ali bin Abi Talib used to guarantee the pigment and the goldsmithh, and he says: "It is not suitable for people except that," so it became clear that the Islamic economy has filled every gap infiltrated by manipulation. of people's rights. The negligence and its consequences also deal with the position of the factory guard, as well as the position of the shepherd, who fatwas some scholars that he does not guarantee, if not excessive, and in the guard, Al-Wansharisi says: «There is no guarantee for the guard if he sleeps at his usual time, not at the time of Al-Assas and the guard» and [525] if he is required, or if the guard system is not to sleep, he sleeps, it seems that he is guaranteed; because by sleeping he has become excessive.

---

[524] Singer 5/5 Persuasion in the jurisprudence of Imam Ahmed 271/2
[525] Ghaniya al-Ma 'ar and the following on the documents of al-Fasttali, p. 232

Its Activity in the Field of Transport

Third- The business company for carrying or transporting and delivering goods and persons, including air, land and sea means of transport... It falls within the framework of leasing, renting and renting... It has been proposed that renting is a type of leasing, based on a difference in how and when it is due, and rent is given in the sense of renting, and rent is given in the sense of renting. Although it is often used for leasing in persons, and renting in property.

Since legitimate contracts do not differ in the provision of their permissibility and prohibition, as between the individual and the company, we do not need to repeat what has already been explained. Rather, we come tothe conclusion that the transport company is legitimate, as other subsidiaries of the business company have legislated... In its origin, Ibn Qudamah said about the jurisprudence of Imam Ahmed: Ahmed said: "There is no need for people to share their bodies, and they have no money. Such as fishermen, carriers and porters."[526] Allah says:"**As for the ship, the poor used to work at sea. "If they worked in fishing, then the business company was in fishing, and if they worked in transportation, then the business company was in transportation.**[527] The transfer is either related to the lease of the tanker, which is the responsibility of the lessor, or it is related to the liability of the obligor of the transfer, which is his responsibility. Ibn Jizi says on the subject:

Renting ships and animals on two sides: a certain animal or a certain ship or a certain content, such as saying: I am more than you a animal or a ship, and it is permissible to criticize and delay the rents together, if he begins to ride, and if the animal dies, the rent will be dissolved, unless it is in a guaranteed animal that is not specified, he must come with another animal. "[528]

In light of the difference between the lease of a certain animal or ship, or the guaranteed transport, we note that there are companies that hate cars in their own right; if they are burned or damaged, they are not obliged to bring another car, and companies that hate renting are guaranteed. Its guarantee is notrelated to the eyes of the car as much as it is related to its obligations towards transportation, so it is obligated to bring another car, in fulfillment of those obligations. However, in the first case, the person gave the fare in exchange for obtaining a specific car; if it perished with his hand, the contract stopped working, and in the second he gave it in exchange for the guarantee of his transport or the transport of his goods, which made the right of guarantee continue to the end of the usual distance, and it is valid to provide the fare and delay it and whatwas done with the work today of providing it does notcontradict with jurisprudential laws.

---

[526] Singer 3/5
[527] Surat Al-Kahf 79
[528] Jurisprudential Laws of Ibn Jazī, p. 203

Then it becomes clear that the transport has two faces: one is to be by renting a certain tanker, such as a certain animal, ship, car or truck... The responsibility for the arrival of the thing or not lies with the lessee, as well as the responsibility for spending and the responsibility to ensure it, if it is lost or damaged by infringement or negligence, and if it is destroyed by a divine order, the contract shall be rescinded, and the second is to be through the guaranteed transfer in which the responsibility for access lies with the obligor of the transfer, in exchange for the consideration he takes. He may inform him in any way he wishes.

The transfer guaranteed in the liability is not of the type of insurance for which ignorance is one of its compensation. Rather, it is a work done to protect something that is guaranteed by the pregnant woman, in return for a wage given to her. He was forced to insure him, as understood from the fatwas of the Hajji [529]jurist and jurist Jawad al-Sikli and the Satisfied Sunni [530]jurist, because the distance[531] is known, the wage is known, and what isreceived at the time of loss is known, unlike the civil liability insurance for the car, in which one of the two compensators is ignorant. He may respond when the accident occurs... The knowledge of the two compensators is a condition for the validity of the netting contracts, but the three jurists have allowed it for necessity, and it is also permissible if it is cooperative.

On the legality of guaranteeing the transport of goods with mosquitoes, and his violation of the insurance system, Al-Bayhaqi narrates that Abu Al-Haytam gave him fat from Basra, and that he rented a porter carrying it, and the price of the bottle was three hundred or four hundred, so the bottle fell and broke. He said: I wanted to reconcile me, so he refused, so I argued with him to the judge Shraheh, and Shraheh said to him: "He only gave the reward to guarantee, so he included Shraheh, and then people did not stop until his goodness."[532]

Ibn Qudamah decides that the thing carried is guaranteed by the pregnant woman, until it reaches its place, and that the acceptance of pregnancy requires its guarantee. This is what he means by saying: "If two men participate, each of whom has a living creature, provided that he rents them, then what God has provided for them is right between them. If they accept the carrying of a known thing to a known place in their liability, then they load it on the two beasts or others, and the wage between them is correct according towhat they have stipulated, because accepting the pregnancy proves the guarantee against them. They may carry it at any back. The company is contracted on the guarantee[533], "which is the same as what Musa Al-Hajjawidecided. To focus on the convening of the company on the agency and guarantee, Musa Al-Hijjawi banned Al-

---

[529]Semitic Thought in the History of Islamic Jurisprudence 306/2
[530]Al-Iman Magazine, p. 11, No. 8- September 1967
[531]Anomalies 244 / 2 See the three fatwas in the Islamic economics curriculum 392/1 -404
[532]Grand Sunnah 122/6
[533]Singer 6/5

Dalalin Company. He said: "Al-Dalalin Company is not valid, because the legitimate company is notoutside the agency and guarantee. There is no agency here. It is notpossible to authorize one of them to sell the property of others. There is noguarantee that the debtors will be in the hands of one ofthem. "[534]

The reasoning is unclearbecause the agency exists between the company and the owner of the thing, notbetween the partners among themselves. Considering that the sale of an individual is the property of another, and what istrue is between an individual and an individual, it is true that it is between the individual and the company, as well as the guarantee, as the company is the one that guarantees whatis lost by infringement or negligence, and not one of the partners against its owner, as they are all considered an agent of the Lord of the thing. We have not identified among the jurisprudential laws thatprevent the activity of companies that rely on selling, renting shops, buildings and others. As long as its activity does not go outside the framework of proxy, in exchange for compensation. And the agency is a reward mosquito, as Ibn Jazzi said.

As for dividing the profit, whether in the income of what is paid,accomplished, made for a fee or for sale, two opinions are known: The first is to divide it equally, considering the work... As a principle by which entitlement is made, and then if the shares of the participants in the processing differ, they negotiate about it, as Ibn al-Qasim said about the Maliki doctrine, and the second is that it should be the subject of the agreement, and the agreement would lead to equality or differentiation, given the differentiation or equality that may occur in the work itself.

In it, Ibn Qudamah said: "Profit in the company of the bodies according to what they agreed upon, in terms of equality or differentiation; because the work is worthy of profit, and it is permissible for them to differentiate in the work, so it is permissible for them to differentiate in the profit obtained by it." [535] He said elsewhere, "All other companies to profit in it according to what they agree upon." [536]

The work concerned in the business company is readiness and directness, not obtaining results; as everyone may work, so one individual wins and the other loses, and the profit and loss is from the luck and responsibility of the company, notfrom the luck and responsibility of the individual, especially since the individual is entitled to profit by membership, as long as the membership exists, the profit is worthy, and the partner may demand from his partner what he owes, or terminate the contract, and he has no right to prevent the profit after it occurs. Ibn Qudamah says in the subject:

"And that one of them is without his companion, so the gain between them, Ibn Aqeel said: It was stipulated by Ahmed in the narration of Ishaq ibn Hani.

---
[534]Persuasion in the jurisprudence of Imam Ahmed 273/2
[535]Singer 5/ 5
[536]Same source 27/ 5

He was asked about two men who share the work of the bodies, and one of them comes up with something and the othercomes up with nothing. He said: "Yes, this is like the hadith of Ibn Mas 'ud, Sa 'id [537] and Ammar." Ibn Mas 'ud got the result and his companions participated with him. Musa al-Hijjawi says: "If one of them gets sick or leaves work, even without an excuse, the gain is between them. If his rightful student is to work or to take his place, he must do so. If he refuses, the other has the right to rescind."[538]

It was stated in the book of jurisprudence on the four doctrines " about their division into negotiation and Anan that they say: "The company of the bodies is divided into negotiation and Anan: negotiation is to be equal in work, profit and loss, and to differ in work, profit and loss, such as a third of work with a third of profit and loss. " [539]

What isstated in this textonly reflects one of the aspects of the dispute over the requirement of equality and its absence. What is new is that he divided the company of the bodies into a negotiation and an unleashed. Although they are made up of money and work.It consists of work, as it is understood to be called bodies. It has been submitted that the partner is an agent who disposes of evil property with his permission, and that - in the opinion of some - it is called the unleashing of the requirement of equal shares, as equal to the unleashing of the horse. Contrary to what wasdecided by the text and in the negotiation, each partner acts in his partner's money with his authorization, so her name was derived from the characteristic of disposing of hermoney, and in the bodies there is no money in which the disposal occurs with permission or authorization, and then dividing it into negotiation and unclear. Perhaps it is clearly an independent company: engaged in the field of marine fishing, the completion of urban projects, the search for solid and liquid minerals, as well as work in the industrial field, air, land and sea transport and allthat is legitimate work... It is also presented when analyzing the aspects of its activity.

Thus, it is clear, through these and other companies, that the Islamic economy, in its principles and laws, has absorbed all aspects of life that concern Muslims as Muslims. If lagging behind global economic development occurs, it is human beings, not principlesand laws. May Allah guide Muslims to practice the righteous law of their religion for every time and place.

---

[537] Idem 5/5
[538] Persuasion in the jurisprudence of Imam Ahmed 271/2
[539] Kitāb al-Fiqh 'alá al-Madhāhib al-Arba'ah 68

FOUNDATIONS OF THE COMPANY FORMATION, AND ITS GENERAL RULES

ESTABLISHMENT OF THE COMPANY AND ITS DIVISIONS

Private and traditional projects are the first brick of the capitalist economy, as we saw in Part Two, and they have developed in the agricultural, commercial and industrial fields, and the completion of services, and they have continued to perform their mission and are still... However, individual projects with limited capabilities, in front of economic development and its means, have not been able to keep pace with technical progress (modern technology, which requires financial, technical and technological capabilities, may exceed the capacity of individuals and their limited capabilities. It was natural for companies in different directions to emerge. Raising capital and technical capabilities in a huge project. It is based on the use of various tools and machines, and it is strong to divide the work, and organize it in an organization that responds to the production capacity of the project, knowing that the huge projectis not considered successful, until it produces the amount of energy spent on it.

Before the eighteenth century, the world did not know whatit knew today of the types of commercial, civil, personal, financial and cooperative companies, organized by commercial, civil and cooperative laws.Although he knows a form of cooperation and participation. According to what the circumstances of time and place allow, as the Almighty says: "As for the ship, the poor were working at sea."[540]If it is advanced that Islamic companies are companies of people, work began with the beginning of the Islamic economy in the seventh century AD... Modern companies are financial and personal.

Money companies emerged in France and England, since the beginning of the eighteenth century as large companies, engaged in navigation, trade and industry, but they did not spread until the second half of it when the English Parliament decided in 1855 - the freedom to establish them, followed by the French legislator in 1867 - and in the forefront of the money companies of the joint-stock company. It played a national and international role, and attracted the international economy... It may contribute to the demand for its establishment that its debts do notexceed its capital to the shareholders' funds, and its bankruptcy does notlead to their bankruptcy. They are less risky to the shareholder's capital.

People companies, although effective, did not play a significant role in developing the size of production units. This is due to the shrinking number of participants, resulting from the excess of responsibility for its debts and its commitment of its capital to their money, and its bankruptcy leads to their bankruptcy. It was natural to be weakened, in the face of raising huge funds, enough to use modern technology in the field of production and work. Limited liability companies were established in Germany. Based on the law of April 20,

---

[540]Surat Al-Kahf presents.

1892, this type – if developed - is close to contributing to the relatively wide circle, and its ability to move the medium trade mechanism. It has known remarkable success because it, too, has debts that do notexceed the shares of the participants.

There are six types of personal and financial companies: Joint Liability Company, Limited Partnership Company, Joint Stock Company, Limited Partnership Company and Limited Liability Company. However, the joint venture company is not regulated by law. It is by agreement of the partners. It is determined at the level of legal organization in five types. According to its purposes and competences, it is divided into commercial, civil and commercial, which is competent to carry out commercial business, and it has been defined by the Moroccan Commercial Law "Article -30" in the joint liability, partnership and shareholding company. He said before enumerating it: "The legally recognized commercial companies are three and the civil ones are the ones that are established in order to achieve civil purposes, which benefit them for material profit, without falling within the framework of commercial business. Among the civil works, works related to real estate, agricultural crops, mines, canal digging and dam construction ... as well as artistic, scientific, medical and sports works... Whenever it is intended to make a financial profit. Hence, companies that buy land, sell it, exploit it, build houses and sell it... Civil companies[541].

There are civil companies, with projects, that do notenter into business but take the commercial form, to support their system and facilitate their business. This is so that it can raise enough money to carry out its projects, and the liability of the partners remains specified in the shares held by each partner. They shall not be responsible for the debts or losses incurred by the company in their own funds[542].

As it is divided according to its purposes and competencies into commercial and civil, it is divided according to its regulations, laws and obligations into companies of persons and companies of funds. Individual companies that focus on the personal consideration, represented by joint venture, limited partnership and joint venture companies, and Amwal companies that focus on the financial consideration, represented by joint stock, share recommendation and limited liability companies. Although the limited liability is disputed in its entity, considerations and financial consideration prevail.

THE CONTRACT AND ITS REQUIREMENTS AND REQUIREMENTS

All personal and financial companies, with the exception of joint ventures, shall be subject at the time of their incorporation to a written contract, a constitutional system, general and special rules, and legal procedures. They

---

[541] The Mediator in Explaining the Civil Law 233/2 by Dr. Abdul Razzaq Ahmed Al-Sanhouri
[542] Companies in the Light of Islam, p. 35 by Dr. Abdulaziz Al-Khayyat

should be fully applied, as will be detailed when analyzing each company's system separately. The Moroccan Civil Code of Obligations and Contracts focused in «Article-682» when defining the company on the contract, as the first rule of incorporation. He said: «The company is a contract according to which two or more persons put their money or work or they are together to be shared between them for the purpose of dividing the profit that may arise from it. The definition does notinclude the contribution, unless the number rises to seven, because it does notconsist of less than seven. Dr. Abdul Razzaq Ahmed Al-Sanhouri walked the same line and said: «Article -505 of the Civil Codification states that the company is a contract under which two or more persons are obligated to contribute to a financial project, by providing a share of money orwork, sharing whatmay arise from this project of profit or loss» and in the considerations of the contract, the Commercial[543] Law saysin «Article -29-»: «The company's contract is subject to the rules of the Civil Code, the commercial laws and the agreements of the parties».

The company's contract is an optional contract that is binding on the parties or the parties agreeing to conclude it, whenever the work it carries out is legally permissible. It is concluded by mutual consent, as confirmed by the Law of Obligations and Contracts in Article 987, where he said: "The company is held with the consent of its parties to its establishment, and on the terms of the contract," [544]which is what Dr. Al-Sanouri wants to say: "The company is held only with the consent of the partners on its subject matter and the share of each partner, in accordance with the rules established in the contract theory."[545]If the general pillars of the company's contract are the availability of satisfaction, eligibility, location and reason, Dr. Shukri Ahmed Al-Sibai says: "The basis is that satisfaction is the basis of the contract."[546]

Consensual or personal agreement, shall notaffect the requirement of the provision and the law. It does not fall on what is prohibited by Sharia and law. If the company signs the nullity of the contract. In this regard, the Law of Obligations and Contracts states in Article (986): "Every company whose place is prohibited by Islamic Sharia shall be void by the force of law among Muslims... Among all people, every company is subject to things that are outside the scope of dealing. " He says in Article -985:" Every company should have a legitimate purpose, and every company whose purpose is contrary to good morals, the law, or public order shall be null and void by force of law. " It became clear that the law is clean and people's actions are what make it dirty.

Regarding the appointment of the legally and Sharia prohibited shop, Dr. Al-Sanhouri says after clarifying the permissible: «It follows that the company is void, if the shares of the partners are not allowed to deal in it, and they are also

---

[543]Mediator in explaining the Civil Code 217/2
[544]Code of Obligations and Contracts p. 208
[545]Mediator in explaining the Civil Code 244/2
[546]Companies p.22 - Dr. Shukri Ahmed Al-Sibai

void, if the works carried out by the company according to its articles of incorporation are illegal, such as smuggling contraband, trafficking in hashish or drugs, managing a prostitution shop, or managing gambling, selling goods that are not licensed in their circulation, forging papers and documents, to reduce the taxes due, dealing in obscene usury or slave trafficking, publishing books or images that are indecent, distributing share papers without a license, or obtaining decorations or jobs from the state in exchange for sums paid to the company»,[547] which is an Islamic principle, if we exclude the expression of obscene usury, and distributing share papers without a license as long as the prohibition includes little, and does not rise with a license.

Since the company's contract is subject, as decided in Article 29 of the Commercial Law, to the rules of the Civil Code, the commercial laws, and the agreements of the parties, and it is distinguished from the rest of the contracts by a basic phenomenon. It manifests itself in that it creates a legal personality. By virtue of which a company with nationality, address, social headquarters, and independent financial assets is formed... It would be the subject of several obligations: the commitment of the partners among themselves, their commitment to the company and the company's commitment to others, and sometimes the partners' commitment to others.

Therefore, the eligibility of the contract means the eligibility of the obligation, and it is invalidated if it is signed with a minor, as it is a condition of the company's validity that the partner is eligible for the obligation, as long as he is personally obligated. Under the contract, and the obligations and debts arising from it, even from its own money, as it occurs in companies of persons...

Hence, the boy, the insane, the imbecile, and the one who is interdicted for his sins or dementiamay not be partners. Rather, the guardian or trustee may participate on behalf of the guardian of his property. The Prophet (peace and blessings of Allaah be upon him) said: "No orphan's guardian has wealth, so let him trade in it, and do notleave it until charity has eaten him." That is, Zakah, and if the testator or his guardian reaches the age of majority, or his dementia disappears, he becomes a partner committed to his name, and it is permissible for him to conclude a new contract. If the other party was his spouse, based on what wasdecided by Egyptian law, in accordance with Sharia law, and French law prohibited it.[548]

The Law of Obligations and Contracts in Article (984) prohibited cases in which responsibilities and compliance factors overlap, saying: The company may not be contracted:

i. between **the** father and the son under his jurisdiction;

---

[547] Mediator in explaining the Civil Code 254/2 and20
[548] The Mediator in Explaining the Civil Law 251/2

2. Between the guardian and the minor until the latter reaches his majority, and the guardian submits the account for the period of his guardianship, and this account is approved.

3. Between an applicant who lacks capacity, or a disposer in a charitable institution, and the person whose property is managed by that provider or disposer.

It is clear from the foregoing that the capacity of the obligation, its circumstances and requirements, is the first door to the conclusion of the Memorandum of Association. If the conditions of the commitment are met, and it is agreed to conclude it, it will not have credibility, until it takes into account the legally established rules and conditions, and it has been ratified. It will be detailed when analyzing the elements of the contract of the joint liability company, as the first company to put forward its system, as stipulated in the Commercial Law in "Article -36-" and in general - and within the general rules - it is required that the contract be in writing. The data includes the personal and family name of each partner, the address of the company, the names of the partners authorized to sign in its name, its purpose, its type, the share of each partner, the amount of capital, the share of the partner in profit and loss, and the date of the start and end of the company, if it is for a certain period.

Article (993) of the Civil Code stipulates that it is permissible to determine the age of the company or not. He said, "It is permissible to contract the company for a specific or indefinite period. If it is held for the purpose of conducting a work, its implementation takes a certain period, which is considered to have been concluded for all the period during which this work continues to be completed. " He said in" Article -994- "about the starting point:" The company starts from the time of concluding the contract, unless the partners decide to start it on another date, and this date is justified before the contract. "The conclusion of the contract does not mean the initial agreement, orwhat is expressed in the draft or project. Rather, it means his resurrection.

As is known, once a company is formed, it is considered a legal person, but its personality is not invoked against others, except after fulfilling the publication procedures prescribed in the law. However, if the publication procedures are not implemented, third parties have the right to adhere to their personality. It will come - within the legal procedures - to deposit a copy of the constitutive contract when writing the seizure of the court of first instance in which the company's headquarters is located, within a period of fifteen days, and registering it in the commercial register, and pasting its summary on the court building board, and publishing it in the Official Gazette and the Announcements Gazette, which is issued in the Judicial Department pursuant to the due publicity.

If the general pillars of the contract are determined in the availability of satisfaction, eligibility, location and reason, the special pillars are specified in the multiplicity of partners and the contribution to the capital by providing a share, achieving profit and dividing it, and the intention to participate is added from the work of jurisprudence.[549]

The Commercial Law has summarized the statement in Article -38- "On the due observanceof theforegoing and the legal procedures arising from the contract and its requirements:" Every change in the partners, the exit of one of them, orhis dismissal from the company, and every change in the company's address, position, or purpose, or in the partners assigned to sign on behalf of the company. Any change in the capital and any reduction or increase in the share of the limited partners, as well as the dissolution of the company before the specified date, its merger into other companies, its continuation after the expiry of its term, or the inclusion of a new partner in it. In general, any change in the constitutive contract must be the result of a declaration or agreement issued by the partners and recorded in a special document. This document shall be deposited, registered and publicized in the same manner and within the same terms stipulated in connection with the constitutive contract. He added in Article 39: "Any change in the company's contractthat does not respect the formalities stipulated in the previous chapter shall be null and void for others."

What the legislator has outlined in this text focuses on issues related to the entity of the company after its incorporation. Its articles did not concern a single case, a single judgment, or a particular company. Rather, it dealt with the topic in general. We will work to put each issue in its place, and analyze it within the system of the company that concerns it.

SOURCE OF CAPITAL, NATURE OF SHARES AND PARTNER OBLIGATIONS

Perhaps the most important element on which companies are based is that of capital... The capital is formed by shares in the companies of persons and by shares in the companies of capital, and it is required - as mentioned above – to be of the type of legitimate property, and to operate within the activity of the company in the legally legitimate fields.

The share may be cash, securities, a business, a trade name, a certificate of invention, or a debt owed by others... All thatis valid to be the subject of the obligation is valid to be a share in the company, and it is not required that it be equal or homogeneous. It is required to be specified. If no share is specified for each partner, the company is void. On the possibility of different quotas, Dr. Al-Sanhouri says: «It is not necessary for the shares of the partners to be homogeneous in nature or equal in value, but it is true that one of the partners provides an amount of money and the other provides securities, and the third provides real estate, and the fourth provides work, and thus the value of each share is not returnedto the values of the other shares, and the share of each

---

[549]Companies p. 30 by Dr. Shukri Ahmed Al-Sibai

partner is estimated at its value. Determining the value of each partner's share is important in the company's contract, as this value oftendepends on knowing the partner's share in profit and loss[550].

The Law of Obligations and Contracts stipulates this principle in Article 990: "It is true that the shares of the partners in the capital vary in value and different in nature. When in doubt, it is considered that the partners provided equal shares. In the Islamic Mudaraba Company, it is true that the shares are of different value and the worker participates in the work, and with it he is entitled to profit without bearing the loss, unless he is infringing or excessive, but his workis not considered a listed share in the capital; because the share in the capital of the Islamic company, isaccepted only in the form of money for its discipline or goods denominated in it, as will come.

On determining the share of each partner, the permissibility of its variation, and the division of profit and loss by quotas on their amounts, modern and Islamic companies meet, and they differ in that the share in Islamic companies isaccepted only in the form of money, or valued goods, the participation is at a price, and it is not accepted without the valued, because of its ignorance of capital, nor of absent money.

Until he comes, nor outside the possession of the owner such as debt, mortgage and deposit with others, until he recovers... And Islamic contracts are characterized exactly, and fill every gap from which the imbalance flows, or lead to confusion.

According to the chapters of the Civil Code on participation or contribution to capital formation, each partner is indebted to the partners for all thathe has promised to provide, and he must deliver it at the agreed time. If he procrastinates in submitting it, the partners may request a judgment to remove him, or oblige him to implement his pledge, while preserving the right to compensation (Article 995-996 Civil). If his share in the capital includes a debt owed to him by others, his liability shall not bedischarged until after the company has paid the full amount, and he shall be liable to the company, if the debt is not paid, when it is due (997 Civil).

If his share is the right of ownership of a specific property, he bears the same guarantee that the seller bears the responsibility for hidden defects, which may affect the property and its entitlement to «8 and civil».

If he commits to provide his share in the form of work he accomplishes, he must perform all the services he has promised, with an account for all that he has acquired, since the conclusion of the contract "999 Civilians".

If his share perishes, or is defective due to a sudden or force majeure after the conclusion of the contract, and before the actual or judgmental delivery, his orderis not without: Either the share is in cash orsomething from lesbians, or the

---

[550]Mediator in explaining the Civil Code 258/2

benefit of a specific thing, the risk of perishing or defecting falls on him, or it is a certain thing, which has been transferred to the ownership of the company, the partners bear that responsibility «1000 civil» and no partner isrequired in the event of perishing to submit his share again, nor to increase the amount of the share over the amount prescribed under the contract «1001 civil» and does the perishing of the share provided in the form of the benefit of a certain thing lead to the company's expiry? The Civil Code answers in Article -1052«and says: "If one of the partners, as a share in the capital, provides the benefit of a certain thing, the destruction of this thing that occurs before or after delivery leads to the dissolution of the company for all partners.

It is not permissible for the partner to set off the losses, for which he bears responsibility towards the company, from what he may have achieved for it from profits in another deal (1002 civilians), nor is it permissible for him to delegate him in the implementation of the works and undertakings he has committed to. In all cases, he shall be responsible for the mistakes committed by whoever deputizes oruses him from the mistakes of "1003 civilians".

Any partnermay not, without the consent of his partners, carry out for his own account or for the account of others similar operations to the same operations carried out by the company, if they harm its interests. If a partner violates this obligation, the partners have the choice between claiming compensation, combining the operations he has completed, and taking the profits he has achieved, with the right of the partners to request his removal from the company remaining, but they lose the opportunity to choose after three months. After its passage, they haveonly the right to claim compensation. If it has a positive "Article -1004- Civil".

If a partner uses, without the written permission of his partners, the common funds or things for his benefit or for the benefit of others, he is obliged to return them with the profits he has made, with the right to claim compensation and to file a criminal lawsuit, if the case requires (Article 1009 Civil).

Each partner shall provide the account within the same limits as the agent is obliged to provide it. This is for the amounts or values he took from the company's money, for joint operations, for what he received for the common interests, oron the occasion of the operations that are the subject of the company, and for every action he undertakes for the common interest. Every condition that exempts him from submitting the account shall be null and void and without effect (Article 1007 - Civil).

If the partner takes or withholds an amount of the company's money, his benefits shall be due from the day he takes or withholds it without the need for a judicial claim. If he supplies it from his money or spends in its interest some of the beneficial expenses in good faith and foresight, he shall be liable to the company for the benefits of these amounts from the day they are paid.[551]

---

[551] Mediator in explaining the Civil Code 329/ 2 -332

Every partner is obliged to perform his obligations towards the company, with the same care and diligence that he exerts in his own business, and to refrain from any activity that harms the company or is contrary to the purpose for which it was established. Any negligence by him is considered a mistake, and he bears responsibility towards others, and he also bears responsibility for not implementing the obligations arising from the contract, and for what results from the abuse of the powers granted to him, but he does notbear responsibility for whathappens due to a sudden accident and force majeure, unless it is due to a mistake committed by «Article -1006- Civil»

The partner has the right to take from the company's money the amount granted by the contract for his personal expenses. It is not permissible for him to take more than «Article 1008- Civilian».

If a new partner replaces an old partner, this is done with the consent of the partners or by virtue of the company's contract, he shall subordinate his rights and obligations, without increase or decrease. This is within the limits required by the nature of the company (Article 1011 Civil).

This provision does not change bychanging the name of the company or its commercial address, as stipulated in Article 1047 of the Civil Code, where it said: "Whoever enters into a previously established company shall be responsible with the other partners, and within the limits required by the nature of the company, for the obligations entered into before entering into it. Even if there is a change in the name of the company or in its commercial address. "

The quota must be assigned and determined. If all the partner's funds - old or new - are included, they must be counted, and if they are things other than money, they must be estimated, according to their value, on the date of their placement in the capital. If it is not based on this consideration, the partners' consent shall be referred to the current price, and if it does not have a price, its value shall be estimated according to what the experts decide(Article 991- Civilian).

These were the general rules, the legal procedures related to the conclusion of the contract and its requirements, the formation of the capital, its laws and considerations, and the obligations arising from the contract from the partners' commitment among themselves, their commitment to the company, and then the company's commitment to them and to others... As for the details related to the division or arrangement of the terms of the contract, the subscription of the capital, the competencies of the management body, the monitoring board, or the ordinary, extraordinary or exceptional general assembly, we will try to analyze each issue in the place or within the company's system that suits it, due to the difference in the nature, characteristics and advantages of companies, despite their agreement in the principle of public order. After the first foundations, it moves to the second topic to complete the overall picture of the general system of establishing the company...

Management, Expiry, Liquidation, Profits and Losses of the Company

Administrative system

The company is managed mainly by the management, and the management in the positive sense is represented in the efficiency of the manager, and those who help him from the acting agents and observers... As long as itis not managed on its own, or by the helpless... The task of the partners, whether by the ordinary, extraordinary, orextraordinary general assembly, as will be explained, is limited to planning, directing, and issuing decisions. If the administrative body is unable to implement decisions, complete projects accurately and firmly, or is the subject of negligence, dependence and indifference... It was a loss. It could be bankruptcy. May Allah have mercy on the poetHassan Al-Bunmani, who says:

If the administration does not find its competencies, it will bring every misfortune and scourge of administrative management from all partners... And whoever of them does so with their permission and on behalf of the rest. He followed any of them to monopolize it. Under any consideration, the Law of Obligations and Contracts states in Article (1015): "The right to manage the affairs of the company shall be for all partners collectively, and it is not permissible for any one of them to exercise this right alone, unless others authorize him to do so. He said in Article (1016) on the power to represent the partners before third parties: " The power of management includes the power to represent the partners before third parties, unless otherwise required. "

The appointment of the director may be stipulated in the Memorandum of Association of the Company by agreement of all the partners. The choice lies with one or more partners assigned to the administration, or with a foreigner who is not a partner. His appointment may then come with a subsequent agreement to the company's articles of incorporation. The partners shall all agree on one or more partners or one or more foreigners as required by the activity of the company, and the work of the director or directors shall be paid or unpaid [552]if they are partners.

If the director is a partner, and he is appointed in the company's memorandum of association or by an amendment in the same contract, and the amended contract months such as the announcement of the original contract, he shall be considered part of the contract, and he shall be called the contractual or contractual director. In this regard, he shall have the right - despite the opposition of the partners - to carry out all the work of the administration, and all the actions included in the purpose of the company, Article -1023 - Civil » provided that it is free from fraud, and that it falls within the limits of the powers prescribed by the contract and granted to it [553]. This type of director is

---

[552]Mediator in explaining the Civil Code 302/2
[553]Companies p. 106 by Dr. Shukri Ahmed Al-Sibai

notdismissed without justification, as long as the company exists.[554] As for directors who are not partners, they are always subject to dismissal, but some laws allow the dismissal of the appointed partner by a subsequent agreement, such aswhat dismisses the non-partner, without the specified in the constitutive contract.

Dr. Al-Sanhouri concluded from those laws that the director, if he is a foreigner, may be dismissed and the agent may be dismissed because he is only an agent for the company. Whether the appointment is stipulated in the company's memorandum of associationor bya subsequent agreement. However, if he is a partner, and if he is appointed by a subsequent agreement to the company's articles of incorporation, he may also be dismissed, and the agent may also be dismissed. If he is specified in the company's articles of incorporation, he may not be dismissed, unless there is a justification for dismissal from treason, mismanagement or major default... His appointment in the company's articles of incorporation makes his appointment part of its system, and gives him the same stability, credibility and continuity... These provisions are not of public order. It is permitted to agree between the partners that the appointed partner shall be a director in the memorandum of association of the company. It is permitted to dismiss as the ordinary agent. It is also permitted to agree that the appointed partner shall be a director by a subsequent agreement, or the foreigner appointed as a director in the memorandum of association of the company or by a subsequent agreement, which is not permitted to dismiss as the ordinary agent.[555]

The considerations of the permissibility and non-removal, on the other hand, are reflected in the right of directors or disposers to abandon their duties or not. Those whomay not be dismissed without justification shall be subject to unjustified abandonment, and those who may be dismissed shall have the right to abandon in accordance with the will of the partners and within the limits prescribed for the agents.

Article (1030) of the Civil Code stipulates the above about who may be dismissed and whomay not, and about the possibility of changing the rule of dismissal or not, and who may abandon and who may not say: «It is notpermissible to dismiss thedisposers appointed in the company's contract, unless there are reasonable justifications for it, and provided that it is done by consensus of the partners, but it is permissible to stipulate in the company's contract that this right is granted to the majority or that the disposers appointed in the contract can be dismissed, as if they were only agents. Justifications for dismissal are considered acts that include mismanagement, serious disputes that occur between the disposers, serious breach by one or more of them in the performance of the duties of their duties, and the impossibility for them to carry out these duties. On the other hand, the disposers appointed under the company's

---

[554] Mediator in explaining the Civil Code 302/2
[555] Mediator in explaining the Civil Code 304/2

contract may not abandon the performance of their functions, unless there are significant reasons that prevent them from doing so. Otherwise, they must be exposed to the rest of the partners.However, it entitles the disposers who can be dismissed, according to the will of the partners, to give up their jobs within the limits prescribed for the agents. "

If nothing is decided and the contract is silent about the circumstances of the appointment and dismissal of the director, Article -1032 of the Civil Code describes the company in this case as Annan Company, and refers in its organization to what is stated in Article - 1030 - which we have finished recording its content. In the Islamic concept, Annan Company is the company in which all partners work on their own. According to Article 1032, "If nothing is decided regarding the management of the company's affairs, the company considered Annan's company, and organized the relationship of the partners in accordance with the provisions of Chapter 1030." He said in Article 1017 on administrative delegation: "When the partners delegate each other in the administration with the statement that anyone can work alone without consulting with others, the company is called the negotiation company or the comprehensive delegation company." It was presented in Islamic companies that the negotiation company in the Islamic concept means the exchange of full delegation to the extent that everything owned by a partner or his work is considered the property of the other and his work. Therefore, Imam Shafi 'i strongly invalidated it.

Manager's Authority and Responsibility

The director has powers specified by the partners in the constitutive contract or in a subsequent contract and whether he is appointed in the constitutive contract. Or in a subsequent contract, he has the sole right to manage the company. Its system usually includes provisions defining its powers. They must be adhered to, and not exceeded. The powers and authorities of the directors may vary according to the forms and size of the management, as well as according to the directors in consideration and reflected in the difference between the partner appointed in the constitutive contract and others.

The non-manager partner is prohibited from interfering in the affairs of management, but he may access the company's books and documents. He shall not have the right to object to the work of the director, unless it exceeds the purposes of the company, violates its statute, or contradicts the law.... Article (1027) Civilians, and then he returns to the partners, and he may resort to the judiciary, and he may also request an account for the management of the company's business at periodic times, or at the time stipulated in the company's system. The right of the partner to see in person the books and documents of the company from the general system. It is not permissible to agree on what iscontrary to it.[556]

Just as the director has power and authority, he also has direct responsibility, which falls on him, and is subject to the general rules, and to the principle of judicial work. They may be civil and they may be criminal. He asks a civilian about the mistakes he makes towards the company. This is like misusing its commercial address, thus exceeding the limits of its authority, and it is also asked towards the company, partners, or others about what arises from the illegal act it engages in. The gravity of his responsibility varies between whether he is a wage earner or anon-wage earner, and he is arrogant towards the company, if his mistake causes damage that affects its financial liability. She has the right to register the lawsuit against him, and each partner has the right to register it in her name and for her account.

His criminal responsibility shall be if the acts he has committed are considered violations or criminal misdemeanors, such as fraud or breach of trust, distributing fictitious profits, or listing his surname as a former employee of the government.[557]

Administrative management may be paid and without it. The principle in the Moroccan Civil Code is that it should be voluntary unless it is agreed to grant it. In this regard, Article (1013) states: "The partner who takes over the management of the companyis not entitled to a remuneration for his management, unless it is expressly agreed to grant him this remuneration. This provision applies to the rest of the partners in relation to the work they perform in the interest of everyone, or in relation to the special services they perform for the company, without being obligated to perform it as partners." In this point, the Islamic Mudaraba Company meets with the relatively modern. The worker in the mudaraba propertyis not entitled to the wage as a partner, but he has the right to spend on himself, if he is conditioned or authorized by the owner of the property or if the custom or custom takes place, as the son of the guardian believes.

THE COMPANY'S JUDICIARY, ITS CIRCUMSTANCES AND REASONS

The company is a legal person. It is born by contract, lasts long or short, and then dies by its dissolution, dissolution, or expiry. She settles her estate, pays offher debts, and distributes the rest to the partners, as a person is born, lives long or short, and then dies at the end of his term. His estate is liquidated, his debts are paid, and the rest is distributed to the heirs.

Expiration of companies for general and specific reasons. It was stipulated in the Commercial Law in "Article -44-" in general, and stipulated in the Law of

---

[556]Mediator in explaining the Civil Code 317/2
[557]Companies p. 119 by Dr. Shukri Ahmed Al-Sibai

Obligations and Contracts in "Article -1051-" andthereafter in detail. It is stipulated in Article (1051) that the company shall terminate:

First: The expiry of the period for it, or the occurrence of any condition or other that requires its rescission

Second: By achieving the thing for which it was established, or by the impossibility of achieving it

Third: By the total destruction of the common property, or by its partial destruction. It is of such magnitude that it prevents beneficial exploitation.

Fourth - The death of one of the partners, or by a declaration of judicial loss, or by seizure, unless an agreement has been signed on the continuation of the company with his heirs or deputies, or on its continuation among the surviving partners.

Fifth: The declaration of bankruptcy or judicial liquidation of one of the partners sixth -with theagreement of all partners.

Seventh: Withdrawal of one or more partners, in the event that the duration of the unlimited company. Either under the contract, or according to the nature of the work, for which the company was established.

Eighth: By virtue of the judiciary in the cases stipulated in the law. It also ends with the destruction of the share that is provided in the form of the benefit of a certain thing. Perished before or after delivery, or provided in the form of the partner's promise to carry out work and services and inability to perform them, as stipulated in Article (1052) Civil.

It is dissolved by force of law, if the losses amount to half of its capital, and the partners do not decide to reconstitute it and raise it to what it was, or decide to reduce it to the level of the amount that already exists (Article -1053- Civilian).

Regarding the reduction of the capital, the Commercial Law says in Article -40-: "The reduction of the capital cannot have any legal effect, except after the expiry of three months, since the date of its publication in the Official Gazette, and in the Local Judicial Announcements Gazette, with this publication attached to an invitation addressed to everyone concerned to submit an offer within the aforementioned period. The exposure shall stop the implementation of the reduction, unless it is revoked or rejected by virtue of the power of the decreed thing. "

The commercial and civil law meet about its dissolution by the force of law in the event of its expiry, the end of the work for which it was established, or the merger process. They also meet about general reasons, especially what companies of persons are dissolved by. The Commercial Law summarized the statement in Article 44, focusing on the joint liability and partnership companies, saying: "The joint liability company and the partnership company end up with the same reasons as other companies. Moreover, the merger into other companies. "

The merger occurs when one company dissolves to join another, or two companies dissolve to form a new company «Article 45Commercial» andmay not legally occur, except with the agreement of all partners on its report, and in each company separately «Article 46Commercial» and shall not beimplemented until three months after the declaration procedure stipulated in «Article 38 Commercial» It relates to the publication of the budget and the manner prescribed for the payment of debts, if it is not proven that they have been paid, or deposited at the writing of the court of first instance. Each company invited to merge may continue its business during the period of exposures. Provided that you carry out these actions without fraud «Article -48 -Commercial».

If, in addition to the merger, the company dissolves on its own with the loss of its capital, the expiration of its term, the expiration of its work, the death, interdiction, insolvency, bankruptcy or withdrawal of one of the partners, with the possibility of agreeing on its continuation, with the heirs of the deceased, or between the rest in the event of interdiction, insolvency, bankruptcy or withdrawal, [558] it shall also be dissolved by a judicial ruling. It shall be at the request of one of the partners, due to the failure of one of the partners to fulfill his obligations, or his default in the work he undertook for the benefit of the company, or the partner was an irremovable director, as if he had been appointed in the company's articles of incorporation, neglected the affairs of the administration, or violated the company's purpose or system, or the provisions of the prescribed laws. The partner may also request the judiciary to dissolve the company, if it is proven that one of the partners has cheated, defrauded, or committed a serious error that justifies its dissolution. The right of the partner to request the dissolution of the company by judicial dissolution from the public system. Any agreement to the contrary shall be void and may not be waived before its cause occurs.[559]

Article (1056) of the Code of Obligations and Contracts stipulates this provision. He said: "It is permissible for each partner to request the dissolution of the company. Even before the expiry of the period prescribed for it, if there are significant reasons for this, such as serious differences between the partners, the actual breach by one or more of them of the obligations arising from the contract, and the impossibility for them to perform these obligations. It is not permissible for the partners to waive in advance their right to request the dissolution of the company in the cases mentioned in this chapter.

Any partner has the right to request the judiciary to rule to dismiss a partner who has raised an objection to the extension of the company's term, or whose actions are considered a justifiable reason for its dissolution, provided that –

---

[558] Mediator in explaining the Civil Code 361/2
[559] Mediator in explaining the Civil Code 377/ 2 -379

after his dismissal – it remains continuous among the rest. Any partner has the right to request the judiciary to rule to remove him from the company, provided that he supports the request to remove him with reasonable reasons and justifications, such as his financial situation is disturbed and he is forced to liquidate his share, in order to seek his help to repair his condition, or his health conditioncalls for his retirement from work, so he liquidates all his business, including his share in the company... His removal does notmean the dissolution and liquidation of the company, as much asit means the liquidation of his share. The right to request dismissal and removal does notmean the right to issue a judgment as long as it is related to the consideration of the reasons and justifications that the matter of evaluation is due to the jurisprudence of the judiciary.[560]

With regard to the withdrawal of the partner, which is the only one that is the subject of suspicion and suspicion, and raises questions, Article 1057 of the Civil Code states that if the duration of the company is not specified, neitherby virtue of the contract, nor by thenature of the work for which it was held, any of the partners can withdraw from it by informing the rest of its partners of its withdrawal, provided that this withdrawal occurs in good faith and at an appropriate time. Withdrawal shall not be in good faith if it occurs from the partner with the intention of taking advantage of the benefit that the partners were aiming to achieve for the benefit of all of them. It occurs at an inappropriate time, if the business of the company is not completed, and it is in the interest of the company to dissolve it. In any case, the withdrawal of the partner does notproduce its effect, except after the end of the current fiscal year of the company's years of establishment, and provided that the partners are notified at least three months before the end of this year, unless there are serious reasons.

With some classification, it can be said that the partnerships of persons are terminated by the death, disqualification, interdiction, bankruptcy, insolvency, withdrawal or judicial liquidation of one of the partners.As for money companies - although they meet in the general causes of the lapse of civil and commercial companies, such as the loss of capital and merger, the expiration of the term or work, or the existence of serious disputes that threaten their existence. According to Articles 1051 and 1056 of the Civil Code and Article 44 of the Commercial Code, they are notentirely subject to the reasons for the companies of persons, especially joint stock companies, because they are based on financial consideration, before human consideration.

A joint-stock company is dissolved by the general assembly, if three quarters of its capital is damaged, the number of partners falls below seven, or the extraordinary or extraordinary general assembly decides to dissolve it... The partnership company, which consists of testators funded on one side, and joint

---

[560]Mediator in explaining the Civil Code 383/2

officers on the other, suffers from duplication in the causes of expiration, as a result of financial and personal duplication in its formation. They are dissolved as companies of persons - by the death, disqualification, interdiction, insolvency, bankruptcy or withdrawal of one of the jointly liable partners, andthey are not dissolved by the death, disqualification, interdiction, insolvency, bankruptcy or withdrawal of one of the limited partners or the financier shareholders. Rather, they dissolve in the financial aspect for the general reasons mentioned above... A limited liability company, which is disputed by financial and personal consideration, and the predominance of financial over personal, also lapses for general reasons. Including the meeting of all classes in one hand. This means that the number of partners falls below two, and the contribution lapses if it falls below seven.

However, the Civil Code says in Article (1061): "If the company is between two people only, whoever issues the cause of dissolution on his part in the cases mentioned in chapters (1056) and (1057) shall have the right to seek permission to compensate the other partner for what he deserves, and to continue alone to carry out the activity that the companywas doing, while bearing the company's assets and liabilities."

Then if it disintegrates by the force of law and continues its work. What is the verdict? The Civil Code answers this question, andsays: "The company shall be dissolved by the force of law upon the expiry of the period specified for it, or upon the end of the work for which it was convened. If the company continues, despite the expiry of the agreed period, or the implementation of the purpose for which the company was convened, to carry out the operations that were the subject of the company, the company implicitly extends, and the implicit extension is considered the occurrence of year by year. "Article -1054- Civil".

LIQUIDATION OF THE COMPANY, PERFORMANCE OF ITS DEBTS AND DIVISION OF ITS PROFITS

As the company offers as a financial and practical entity, it is born with the consensual contract, and acquires, with the availability of its elements, conditions and procedures, and its ratification, a binding legal person... After the expiry of its term, dissolution or dissolution by the force of law, its estate shall be liquidated and its debts paid, and the rest shall be distributed to the partners in the amount of their shares or shares in the capital, and the subjective person - as a living creature of the mind - is born of parents, and acquires, with the conditions of eligibility, all national, legal, constitutional, political, economic, social and practical rights... After the expiry of his term, his estate is liquidated, his debts are paid, and the rest is distributed to the heirs in proportion to their shares in the inheritance. Either way.

After the expiry of the term of the company, its dissolution or dissolution, and its entry into the liquidation stage, its legal personality shall remain in existence to the extent necessary for liquidation.[561] The law has authorized its survival throughout the time during which the liquidation works are carried out, so that the liquidator can fulfill its rights from third parties, and pay its debts. However, it is notpermissible for him, under the cover of its survival, to carry out for its account works other than liquidation works.

As for the authority of directors or disposers, it ends as soon as the company ends, and if they violate and do business, it is under their own responsibility. This is stipulated in Article (1063) of the Law of Obligations and Contracts, where it said: "After the dissolution of the company, the disposers are notallowed to carry out any new works, unless these works are necessary to liquidate the qualities that have already been initiated. In the event of a violation, the directors shall be personally responsible, as a matter of solidarity, for their actions. The previous prohibition shall be imposed from the day of expiry of the specified period of the company, from the day of completion of the work for which it was established, or from the day of the occurrence of the event giving rise to the dissolution of the company, as required by law.

The liquidation and division of the company's funds, and how to divide profits and losses, shall be carried out in the manner set out in the constitutive contract. If the contract does not contain a special provision or agreement, the rule of law shall prevail. He performs the liquidation function when necessary: either all the partners, or one or more liquidators, appointed by the majority of the partners. If the partners do not agree on the appointment of the liquidator, the judge shall appoint him, at the request of one of them. In the event that the company is invalid, the court shall appoint the liquidator and determine the method of liquidation, at the request of any interested party.[562]

The Civil Code has decided in Article + -1065 » that all partners, even those who were not involved in the management, have the right to participate in the liquidation procedure, and that it is carried out either by all of them or by a liquidator they agree to appoint, unless this is specified in the company's contract.

Otherwise, the authority of the directors shall be transferred to the liquidator. He represents the company, and manages it, until the end of his mission, and the company - in the event of liquidation - retains its financial liability as it is the general guarantee for all creditors... The method of liquidation may be | optional contractual, it returns to the agreement of the partners under the constitutive contract or by a special collective agreement, and it may be judicial, if the case requires, it is conducted under the law.[563]

If the majority of the partners decide to appoint one or more liquidators, the numerical majority shall dispense with unanimity, according to whatDr. Al-

---

[561] Companies p. 152 by Dr. Shukri Ahmed Al-Sibai
[562] Mediator in explaining the Civil Code 390/ 2
[563] Companies p. 154 by Dr. Shukri Ahmed Al-Sabaa

Sanhouri mentioned, and whoever she appoints may be a partner or a foreigner. Rather, in the case where there are many liquidators, their decisions must be unanimous or majority... It is customary for each liquidator to appoint the type of work that he liquidates, and if he is not appointed, each liquidator can unilaterally liquidate any business of the company. Provided that others have the right to object to his work before[564] its completion, accordingto Dr. Al-Sanhouri. She said: "Article -1068 of the Code of Obligations and Contracts:"If there are multiple liquidators, they are not allowed to work alone, unless they are explicitly authorized to do so, " which is required by the Labor Law, and harmony in the program of its performance. What is noticeable in positive laws is that - within the Arab world - they differ from state to state... Knowing that the agreement of the law depends on the agreement of the one who sets it, and works in accordance with it.

If the liquidator cannot be appointed by the partners who have the right to appoint him, Article - 1065 of the Civil Code | says: «If it is not possible for those concerned to agree on the selection of the liquidator, or if there are significant reasons, the liquidation task shall not be entrusted to the persons appointed in the company's contract, the liquidation shall be carried out, at the request of any of the partners» ...

The liquidator must provide the partners with the account on the liquidation works. If one of the partners requests during the liquidation information about its procedures, he must submit it «Article + -1077 *Civilian» and he may delegate him to conduct one or more specific work, and he is responsible for the work of his delegate «Article -1075- Civilian» and he may not - even if he is appointed by the court to violate the decisions taken unanimously by stakeholders, related to the management of joint property «Article -1076 - Civilian».

It is permitted,as an agent, to work for a wage or volunteer. He is likely to work for pay, especially if he is a non-partner foreigner. His wage shall be appointed with the text of his appointment, and it shall be issued by a majority of the partners or by the judiciary. [565]If he is appointed by a majority of the partners or by the judiciary and he comes up with what requires his dismissal as if he committed fraud, error, disability, interdiction, or bankruptcy, then the body that appointed him is the one that owns his dismissal: the majority or the judiciary, and it shall be at the request of any partner. If appointed by the majority, if it is related to the judiciary [566]

The liquidator, whether judicial or non-judicial, begins his work by taking the necessary preliminary measures. It strips the company's funds, draws up an inventory list, and makes a detailed statement, indicating the company's rights, obligations, and debts. After receiving her books, papers and documents... He

---

[564] Mediator in explaining the Civil Code 393/2 in the two cases
[565] Mediator in explaining the Civil Code 408/2
[566] Id. 395/2

shall seek the help of those who took charge of the administration before its expiry. After that, he undertakes to collect the rights of the company from third parties and to pay its debts. After he publishes the necessary announcements to invite the company's creditors to apply. With their documents, in the case of creditors, whose debt has dissolved, before the dissolution of the company or during liquidation. As for debts that are not maturing, they are not due for liquidation, unlike whatoccurs in bankruptcy. Rather, its values, and the values of the disputed, shall be placed in a trustworthy place, until the deadline comes and the dispute is resolved, Article -1071- Civilian. "

The liquidator may sell the company's property, whether movables or real estate, in order to pay its debts, and if the remaining money in its capital is not paid by its performance, and the price of its assets and property after its sale doesnot cover all its debts. Here, the difference is raised between the financial joint stock company, and whathappens to it in the fact that its debts do notexceed its capital to the shareholders' funds, and between the personal joint liability company, and what happens to it in the fact that its debts exceed its capital to the funds of the participants jointly and responsibly, and the obligation. In the second category, it says : «Article -1072-» of the Law of Obligations and Contracts: «If the company's funds are not sufficient to pay its outstanding debts, the liquidator must ask the partners for the necessary amounts if they are obligated to provide them according to the nature of the company, or if they still owe their shares in the capital in whole or in part, and the shares of the insolvent partners are distributed to the rest, in proportion to the losses they bear».

The creditors are of two types: the creditors of the company, and the creditors of the partners personally: the creditors of the company have the right of precedence over its money; because it is the legal person committed to their rights, and then after the inability of its money to pay, their right is transferred to the funds of the responsible partners committed in its name, if its contract is based on solidarity, responsibility and commitment... The right of privilege over the creditors of the partners shall be established for them in person. In this regard, the Civil Code states in Article 1048: "The creditors of the company may initiate their claims against it represented by the person of its disposers, and they may also initiate them against the partners in person, but it is necessary to start implementing the judgments issued to them on the company's funds, and these funds prove to them the right of privilege over the creditors of the personal partners, and when the company's funds are insufficient, they are entitled to follow up the partners personally, to fulfill their rights from them, within the limits required by the nature of the company."

As for the creditors of the partners, after the expiry of the company and its dissolution, they may exercise their rights over the share of their debtor in the assets of the company, after deducting from it the debts due from it. Before any liquidation, they have the right to impose a precautionary attachment on this share (Article 1050- Civil). The Commercial Law stipulates in Article 43 that the partners' personal creditors are considered as third parties.

After liquidation, payment of debts and expenses, and all rights owed by the company, the remainder shall be divided among allpartners according to the amount of their shares or shares in the capital. With the same account in which profits and losses are divided, as long as the shortfall in capital is considered a loss. It has been submitted that it is the amount of shares or shares involved in the capital that determines the amount of profit and loss. The provisions of the law say: The share of each partner in profits and losses shall be in proportion to his share in the capital "Article -1033 Civil" "Every condition that would grant one of the partners a share in profits and losses greater than the share that is commensurate with his share in the capital shall be null and void and void of the company's contract itself" "Article -1034 Civil" "If the contract includes granting one of the partners all the profit, the company shall be void" Article -1035 Civil ".

This was the overall view of the formative foundations, the necessary conditions and basic laws, judicial rulings, contractual agreements, and general and special rules...

which represents the general framework for the establishment of the company. As for the nature of each company, its characteristics and provisions, and whatdistinguishes this system from that, we will see it when analyzing its systems, focusing on the operative part of the law, and starting with people's companies.

JOINT LIABILITY COMPANY

CONTRACT, COMMITMENT AND CAPITAL

The commercial companies of persons are three: the general partnership company, the limited partnership company, and the joint venture company. The Moroccan Commercial Code, in Article 30, defines commercial companies legally considered in three types: the joint liability company, the partnership company of personal companies, and the joint-stock company of capital companies. The joint venture company is not regulated by the Commercial Law. even if it is considered commercial. Rather, by the agreements of the partners, and it works in civil and commercial purposes, as will come, and the limited partnership company, if its capital is in shares instead of shares, has been transformed into a company limited by shares. It was considered a money company, as it will come.

The Commercial Code in Article 31 defines a joint liability company as "a company held between two or more persons with the intention of trading on the face of the company with a special address. Its name shall be "and it is stated in Article 32 that the partners in the joint liability company, whose names are mentioned in the company's contract, are joint in all its undertakings and obligations. Even if the signature status occurs only from one of them, provided that it is signed in the name and address of the company.

Thus, all partners are jointly liable for all the obligations of the company, its debts and undertakings, and the rights of third parties towards it. The fulfillment of their own funds[567] and every condition that determines the liability of the partners shall be considered null and void, and shall not beinvoked against others, without requiring the nullity of the company.

The joint liability company, in its formation, foundations, management, distribution of its profits and losses, nullity, expiry, dissolution, and liquidation, shall be subject to the rules and laws prescribed in the commercial and civil law.

Formation of a partnership company, such as a partnership company, requires that the contract be written on an official orcustomary paper and [568] dated, and it must include the data listed in the Commercial Law (Article 36), whichare as follows:

1- The personal and family name of each of the partners and his place of residence 2- The company's address and headquarters. The address consists of the names of the partners 3. The names of the partners authorized to sign in the name of the company.

---

[567] Mediator in explaining the Civil Code 235/ 2
[568] Mediator in explaining the Civil Code 247/2

4- The purpose of the company, its type, the amount of its capital, and the share provided or to be provided by each partner. It is from the shares that the capital is formed.

5- Evaluating the shares when theyare not in cash, whether they are in kind and how the evaluation took place

6- A statement of the share of each partner in the profit and loss.

7- The date on which the company starts, and the date on which it ends, if it is fixed-term.

8. Special agreements relating to the operation of the company, and the powers of the director.

In addition to writing, the contract of the joint liability company - such as the partnership company - is subject to the filing system, registration in the Commercial Register and publication. Legal measures A sentence was decided in "Article -37-" of the Commercial Law. It must fall within the fifteen-day period. It is calculated from the date of the contract and its omission results in nullity based on Article 20 of the Commercial Code, which is as follows:

1-Deposit a certified copy of the constitutive contract, if notarized or its counterpart if customary, within a period of fifteen days. It is calculated from the date of the contract «Article 37 Commercial».

2- The deposit shall be made at the time of writing the seizure of the court of first instance in which the company's headquarters are located, so that those who wish to know the conditions of the company can view it.

3- The contract shall be deposited and registered in the Commercial Register pursuant to Article19 of the Commercial Law. 4- Attach or paste a summary of the contract on the court building board.

5- The summary shall be published in the Official Gazette, and in the Announcements Gazette, which shall be issued in the Judicial Department located within the company's headquarters «Article 20 Commercial».

Article 41 of the Commercial Law stipulates that the failure to prove the company in a written fee or the lack of publicity does notprevent the company's contract from producing all its legal effects in the relations of the partners with each other, and they may prove the existence of the company by all means of proof, but if a written fee or publicity is not drawn up, each of the partners may request the dissolution of the company whenever he wishes and the dissolution has its legal effect between the partners, starting from the date of submitting the petition containing the request for dissolution. Article 42 states that the partners may not protest against others for the absence of a written contract or thelack of publicity. The joint liability company has four characteristics:

1- With an address consisting of the names of all or some of the partners. If one of them adds the word "and his partners" and therefore the company requests in its obligations the collective name.

2- All other partners acquire the status of merchant. Whenever it is commercial, its purpose is commercial. Even those who have not previously held that capacity, or have not been explicitly mentioned in the contract. His name is included in the formation of the company's address by force of law.Merchant's legal capacity benefits from its business activity.

3-That the partners are all responsible for their debts as an absolute personal liability in solidarity.

4- That the share of the partner does notaccept the transfer except by consensus of the partners as follows, because it is a closed company.[569] Joint liability means that the partners are jointly liable for the debts of the company. even from their own funds, if its capital is unable to pay it. Creditors have a primary formal guarantee that falls under the responsibility of the company, mainly its capital, and a secondary reserve guarantee. It falls on the partners' receivables, and performs, when necessary, from their own funds...

Solidarity obligations, in their considerations, mean that the partners are committed to solidarity among themselves, and between them and the company under the contract, and are committed to its name with others. The partner must fulfill all his obligations.

Creditors have the right to register their claim against the company represented by its disposers, or against the partners in person. Rather, it is necessary to start the company as the source of the obligation, even if its capital does not meet their rights, they move to follow up with the partners in order to meet therest of their debts. The result of joint and several liability... If it occurs that one of the joint partners owes the debt of the company, it shall be discharged, and the partners shall be discharged.The partner who has paid the debt of the company shall have the right to recourse against it, and then the partners shall each have to the extent of their share in the debt. If one of them is insolvent, his share is divided among the solvent partners.[570]

The partner is bound by all the undertakings of the company, its obligations in the period in which it is considered a member under the contract, as well as the partner who re-enters the company. It asks for all previous and subsequent commitments, pledges and debts. Even if there is a change in its name or commercial address, because this happened in the name of the company as a legal person independent of the partners, except in terms of guaranteeing its debts. Every condition that exempts a partner, whether a founder or a new one, or limits the liability of the company to third parties is null and void and has no effect on him.

---

[569]Companies in the Light of Islam, p. 36 by Dr. Abdulaziz Al-Khayyat
[570]Companies p. 209 by Dr. Shukri Ahmed Al-Sibai

The partner commits to the company, and the company commits to the partner with certain obligations. Hence, the company contract is a consensual contract, and a formal contract. It must be in writing, otherwise it is invalid. It is one of the netting contracts, one of the contracts binding on both sides, and one of the specific contracts and the specific [571] meaning that it is not a probabilistic contract such as the probability of profit or loss. The possibility does notaffect the requirement of the contract. It has been submitted that one of its advantages among contracts is that it creates a legal person. The company acquires it as soon as it is formed and it is subject to obligation and obligation.

Therefore, if a partner withdraws with the agreement and consent of the partners. He remains responsible for the debts that occurred before his withdrawal, and he is notasked what happens after him, provided that he announces his withdrawal, and the date of the announcement is taken into account in Article 38-39 Commercial.

Non-transferability of the Share and Dividing the Profit

It isnot permissible for a joint partner, even if he is a director, to assign, in whole or in part, his share in the company to others, except after the consensus of the partners, and it is nottransferred to the heirs, because death is one of the reasons for the dissolution or expiry of the company, and the reason for the inability of the share to be assigned and transferred is due to the maintenance of the principle of personal consideration, on which the companies of persons are based, and the inability to transfer it to the heir, meaning that it is not permissible to become a partner by its transfer and the company continues without being dissolved by the death of the heir.

Rather, the partners have the right to agree at the time of contracting or after that on the continuation of the company with the heirs, with the condition of eligibility, or the permissibility of transferring the share to others under predetermined conditions, such as requiring the approval of the majority, or proving the right of objection to the rest of the partners during a certain period, or theright of priority of the partners to own the assigned share, in exchange for paying its price.

In an Islamic Mudaraba company, which is a joint venture of another kind, the company may continue to agree with the heir immediately after death and not on the basis of the agreement of the partners when contracting. They saw that its continuation would be with the same contract, and I saw that it would be again; because the worker in the mudaraba money works by proxy for the owner of the money and the proxy is invalidated by the death of the principal, as it is invalidated by the death of the agent, and whatis said in the heir of the owner of the money is said in the heir of the worker in it.

---

[571] Mediator in explaining the Civil Code 225/2

Moroccan legislation in 1058 of the Code of Obligations and Contracts allows agreement on the continuation of the company with the heirs, provided that one of them is not incompetent. The agreement shall be void, unless the judge authorizes the minors or the incompetent to continue the company, whenever its continuation is in their interest, while taking all measures to preserve their rights.[572]

If this condition is not met, the partners can agree on the continuation of the company. by issuing a judicial ruling. The partner who is incompetent shall be discharged, with his share of the company's capital and profit being fulfilled «Article 1060 Civil».

If the deceased does not leave an heir, the Tunisian Commercial Code allows the continuation of the company between the rest of the partners if there is nothing in the contract thatcontradicts its continuation, and if he leaves an heir, he has the status of a lender. So that only within the limits of the share of the deceased[573] is asked this image, and if they include it in the system of the joint liability company, it may apply to the heir of the testator in the limited partnership more than the heir of the partner in the joint liability company.

As stipulated in the law, it is not permitted for a partner, even if he is adirector or a disposer, to include anyone in the company in his capacity as a partner, without the consent of all partners or based on permission in the contract. Rather, it is permissible for him to share his share with him, or to transfer tohim what he will receive upon division. Unless the contract stipulates otherwise.

This is confirmed by the Law of Obligations and Contracts in Article (1010), where he said: "It is not permissible for a partner, even if he acts for the company without the consent of all his other partners, to include a third party in the company as a partner in it. Unless the company's contract authorizes it to do so. Rather, he may share his share with others or transfer to him, and he may also transfer to others his share, which will affect him from the capital upon division. And all this, unless the agreement stipulates otherwise. "

Involving the third party in his share, known as the rider agreement, is similar to the rider's rider, and he hides behind him. His relationship, as it is understood from the text, is between him and the partner who added him, and their agreement does notcreate any legal relationship, linking the partner to the company, as he does not have the right to file a lawsuit against it orclaim it for profits or interfere in the affairs of management or access to the books.Unlike the death, loss, bankruptcy, insolvency, withdrawal or interdiction of the partner. This leads to the dissolution and liquidation of the company, if its continuation is notagreed with the heirs or among the rest. His death and its aftermath do nothave any impact on the existence of the company and its system, nor does it have the right to claim the loss or the rest of the share in the custody of the

---

[572] Companies p. 211 for Dr. Sibai
[573] Companies p. 211 for Dr. Sibai

partner. As long as she is committed, she knows the partner, and she is ignorant of the partner.

In connection with the analysis of the general system of the company, it has been provided with regard to the constituent, regulatory, formal and objective laws dealing with its life, its dissolution, liquidation, the payment of its debts and the division of its profit... Perhaps the most important element related to her life is the capital, as it onlyexists, and dissolves when it is destroyed. The capital in the joint liability company shall be formed by shares. Shares donot require homogeneity orsimilar value, and they may differ in their nature and value.

The Law of Obligations and Contracts stipulates in Article 988 that the share in the capital may not be in cash, movable or real things, or moral rights, as it may be the work of one of the partners or all of them. In particular, he said: It is not permissible among Muslims for this share to be foodstuffs.

It's an unfounded opinion. What has advanced in the formation of the capital of the Islamic Mudaraba Company is to be in cash, to discipline its values, and they have authorized it with goods denominated in it. and foodstuffs are commodities. The statement of Hisham bin Abdullah bin Hisham: «It is not okay for one of them to go out for food or an offer, and the other dinars or dirhams, and share values, and between them profit and loss by quotas» and the statement of Ibn Ghazi «Every company that signed the goods on the values is correct», which is notpermissible among Muslims is to be forbidden materials or to share undervalued goods. Food or other, because of the ignorance of the capital, which is one of its conditions to be known or otherwise void[574].

One of the advantages of Islamic contracts in terms of control and discipline is that they do notfall on the nonexistent or the unknown as much as a recipe or the legally prohibited, or unspecified, that can be inspected, or thatwhich is not in the possession of the owner in other than the sale of goods orwhatleads to confusion, oropening a hole from which the defect may flow, or cause the loss of rights. Foreigners have admitted that Islamic contracts are more disciplined than others.

Article 1037 of the Civil Code stipulates that the company's account shall be held at the end of each fiscal year, with the aim of counting and editing the budget, in order to extract the profit and loss account by taking an inventory of the positive and negative elements or what is known as the company's assets and liabilities. However, if the company was established in order to carry out a work or complete a fixed-term project, the final liquidation of the accounts and the distribution of profits shall not take place until after the work is carried out or the project is completed.

In other than this case, it is necessary to prepare the budget to identify the position of the company, its profits or losses. This is to know exactly how much net profits will be distributed to the partners, after deducting costs, and

---

[574] See my book The Approach of Islamic Economy in the Production and Consumption of Wealth 103/ 2

deducting one twentieth of the net profits of each fiscal year, to be used to form a reserve fund. The deduction continues until the reserve amount reaches one-fifth of the capital (Article -1038 - Civilian), and thatconfrontationmay occur from recession or loss and loss is forced from the profit before dividing it, as the profitsare not distributed, until after the full return of the capital, if the partners do not decide to reduce it to the extent of the already existing amount and the share of the partner in the profit and loss is determined by the percentage of his share in the capital. The rule that applies in the distribution of profit, is the same applied in the loss. If the profit is specified in the contract, and the loss is not specified or vice versa, the unspecified shall be measured according to Article 1033 - Civilian.

Each partner, after determining his share of the profit, has the right to withdraw it. If it does not, it shall be considered a deposit with the company and may not be added to its capital except with the consent of the partners. If he receives it in good faith and according to a duly edited budget, he is not obliged to return it to the capital for a previous financial year, if the company suffers a subsequent loss. If he is not acting, and he is forced to return to the company the profits that he previously received in good faith, as a result of not properly editing the budget, or because its editing was tainted in bad faith, he has the right to return to the company's disposers to compensate for the damages caused by «Article -1040- Civilian».

If the contract includes a condition that grants one of the partners all the profits, the company shall be nullified and the contract shall be converted into a donation. If it includes a condition that exempts one of the partners from bearing his share in the loss, the condition shall be null and void without the contract. If one of the partners is exempted from his share in bearing the loss with sharing his profits, or he forbids sharing the profits with bearing the loss, the company shall be called Al-Assad Company and it shall be void[575]. The company must distribute to the partners the profits resulting from the increase in assets over liabilities, but it is prohibited for it to distribute fictitious profits. They are distributed before the calculations are made and the budget is achieved.[576]

Regarding the end of the partnership company, such as the partnership company for general reasons or merger, the Commercial Law says in Article 44: "The partnership company and the partnership company end with the same reasons that other companies end with or merge with other companies." It was better to refer to the above in the general system of the company about the reasons that companies end with, in order to avoid repetition. And that's from the research methodology.

---

[575] The Mediator in Explaining the Civil Law 282/2 and Beyond
[576] Companies p. 216 for Dr. Sibai

Limited Partnership Company

Simple recommendation company contract

Under Article 33 of the Moroccan Commercial Code, a limited partnership company is held between one or more partners who are responsible and joint partners, and between one or more partners in which they are owners of funds, and they are called limited partners or | partners by recommendation. It is a joint liability company by the officials, and it is distinguished by the fact that it brings together the owners of financial shares, who are outside the management andare not accountable except within the limits of their shares of the capital, and between those responsible for their obligations and debts jointly with each other.

In its system, it is subject to the general rules governing companies, and the special rules relating to the establishment of a joint liability company. We have finished analyzing them, so we do not need to repeat them. It is a partnership company for general partners, and a capital company for limited partners, and if participation in shares - instead of shares - is transferred to a partnership limited by shares .[577]

Thus, it branches into two types: the limited partnership company, whose capital consists of shares that do notaccept trading and transfer, and the limited partnership company with shares in which it moves and trades. Article (138) of the Tunisian Commercial Code gave them the name of the simple muqaddah company and the shares of the muqaddah company, in[578] a similar way to the Islamic mudaraba and loans company.

However, the analogy is not perfect, as it did not occur, except in terms of its composition of money on one side and work on one side. Otherwise, they differ in the fact that the employees of Mudaraba and Al-Muqarrada Al-Islamiya do notbear any responsibility resulting from the loss of capital. Unless they are infringing,excessive or in violation of one of the prescribed conditions. Unlike the joint employees of a limited partnership company who have to pay their debts, even from their own money. The fundamentalist rule says: "There isno measurement with the difference."

If a limited partnership is divided into a simple recommendation and a stock recommendation and together they are made up of money, on the one side and work on the other side, then the simple recommendation that is most important to us now is a personal consideration. which is the consideration that made it a people company. The same as the joint liability company. So that it is notpermissible for the partner, whether jointly liable, or a financial testator, to assign his share to others except with the consent of all partners. As is the case with the joint liability company, unless the permissibility is authorized in the contract.

---

[577] Mediator in explaining the Civil Code 235/ 2
[578] Companies p. 218 for Dr. Sibai

The limited partnership is terminated by the reasons that the partnership expires, such as the death, loss, bankruptcy, insolvency, withdrawal, interdiction or judicial liquidation of the limited partner... The personality of the silent partner is a consideration for the joint partner. As for the company limited by shares, it differs from the limited partnershipin that the limited partner is subject to the legal system, which governs the shareholder in the financial shareholding company, and that its capital is divided into shares of equal value that are transferable, negotiable and transferable. Unlike the quotas in the simple recommendation, which do notaccept neitherwaiver nortrading. and no transition. It was natural for a company limited by shares to be considered a capital company, and a limited partnership company to be a personal company. It is noticeable that there is overlap between the two companies, so we tried to disengage, so that the same shares of the same shares become clear. So, the advantage of a limited partnership is that it consists of two types of partners:

1-From joint working co-founders. They ask about the company's debts, obligations and undertakings as an absolute joint liability. Like the partners in the joint liability company, they acquire the capacity of a merchant, and the bankruptcy of the company results in their bankruptcy, and their names are included in the formation of the company's address - unlike the limited partners - and they have the right to participate in the management of its management.

2- Financial limited partners, whoare not responsible for the debts of the company, except within the limits of the share they have provided in the capital. Article 49 of the Commercial Law stipulates that the limited partner shall not beliable for losses, except to the extent of the amount he has provided or must provide to the company, and he cannot carry out any act of management, even if he has an agency, which led to the designation of the testators as money providers or owners of money, andthey do not acquire the status of merchant, and the bankruptcy of the company does notresult in their bankruptcy, and their names are notincluded in the formation of the company's address, or the assignment of management to them. They are forbidden. Although they have the right to supervise and monitor. It is stated in Article 33 of the Commercial Law that the management of this company shall be entitled, and this address must be the name of one or more of the jointly liable partners, and it is not permissible to include within the title one of the limited partners.

Therefore, the liability of the limited partner in the loss is determined by the amount of the amount he has provided.He has no right to engage in any work of administration and management. even by proxy under his hand. If some companies allow participation in a work quota instead of the financial quota. The limited partnership is simple or by shares, it is notpermissible for the testator to participate in the work in lieu of money, pursuant to the Commercial Law (Article 33), which classified the testator or the partners in the recommendation among the owners of the funds. Their liability is limited to the amount of shares in which they participate or contribute to capital formation.

The pronunciation of money to include work except by a legal text that includes it. With the exception of participating in shares and bearing the lossthat may be incurred. In returnfor its profit, the limited partners are considered as foreigners of the company.

The limited partner must provide the full share he commits to participate in the capital formation. In the agreed term, he is discharged from his obligation to the company and its creditors, because he is notliable for the company's obligations and debts, except within the limits of the share he is obligated to provide. If he fails to submit the share in whole or in part, the company has the right to claim judicial execution and compensation, and the benefits resulting from the delay... Some laws considerthat creditors have the right to initiate a lawsuit against him [579] as long as extracting their right from the company, and fulfilling its obligations towards them, depends on fulfilling the obligation to provide the share.

And is providing the share in the limited partnership a commercial orcivil business? Dr. Shukri Ahmed Al-Sibai answers this question, and says: "We believe that the obligation of the testator to provide the share is a commercial obligation, because the motive for it is a commercial motive, but the testatoris not considered a trader on the basis that his obligation to provide the share is an offer and for one time, in other words, he does notaccept professionalism.[580]

As for the jointly liable partner, it is not necessary to mention the share he participates in the capital: because he is absolutely responsible for the company's obligations and debts. This made his responsibility include his share, and exceed it to his own funds if necessary.

The partnership company meets with the joint liability company in the basic, legal and final rules... and their divergence in regulatory laws, the nature of liability, and financial consideration. This is because the joint liability company consists entirely of joint and several liable financiers, and the recommendation consists of joint and several officers on one side, and financial testators who are not liable on the other side.

Therefore, we note that the law combines them, as reflected in what was decided by the Commercial Law in Article 35, where it said: «Partnership companies and partnership companies may acquire rights under their title. Even if this acquisition is by means of a contract without consideration or will, and to undertake obligations, acquire the right of ownership, and other in-kind rights over real estate, and plead with the courts, whether as a plaintiff or a defendant. "He said in "Article 36 ":" The founding contract of the joint liability company or the limited partnership must be in writing, and be dated. "He said in" Article 37 ": " A certified copy of the constitutive contract of the joint liability company

---

[579] Companies p. 225 for Dr. Sibai
[580] Id., p. 224

or the limited partnership shall be deposited whether it is notarized or a counterpart of it, if it is customary for him to write the record of the court of first instance, in whose jurisdiction the headquarters of the company is located. within a period of fifteen days. As of the date of the aforementioned contract, as provided upon the incorporation of the joint liability company.

Thus, if we exclude some of the differences referred to, it can be said that what is required and stipulated in the joint liability company is required and stipulated in the partnership company and what isproven for one of them is proven for the other, and whatends with one of them ends with the other... By referring to the above, we will remove from the shoulders of the reader thedrowning of repetition and repetition.

Management and the role of the company's address in the conduct of its affairs

A limited partnership company-as a general partnership-is managed by an address consisting of the name of one or more general liable partners. It is not legallypermissible to include in the title the name of one of the limited partners (Article 33 Commercial), as the inclusion of his name in the title will distract others from his personal responsibility and involve him in administrative responsibility. While he is not legallyresponsible, neither for debts nor for the company's undertakings and obligations. He is asking about the share he is committed to providing.

It is mentioned in Article 34 of the Commercial Law when there are several joint partners under a collective name, whether they all take over the management collectively, or one or more of them takes over on behalf of all, the company is at the same time a joint venture company for them, and a recommendation company for the owners of the funds in it.

If the limited partnership is formed by one joint liable partner and one partner or a number of limited partners, the word "and his partner" must be added to the title that was formed only by the joint partner if the limited partner is one or "and his partners" if they are multiple. This is only in order to sort the papers before others, so that he can distinguish between undertakings in the name of the company and undertakings in the name of the partner or distinguish between the company in whose name the partner is obligated, such as a joint venture company, and the company with a legal personality in whose name the obligation falls.

On the omission of the company to take an address for its management, Dr. Shukri Ahmed Al-Sibai quotes Ali Hassan Younis as saying: The address - even if it is useful to the company –is not considered essential in it, so there is no risk to the company, and this does notaffect its consideration as a limited partnership, when it appears from the contract that it includes two types of partners: joint partners and limited partners. Some of them shall be personally and jointly liable, and others shall be liable only within the limits of their share. In this case, the manager shall indicate, when contracting, the capacity of the joint partners from whom the company is formed without the names of the testators.[581]

This opinion is not without contradiction and violation of the law as evidenced in the Commercial Law "Article 33", where he said regarding the limited partnership company: "The management of this company shall be entitled, and this address must be the name of one or more partners jointly responsible, and itis not permissible to include within the title the name of one of the limited partners» The company is notmanaged, and the transaction and obligation are only with its commercial address. The professor says: «In this case, the manager must indicate when contracting the capacity of the joint partners that make up the company, without the names of the testators» that the company is made up of all the partners, which is made up of the joint partners, without the testators being the address. The manager from whom this procedure was requested, does not exist in the case of contracting. but the practical presence of partners. Even if appointed in the founding contract. His administration does notmove until it is approved, and the company acquires a legal personality working under its title ...

If he had said: If his omission had occurred in the founding contract, he would have been more correct in a subsequent contract...

If the limited partner authorizes the inclusion of his name in the address of the company, or he is included and aware of it and does not object, this results in him being responsible for the debts of the company as a joint personal liability, as are the joint partners because the liability of debts in the limited partnership company is related to the administrative structure represented by the composition of the address, more than it isrelated to the capital.

Conversely, if the silent partner enters the address without his knowledge ordespite his opposition. He shall not beliable for the debts of the company or for its undertakings and obligations, except within the limits of the share he has provided in the capital. In addition, he shall have the right to follow up on the joint partners. The right to claim compensation for damages incurred as a result of their unlawful conduct. Based on "Article 25" of the Commercial Law, he has the right to oblige whoever enters his name to change what he hasregistered.

The management of a limited partnership company shall be subject to the same general rules and special laws governing the administration and management of a general partnership company. Rather, the external work and administrative management of the partnership company is the responsibility of the joint partners. As for the limited partners, as mentioned above, they are prohibited by law. However, the prohibition does not concernthe external management, which is based on representing the company before others, such as signing its undertakings and acquiring in its name.

---

[581] Companies p. 128 for Dr. Sibai.

As for internal management or internal management, the limited partners have the right. Such as participating in voting on the appointment or dismissal of the director, the right of monitoring and inspection, directing the company towards its purpose or other internal management work. In view of this, the limited partner can contract with the company as a user, computer or technical... Provided that the work he carries out within the company is not related to others, and he may also contract with it to lend or sell goods.

If the limited partner violates the requirement of the law and enters into business within the competence of the external administration, this shall result in him being jointly liable for the debts and undertakings resulting from the work he undertook. This responsibility falls within the framework of his relationship with others. As for his relationship with the company and the partners, it remains in its nature, as a limited partnerwho does not ask for debts, except within the limits of his share. He has the right to claim what he paid in excess of his share, if he commences those works by commission or power of attorney.

The company's position is that it is not responsible for the actions of the limited partner, if he violates the law and interferes in the work of the external management without assignment. Its argument is that its contract and law have defined its framework and character. She has the right to ask him to repair the damage she has suffered as a result of his act.

This was the general and illustrative view of the contract of the limited partnership company, its system and characteristics, and the role of the installation of the address in its management and conduct of its affairs ... As for what itends up with, the methods of liquidating it, and dividing its profits and losses, after conducting the calculations, achieving the budget, and deducting part of twenty of the net profits of each fiscal year to be used in forming a reserve fund, it has progressed, and there is no need to ruminate and repeat it again.

Joint Venture Company

Nature and Characteristics of a Joint Venture Company

A joint venture company is a company established between the partners, alone, and is not a company against third parties. Whoever makes a contract from the partners covered by a contract, or undertakes an obligation for which he is responsible, the [582] obligations and agreements concluded by one of the partners shall be personal to others. The joint venture company is not legally obligated, nor is it a legal person to whom the letter is addressed. Despite its multiplication in the valleys and cities, it was not known socially by the company. Rather, it is said: So-and-so trade in wool, and so-and-so trade in love, and so-and-so and so-and-so trade in sheep, or build or cultivate, or do so...

The joint venture company is one of the easiest and most common commercial companies in the popular circles, as a result of the ease and lack of complexity in its formation; because the law did not regulate it and did not require its existence in a specific form, nor a written contract, nor an advertisement nora commercial register to be seen by others. They are hidden and hidden, without a business address, social headquarters, or capital of limited value.

Because of its weakness and inability to face mega projects, and in the long run some called it the temporary company. They saw that it onlyarises in order to achieve a quick business process. They are often seasonal. Such as buying and selling vegetables and fruits, and buying and selling love ordates. It has been advanced in Islamic companies that Hanafi allowed the speculation period to be set in the same way as the season of dates, love or cotton... If Mudaraba is a contract and joint venture company without a legal contract, its system shall take into account what the partnersagree upon in terms of purpose and form, estimating shares and dividing profit and loss. In it, before others, the common phrase "the Convention is the law of the contracting parties" is ratified.

The Law of Obligations and Contracts was discussed in Article 1018 within the activity of the partners within the bargaining company. He said: It is permissible in the bargaining company for each of the partners to carry out alone the management work and even the work of missing the purpose of the company. In particular, he may conclude, for the interests of all, with a third party, a joint venture company. Its place shall be to carry out one or more commercial transactions. "

It has now come to me that I have already started her work - and I am a student to participate with another student. It was agreed that each of us would provide a share of the cash with the intention of buying and selling the rams of the Eid sacrifice. Dividing the profit or lossresulting from the transaction, without intending to form the company or knowing what happened.

---

[582] **Mediator in explaining the Civil Code 235/2**

The joint venture company - also called the joint venture association - is distinguished from the commercial companies of which it is a member by beinglimited between the contractors. It is a partnership between them and not between them and others. Hence, the lack of announcement of its existence and keeping it hidden from the public. It is required to be anonymous andknown only to the co-founders. As long as the joint venture partners adhere to the side of caution and do not declare their will and act in its name, it is a joint venture company that concernsthem and no one else. Its purpose, although classified as a commercial company, may be civil and may be commercial. It is mostly commercial and practically and socially [583]observed that it works in civil and commercial purposes, and each partner takes over an aspect that he knows about, and some believe that covering them and distributing the work among them benefits them in not paying taxes in the name of the company. It may nothelp, as long as each partner performs what he knows.

One of the characteristics of a joint venture company - besides the fact that it is hidden - is that it arises temporarily, ends with the end of the purpose for which it was established, and is concerned with one or more business activities. Mustafa Kamal Taha has seen that the hidden and hidden nature is the only one that distinguishes it from other companies [584]because the timing is not a steady control, as it can continue with the work or end with its completion. Therefore, it does not exist for others, and dealing with one of the partners is personal, and an individual commitment. It is subject to the laws and provisions that regulate relations between individuals, not the laws and provisions that regulate them between individuals and companies.

If it is known to those who deal with it that it is a visible company that is not hidden, and it is dealt with in the name of two or more partners, and not in the name of one partner. Then it goes outside the framework of the joint venture company, and it is offered at the level of the joint liability company in what it has and what it has.With regard to the right to prove it in the context of joint venture, Article 53 of the Commercial Code states: "It is permissible to prove the existence of joint venture companies by presenting books and correspondence or by witnesses if the court considers that it is possible to accept proof in the last way," although it is not subject to the formal procedures prescribed for companies and justifies its proof by all means of proof, including evidence and presumptions. "The Commercial [585] Code did not require writing to prove except in contracts of joint, limited and joint-stock companies... As for the joint venture company, it may be proven by evidence.

---

[583]Companies p. 242 for Dr. Sibai
[584]Companies p. 239 for Dr. Sibai
[585]Id., p. 250

Management of the joint venture company and personal commitment within it

Administrative management in a joint venture company is different from management in other types of companies. The difference comes from the fact that the joint venture does nothave a legal personality, an independent financialliability,a commercial address, or a socialheadquarters... This made the issue of management the issue of partners, not theissue of others, who are unaware of its existence. It was called anonymously or anonymously, so the word moved to contribution, and remained suspended.

If any private partner has the right to carry out in his personal name all works and activities that fall within the purpose of the company, due to its lack of moral personality, he alone is personally responsible for what results from the results of the work he undertook, unless one of the partners works with him, or interferes in the operations of completion, so he is asked with him in personal solidarity. The result is that the responsibility lies with the one who personally undertook the work, one, two or three.... Even if this is not decided in the contract concluded between them, because solidarity is imposed in commercial materials, and it is raised only by an explicit text.

The quota partners may determine the administrative responsibility, so they choose one of the partners or a foreign person to take over the management and administration affairs, but the quota manager in turn does notrepresent the company, and does not deal with others in its name, as long as it does not exist for others, because it does not have a legal legal personality. He acts in his own name, and under his own responsibility. As for the relationship of the partners with the manager and their relations with each other, they remain subject to the terms of the contract. Personal interaction is for others, to secure the rights of people, and collective for partners. Therefore, profits and losses resulting from their business are divided among them. Whether you get them together or individually... As for the corporate system in the Islamic economy, which does notrequire any of the Islamic contract companies to be anonymous or hidden, and does not allow its regulation by personal agreements, instead of written Sharia laws, the joint venture company with its wording, conditions, disappearance and non-regulation by law is non-existent, andit is not valid until it is placed either within the framework of the speculation and loans company, the unleashing company, the faces company, the bargaining company or the business company, according to theforegoing in its regulations with the dispute between the imams in other than speculation and unleashing.

The position of the commercial law on the joint venture company may not be without weakness and contradiction, as it recognized and approved it, without regulating it. Although she is an analyst and circulating among economists and lawmen and is determined in the commercial laws of countries such as French, Egyptian, Tunisian and Moroccan law... On the subject, the Moroccan

Commercial Code says inArticle 52" Based on the Dahir - June 18 - 1927: " In addition to the three types of companies mentioned above, the law also considers commercial companies with joint ventures that specialize in the work of one or more commercial businesses, and these companies take into account what the partnersagree on in terms of purpose, form, shares belonging to each one and conditions " and the aforementioned commercial companies solidarity, recommendation and contribution.

This is an acknowledgement, and the acknowledgement in the language of the law is not without a declaratory text that is adopted when the judgment is issued... The text imposes its subject matter. And the subject means organization. It is known that the company recognized and approved by the law is the one that acquires legal personality, after the availability of the elements, conditions, written contract and publication procedures, which it approves and imposes. As Dr. Al-Sanhouri said: "The company is considered merely for its formation as a legal person, but this personality is notinvoked against others, except after fulfilling the publishing procedures prescribed by law[586], which exempted it from all legal procedures. However, it was approved and classified as a commercial company regulated by commercial laws, and as a person company. As mentioned by Dr. Al-Sanhouri in Al-Waseet 234/2, the jointliability company, the partnership company and the joint venture company.

Perhaps it is right with those who called it the Joint Venture Association. As a company, we do notknow how the law classifies it as a commercial company, and the judiciary is required to deal with the obligation of each partner separately, and how it fills a space in the books of the law and the analyses of its men, and it is permissible to prove it before the judiciary and the law by all means and it is required to be hidden. Subject to the agreements of the partners, is it not considered necessary to prove it before the courts? After proving it, will it remain a joint venture or move to solidarity? And do you move to solidarity with the same contract or a new contract? And how does the judiciary deal with the obligations that occurred before and after the proof? Or how does it deal with problems and issues arising from confidentiality agreements? They are questions that need to be answered...

It seems that the deduction and invocation of its provisions -which are more common and pervasive in society - may find a source in customary law more than codified law. Which I did not see who mentioned. Although custom, has known its way to Sharia law, civil and commercial, internal and constitutional, international, criminal and maritime... It is attracted towards the public and the private, and it is legally accepted, if there is no Sharia text, and legally, if there is no written law text, as I explained in my book "The joint usufruct between Sharia, custom and law in the territories of the communities in Morocco, p. 106" and the book is in print.

---

[586]Mediator in the Civil Code 288/ 2 Mediator in the Civil Code 288/ 2

If it is decided to refer in the joint venture system to the agreements of the partners regarding the formation, management, administration and share in the capital, it may also be decided that they expire, liquidate and divide their profits, losses and debts in any way they agreed to use... We hope that they will all be at the level of concluding economic agreements that secure rights, and do notdisturb the judiciary.

JOINT-STOCK COMPANY

IMPORTANCE AND CHARACTERISTICS OF A JOINT STOCK COMPANY, AND ITS ARTICLES OF ASSOCIATION

The joint-stock company was not known for anonymous,anonymous or anonymous companies, because it is a description of a joint venture company, which does nothavea legal personality, an independent financialliability, or a commercial address. However, the matter has changed, so legislation has become required to give this name to joint-stock companies and more, it obliges the founders to add to its title a "anonymous contribution" due to its financial nature, and the number of shareholders who are ignorant of each other, so it was also called anonymous. Dr. Al-Sanhouri described it as the most important company in money companies, and that the partners vary greatly in the number of shares they own, and we [587] have explained its system, within the general system of incorporation of companies. And here - as we have done and are doing - in other companies, we are trying to highlight the characteristics, and what a company can stand out from the other.

Joint-stock companies in the present era are one of the most important pillars of commercial and industrial progress, the most powerful tool for achieving major economic projects, the most effective way to huge investments, and obtaining huge profits... All of these are positive considerations, and powerful factors. It prompted the world's venture capitalists to found it.

However, although it has a positive role at the level of the national and international economy, it is considered the most powerful means of monopoly, influence, domination and influence... It is the largest field in which the meaning of political economy is manifested, and it has spent a weapon used by developed countries in addition to the weapon of the monetary system and "modern technology, in the face of the confinement of the economies of third world countries, including Arab and Islamic countries, in a narrow field. Although its establishment is easy, both legally and financially. Most Arab and Islamic countries, combined in an integrated economic bloc, should establish international civil, commercial and industrial companies. Do you go to halal, avoid haram, and attract the international economy? We lack only sincerity and sincerity, and wise and foresighted hands.

As for the system of the joint-stock company, it is subject to the general principles, and the rules of the civil and commercial law... The general rule is that every company is anonymous or anonymous. Whatever its subject matter, it is subject to the laws of commerce and its customary origins. The expression of contribution means that it is open to everyone, anonymous, anonymous oranonymous, meaning that it is naked from the collective name. It is

---
[587]Mediator in explaining the Civil Code 235/2

established by seven natural or legal persons by subscribing to shares, i.e. negotiable instruments, as a number that responds to the constitutive condition, without having a personal presence at the address.

Characteristics of a joint-stock company include:

1- The partner shall not be liable for its debts, except within the limitsof the shares it owns and shall not acquire the capacity of a merchant, and its bankruptcy shall not result in its bankruptcy.

2 - It is based on the financial element, not on the human element, and the capital is required to be sufficient to achieve its purpose, and to be divided into shares of equal value, and negotiable. It must be valued within Morocco in national currency or its value. The same applies to debts related to public order, and the estimate[588] is subject to an initial meeting of the constituent assembly, to appoint an observer or observers to estimate the in-kind shares, in which the amount of the capital is not known before it is estimated.

3- That the partners provide shares, in exchange for bonds, to be called shares.

4-Considering it as a commercial company regardless of the purpose it aims to achieve. Is it civil or commercial?

5- It does nothave a title consisting of the names of the partners or one of them, as is the case with personal companies. Rather, it bears a name derived from its purpose. In this regard, the Commercial Law states in Article 50: "It is not permissible for an anonymous company to be established under the name of the partners, nor to be appointed under the name of one of the partners, but it is called its intended purpose as its address."

6- Itcannot be established in less than seven persons, with the exception that the state may use the weapon of nationalization, own all the shares, or authorize the public institution to establish a joint stock company on its own. Whenever it is in the public interest to close the door to private capital,[589] especially when it comes to a necessary national institution, all citizens benefit from it. Nationalization may be necessary, as Morocco did some time ago in nationalizing the trade in tea, as it is a substance consumed in almost fictional numbers...

7.It is not sufficient to establish the agreement of the partners. Rather, the incorporation procedures must pass through many stages and respond to the prescribed regulations, which have already been clarified, within the general system of establishing the company.

8- It is its competence to issue securities. They are stocks, bonds, incorporation shares and dividends, as will be explained.

---

[588] Companies p. 278 for Dr. Sibai
[589] Companies p. 273 for Dr. Sibai

In sum, the establishment of a joint-stock company requires the founders to perform a number of complex procedures. It may take a long time to complete. Such as editing the draft basic laws, the statute, subscription and capital, calling the Constituent General Assembly to convene, and proceeding with filing, publicity, registration and publication procedures...

It seems that Moroccan law did not require government permission before submitting its establishment project, but Dr. Al-Sanhouri says: "It is onlyestablished by order of the supreme authority." Submitting the project[590] may be considered as an application and approving it as an authorization.

And the liberation of the statute from the task of the founders, who depend on the liberation of the draft statutes, and the preparation of subscription, in the capital, and certify its validity and deposit with a notary, orwrite the seizure of the Court of First Instance and deliver copies of it identical to the original to each person or institution entrusted with receiving the subscription, and to invite the General Assembly to appoint the first disposers. Dr. Ahmed Shukri Al-Sibai quoted the French jurisprudence in the capacity of the founder as "a person who carries out on his own, and without prior authorization from others, the material and legal works necessary to establish the company, and to find subscribers in its capital." He[591] quoted the Syrian judiciary in the same subject that if the founder stops the establishment of the company without an acceptable reason, he must compensate those affected by his work, and if he has already received money calculated on the value of the shares, he must return it, and his action results in bearing all the expenses he spent.

The written instrument for the incorporation of a joint-stock company is fundamentally different from the incorporation of types of companies in that it is nothing more than a draft of the articles of association, prepared and signed by the founders, and certifies its validity, and includes the basic data related to the capital, its division into shares, the bond statement, the rules of management and distribution of profits | and losses, the regulation of accounting control, and other rules on the basis of which the public subscribes. It remains a mere draft until it is ratified by the Constituent Assembly. | Violation of the rules and principles of the laws of the joint-stock company shall be void. These violations include:

- 1Non-filing of the draft laws

2- Not to subscribe to all the capital, and to demand the payment of a cash amount representing at least a quarter of the value of the shares.

3-Failure to prove subscription, and payment of funds in a declaration issued by the notary

4-The number of founders should be less than seven people

---

[590] Mediator in explaining the Civil Code 235/ 2
[591] Companies p. 272 for Dr. Sibai

5- Trading of shares, before the performance of the quarter of their value

6- The shares do not remain nominal, until their price is fully paid, or the in-kind shares are fully paid at the time of incorporation.

7- Failure to correctly estimate the in-kind shares legally

8. Failure to respect the legal requirements related to the convening of a constituent general assembly and the appointment of the first administrators and observers

9. Failure to respect the rules for appointing and dismissing an agent or agents of management

10- Failure to respect the deposit and publication procedures.

CAPITAL FORMATION

Joint-stock companies of different nationalities are those that express economically, politically and internationally the meaning of large capitalism. The most important element in its establishment is the formation of capital at a level that responds to the achievement of its purpose... The formation of share capital may be offered to the public by way of an IPO. The founders themselves may prefer to subscribe for all the shares, called closed shareholding, and often resort to closing, if they have sufficient funds to own them.

Thus, the subscription is divided into a closed subscription, which falls between the founders alone, and an open subscription, which falls in front of the public. The founders must, if they choose to go public, send an invitation to the public by issuing a statement to be published in the Official Gazette, which includes thefollowing:

1- Company Name

2- Her social headquarters

3. Its purpose

4. Duration if deferred

5. Amount of capital

6. Price of each class of shares

7- The amount of paid-upcapital

8. A statement of the benefits granted to the founders, or to other persons and the conditions for recovery, if any

10- In-Kind Shares and their Estimation

11. How to call a general meeting

12. A statement of whether the company has offered shares abroad, and the number of those shares

13- The names of the founders, their crafts, and their place of residence. The number of subscribed partners must not be less than seven, and the subscription must be with the consent of the subscribers, and it must be completed in total in each capital of the company, and each subscriber must pay a cash amount, representing one quarter of the value of the shares in which he subscribed. Dr. Shukri Ahmed Al-Sibai quoted Mustafa Kamal Taha in the definition of the IPO as "declaring the will to participate in the company's project with a pledge to provide a share in the money. is a certain number of shares» [592]

They disagreed about the subscription, is it a civil or commercial business? Some saw it as a civil act, because the liability of the shareholder is limited in its shares, and others saw it as commercial as long as the shareholding is a commercial company. Whether considered civil or commercial, the subscriberis not considered a partner until he practically contributes to the formation of the capital with a share he provides. It determines the amount of his share in the profit and loss.

The share, as mentioned above, may be cash, securities, movables, real estate, usufruct, business or trade name, or a certificate of invention or debt owed by others...All that isfit to be the object of theobligation is fit to be a share in the capital of the company. The Law of Obligations and Contracts stipulates in Article 992 that the capital of the company consists of the total shares provided by the partners, and of the things acquired through it, including compensation for the destruction, defect, or expropriation of one of the things included in the capital. This is from the perspective of positive law in the concept of share. As for the Sharia law, it has been submitted – in defense of the reasons for the defect – that it accepts only cash or goods that it carries out.

In this regard, it is a cash quota, which is set at the calendar and at liquidation. If the capital includes non-cash shares, such as movables, real estate, moral rights, and others mentioned above, the situation requires the meeting of the Constituent General Assembly, which consists of all subscribers, and its meeting shall be held after the end of the subscription process, and the performance of the cash quarter of the capital. - And her mission?

1- Examination of the subscription fee, issued by the notary, and payment of funds

2. Appointment of the First Disposers

3. Appointment of an observer or observers

4- Granting permission to the disposers

5- Giving discharge to the founders, and the final announcement of the establishment of the company, but the meeting of the Constituent Assembly is not necessary, if the company arises between the founders alone. Each shareholder participating in the IPO shall have the right to attend the sessions of the Constituent General Assembly. Even if he owns onlyone share, and he does not have to vote himself, and it is permitted legally to appoint a proxy for him.

---

[592] Companies p. 285 for Dr. Sibai

Only shareholders who have provided in-kind shares, such as real estate, or who have stipulated for themselves special benefits or advantages, are excluded from the right of agency and delegation.

All this is when the conditions of the IPO, which represents the spearhead in the formation of the company, aregoing well. As for the control of revenues, starting from the subscription and until the final announcement of the establishment of the company, it is due to the fact that the subscriptionis only carried out by a bank, a payment for each fraud or fraud and all revenues are deposited in the current account of the company. If the company is not established within six months, its date shall start from the day of depositing the project, the funds shall be withdrawn from the bank, and paid to those who request them from the subscribers, and the withdrawal shall be made with the signature of the company's agent, if a copy of the report of the founding meeting, attested to its authenticity, is submitted against the withdrawal.

Administrative System

The rules that govern institutions vary from institution to institution and from company to company. For example, the management of Bank Al-Maghrib consists of:

1- Wali

2- The Board of Directors of the Bank

3- SteeringCommittee

4-Government Delegate

5-Observers

The management of the joint-stock company consists mainly of:

1- Board of Directors

2-The General Assembly

3. General Manager

4-Disposers

5-Auditors

The election of the members of the board of directors shall be by majority by the ordinary general assembly of the participants or shareholders, and he shall exercise in his authority and responsibility all the competences entrusted to him, relating to the management of the company and its affairs, except for those that were within the competence of the general or extraordinary assembly. The collective management method stipulates that the disposersshall not be given any individual personal opportunity to be independent in carrying out the administrative activity, unless the council authorizes one of its members to carry out or supervise a specific work. In the sense that the first gesture is the competence of the Council.

The President elected from among the members of the Council shall be the main driver of the Council's activity. He is the one who summons the members to the meeting on a date he appoints, determines the agenda of deliberations, conducts the sessions, takes the necessary financial and economic initiatives to achieve the company's objectives, supervises the minutes, and other management work arranged in the company's articles of association. [593]

Reference has been made to what isstated in the Law of Obligations and Contracts (Article 1023), which stipulates that "the partner in charge of management, under the company's contract, may, despite the opposition of the rest of his partners, conduct all the work of management, but rather all the acts ofdisposition within the purpose of the company as indicated in Chapter 1026, provided that he conducts them without fraud, and taking into account the restrictions imposed by the contract, which gives him his powers" and indicated in Chapter 1026, that "it does notjustify the disposers. If they are unanimous, and it is not permissible for the majority of the partners to carry out works other than those that fall within the purpose of the company, as required by its nature and the custom of trade.

The expression of the text by the partner assigned to the management under the company's contract is not without flexibility, because the authority given to him in the text isgiven in some laws only to the director appointed from among the partners in the constitutive contract, or by an amendment in the same contract, and months such as the declaration of the original. Whereas the term of the person in charge of the administration falls on the director, the president and the disposer, with their different responsibilities, competence and degree of authority... The Disposers shall act in accordance with the Contract. The manager is acting in the first instance. Although "despite the opposition of the rest of the partners" goes to his authority, but theperson entrusted with management under the company's contract " does not necessarilymean the manager appointed in the constitutive contract alone, as long as the assignment has many methods and considerations.

The first disposers and agents shall be appointed and dismissed by the General Assembly of Shareholders. They have the right to resign from their duties whenever they wish, and to work for a wage. The disposer is not entitled to hold a position in the management of the board for a period exceeding six years, but the Companies Law allows the renewal of his election, if the constitutive system does not provide for prohibition. The delegated disposer, such as the president and general manager,may only be elected from among the contributing partners, but Tunisian law allows the disposers to elect from among themselves a director.

---

[593]Companies p. 391 for Dr. Sibai

The company, as a legal person, is responsible for the work carried out by the delegated administrator within the framework of the competences granted to him by the Board of Directors. Its responsibility may extend to external acts, whenever the dealer with the delegated disposer is a victim of good faith.

The Law of Obligations and Contracts expressed in "Article 1046" the partners instead of the company, saying: "The partners are responsible towards bona fide third parties for fraud and fraud committed by the actor, who represents the company. They are obliged to compensate the damage resulting from it to that third party, while retaining the right to recourse against the perpetrator of the harmful act. "

The first observers, in turn, are appointed by the Constituent General Assembly, from among the partners or others for one first year, and their names are published in the Official Gazette, or one of the newspapers appointed to publish judicial notices. Provided that the Ordinary General Assembly shall make subsequent appointments and renew the position of the appointees for the same period, that is, forone fiscal year.

ISSUANCE OF SHARES AND BONDS

The joint-stock company is characterized by the issuance of stocks and bonds on the widest scale and stocks are among the most important securities in which money companies are active, and the strongest relationship with shareholders. The share, as mentioned above, represents the share or part of the capital of the ownership of the joint stock company with its profit and loss, and it is in the capacity of a negotiable and transferable financial document, and it is often purchased at the nominal value, that is, the price recorded or printed on its face. The research methodology required that we introduce the activity of the stock exchange, the types of stocks and bonds and their laws, and consider their trading, within the exchange in free markets in order to compare between the traditional markets, in which commodities are sold, and the financial markets in which stocks and bonds are sold. Go back there.

The shares of participation or incorporation are divided into cash shares and in-kind shares. The first type represents the cash share, and the second represents the in-kind share. Its issuance and trading is the primary control, which determines the nature of money companies from the nature of companies of persons, and if the shares lose the character of trading, the company loses its shareholding status and focuses on financial consideration. Dr. Abdulaziz Al-Khayyat did not distinguish between the shares of incorporation or the shares of the participant, which may not be traded before the scheduled time, and the shares issued by the company for trading and conversion. He said: The shares are in cash and in kind, work, incorporation shares or mixed.[594] The same applies to incorporation. It may be clearer to express the cash, in-kind, practical

---

[594]Companies in the Light of Islam, p. 41 by Dr. Abdulaziz Al-Khaya

and legal shares or shares of participation... At the will of incorporation, we express stocks and bonds when tradingoccurs, and they are bought and sold and known as securities.

Among the rights arising from owning shares are the right to remain in the company until it expires, the right to share the profit, the right to vest in its assets upon liquidation, the right to participate in deliberations and vote on decisions, and directing the company towards its purpose...

There are what isknown as incorporation shares and profits, and it means rewarding shareholders of business and government authorities for services, which helped the success of the company. The excessive use of these shares, which have become a means of manipulating manipulators, and a tool that has led to illicit profits.The degree of giving founding shares and dividends to people who did not provide any service except to take refuge in their face, to eliminate the need, and to evade the performance of rights. It was from the French law of 1966that it was forbidden. Ore

For practical and positive services, some saw that the owner of the incorporation share or the profit share is considered a partner, even if he does not provide a share in cash or in kind. This is the rewardfor the service that helps to establish. The share of incorporation or profits is notional. They do notfall within the framework of cash and in-kind shares, however, they are considered asindivisible securities towards thecompany. Although they do nothave a nominal value, and trade by commercial methods.And its owner - a founding share or a dividend - enjoys some rights, which may be specified in the articles of association, or by virtue of the decision, taken by the general assembly at a later date to establish those shares.

As a joint-stock company, bonds are issued, and their origins in France date back to 1850 - when the major railway companies ordered their issuance. As mentioned above, the bond is a paper of financial value purchased at its nominal value, which is issued by governments and some companies and includes an undertaking by its issuer to pay a specified periodic interest on a date below ninety days and above. It is a document whose holder is treated as a lender, and to which the laws governing the relationship between the creditor and the debtor apply.

If it is submitted that the amount of the partner's share or share determines the amount of his share in the profit and loss, and that the negatives and positives are related to the efficiency of the company's management, and its ability to control and monitor well, the joint stock company – such as the company limited by shares - places its responsibility within the framework of achieving the budget and profit account:

1- To make a brief statement every six months on the status of the company's assets and liabilities.

2 - To draw up each year a census or inventory that includes a statement of all movable and fixed values.

3- Prepare the budget for the fiscal year.

4- Prepare the profit and loss account. As for the expiry or dissolution of the joint-stock company, its liquidation methods, the payment of its debts, and how to divide its profits and losses, it was submitted in the general system, which means the joint-stock company, before others, there is no need to repeat it.

INCORPORATION OF A COMPANY LIMITED BY SHARES AND ITS CHARACTERISTICS

The company limited by shares, in the requirements of the contract and the incorporation procedures, is subject to the aforementioned rules, especially for the limited partnership company, so let's solve it to avoid repetition... As mentioned in the simple recommendation, a contract is concluded between one or more partners. They shall be jointly liable, and between one or more partners they shall be owners of funds. It differs from a limited partnership in that its speculators are shareholders or shareholders. Contributing shares means that they are money companies. As for the limited partnership company, its speculators with funds provide shares, and they are partners by recommendation or testators, and it means that it is a partnership of persons, as a result of the difference between shares and the share.

One of the advantages of a company limited by shares is that it is in law a money company. It has the right to monitor and supervise. Even if you combine the characteristics of companies of people and companies of money. It seems that the legislator wanted to respond to freedom of choice, so he put in front of the businessmen two similar forms of the two partnership companies: the recommendation of shares and the simple recommendation, so the first type prevailed over the characteristics of money companies: management and trading of shares, and the second type prevailed over the characteristics of people companies: management and non-transfer of shares.

Of course, the freedom to contribute is greater than the freedom of the testator. Although together they do notask about debts, except within the limits of the share offered by the testator, and the shares owned by the shareholder. The difference is clearly evident in the fact that the recommender in the simple recommendationdoes not have the freedom to assign or trade his share, unlike the shareholder in the stock recommendation who has full freedom to trade his shares, as traded by the shareholder in the joint-stock company. However, the size of the company limited by shares is smaller than the size of the joint stock company.

A company limited by shares is of a dual nature, subject to the rules of companies of persons on the one hand, and the rules of companies of funds on the other. The matter of its submission to the rules of partnerships is evident in the fact that all joint partners in it are responsible for their debts, obligations and undertakings. Such as the liability of joint officers in the joint liability and limited partnership companies and they acquire the status of merchant, and their bankruptcy leads to the bankruptcy of all of them, and the bankruptcy of one of them or the like results in its dissolution, if the constitutive contract does not stipulate otherwise. It consists of a title consisting of the name of one or more joint partners. They are the only ones who have the right to manage, as provided in the joint liability and limited partnership companies.

On the other hand, the recommendation of shares is subject to the comprehensive system, which applies to the shareholders of a financial shareholding company. Whether with regard to the system of shares and their circulation, the procedures for incorporation, the competence of the General Assembly, or the supervision of its administrative bodies, with some differences. Among them is that the debts of the shareholding are specified inits capital, which does notexceed it to the funds of the shareholders, if it does not meet its coverage, theremainder of it is divided among the creditors, and the debts of the company limited by shares are specified in the shares and shares for the limited partners, and all of them are guaranteed by the joint liable partners, if its capital does not cover them, they pay the rest of their own funds.

As provided in the joint stock company, the incorporation of a company limited by shares is subject to the rules relating to the division of the capital into shares of equal value, the subscription of all capital, the performance of one quarter of the cash contributions, the negotiability of shares after the performance of one quarter of their value, the payment of contributions in kind in full, their correct appreciation, the survival of nominal shares until their price, the[595] consideration of special conditional advantages for the benefit of one or more shareholders, the ratification of the appreciation and the requirement to establish the company permanently, the certification of the founder of the validity of the draft articles of association, depositing it with a notary, or the seizure of the court of first instance, the deposit of subscription funds for the account of the company that has one of the refineries or banks, and the rules of publicity.[596] Dr. Abdulaziz Al-Khayyat summed up the statement, saying:"The laws of the joint stock company apply to it in the establishment, management, monitoring, general assembly and distribution of profits."[597]

Violation of these rules results in the invalidity of the company, and considers it without effect for the partners, but they may not adhere to the issue of invalidity for others, because the rights of those who are not secured by a law, its requirementsare not affected by the results of its violation.

Management and Supervisory Board

At the level of administrative management, it is legally determined that the company limited by shares is managed by one or more joint partners, and it is

---

[595]- The nominal value of the share or bond is the registered, or the price printed on its page and is subject to change up or down according to the market conditions of the values, and according to the importance of the issuing company in the issuance market.
[596]- Companies, p. 485, by Dr. Al-Sibai.
[597]Companies in the Light of Islam, p. 45 by Dr. Abdulaziz Al-Khayyat.

not permitted for him to be a foreigner or a shareholder, even if he has a power of attorney. The presence of the director at the head of the department shall be done by agreement of the partners, and shall be exempted from the guarantee to which the disposers of the joint stock company are subject, unless the articles of association stipulate otherwise, and hecan only be removed by amending the articles of association of the company. His resignation depends on its acceptance by the general assembly, but it justifies that the company's system includes the possibility of his dismissal, or allowing his resignation.

The Supervisory Board shall be established in addition to the governing body and shall have the force of law and shall be composed of shareholders only. Thus, the legislation has produced a fair balance. It took into account the interests of both the joint holders and the shareholders, putting the right of management in the hands of the joint holders, and the right of control in the hands of the shareholders.

The Supervisory Board shall be composed of at least three shareholders, who shall receive a fixed remuneration or a percentage of the profits. determined by the Constituent Statute or the General Assembly. The Ordinary General Assembly shall appoint its members immediately upon the incorporation of the company and before the commencement of any of its business. Their assignment shall notexceed one year. Provided that the election of the Board shall be determined by the Ordinary General Assembly on the dates and in accordance with the conditions prescribed in the Articles of Association, and the appointment may be for a period specified in the Articles of Association of the Company. It may be indefinite.

The director and members of the supervisory board shall, if an impediment arises, or in the event of the death of a member of the board or hisresignation, invite the general assembly to convene in order to consider the appointment of a new member filling the vacant position.

The Supervisory Board exercises a number of tasks and competences, as it investigates, immediately upon its appointment, whether the legal requirements for the incorporation of the company have been observed, examines the company's books, fund, commercial and financial papers, and submits each year a report to the general assembly. In it, he shall indicate the violations and errors discovered in the statistics and inventory, and prove, if necessary, the reasons that prevent him from distributing the dividends proposed by the director, and[598] he may summon the general assembly, and take the necessary measures to dissolve the company, in accordance with its decision, and it is not necessary to submit a special statement to the general assembly, about the implementation of deals or contracting. Because that is theprerogative of the joint stock company.

---

[598] - Companies, p. 489 for Dr. Sibai.

The members of the Supervisory Board, as owners of funds, do not have the right to intervene in matters of administrative management. Otherwise, they bear responsibility before others, and before the company and partners, especially since the legislation has exempted them and stipulated against them that they do notbear any responsibility for what arises from the management and its results, and they are not civilly responsible for any crime committed by the director. Instead, they ask contributors what personal mistakes they make while performing their tasks. Dr. Shukri Ahmed Al-Sibai explained that the French legislation "Article 254" has brought about a fundamental amendment in the management of the company limited by shares. It established the auditor's center, and its organization was subject to the same rules governing the auditor's center in the joint-stock company.[599]

The ordinary general assembly in a company limited by shares shall exercise the same competences entrusted to the ordinary general assembly in the joint-stock company, and shall be attended by the shareholder partners, without the joint partners. The extraordinary or extraordinary general meeting is concerned with amending the company's articles of association, but the amendment - unlike joint-stock companies - must be signed by all joint partners, unless the law stipulates otherwise.

As for the method of issuing securities, controlling and trading them, the termination and liquidation of the company, the payment of its debts, and the system of distributing profits and losses... It is subject to the same rules that have already been mentioned, and it applies to the company limited by shares, as it applies to the joint-stock company, so there is noneed to return it, exempting the reader from the boring repetition that he feels in some studies.We have intended - after submitting the general system for the establishment and end of the company - to limit - the effort of the possible - to the bases, characteristics and advantages of each company and torefer only to whatis not explained except by him.

---

[599]- The same source, p. 491.

Origin, Nature and Characteristics of a Limited Liability Company

A limited liability company, too, combines the qualities of companies of persons, and companies of money to the extent that it is difficult to classify them into one of the two types. Which forces its clarification. One of the characteristics that makes it a money company is that the partner inside it is not responsiblefor its debts, except within the limits of the share it provides in the capital, and it is close to the partnership that it does notaddress the public through public subscription or issue negotiable securities. However, it is considered a money company due to its nature. In France, by virtue of the Law of March 7, 1925, it was added to the types of commercial company, taking into account the German legislation issued since 1892.

It has spread in France, due to its ability to face medium trade while maintaining personal consideration and family participation, but its prosperity, and the public's interest in business and trade to establish it, with the emergence of some dangers that are not equal to the dangers of the joint-stock company, prompted the legislation to reconsider the legal legislation that governs it. Among the amendments made to its organizational laws are not taking an address consisting of the names of the partners, raising the minimum capital, the solidarity of the management body in the event of bankruptcy, adopting the filing system, subjecting the in-kind shares to estimation and management provisions, and mitigating the principle of transferring the share... These are modifications that brought it closer to Amwal. Jocar and Apolito described them as "small money companies."[600]

Legislation related to limited liability companies has moved to Arab legislation, and Egyptian commercial legislation, Tunisian commercial legislation, and Syrian commercial legislation have adopted it, and the earliest Arab legislation adopted is Moroccan legislation. Where it was adopted, after the French legislation in theyear -1925-1926-

A liability company has been defined from the definitions as a commercial company in which the number of partners does notexceed fifty, and each of themis not liable except to the extent of his share in the capital. It is not permitted for the formation of its capital, increasing it, or borrowing for its account to take place through public subscription, and it is not permitted for it to issue negotiable shares or bonds. The transfer of shares within it shall be subject to the recovery of the partners and to the conditions prescribed in the contract. " All of them are legislations that contribute to understanding the meaning of limited liability.

---

[600]- Companies, p. 495 Dr. Al-Sibai.

Some legislations considered that its designation as a limited liability company came from the fact that the partner's liability is limited in the amount of his share of the capital. In view of the foregoing, the liability of the limited partner in the simple recommendation, or the shareholder in the recommendation of shares is also limited in the amount of the share of the first, or the shares of the second in the capital. Besides, it is legally limited, as we have seen, and financially limited. The minimum capital was initially set at 20,000 francs.

Therefore, its liability is legally and financially limited to the extent that banks in France refuse to grant it the guarantee, unless the managers personally pledge to fulfill, which led Leon Mazzo to say that the limited liability company in this case is approaching the partnership company, in which a team of partners - who are owners of funds - isasked only within the limits of their shares. While the solidarity officials, they ask for all her debts is an absolute personal responsibility.

If the motive that led the children in France to ask for the pledge of the directors in person in granting the guarantee, is that it is oftenestablished with weak capital. Itis not able to face the general guarantee of the group of creditors. legislators in different countries may be alerted to this gap, and try to fill it. by requiring the minimum that he can be assured of. Moroccan legislation set it at one million centimes, Egyptian legislation at one thousand pounds, Syrian legislation at twenty-five Syrian pounds, Tunisian legislation at one thousand dinars, and French legislation at twenty thousand francs.

It should be noted that these quantities are weak again. As a result of inflation and the continuous melting in the value of money, as a result of the continuous rise in the value of materials, due to the continuous activity in demographic growth. The percentage that rises in the value of materials decreases or falls in the value of money. For example, beef in 1956 was equal to two dirhams and today it is equal tobetween forty and fifty dirhams. This is at the expense of the qualitative and quantitative capital, and therefore these amounts are insufficient to launch the company, as mentioned above.

The activity of a limited liability company is determined by the fact that it does not have the right to offer shares for public subscription, and addresses the public in the formation of its capital. In other words, it is not entitled, even if it is classified as a money company, to issue shares, bonds, incorporation shares orother negotiable securities issuedby money companies, or by commercial means. And this is where you meet with the company of people.

If the shares of the partners in the limited liability, such as the shares of the partners in companies of persons, do notaccept transfer and trading by commercial methods. Is it possible to transfer by ordinary or civil means by transferring the right in which the transfer depends on the consent of the debtor of the right? The Moroccan Law of Obligations and Contracts, Article 195, " based on the Dahir of May 20, 1939, provides a general answer to this question and says: " The transfer of rights in a company must be notified to the company, or accepted from it in an official document, or a customary document registered within the Kingdom. "

Legislation before the dual character of the limited liability company tried to alleviate as much as possible the complexity arising from the combination of the characteristics of personal companies and money companies in its system, and introduced flexibility on the principle of the non-transferability of the share, and on the conditions necessary for the transfer process. However, this flexibility has not reached the point of releasing freedom of movement as it is done in money companies. In order for the transfer to be permissible and the shares of the partners to be forfeited to foreigners on behalf of the company, the majority of the partners representing three quarters of the capital must agree.

The limited liability company, even if it is linked to personal consideration in several answers, does notdissolve by interdiction, bankruptcy, insolvency, death or judicial liquidation of the partner... Unless the Constitutive Act so provides, in the event of death.

It is commercial in form, regardless of its purpose. Was it commercial or civil? Commercial rules and customs are subject, but the partners within them are not consideredmerchants. However, the contracts that bind them to the company are commercial. It may take a name, derived from its purpose, as is the case for a joint-stock company, or an address that includes one or more partners, as was the case in the joint venture and partnership companies, which made it combine the characteristics of money companies and partnerships.

However, they do nothave the freedom to do all the work, as the legislation prevented them from doing work that is notcommensurate with their financial ability. Because of the weakness of its capital and the body supervising its management, it was prevented in Morocco from banking, loan, insurance, saving and investing money for the account of others... Thus, it was limited in responsibility and limited in activity. And I was tired or the legislator was tired.

INCORPORATION PROCEDURES

The establishment of a limited liability company is subject to the same conditions as those necessary for the establishment of types of companies in general... For some complexity in its system and nature, we mention what is necessary with the addition ofits own, and it is divided into objective and formal conditions. Objectivity is as follows:

1- The capital in Morocco should be at least one million centimes and divided into equal shares. Don't say about fifty dirhams. They may not be in the form of negotiable papers or debentures.

2- That the incorporationshall not take place unless all the shares in the memorandum of association are distributed among the partners, and their value is paid in full, whether they are cash or in-kind shares.

3- Determining and stating the purpose of the company, and it can exercise all commercial and civil purposes. Except for the acts from which it is prohibited by law. It has the right – such as a simple recommendation - to deal even with the business of the stock exchange, and if it produces pharmaceutical materials or sells them in bulk, the manager and technicians must be pharmacists.

4- Provide an address consisting of the purpose or the name of one or more partners.

5 -Statement of the number of founding partners. It consists of a minimum of two partners, and the maximum limit set by some commercial legislation is fifty. If the number exceeds fifty within two years, it shall be transferred from the same limited liability to the shareholding.

Those were the objective conditions. Formality. Theyare as follows:

1-The contract must be in writing. Either formally or customarily. It must include the prescribed data that must be mentioned, and if it is not in writing, the company shall be nullified.

2- The personal and family name, address and profession of each of the partners.

3- Stipulating that the company is a limited liability.

4- A statement of the company's headquarters and social headquarters.

5-By the persons authorized to manage the company, and to sign its obligations.

6- A statement of the amount of the capital, and dividing it into shares of equal value. Dr. Shukri Ahmed Al-Sibai has quoted from the French law dated July 24, 1867 that the partners may make the capital increaseable by means of successive performance, by the partners, or by accepting new partners, or decreaseable by means ofthe return of shares, in whole or in part. It is permitted for joint liability, partnership and shareholding companies established before or after this law to be transformed into a limited liability company. A limited liability company established under the same law can only be transformed into a joint-stock company.[601]

7. Type and value of in-kind shares.

8. A statement of the condition under which interest is granted to the partners, even in the absence of profits.

---

[601]- Companies, p. 535 for Dr. Sibai.

9- The date of commencement of the company, and the date of its termination, if it is fixed-term.

10- The date of filing at the writing of the court of first instance.

11. Provision for participation in the distribution of profits and losses

12- Forming the legal reserve, which consists of deducting annually the part of twenty of the net profits, and continues until it reaches one tenth of the capital, in order to face the problems.

13. Organization of the Supervisory Board and the deliberations of the Assembly, as prescribed in each company whose number of partners exceeds twenty.

14- A statement of the reasons for the dissolution of the company and the methods of its liquidation.

15- Indicating the number of participating partners.

16- Distribution of shares in the Memorandum of Association among the partners.

These were the procedures related to the writing of the constitutive contract and the data to be mentioned, and it must be publicized in the sameway as the work is done in all companies, and the publicity is as follows:

1- Creating a copy of the constitutive contract if it is notarized, or one of the original counterparts, if it is customary, when writing the court of first instance, in whose jurisdiction the company's headquarters is located within a period of one month from the constitutive date.

2- Publishing a summary copy of the constitutive contract in the Official Gazette and in the newspapers that publish advertisements within a period of one month.

3- Registration of the company in the Commercial Register within the period legally specified in the commercial legislation.

These were the procedures related to filing, publication and registration in the Commercial Register after the contract, and the consequences thereof, and the limited liability company is nullified by the following:

1-Violation of the requirements of the laws that prevent it from transacting the business of banks, insurance and savings, and investing funds in the account of others.

2- Not to enter into a formal or customary contract, and the rest of the requirements governing the subject matter.

3- Issuing negotiable documents.

4- Its capital shall be less than one million centimes in Morocco.

5- The capital shall not be divided into shares of equal value, or the value of the share shall not be less than five thousand centimes.

6- It should consist of less than two partners.

7- Not to distribute all the shares in the Memorandum of Association among the partners.

8 - Lack of real report of in-kind shares.

9- Legal publicityshall not take place. If the nullity occurs, the partners and the first agents who, because of their conduct, are liable jointly for the damages that may be caused by the rest of the partners or others, as they are criminally liable before the law.

A limited liability company, like all companies, has management structures. It manages its affairs, and it consists of three bodies: the management body, which consists of one or more directors, the monitoring body, and it is obligatory if the number of partners exceeds twenty, and the general assembly body, and it is also obligatory if the number exceeds its details as follows:

First -The administrative management body, which is assumed by one or more managers, depending on the size of the company's activity. In Moroccan law, it may be chosen from among the partners or others as decided in the Contracts and Obligations Law (Article 1022). If it is chosen from among the partners, itis not entitled to remuneration except by explicit agreement, as decided in Article 1013 of the same law. It is appointed by a majority of the partners: either in the constitutive contract, or in a subsequent contract, and it is appointed for a limited or unlimited period, and it does notacquire the status of a trader, and it is notpersonally responsible for the company's debts. Therefore, the legislation allowed the position of director to be assigned to legal or juridical persons. Whether appointed in the constitutive contract or in a subsequent contract, he shall not bedismissed except for legitimate reasons, such as exceeding the limits of his authority or misusing it, or committing a serious error or negligence in the management of the company, as stated in Article 1013of the Civil Code. The director of a limited liability company has wide powers in the conduct of the affairs of the company, and the partners may limit his authority. Either in the articles of association or in the company's contract, but the order of limitation from the authority is notinvoked against third parties. All acts and deeds carried out by the director shall bind the company. If it falls outside his authority, in order to secure the rights of the people.

Civilly, the directors are asked individually and jointly towards the company and third parties to the rules of ordinary law - for the mistakes they commit in the measure, and for violating the legal requirements, and the company's articles of association, and criminally they are asked - as the founders are asked - about committing the acts and violations punishable by law.

Those who are subject to punishment - whether at the level of incorporation or management and administration - the founders who make a false declaration in the memorandum of association and related to the distribution of shares among all partners, or discharging them... Managers who open directly, or through intermediaries subscribe to the public in values transferred to the account of the company, and who reach by fraudulent measures to assign the value of shares in kind, exceeding their real value, and managers who distribute fictitious profits, without conducting any census, or based on a census in which fraud has occurred...

Second: The Supervisory Authority. The law did not initiate the establishment of the Supervisory Board, in the limited liability company, and in all companies, unless the number of partners exceeds twenty as mentioned above. If the number is less than twenty, the company has the absolute freedom to choose the individual or collective method, which it deems most appropriate to monitor the progress of its business. The board, if its conditions are met, consists of at least three members, and the first board is appointed in the company's contract, provided that it renews the election of its members, in accordance with the rules prescribed in the constitutive system. and to elect or appoint members. Removing them from the competence of the partners. The partner has the right to inform himself at the company's headquarters or through his agent of the company's statistics, budget, and the report of the monitoring board.

One of the basic competences of the Supervisory Board is to examine the company's books, fund, commercial and financial papers, and to submit a report to the annual ordinary general assembly. In it, he shall indicate the irregularities and errors in the statistics he discovered, and shall invite the Ordinary General Assembly, whenever necessary, as mentioned above.

The members of the Supervisory Board are not accountable for the actions of the directors and their results. Rather, each member asks himself towards others, and towards the company, about the mistakes he made during the execution of his mission.

Third - The General Assembly, which is considered the source of powers in a limited liability company, as is the case for various companies. Through its convening, the partners intervene in the affairs of the company and its activity, in order to issue the necessary decisions for its proper functioning. Since the legislation did not oblige the partners to hold the general assembly, unless their number exceeds twenty, the legal answer is that if it is less than twenty, the directors may only direct the text of the proposed decisions to be taken in a clear manner to each partner, to be ratified in writing. However, if the quorum of twenty is met, the general assembly must convene once a year, and at the date specified in the constitution, in order to approve the budget and the profit and loss account.

The meeting shall be convened upon an invitation addressed either by the director, the supervisory board, or by a number of partners, if they represent more than half of the capital of the company. Resolutions are issued by a majority of votes, and all shall have a vote share, and any partner shall have the right to contribute to the vote. Even if the Memorandum of Association stipulates otherwise, because it is from the publicorder, which invalidates every condition that violates it. The absentee may vote in writing, or represent him who attends the deliberations of the general assembly by special authorization, unless the company's contract stipulates otherwise.

The conditions relating to the quorum and the necessary majority do not differ depending on whether the decisions are ordinary or aim to amend the company's articles of association on the one hand, and whether they are issued by the ordinary, extraordinary or extraordinary general assembly on the other hand.

In order for the resolutions of the Ordinary General Assembly to be valid and effective, it is necessary to obtain in the first deliberations an absolute majority of the capital. It means that the number of partners voting on the resolutions represents more than half of the company's capital at a rate of 51%. However, if the resolutions are issued by the extraordinary or extraordinary meeting, the matter is differentbecause it is related to amending the company's articles of association. It requires two majorities: an absolute numerical majority. It is represented by the majority of partners with a rateof 51% and a financial value majority. Represented by the ownership of this numerical majority of three quarters of the capital, unless the company's statute stipulates otherwise.

By majority, the Extraordinary General Assembly can exercise all modifications, except for the increase in the shareof the partner, and change the nationality of the company. This can only be done by consensus of the partners.

From theforegoing during these investigations, it is noted that the general rules and laws governing the Steering Board, the Supervisory Board and the General Assembly... Or the contract and its requirements, or the procedures for incorporation, or the system of shares and shares, or what the companyends up with and liquidates and performsits debts and distributes its profits and losses... In the sentence, it refers to the general system on which companies are established, with some natural differences, especially between companies of people and companies of money, and what isnecessary in this case and notnecessary in those... We have tried - as best we can - to avoid unnecessary complexity, digression and repetition, as required by the methodology in the brief studies. It is a complete methodology to focus, when analyzing the system of each company separately, on its nature, characteristics and advantages ...

With deriving from the general rules what is required by the circumstances of the clarification and the statement, as manifested in the nature, characteristics and advantages of the limited liability company, which requires shedding light on its aspects.

It is noticeable that a limited liability company arises modestly. They may grow close to the size of the contribution, or move into their system. It alone has the right to move to the contribution system and its system in front of its modest size at first, like something with a thread shirt for a man and a boy wearing it, and then the body grows until it fills the shirt. It is a key factor in the development of economic activity. Dr. Abdulaziz Al-Khayyat summarized it in words and said: "It is a commercial company consisting of two or more partners, each of whom is responsible to the extent of his share in the capital, and it is notestablished in the manner of public subscription, and the capital is not divided into negotiable shares, and bonds are not issued,and the transfer of shares is subject to the recovery of the partners under the conditions specified, as it is a company exempted from the most restrictions of participation."[602]

That was the picture of modern businesses after Islamic businesses. We tried to bring the subject together and focus on the rules and laws that govern it. And never once did we deliberately let the law express itself; because that called for persuasion, and silenced the tongues.

The most important Islamic company seems to be the speculative and loan company. The most important thing is the modernity of the joint-stock company, and we tried when analyzing the system of the Mudaraba company to compare their systems. We met them in some principles, and they differ in others.[603] If the companies organized by Sharia laws are five: speculation, unleashing, faces and bargaining, business, and organized by positive laws are five: solidarity, simple recommendation, contribution and recommendation of shares and limited liability, the conditions in which the world lives, and the attempt of each side to establish its own identity and status. Even at the expense of others, and inthe face of the positivity, mediation and moderation of the Islamic economy, Islamic countries must return to their subjectivity, wealth and elements, and think objectively and practically how to move from five Western companies to five Islamic ones.

As for the issue of Muslim participation in modern companies, it was the subject of disagreement and we agreed with the authorized team such as Muhammad Abdo, Dr. Muhammad Yusuf Musa, Sheikh Muhammad Al-Khalisi, Sheikh Abdul Wahab Khallafy, and Sheikh Ali Al-Khafifi[604] because he is closer to the right, and more responsive to the Department of Economic

---

[602] Companies in the Light of Islam, p. 46 by Dr. Abdulaziz Al-Khayyat.
[603] - See my book The Approach of Islamic Economics in the Production and Consumption of Wealth 2/141.
[604] Companies in the Light of Islam, p. 59 by Dr. Abdulaziz Al-Khayyat.

Development, especially for Muslims outside the Islamic world. And if the alternative is not available enough within it... With regard to Islam's position on the purchase of shares by a Muslim from the stock exchange, I have already explained that civil and commercial companies that avoid Sharia prohibited transactions such as dealing in usury and trafficking in alcohol, as Dr. Abdulaziz Al-Khayyat sees with us and[605] works in the permissible legally and legally, and their purposes, laws and transactions are moral in accordance with what is stated in the Islamic Sharia, a Muslim may participate in its establishment and buy its shares, as evidenced by the work of the Prophet (PBUH) in the participation of Jews in Khaybar, with emphasis on what we havealready said that it is difficult for a Muslim to see the conditions of a company of different nationalities, especially if it operates in several countries. The problem is mostly related to commercial companies. Otherwise, we knew a scientist who owned shares in air transport, a civilian company.

The issue of the participation of the Prophet (peace and blessings of Allah be upon him) to the Jews in Khyber was mentioned as a principle; because the peasant company is civil and the shareholding that issues the shares - as issued by the recommendation of the shares - is commercial, and it can be said that the door may be open but with the condition that it is permissible to work and verify its existence, knowing that scientific diligence, or the responsibility of scientists ends with clarification, and the responsibility of personal applied diligence is transferred to the concerned person. For example, the task of the world in Ramadan is to clarify the ruling on the permissibility of Iftar for the patient, and it is not his task to investigate the existence of the disease and to clarify the permissibility ofdealing with usury or taboos for legitimate necessity, without the permissibility of dealing with the need or necessities of life, and it is not his task to investigate the availability of the conditions of legitimate necessity at the level at which it is permissible to deal with taboos, such as eating the dead. And remove the straw with wine; because that is a metaphysical matter in which the responsibility is placed on the person concerned. Necessity may be apparent, as manifested in the circumstances of some African countries where thousands die of starvation, nakedness and disease...

Undoubtedly, the first task of scholars is to clarify, especially in this era, in which values were established, laws were mixed, and Sharia rulings were wanted to respond to personal interests. Allah the Almighty says to His Prophet, "We have revealed to **you the Reminder so that you may make clear to people what** has **been revealed to them.**" The[606] scholars are the heirs of the prophets, the heirs of the prophets in behavior, morals and good treatment, and to clarify what Allah has revealed in the absence of taking into account human beings...Their authority is moral. Their responsibility after clarifying what must

---

[605]- The same source, p. 57.
[606]- Surat Al-Nahl, 44.

be clarifiedis to collect evidence and extrapolate judgments... The fatwa is one of the most dangerous thingsfacing the world, knowledge, religion, honesty, and creation... It is the responsibility of leaders to implement what can only be implemented by authority... It is the responsibility of those concerned to psychologically verify the existence of the circumstances and requirements of the judgment in what is personally applied... It is up to the verification of the subject matter: either to verify the circumstances of the permissibility or prohibition, such as the consideration of the company's transactions and laws, or to investigate the circumstances of the permissibility of dealing with the prohibited in advance, such as the heart referendum in the presence of a legitimate necessity... God is the Arbiter of righteousness...

Conclusion

This study tries to compare the political economy: Islamic and modern, while the comparison comes naturally without cost, analysis or loading texts that do not bear either in issues, ideas or topics. It also tries to put the concept of political economy in its real context and make its train cars go on the track of reality. The actions of yesterday are far away. In the last two decades, our children have been studying economics on professors who were imbued with Marxism when it was exported to the Third World and have deluded them that political economy is Marxism in order to empty them of its extremist mold. Although political economy in its general and broad sense does not mean a special ideology as much asit means that it is subordinate to the policy of an Eastern, Western or Islamic state or to the policy of an international association such as thepolicy of the European Community as long as each country has a policy that responds to its capabilities, resources, system, choices, orientations and links to various countries of the world. At the heart of the matter, we have seen that the first to subject the economy to the policy of the state and the fact that collective ownership in its name is the caliph Omar bin Al-Khattab. If the sources and the prevailing expression at the time are known about Omar's fiscal policy, Omar does notplan for the individual or family economy, which is not linked to politics except in terms of good governance in living. He is planning a sprawling state. Its authority and economic system extendsbetween Al-Jazeera, the Levant, Iraq and Egypt and covered the positions of influenceof Kasra and Hercules... On the basis of its principles and laws, the Islamic economy and the structures of Islamic civilization have been established on three continents... In planning this study, we deliberately:

1- To be graduated from the basic issues on which the concepts and theses that may be put forward and notunderstood without them. Such as the concept of the word economy in the original, language and terminology and its scientific or ideological perspective between the capitalist and communist doctrine and the Islamic economy and what does the expression mean by political economy? And what policy? Then introduce the science of economics and its branches and its relations with other sciences.

2-To start the analysis from the economic reality as a "living" reality, starting with what they called the economic problem as the biggest problem that concerns the world. Individuals, countries and societies: their human and natural causes, ways of solving them, and their connection with the proliferating and increasing human needs in front of the scarcity of resources on the one hand and with economic activity - production, exchange and consumption - and what it imposes of a clear continent policy that ends with good governance on the other hand.

3- To study the history of economic thought: capitalist, socialist and Islamic from its beginning to the sixteenth centuryand from it until modern doctrines imposed its existence on the economic field - a brief, focused study accompanied by as much analysis and commentary as possible away from the rumination of abstract historical events... This is in order to derive the principles, laws and positive and scientific theories that are valid for application from among the negative theories that have entered the midst of history without leaving their impact on the pages of life. Knowing that the successor benefits from the experience of the former negatively and positively, he is guided by his successes and avoids his failures for the gain of time, which is the lost time in the Arab world

The result of failed new experiments. If the goal of studying the history of economic thought is not to obtain positive results. Helps to fold the fun, so the study and reading in it are alike. - Put in front of businessmen and trade models of Islamic companies with their systems and laws and modern companies with their systems and laws and compare, comment or analyze whatneeds to be analyzed, comment or allow comparison with the warning on what ispermissible and what is not, even if the majority of Arab and Islamic capital is found - apparentlywithin modern companies spread within the Arab and Islamic world if we exclude what is found within about forty Islamic institutions distributedbetween Europe, Asia and Africa began to exercise their economic activity and did not impose their presence strongly. At the forefront of these institutions and the most widespread of which are the institutions of the Islamic Bank and the Islamic Bank in its legitimacy and Islamic system and its laws is the Mudaraba and Lending Company, which consists of money on one side and work on the side of the financier is responsible for the loss, and the working side is responsible for the work and whatresults from an infringement of it or negligence and the profit is divided by the amounts of money and the amounts of business. I presented his entire system in the second part of the book "The Approach of Islamic Economics in the Production and Consumption of Wealth"asa starting point for what they wrote and criticized. We ask you, the Lord of the heavens and the earth, and those among them, to accept from us the rightness, overlook the mistake, and pardon the slip of thought, tongue, and pen, as we ask you, thanks to your grace and generosity, to unite this nation and return it to work with your book and the Sunnah of your Prophet, and prayers and peace be upon the face of the pious and the intercessor of the sinners, our master Muhammad, his family and companions, and peace be upon him.

INDEX

Introduction 1

Capitalist system 4

Communist system 5

Islamic Economic System 9

Definition of Economics 25

I. Theoretical Economics 26

II. Applied Economics 27

III. Social economy, ... 27

IV. The national economy 30

V. The international economy 30

I. Social Sciences 34

II. Legal Sciences 37

III. Natural Sciences 37

I. Work 48

II. Themes 48

III. Means 48

Share 63

Option and Undertaking Sale and Purchase of Shares 64

Bond 66

Transferable and Recallable Deed of Engagement 66

The beginning of ownership between individual and collective 80

Greece 83

Plato 84

Aristotle and his views on economics 86

In the Romans and in the Middle Ages 87

Islam and the Beginning of Arab Economic Thought 91

Revoke the usurious system and establish Islamic commerce in its place	93
Reform in the peasant economy	95
Advocacy for economic development and action	96
I. Spanish Mercantilism	99
Second- French Mercantilism	101
III- English Mercantilism	101
Adam Smith	109
Robert Malthus	111
David Ricardo	113
Caliph Umar ibn al-Khattab was the first to establish collective ownership.	137
Anarchism and the Rejection of State Power	142
A glimpse into Marx's life and what people think of him	150
Theory of value, its surplus, overtime and its take-off	152
Scientific socialism and the elimination of surplus value	159
Theory of Evolution between Economics and Philosophy	161
The theory of art and the views of scientists, philosophers and naturalists on the subject	166
Ruling	184
Its pillars	187
Terms	187
Foundations of its formation	190
What is the Lord of the world and what is not his	191
What is for the worker, and what is not for him	195
Cancellation	199
Her loss and her debts	200
Split her winnings	201
Composition	206
Its pillars	207
Terms	208
Cancellation	212
Earned	213
Her loss?	215
Partner's Right to Act	215
Establishment of the company and its divisions	242
The Contract and its Requirements and Requirements	243
Source of Capital, Nature of Shares and Partner Obligations	247
Administrative system	251

Manager's Authority and Responsibility 253

The company's judiciary, its circumstances and reasons 254

Liquidation of the company, performance of its debts and division of its profits 258

Contract, Commitment and Capital 263

Non-transferability of the share and dividing the profit 266

Simple recommendation company contract 270

Management and the role of the company's address in the conduct of its affairs 273

Nature and Characteristics of a Joint Venture Company 276

Management of the joint venture company and personal commitment within it 278

Importance and Characteristics of a Joint Stock Company, and its Articles of Association 281

Capital formation 284

Administrative System 286

Issuance of Shares and Bonds 288

Incorporation of a company limited by shares and its characteristics 291

Management and Supervisory Board 292

Origin, Nature and Characteristics of a Limited Liability Company 295

Incorporation Procedures 297

Conclusion 306

List of Manuscript Sources

We start the list of sources and references with manuscripts supported by symbols, which symbolize their places, unless they are in the property of a person, so he writes in front of them "personal " and the symbols are as follows :

- (3 AD) and (4 AD) : The third and fourth exhibitions of the Hassan II Prize for Manuscripts and Documents.
- 64c - Under No. 64 in Al-Jalawi Treasury
- 13 D- Under No. 13 in the State Treasury
- 98 S - under No. 98 in the Awqaf Treasury
- 896 under No. 896 in the linen cabinet
- To comply with the provisions of feudalism (13d) Judge Abbas Ibrahim Al-Taraji.
- Sufficiency in the news of the caliphs (personal) Abd al-Malik ibn Muhammad ibn al-Kardbus
- Aḥkām al-Zakāt (76 BC) Abū Bakr Muḥammad ibn ʻAbd Allāh Ibn al-J
- Completion of the advertiser: Layadh Ali Sharh Muslim(M 3 Jah - 54 - Al-Bayda) by Imam Abu Abdullah Al-Mazri.
- Answers of Jurisprudence (Article 4 Jah - 318 T) Ahmed bin Ali Al-Manjour
- The answers of the late jurists (M 3 Jah - 15 - Blood) Abdullah bin Ibrahim Al-Tamli. - Ajwab Al-Abbasi (P3JH-13D)
- Badie Al-Salak in the natures of King(64c) Abu Abdullah Muhammad bin Ali Ibn Al-Azraq printed after its adoption.
- Tuḥfat al-Nāḍir(d. 3 Jah 7d) Muḥammad ibn Aḥmad al-ʻAqbānī.
- Doha, which is confused in the controls of Dar al-Sikka, which was extracted from Al-Rawdha al-Sfarda in the rulings of gold and silver (231d) Ali bin Yusuf al-Fasi.
- The Bright Meteors in Beneficial Politics (908 c) Abu al-Qasim Ali bin Salmon.
- Ghaniyat al-Maʻāṣir wa al-Talī ʻalá al-Fashtālī (2479 d) Abū al-ʻAbbās Aḥmad ibn Yaḥyá al-Wansh
- The Book of Money (98 BC) Abu Jaafar Ahmed bin Nasr Al-Dawoudi Al-Asadi printed after its adoption.
- Faculties in matters under work in the Maliki school (1729 d) Muhammad ibn Aḥmad ibn Ghāzī.
- (877D) Abu Al-Walid Hisham bin Abdullah bin Hisham.

- Sub-Mukhtaṣar Ibn al-Ḥājib (2334 d) Abū 'Amr and 'Uthmān ibn Abī Bakrīn Yūnis Ibn al-Ḥājib .
- Nawazil al-Abbasi (896 k) compiled by Ahmed bin Ibrahim al-Samlali.
- Nawazel Al-Nasiri(1045 c) Muhammad bin Abdul Salam Al-Nasiri .
- Nawazel Company (M4 - C 64 AD) Abdulaziz bin Al-Hassan bin Youssef bin Mahdi Al-Zayati.

List of Printed Sources and References	
The Qur 'an and its Interpretations	
The Qur 'an and its commentaries on the Holy Qur 'an by the narration of Imam Warsh	
- Provisions of the Qur 'an - I 11376 - 5 - 1957	Judge Abu Bakr Al-Arabi
- In the shadows of the Qur 'an - 13651946 m Tehran	Mr. Qutb
- The Exegetical Qur 'an - i-1- 1377 AH	Mohamed Farid Wajdi:
- Sahih Imam Al-Bukhari	Muḥammad ibn Ismā'īl al-Najārī
- The printed version with Fath Al-Bari on 1378, 1959, and we express it in the Fath copy - Sahih Imam Muslim	Muslim ibn al-Hajjaj
I - 1- The printed version with the explanations of the father and the Sunnis on 1327 AH, and we express it in the father's version, and the printed version with the explanation of the nuclear 1349 - 1930 AD, and we express it in the nuclear version.	
- Sahih or Al-Tirmidhi Mosque - I - 1 – 1350AH 1931AD Cairo.	Muhammad ibn Isa at-Tirmidhi
- Sunan Al-Nasa 'i - Egyptian Press in Al-Azhar	Aḥmad ibn Shu'ayb al-Nisa'ī
- Sunan Abu Dawood - 2ndEdition - 1369AH 1950AD Egypt	Suleiman bin Al-Ashat Al-Sijistani
- Sunan Ibn Maja	Abū 'Abd Allāh Muḥammad ibn Yazīd
- Musnad Al-Imam Ahmed - I - 1- 1313 AH Egypt	Abū 'Abd Allāh Aḥmad ibn Ḥanbal
- Al-Muwatta, narrated by Yahya bin Yahya Al-Liti	Imam Malik bin Anas

Greater Sunnah - I - 1 - 1350AH India	Abū Bakr Aḥmad ibn ʿAlī al-Bayhqī
Al-Jawāhir al-Munīfah's Contracts in the Evidence of the Doctrine of Abī Ḥanīfah - i - 2 - 1309 AH	Mohammed Mortaqi Al-Husseini
Al-Taj al-Jāmiʿ al-Uṣūl fī Ḥadīth al-Rasūl, 3rd edition, 1381 AH, 1971AD	Sheikh Ali Mansour Ali Nassif
Al-Zu'aydah Complex and the Source of Benefits D - 2nd Edition - 1367AH	Nūr al-Dīn ʿAlī ibn Abī Bakr al-Ḥaytim
Fatah Al-Bari in Al-Bukhari Shirk - I - 1378AH 1959AD Cairo	Al-Hafiz Ibn Hajar Al-Asqalani
Sharḥ al-Abī wa-al-Sanūsī ʿAlī Ṣaḥīḥ Muslim, 1st- 1327 AH, Cairo	Father and Senussi
Sharḥ al-Nawawī ʿAlī Ṣaḥīḥ Muslim, 1st edition, 13491AH, 1930AD, Cairo	Efam Al-Nawawi
The Way of Peace Explanation of Bulgh Al-Maram in the Hadiths of Rulers	Muḥammad ibn Ismāʿīl al-Sanānī
Sharḥ al-Zurqānī ʿalá al-Mawṭā (Commentary on al-Zurqān	Mohammed Al-Zaqani
Absorption - Nahdet Misr Press - Cairo	Abū ʿUmar Yūsuf ibn ʿAbd Allā
Major Classes - 1377AH - 1957AD Beirut	Muḥammad ibn Saʿd
Patriarchal Circuit 1st Edition – 1351AH 1932AD India	Aḥmad ibn ʿAbd Allāh Abū
"Siyar A'lam Al-Nubala".	Shams al-Dīn Muḥammad ibn Aḥmad ibn ʿUthmā
Life of the Companions	Yousaf, Mohammed /
Jurisprudence, the biography of the Prophet, and his life.	
Grand CodeI-1-1324 AH Egypt	Sahnoun's narration on ʿAbd al-Raḥmān ibn al-Q
Introductions of Ibn RushdI-1-1334AH Egypt	Ibn Rushd the grandfather
Bidaya Al-Mujtahid – Al-Istiqamah Library Cairo	Abu Al-Walid Muhammad Ibn Rushd, grandson
Rulers' Masterpiece	Judge Ibn Asim
Mukhtaṣar al-Muzzīnī ʿalá al-Mawdūn al-Kubrī	Efmam Al Muzni
Mother's Book – I-1-1331AH Egypt	Imam Muḥammad ibn Idrīs al-

	Shāfi'ī
The Book of Jurisprudence on the Four Madhhabs – I-2 1349AH 1931AD – Egyptian Ministry of Religious Endowments	Presented by Abdulrahman Al-Jazari
Manar al-Sabil in Sharḥ al-Dalīl 'alá Madhhab al-Imām Aḥmad – i-1-1378AH.	Ibrahim ibn Muhammed ibn Salim ibn Dhawyan
Persuasion in the jurisprudence of Imam Ahmed – Egyptian Press – Al-Azhar	Abū al-Najā Mūsá al-Ḥijāw
Al-Mughni I-2-1367AH Cairo	Abu Muhammad Abdullah Ibn Qudamah
Inform the signatories about the Lord of the Worlds –I-1- Al-Munirah Printing Press - Cairo	Shams al-Dīn Muḥammad ibn Abī Bakr Ibn al-Qay
Local – I – 1-1351 AH Egypt	Abū 'Alī Muḥammad ibn Aḥmad ibn Sa'īd
Islamic Thought in the History of Islamic JurisprudenceI-1-1345 Fez	Muḥammad ibn al-Ḥusayn al-Ḥaj
Jurisprudence of Zakat – 1st edition -1379 AH 1969 AD Beirut	Youssef Al-Qaradaweed
Jurisprudence of the Year I-1-1397 AH 1977AD Beirut	Mr. Sabeq
Nuggets, Interest Capture and Returns Delinquency I-1- Al-Najah Press - Morocco	The Satisfied Mufti of Sinani
Fatwas by Sheikh Shaltout - Dar Al-Qalam Press, Cairo	Sheikh Mohammed Shaltout
Jurisprudential Laws	Ibn Jizi
Zad Al-Maad – I- 137- E Cairo	Shams al-Dīn Ibn al-Qayyim al-Jawzī
Nour Al-Yaqeen in the biography of Sayyid Al-Mursalin, 12-1955 Cairo	Sheikh Mohammed Al-Khudari Bey
Al-Shamā'il al-Muhammadiyyah - 2nd Edition– 1396 AH 1976 Cairo	Abu 'Isa Muḥammad ibn Surat al-Tirmidhī
Muhammad al-Muwallal al-Kamil – 5th edition- 1370 AH 1961AD Cairo	Muhammad Ahmad Jad Al-Mawla Bey
The Life ofMuhammadT-8-1963 Cairo	Mohamed Hassan Heikal
Economics and law	
The Money Book of Abu 'Ubayd	Abū 'Ubayd al-Qāsim ibn S

Kitāb al-Kharjāj li-Ab	Judge Abu Yusuf
Kitāb al-Kharjāj li-Ibn	Yahya bin Adam
Kitāb al-'Amūl li-Dāwūdī – Submitted in Manuscripts and Printed after Approval	Abu Jaafar Ahmad bin Nasr Al-Daoudi
Royal RulingsI-1-1327AH-1909AD	Mawardi
Extracting Output Judgments	Abū al-Farāj 'Abd al-Raḥmān ibn A
Al-Kharj in the Islamic State	Mohammed Ziauddin Al-Rayes.
Main Lines in Islamic EconomicsI-1-1385AH 1965AD	Dr. Mahmoud Abu Al-Saud
Introduction to Economic Theory in the IslamicCurriculumI-1-1973	Dr. Ahmed Al-Najjar
OurEconomyI-3-1389AH 1969AD Beirut	Mohammed Baqir Al-Sadr
Islamic Economist – Book 7 of the Series	Sadiq Al Abawi
The Theory of Forbidden Usury in Islamic LawI-1-1383AH 1964AD	Zakī al-Dīn Badawī
Cash andCreditI-3-1996 Egypt	Dr. Hussein Omar
Companies in Moroccan and Comparative LegislationI-1-1976AD	Dr. Shukri Ahmed Al-Sibai
Companies in light of Islam -Dar Al Salam for Printing, Publishing and Distribution	Dr. Abdulaziz Al-Khayyat
Curriculum of Islamic Economics in the Production and Consumption of Wealth, 1/1987	By Ahmed Lisan Al-Haq
Their Socialism and Our Islam, 1/1966	Al-Bashir Al-Auf
Economics I-2-1979AD	Dr. Abdullah Asim
The Origins of Political Economy -1979AD	Dr. El Sayed Abdel Mawla
Accumulation at the global levelI-2-1978AD	Dr. Samir Amin Translated by Hussain Qubaisi.
Political Economy - Moroccan Publishing House Press – Casablanca.	Dr. Fathallah Al-Alou
Lecturer in Political Economy, 6/6/1980, Dar Al-Ilm for Klein, Beirut	Dr. Salahuddin Haroun
History of Economic IdeasI-1-1956 Baghdad	Dr. Mohammed Aziz Al-Iraqi

- Economy	Lal Leontief
- Capital – I-1965 Translated by Rashid Al-Barawi	Marx
- Spirit of Socialism	Gustave Le Bon
- Commercial Papers in Moroccan Legislation: Bills Bond – Cheque – 1970	Ali Sulaiman Al-Obaidi
- Fatiyat Tariq and Al-Ghafiqi, "In the Exploitation of Land," 1st-1392AH, 1972AD	Mohammed Al-Muntaser Al-Ketani
Moroccan Civil Contracts and Obligations Law Moroccan Commercial Law – Dahir 12/08/1913 Submitted by Abdelaziz.	
- Mediator in Civil Law Explanation: Contracts that fall on the property	Dr. Abdul Razzaq Ahmed Al-Sanhouri
- Brief on Constitutional Law - I-2 -Hashemite Press – Damascus –	Dr. Mustafa Baroudi.
- Legislative Comparisons between Positive Laws and Islamic Legislation,I-1-1959	Abdullah Ali Hassan
- Administrative Arrangement I-1-1384AH 1952 Rabat	'Abd al-Ḥayy ibn 'Ab
Islamic, Social and Philosophical	
- Islam and Imported Principles 1380 AH 1960AD	Abdul Moneim Al-Nimr
- Islam and SocialismI-1-1968 Beirut	Mohammed Azza Darwaza
- World Peace andIslamI-1386-1967 Beirut	Mr. Qutb
- Islamic Thought and Evolution I-1- Dar Al-Qayyim Press -Cairo	Mohamed Fathi Othman
- Islamic Encyclopedia	Boutros Bustani
- Social Solidarity in IslamI-1-1384 1964 Cairo	Mohammed Abu Zahra
- Fajr al-Islam I-8-1360AH 1961AD Cairo	Ahmed Amin
- Self-Criticism I-1966 Dar Al-Kitab – Casablanca	Allal Al Fassi
- Humanism and Communism	Abbas Mahmoud Al-Aqqad
- New Layer I-1- Dar Al-Kitab Al-Arabi Beirut	Miliovan Djilas
- Risālat al-Imām al-Ghazālī I-1986AD Dar al-Kutub al-I	Imam al-Ghazali
- Islamic Peoples in the Soviet Union	Abdullah Al-Ghafiki

- The Story of Faith I-3- Beirut	Sheikh Nadim Al-Jisr
- The Issue of Divinity between Philosophy andReligion I-1-1382AH 1962AD	Abdul Karim Al-Khatib:
- The Great Cosmic Certainties, Beirut, 2-1390 AH	Mohammed Saeed Ramadan Al-Buti
History & Magazines	
- History of Nations and Kings of TabariI-2 - Dar Al-Maaref Cairo	Abu Jaafar bin Jarir Al-Tabari
- The Beginning and the End in History 1- 1351AH1932AD Egypt	Abu Al-Fida Ismail Ibn Kathir
- Fattouh al-Balad I-1-1350AH 1932AD Egypt	Abu al-Hasan al-Balazari
- Fotouh Egypt and Morocco i-1 -Cairo	Ibn Abdul Hakam
- History ofTetouan01/01/1970 Morocco	Mohammed Daoud
- Lectures on the History of Islamic NationsI-7- 1376AH Cairo	Sheikh Mohammed Al-Khudari Bey
- Introduction of IbnKhaldunI-3-1976 Lebanon	'Abd al-Raḥmān Ibn Kh
- The Story of Civilization	Wall Durant
- Dawa Al-Haq Magazine No. 7- Second Year – April 1959	
- Al-Iman Magazine No. 8- Fourth Year September 1967	
- Journal of Islamic Banks No. 15- January/February 1981	
- Risalat Al-Jihad Magazine Issue -88- May 1990.	

www.ingramcontent.com/pod-product-compliance
Lightning Source LLC
LaVergne TN
LVHW081540070526
838199LV00057B/3723